Cloud Forensics Demystified

Decoding cloud investigation complexities
for digital forensic professionals

Ganesh Ramakrishnan

Mansoor Haqanee

Cloud Forensics Demystified

Group Product Manager: Pavan Ramchandani

Publishing Product Manager: Prachi Sawant

Book Project Manager: Ashwini Gowda

Senior Editor: Romy Dias

Technical Editor: Nithik Cheruvakodan

Copy Editor: Safis Editing

Proofreader: Safis Editing

Indexer: Rekha Nair

Production Designer: Vijay Kamble

Senior DevRel Marketing Coordinator: Marylou Dmello

First published: February 2024

Production reference: 1250124

Published by Packt Publishing Ltd.

Grosvenor House

11 St Paul's Square

Birmingham

B3 1RB, UK

ISBN 978-1-80056-441-1

www.packtpub.com

To my parents and my lovely wife, Priya – thank you for your relentless support and love.

– Ganesh Ramakrishnan

I would like to thank my loving family for their continued support, patience, and encouragement throughout the long process of writing this book.

– Mansoor Haqanee

Contributors

About the authors

Ganesh Ramakrishnan is a senior manager at KPMG Canada's Incident Response team, with over 12 years of incident response experience. He leads a dynamic team focused on responding to and managing incidents for organizations across various industry sectors, working with KPMG's incident response teams globally. He has led numerous incident response cases, including high-profile ones, and collaborated with law enforcement agencies worldwide. Apart from assisting organizations during crises, Ganesh also helps them prepare for incidents and educates them on handling them.

Ganesh has a master's in computer application and an MSc in network and information security. He also holds CISSP, SANS GCFA, and SANS GNFA certifications.

My deepest gratitude to my parents for always being there to motivate me and help me overcome any obstacles. Thank you for your unwavering belief in me. To my incredible wife, Priya – thank you for being my constant source of strength and inspiration. Your unwavering support, patience, and encouragement have been remarkable. I cannot thank you enough. Lastly, to my son, Hridhaan – you are why I wake up every day with renewed purpose and enthusiasm. Thank you for reminding me of the joys of life and for being my greatest motivation.

To the two special people who believed in me from the start and supported the idea of writing this book, Hartaj and Alex – thank you for your relentless support.

Finally, I want to thank the Packt team for allowing Mansoor and me to bring this book to life.

Mansoor Haqanee is a manager with KPMG Canada's Forensic Technology team, with over six years of experience in software development, computer forensics, and incident response. Mansoor has a background in electrical engineering with a bachelor of engineering from Toronto Metropolitan University (formerly Ryerson University). Combining his education with both software development and computer forensic experience, he is equipped to provide organizations with insights into the security of their assets. Mansoor has provided technology consulting services to a wide range of industries in the education, financial services, healthcare, telecommunications, manufacturing, and government sectors, to name a few.

This book is dedicated to my parents, who have always been the roots that keep me grounded and the wings that let me fly. Your sacrifices, love, and wisdom have shaped me in more ways than I can count. To my siblings – thank you for the laughter, the fights, my cute nephews, and your unwavering support. To my partner, Nabila – your love makes every challenge worthwhile. And to my dog, Ace – thank you for the countless walks that cleared my mind. Each of you holds a special place in this journey and my heart.

To Alex, Ganesh, and Chris – your collective wisdom has not only shaped my professional path but has also left an unforgettable mark on my personal growth. Thank you for your generous sharing of knowledge. This book, a milestone in my career, is a testament to the invaluable lessons I've learned from each of you.

About the reviewers

Aby Rao, **Deputy Chief Information Security Officer (CISO)** at a leading financial technology company, oversees multiple security teams with decades of experience in consulting. Specializing in cloud security, IAM, and GRC, Aby actively explores the intersection of cybersecurity with emerging technologies, such as machine learning and artificial intelligence. His diverse skill set and interest in cutting-edge innovations showcase a forward-thinking approach. Aby holds certifications such as CCSK, AWS CCP, CISSP, CISM, CISA, OneTrust Fellow of Privacy Technology, and CDPSE, demonstrating his commitment to staying current in the ever-evolving cybersecurity landscape.

Recognizing the vital role of digital forensics and incident response, I'm committed to contributing in every possible way. I extend heartfelt appreciation to my wife, daughter, and parents for their unwavering support, enabling my modest contribution as a technical reviewer. Special thanks to the authors and the dedicated Packt team – Pavan, Dhruvil, and Ashwini – for their patience and collaborative efforts amid my busy schedule.

Alexander Rau is a partner at one of the big four consulting firms in Canada, focusing on cybersecurity and cyber incident response. Alexander is responsible for leading the firm's cyber response practice, providing cybersecurity services to support and enable clients to better respond to cyber incidents before, during, and after a cyber breach. With 20+ years of experience in cybersecurity, IT, and privacy, Alexander has provided leadership to a number of multinational organizations, leading and delivering incident response and strategic cybersecurity engagements, practice leadership, and business development. His roles have included cybersecurity evangelism, conducting media interviews, keynote speaking, and panelist engagements.

Table of Contents

3

Exploring the Major Cloud Providers   39

4

DFIR Investigations – Logs in AWS   61

Part 2: Forensic Readiness: Tools, Techniques, and Preparation for Cloud Forensics

5

6

7

Cloud Productivity Suites   179

Part 3: Cloud Forensic Analysis – Responding to an Incident in the Cloud

8

The Digital Forensics and Incident Response Process   193

9

Common Attack Vectors and TTPs   241

10

Cloud Evidence Acquisition   267

11

Analyzing Compromised Containers   295

12

Analyzing Compromised Cloud Productivity Suites   311

Preface

The cloud has become a crucial platform to store, process, and manage data in the fast-paced world of digital technology. However, it also poses several complex challenges in the domain of digital forensics. *Cloud Forensics Demystified* is a comprehensive guide that aims to unravel these complexities and provide clarity and insight into the world of cloud forensics.

This book is aimed at professionals and enthusiasts alike, regardless of their prior experience in the field of digital forensics. It starts by establishing a foundational understanding of cloud computing, including its architecture, service models, and deployment types. This background is essential to understanding the unique challenges and opportunities that the cloud presents when it comes to forensic investigations.

The book then shifts focus to the core of cloud forensics, exploring the methodologies and best practices to conduct effective forensic investigations in cloud environments. This includes a detailed examination of data acquisition techniques, artifact analysis, and the legal considerations unique to the cloud. Throughout the book, the balance between technical efficiency and legal compliance is emphasized, reflecting the multifaceted nature of cloud forensics.

One of the unique features of this book is its emphasis on real-world applications. Through case studies and practical scenarios, you are shown how the principles and techniques discussed can be applied in actual forensic investigations. These examples provide a practical context to the theoretical concepts and prepare you for the unpredictable nature of forensic challenges in the cloud.

To ensure that the content remains relevant and up to date, *Cloud Forensics Demystified* also addresses the latest trends and advancements in cloud technology. This forward-looking perspective equips you with the knowledge needed to anticipate and adapt to the dynamic nature of cloud computing.

The book's goal is not only to demystify cloud forensics but also to inspire a new generation of forensic experts who are well versed in the nuances of cloud-based investigations. Whether you are a cybersecurity professional, a legal practitioner, an academic, or simply a technology enthusiast, *Cloud Forensics Demystified* offers a blend of theoretical depth and practical insight, paving your path toward mastering this fascinating field.

As you embark on this journey, you will be equipped with the knowledge and skills necessary to navigate the complexities of digital forensics in the cloud era. Get ready to explore a world where the cloud, once intangible, becomes a tangible source of forensic evidence.

Who this book is for

Cloud Forensics Demystified is a book that is primarily designed for digital forensics practitioners who are looking to broaden their knowledge of cloud-based forensics investigations. However, this book is also suitable for a range of professionals and enthusiasts with varying levels of experience in digital forensics and cloud computing. It is particularly helpful for those who want to learn more about the subject:

- **Digital Forensics and Incident Response (DFIR) practitioners seeking cloud expertise**: This book is aimed at professionals who are already skilled in digital forensics and incident response but want to extend their abilities to work in cloud environments. It covers advanced techniques and strategies to manage cloud-specific challenges and is an essential resource for DFIR experts who want to adapt to the cloud.

- **Cybersecurity professionals**: Those working in cybersecurity can gain valuable insights into conducting forensic investigations in cloud settings, due to the increasing dependence on cloud services.

- **Digital forensic investigators**: This book provides forensic investigators with detailed methodologies to acquire and analyze data in cloud environments.

- **Legal practitioners**: Legal professionals handling digital evidence from cloud sources will gain knowledge about the legal complexities of cloud forensics.

- **IT and cloud computing professionals**: IT and cloud computing professionals can deepen their understanding of the forensic implications of managing cloud services; this is essential for compliance and investigation preparedness.

- **Academics and students**: Educators and students in the fields of cybersecurity, digital forensics, IT, and law will find this book a comprehensive academic resource.

- **Technology enthusiasts**: For those interested in the convergence of technology, law, and security, the book offers an engaging and informative exploration of cloud forensics.

- **Corporate compliance and risk management professionals**: Professionals must understand cloud forensics to effectively mitigate cloud data risks.

What this book covers

Chapter 1, Introduction to the Cloud, presents a fundamental overview of cloud computing, including its architecture, service models (IaaS, PaaS, and SaaS), and deployment types (public, private, and hybrid). Its goal is to refresh or establish basic cloud knowledge, which is essential to comprehend subsequent forensic discussions.

Chapter 2, Trends in Cyber and Privacy Laws and Their Impact on DFIR, provides an in-depth understanding of the legal complexities that arise in cloud-based environments. These complexities include data privacy laws, compliance requirements, and jurisdictional issues. It is crucial to understand the legal framework that governs cloud data and its implications for forensic investigations.

Chapter 3, Exploring the Major Cloud Providers, provides an overview of the major cloud service providers, such as AWS, Azure, and GCP. It explains their unique architectures and services, giving context for how each affects forensic investigations.

Chapter 4, DFIR Investigations – Logs in AWS, provides a detailed guide on conducting DFIR in AWS environments, including accessing, interpreting, and analyzing logs to trace activities and identify security incidents.

Chapter 5, DFIR Investigations – Logs in Azure, focuses on leveraging Azure-specific logging mechanisms for forensic investigations.

Chapter 6, DFIR Investigations – Logs in GCP, is devoted to forensic investigations in GCP, with an emphasis on retrieving and analyzing GCP logs, which are a critical component of investigating incidents in GCP environments.

Chapter 7, Cloud Productivity Suites, discusses the challenges of forensic investigations in cloud-based productivity suites, such as Microsoft 365 and Google Workspace, and explores ways to access and analyze data from these widely used business tools.

Chapter 8, The Digital Forensics and Incident Response Process, provides a comprehensive guide to the DFIR process in cloud environments, including the identification, preservation, analysis, and reporting of digital evidence.

Chapter 9, Common Attack Vectors and TTPs, examines common attack vectors and the **tactics, techniques, and procedures (TTPs)** used in cloud environments to help anticipate and identify potential security incidents.

Chapter 10, Cloud Evidence Acquisition, discusses the challenges of acquiring digital evidence from cloud environments such as AWS, GCP, and Microsoft Azure, emphasizing the best practices to ensure evidence integrity and legal admissibility.

Chapter 11, Analyzing Compromised Containers, is dedicated to the forensic analysis of compromised containers and Kubernetes platforms in cloud environments. This chapter covers how to identify, collect, and analyze evidence from containers that are increasingly used for cloud-based applications.

Chapter 12, Analyzing Compromised Cloud Productivity Suites, discusses forensic strategies to analyze breaches in cloud-based productivity suites.

Each chapter of *Cloud Forensics Demystified* builds upon the previous one, creating a comprehensive guide that covers both the theoretical and practical aspects of cloud forensics, tailored to a variety of professional needs and interests.

To get the most out of this book

To get the most out of this book, consider the following approaches:

- If you are new to cloud computing, *Chapter 1* will provide you with a foundational understanding of basic cloud concepts. This will facilitate your comprehension of the complex topics discussed in later chapters.

- **Understanding the legal context**: It is important to understand the legal context before conducting any forensic work in the cloud. *Chapter 2* provides fundamental knowledge on laws and regulations that must be followed in investigations.

- **Studying specific cloud providers**: Gain insights into different cloud service providers by focusing on *Chapters 3, 4, 5, and 6*. Tailor your learning to the **cloud service providers (CSPs)** you encounter most in your work or are most interested in.

- **Hands-on practice**: It is recommended to apply the concepts and techniques discussed in the book in a practical setting. This can be done through simulations, training environments, or during actual forensic investigations if you already work in the field.

- **Focusing on DFIR processes**: *Chapters 7 and 8* are crucial to understanding the nuances of incident response and investigation in cloud environments. Pay close attention to these whether that's your primary interest.

- **Staying updated on attack vectors**: Review *Chapter 9* to stay ahead of evolving security threats and keep your knowledge current with the latest attack methods.

- **Mastering evidence acquisition**: *Chapters 10 to 12* cover evidence acquisition and analysis, crucial for developing practical skills in real-world forensic cases.

- **Engaging with case studies**: Take the time to thoroughly understand practical examples and case studies, as they provide context to theoretical knowledge and valuable understanding of real-world applications.

- **Participating in community discussions and workshops**: Engage with the cybersecurity and digital forensics community. Discussions, workshops, and conferences can provide additional insights and practical perspectives.

- **Reflecting and applying**: After each chapter, take a moment to reflect on how the information applies to your current knowledge, experience, and professional scenarios. Consider writing down key takeaways or how you might implement new strategies in your work.

Approach *Cloud Forensics Demystified* with a structured mindset to enhance your skills and understanding of cloud forensics.

Conventions used

There are a number of text conventions used throughout this book.

Code in text: Indicates code words in text, database table names, folder names, filenames, file extensions, pathnames, dummy URLs, user input, and Twitter handles. Here is an example: "Commands such as `sort by` and `limit` control the order and the number of records in the output."

A block of code is set as follows:

```
AzureNetworkAnalytics_CL
| where SubType_s == "FlowLog"
| extend FlowDirection = iff(FlowDirection_s == 'O', 'Outbound',
'Inbound')
| extend AllowedOrDenied = iff(FlowStatus_s == 'A', 'Allowed',
'Denied')
```

When we wish to draw your attention to a particular part of a code block, the relevant lines or items are set in bold:

```
StorageBlobLogs
| where TimeGenerated > ago(7d)
| project TimeGenerated, OperationName, AuthenticationType, Uri, _
ResourceId, CallerIpAddress
```

Any command-line input or output is written as follows:

```
$ gsutil iam get gs://test_cf1_test1
```

Bold: Indicates a new term, an important word, or words that you see on screen. For instance, words in menus or dialog boxes appear in bold. Here is an example: "All virtual networks can be accessed directly from the **Virtual networks** service on Azure's **Home** page."

> **Tips or important notes**
> Appear like this.

Get in touch

Feedback from our readers is always welcome.

General feedback: If you have questions about any aspect of this book, email us at customercare@packtpub.com and mention the book title in the subject of your message.

Errata: Although we have taken every care to ensure the accuracy of our content, mistakes do happen. If you have found a mistake in this book, we would be grateful if you would report this to us. Please visit www.packtpub.com/support/errata and fill in the form.

Piracy: If you come across any illegal copies of our works in any form on the internet, we would be grateful if you would provide us with the location address or website name. Please contact us at copyright@packt.com with a link to the material.

If you are interested in becoming an author: If there is a topic that you have expertise in and you are interested in either writing or contributing to a book, please visit authors.packtpub.com.

Share your thoughts

Once you've read *Cloud Forensics Demystified*, we'd love to hear your thoughts! Scan the QR code below to go straight to the Amazon review page for this book and share your feedback.

https://packt.link/r/1800564414

Your review is important to us and the tech community and will help us make sure we're delivering excellent quality content.

Download a free PDF copy of this book

Thanks for purchasing this book!

Do you like to read on the go but are unable to carry your print books everywhere?

Is your eBook purchase not compatible with the device of your choice?

Don't worry, now with every Packt book you get a DRM-free PDF version of that book at no cost.

Read anywhere, any place, on any device. Search, copy, and paste code from your favorite technical books directly into your application.

The perks don't stop there, you can get exclusive access to discounts, newsletters, and great free content in your inbox daily

Follow these simple steps to get the benefits:

1. Scan the QR code or visit the link below

https://packt.link/free-ebook/9781800564411

2. Submit your proof of purchase
3. That's it! We'll send your free PDF and other benefits to your email directly

Part 1: Cloud Fundamentals

In this part, we will look at the fundamental aspects of the cloud. This part is specifically useful for familiarizing yourself with the basics of the cloud and legal challenges regarding cloud technologies, especially when it comes to cross-border investigations and complex cloud infrastructure. We will also introduce some prominent cloud service providers, offering various cloud resources.

This part has the following chapters:

- *Chapter 1, Introduction to the Cloud*
- *Chapter 2, Trends in Cyber and Privacy Laws and Their Impact on DFIR*
- *Chapter 3, Exploring the Major Cloud Providers*

1

Introduction to the Cloud

Cloud computing has been around for years – the concept of computing resources being offered to users or customers over the internet. While the concept is not new, it has been offered in various forms and can be deployed in various ways. The benefit of the cloud is that it natively offers scalability, the flexibility of resources (meaning you can choose how powerful resources you need, depending upon computational requirements), and cost-effectiveness, making it easier for organizations to plan for cloud adoption. As a result, organizations are now migrating their critical data and business applications to the cloud, creating new challenges for incident responders when investigating security incidents and data breaches. According to Gartner's report, 80% of enterprises will be moving to a cloud-only strategy by 2025 and moving away from traditional data centers. Meanwhile, the IDG 2020 Cloud Computing survey indicates that at least 92% of companies are using at least one or more cloud services (for example, Microsoft 365 for emails and so on) for their business operations.

Incident responders need to understand how the cloud works to effectively investigate security incidents. An incident responder is someone or a team who is primarily responsible for handling a security incident related to an **Information Technology** (**IT**) system. Incident responders typically will analyze, investigate, contain, and resolve security incidents. Incident responders have a deep understanding of IT computing concepts and carry a deep understanding of investigative procedures, including digital forensics.

This chapter on the cloud will provide you with a quick refresher on cloud computing, covering important topics such as the history of cloud computing; the advantages and disadvantages of cloud computing; cloud services and deployment models; and the impact cloud adoption has had on several key industries.

Cloud evolution goes as far back as the 1960s when the **Defense Advanced Research Projects Agency** (**DARPA**) tasked MIT with developing a computing environment that could be used by two or more people. In 1969, American psychologist and computer scientist J.C.R. Licklider, as part of his research in the **Advanced Research Project Agency Network** (**ARPANET**), worked on systems that would allow users to connect and share information from anywhere in the world.

Fast-forward to the 1990s, during the mainframe age, when computing resources were provided centrally. The dot-com boom paved the way for web services to be offered over the internet to consumers (**Software as a Service (SaaS)**). As cloud computing has become more complex and distributed, so have the challenges of managing security incidents and conducting forensic investigations. The ability to collect and analyze data across different cloud environments and deployment models is essential for organizations to respond quickly and effectively to security incidents. The following diagram illustrates the evolution of the cloud from a centralized mainframe model to serverless computing and really highlights the importance of continuously developing your forensic methods when responding to cloud-based security incidents.

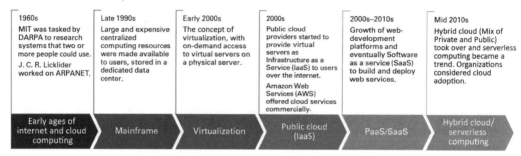

Figure 1.1 – Cloud evolution timeline

Advantages and disadvantages of cloud computing

Every technology comes with its own set of complexities and challenges, and there is always a good and bad side of every technological evolution. Here are some of the advantages and disadvantages of cloud computing.

Advantages:

- **Modernization and innovation**: The cloud promotes new innovations. Cloud service providers investing in advanced infrastructural features allows researchers and enthusiasts to research and innovate new solutions, such as **Artificial Intelligence (AI)**, **Machine Learning (ML)**, robotics, and so on.

- **Scalability**: Clearly, a huge advantage of adopting the cloud for organizations is easier scalability of resources. Storage and computational power can be scaled up or down to suit the needs of the organization, applications, or user demands, and all this without any significant hardware or software investments. Cloud scalability is particularly useful for deploying **endpoint detection and response (EDR)** tools, which can help investigators identify and contain threats and conduct forensics on compromised systems. EDR tools can be resource-intensive, requiring significant computing power and storage capacity to run effectively. With cloud scalability, investigators can quickly allocate additional resources to run EDR (and other forensic) tools on the systems under investigation, allowing them to detect and respond to threats more quickly and efficiently and minimizing business disruption.

- **Flexibility and reach**: You can turn your cloud computing resources on or off; cloud computing offers the flexibility to enable or disable any services based on user demands. Furthermore, you can make your cloud services available through any device with just an internet connection, increasing your application outreach to remote users. Flexibility allows cloud services to be made available in remote parts of the world without any investment in the hardware or software for hosting your applications. Specifically, this allows forensic investigators to gain access to data from across an IT environment fast and efficiently (most commonly through a centralized cloud console). This is critical in identifying and responding to security incidents for organizations that have an IT infrastructure presence in multiple geographic locations.

- **Cost savings**: One of the biggest advantages of using the cloud is a significantly higher return on investments and low costs. There are no upfront investments required in procuring and setting up hardware/software. No capital investments are required to rent a space in a data center, or set up your own data center. There are also minimal operating costs – just cloud operating costs that are billed to the organization. Reduced capital costs mean organizations can budget more for deploying additional resources to mitigate security incidents, such as hiring security experts, acquiring specialized security tools, and increasing the capacity of their IT infrastructure.

- **Disaster recovery**: Another advantage of subscribing to cloud services is disaster recovery and ensuring continuity of service to users. Cloud services are typically replicated, load-balanced, and backed up to ensure continuity of services. Robust disaster recovery policies allow organizations to quickly recover from a security incident, minimize downtime and business disruption, and ensure that there will be backups available for forensic analysis if required.

- **Data security**: Given that cloud service providers invest in the infrastructure to set up and provision cloud services for users, cloud service providers typically use strict security controls, including encryption and advanced access controls. As the cloud operates on a shared security model, it is important to note that customers or enterprises subscribing to the cloud are still responsible for the enablement of encryption, access control configurations, and any other security features offered by the cloud service provider.

Disadvantages:

- **Security and privacy risk**: The fact that cloud providers invest heavily in protecting cloud infrastructure, putting organizational or customer information in the cloud poses a risk of data exposure of records if the cloud systems are misconfigured. There are plenty of such examples out there that reflect this concern.

- **Requirement for an internet connection**: Because cloud resources can be accessed from any part of the world, there is a huge dependency on the internet. Without internet access, you cannot perform any activities on the cloud.

- **Potential vendor lock-in**: Once organizations sign up with a cloud provider to offer their services to users via cloud infrastructure, organizations are often locked in with the same vendor, making it harder to switch to other providers.

- **Potential service disruption**: Service providers will often try to provide new features/products to end users, and in doing so, they can inadvertently affect services, which can lead to outages and service disruptions.

An overview of cloud services

In today's world, there are many services that are virtualized and can be made available in the cloud. The cloud offers scalability of resources and cost-effectiveness, which have been key to its success.

Generally, cloud computing is offered in the following service models:

- **Infrastructure as a Service (IaaS)**: IaaS provides users with access to virtualized resources such as servers, operating systems, storage, and networking. With IaaS, users are also allowed to customize their infrastructure. For example, they can enable storage encryption or configure the server to access a particular segment of the cloud network. This setup is typically applied by organizations who have their corporate data in the cloud and want to safeguard it from being generally accessible on the internet. It is also a security best practice to only allow cloud resources to access specific network connections, including corporate networks. In IaaS, users can create, configure, and manage their virtual infrastructure on the cloud provider's platform, paying only for the resources they use. IaaS provides the highest level of control, as cloud consumers are responsible for securing their operating system, applications, and data—as a result, incident responders will have a larger scope and granular access when responding to security incidents. However, because the cloud provider is responsible for securing the physical cloud infrastructure, incident responders may need to work with the cloud provider if the root cause is determined to be related to physical hosts, the physical network, or the physical data center.

- **Platform as a Service (PaaS)**: PaaS provides application developers with a ready-made environment to build, deploy, and manage applications without having to configure the underlying infrastructure. In PaaS, cloud providers typically package the infrastructure based on the needs and requirements of the applications. Some of the platform configurations will allow developers to use various popular programming languages as well, such as Python, Perl, Go, Ruby, Java, Node.js, and .NET. A PaaS setup typically allows auto-scaling, meaning that, based on the performance demands required for the platform to operate, it can scale and share the load of processing and allow users transparent access to the platform. Some PaaS providers will also provide application monitoring and telemetry to allow developers to troubleshoot and optimize their applications for their customers. PaaS provides a mixed level of control, as the cloud provider manages the operating system, and the cloud consumers are responsible for securing only the applications and data. Incident responders will therefore have to work with the cloud service provider if requesting any evidence at the operating system layer.

- **SaaS**: SaaS provides users with cloud-hosted software applications over the internet as a web service. Examples include payroll processing, accounting software, **Customer Relationship Management (CRM)**, and project management. The cloud provider manages the infrastructure and software, and users can access the software from any device with an internet connection either through a web browser or a dedicated application – for example, an airline ticketing application that accesses the backend services hosted on the cloud. SaaS provides the lowest level of control for a cloud consumer, and as a result, incident responders will have to work with any evidence/artifacts/logging at an application level and work with the cloud provider for anything else (the infrastructure, operating system, etc.). The features of SaaS include the following:

  - **Multi-tenancy**: Software services are made available to multiple users, on multiple separate cloud tenants (shared infrastructure). Tenant refers to an isolated service that is made available specifically for users. With multiple tenants, cloud services are isolated from each other, and one user's data is not available to others, allowing security and privacy of the data stored within the service.

  - **Automatic updates**: SaaS providers manage updates or upgrades to their software applications without any intervention from their users.

  - **Scalability**: SaaS providers can scale and support a large number of users and datasets.

  - **Pay-as-you-go**: SaaS providers typically provide their services as a subscription model, so customers only pay for the resources or the software services they need.

  - **Accessible from anywhere**: SaaS services are usually offered as accessible from anywhere in the world. Some SaaS providers will also offer their services from any device as well. SaaS providers may customize their service offerings based on the location of the user accessing or subscribing to the services.

- **Database as a Service (DBaaS)**: DBaaS provides users with access to managed database services, allowing them to store, manage, and analyze data in the cloud. The cloud provider manages the infrastructure, software, and data backups, providing users with a scalable and secure database solution. For DBaaS, an incident responder's focus would be digital forensics at the database level (i.e., database configuration, database logging, etc.), if customers have enabled database logging including transaction logging.

- **Function as a Service (FaaS)**: FaaS provides specific functions to users. It is also known as serverless computing, allowing developers to execute code without having to manage servers or infrastructure. It is a subset of PaaS; users can write and deploy their code on the cloud provider's platform, paying only for the compute resources used. Examples include chatbots and IoT applications. Some of the serverless features include the following:

- **Event-driven**: Triggered as a result of a particular event and specified by the developer. It can also be configured to trigger when a certain condition is met. This type of setup is usually configured for alerting and notifications, where there is an event that occurs and as a result, users are notified.

- **Scalable**: Automatically scale to manage the function workload and computing demands, without any manual intervention.

- **Pay-per-use**: You only pay for what you use, for example, you will be billed for the compute resources utilized, or volume-based pricing will be used, rather than a fixed fee for computing resources.

- **Stateless**: FaaS services are stateless, and do not retain any context or the state of a user's request between multiple requests from the same user. They simply respond (execute the function) as requested by the user.

- **Short-lived**: Functions are short-lived, meaning they execute the function in a few seconds and exit. You are only billed when the function is executed, as that is when compute resources are utilized.

We will discuss more on some of the services and associated products offered by popular cloud providers in *Chapter 3*.

Cloud deployment models

It is important to understand that cloud services can be deployed through various means and have forensic implications for investigators. These models are a framework for how these services are hosted and delivered to users. We can typically classify cloud deployment into four different models: public, private, hybrid, and community models:

- **Public cloud**: The most popular option for all users and service providers is a public cloud model. In this model, service providers can deliver their applications over a commonly used infrastructure. Typically, the public cloud is used for non-critical tasks, or by developers to develop and test their applications on a public cloud tenant. Some of the public cloud offerings could also include services such as file hosting services, file sharing services, and email services. In some cases, public cloud services are offered over multiple cloud service providers, for example, a public cloud application that is deployed and available to users via **Amazon Web Services (AWS)** and **Google Cloud Platform (GCP)**, depending on the region from which the web service is accessed. The public cloud is typically cheaper for users and is offered on a pay-as-you-go basis, with the ability to scale up or down when required. From a digital forensic standpoint, performing an investigation on a public cloud domain can be challenging because cloud resources are usually shared, and preserving forensic data may be challenging. It can also happen that sometimes you will not find the relevant artifacts you are looking for as some of the resources are terminated and no longer in use, which cloud providers will begin to reallocate, making it harder to gain insight from a digital forensics point of view. The following diagram illustrates some common use cases of the public cloud. Specifically, the following figure highlights the various applications that can be delivered through the public cloud, essentially allowing users access to these applications for free or for a subscription-based fee.

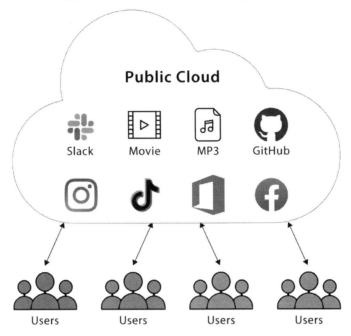

Figure 1.2 – An example of the public cloud

- **Private cloud**: A private cloud is a dedicated setup of cloud infrastructure owned and operated by a single organization to host their application exclusively, making it available to a single customer. An example would be hosting a machine learning application, virtual desktop infrastructure for an organization, and so on. A private cloud setup can be on-premises or hosted by a third party with specific controls. Private clouds are usually expensive to build and maintain and allow organizations to define more granular security controls based on their application needs. As the private cloud demands that the cloud infrastructure is configured and secured appropriately, from a digital forensic standpoint, forensic artifacts are usually available for investigators' review. Since it's a private cloud, cloud resources are not reallocated to other tenants, and, therefore, there are better chances of obtaining the logs/artifacts that are needed for investigation in a private cloud setup. The following diagram illustrates some common use cases of a private cloud model. For example, a commercial shopping application, internal systems such as **Enterprise Resource Planning** (**ERP**) software, and other systems are hosted on dedicated cloud infrastructure that is offered to a limited set of consumers.

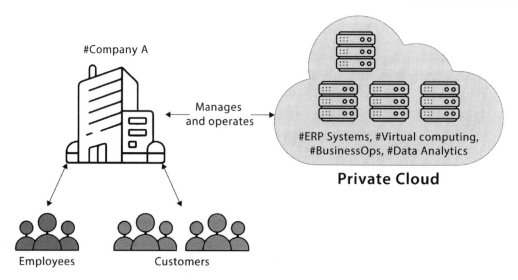

Figure 1.3 – Private cloud setup

- **Hybrid cloud**: This is a mix of public and private cloud infrastructure, where customers or users see the hybrid cloud as a single cloud offering transparently. Hybrid cloud infrastructure is typically used by organizations where they want to offload processing a function or require additional storage during peak times. A hybrid cloud can also be set up by some customers by leveraging on-premises systems and connecting with cloud infrastructure to provide additional services (for example, additional storage, cloud backup, and so on). However, having a hybrid infrastructure across public and private clouds may create challenges for investigators from a digital forensics perspective because of the spread of the data and artifacts between private and public clouds. As a result of the chosen deployment model, blind spots may occur during investigations as some of the artifacts may be lost and resources may be reallocated, specifically those that were hosted within the public cloud tenant. The following diagram shows a private cloud infrastructure that hosts internal applications such as ERP software and any other internal applications, while also offering services such as Dropbox or Netflix for general users. These applications are backed up in private cloud infrastructure.

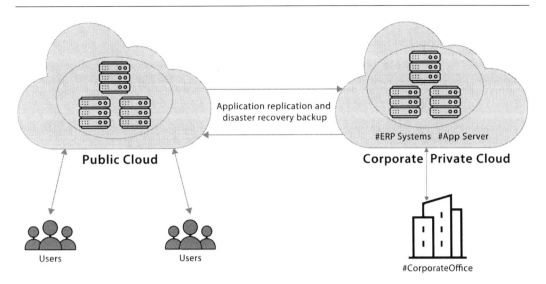

Figure 1.4 – Hybrid cloud deployment model

- **Community cloud**: Organizations with a shared mission may come together to create a joint cloud infrastructure that is made available for a specific user community. Typically, the organizations that are part of this community share the cost of hosting the infrastructure in the cloud. This kind of setup is typically operated by universities or not-for-profit organizations that come together for a joint cause. The upside of such deployment is shared cost and responsibility for hosting and making the data available to users. A community cloud can be hosted on-premises, in a private cloud, or in public cloud tenants. Investigating breaches in the community cloud is more challenging for investigators because of shared infrastructure and resources. Specifically, for **Digital Forensics and Incident Response (DFIR)** teams, it is important to ensure that you obtain legal authorizations prior to commencing an investigation into a community cloud infrastructure as multiple parties and multiple levels of datasets are involved. DFIR teams should consider the challenges in reviewing forensic artifacts that may be stored across various locations and servers. *Figure 1.5* illustrates a community cloud and how various organizations with the same mission may share a joint cloud infrastructure. For example, a consortium of banks come together to establish a cloud infrastructure to jointly provide services to end users, and these can be classified as a banking community offering services to the public. Similarly, government agencies set up a community cloud infrastructure to offer joint services in one place to end users and citizens.

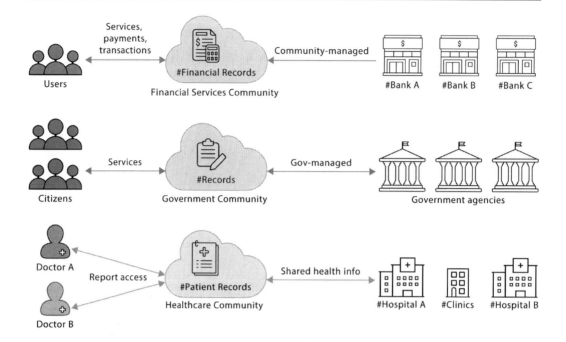

Figure 1.5 – Community cloud model

In summary, forensic data availability depends on the choice of cloud deployment models and logging and preserving relevant data/logs.

Cloud adoption success stories

Many organizations h1ave adopted the cloud as their primary center to provide services to their customers. It is essential to understand how cloud infrastructure and applications differ from traditional on-premises IT environments and how to respond to incidents effectively in the cloud. By studying cloud adoption success stories, security professionals can learn about emerging cloud implementation trends and the associated threats and how to proactively address them.

The following case studies include some of the many examples of organizations that utilize the cloud for their business needs:

- **A large global entertainment streaming platform**: This large streaming enterprise adopted the cloud, specifically **AWS**, to provide its streaming services to end users. As one of the world's leading streaming providers, with more than 200 million members from 190 countries with more than 125 million hours of viewing, it uses AWS for storage, computation resources, and infrastructure to allow quick scalability and meet peak streaming needs. It has also built a virtual studio in the cloud, allowing artistic talents to collaborate seamlessly without any restrictions.

- **Sports entertainment**: Another entertainment company has leveraged AWS to deliver its telemetric analysis that is collected live from their race cars lap by lap. It used the cloud to scale up the number of feeds it receives, process them, apply predictive **ML** modules, and utilize **High-Performance Computing** (**HPC**) to provide insights to end users. This has, of course, driven higher viewership of the sport.

- **Bank of Canada** (**BoC**): BoC owns the responsibility to regulate banking systems in Canada; it is responsible for setting monetary policies and maintaining financial stability. BoC leveraged Microsoft Azure to launch the Canada Skills Program, which aimed to provide Canadians with the skills necessary to thrive in the digital economy. The program used Microsoft's LinkedIn Learning platform to offer free access to online courses and learning paths, covering topics such as cloud computing, data analysis, and cybersecurity. Over 7,500 Canadians participated in the program within its first year, with plans to expand and offer more learning opportunities in the future.

Impact of the cloud and other technologies

Cloud computing has had a significant impact on industries, the economy, and, most importantly, end users. Similar related technological innovations in ML, blockchain and cryptography, the **Internet of Things** (**IoT**), and so on have changed the way we utilize the cloud. The following are some of the impacts of related technological innovations and the cloud:

- **Containers**: Containers are applications and associated dependencies packaged into a portable and lightweight unit that can be deployed and scaled quickly and efficiently. In cloud computing, containers can be used to enable microservices-based architectures, improve application performance and reliability, and enhance DevOps processes. The use of containers has also enabled container orchestration tools such as Kubernetes, which automates the deployment, scaling, and management of containerized applications. These tools provide a way to manage large-scale container deployments and ensure high availability and fault tolerance.

- **DevSecOps**: DevSecOps is an approach to integrating security into the software development life cycle process, right from the ideation phase to the execution and deployment phase. It promotes shift-left security, continuous security testing, automation, collaboration, and the use of cloud-native security tools and practices. DevSecOps improves the security and reliability of cloud-based applications and infrastructure by identifying and addressing security issues early on, promoting consistency and reducing errors, and ensuring that security measures are applied consistently across all stages of the development process. Overall, DevSecOps ensures that security is a top priority throughout the entire life cycle of a cloud application, leading to a more secure and reliable cloud computing environment.

- **ML**: ML models deployed in the cloud can leverage cloud scalability, automation, and accessibility to enable the development of intelligent applications that learn from data and improve over time. ML requires vast amounts of data to train models and make accurate predictions, and cloud computing provides the necessary computing power and storage to process large amounts of data. Cloud-based ML platforms can automate many of the tasks involved in developing ML models, making it easier for developers to build and deploy ML models without requiring significant expertise in data science or machine learning.

- **Quantum computing**: Quantum computing requires massive amounts of hardware and building them on a physical bare-metal system is expensive. It is regarded as one of the most revolutionary computing products by processing complex problems that are currently infeasible in classical computing. Conducting quantum computing enhances ML, cryptography, and simulation applications.

- **Blockchain**: Another technological innovation is the application of blockchain technology, which can enable secure and transparent data sharing and exchange and can be useful in industry sectors, specifically finance, healthcare, and supply chain management. In cloud computing, blockchain can be used to establish trust in distributed environments, enable decentralized applications, and enhance data privacy and security.

- **IoT**: IoT devices generate large volumes of telemetric data that can be processed and analyzed in the cloud. Cloud computing provides the infrastructure and tools to store, manage, and analyze this data, enabling new use cases in areas such as smart homes, industrial automation, and predictive maintenance. The cloud also allows related technologies to complement each other, for example, using IoT telemetric data to train ML models and allow smart homes to be even smarter using these predictive technologies through AI.

- **Identity and access management (IAM)**: Cloud computing has led to the widespread adoption of IAM technologies, which enable organizations to manage user identities and control access to cloud resources. IAM technologies (such as passwordless authentication) can help ensure that only authorized users able to access sensitive data and have made it easier to implement additional security features such as multi-factor authentication and role-based access control. Passwordless authentication is the approach of verifying and authenticating users without requiring them to enter a password. Some of the applications of passwordless authentication include the following:

  - **Biometric authentication**: For example, retina scans, fingerprints, and facial recognition.

  - **Public key cryptography**: Users are required to authenticate using a public-private key combination pair. Private keys are held securely by the user while associated public keys are used to verify the identity.

  - **One-time passwords**: This involves a system generating a one-time token for the purpose of validating the identity of the user.

- **Physical tokens**: A hardware device that has the necessary information to validate the identity of the user. Physical tokens can also be used to store users' private keys for validation.

Summary

This was a quick refresher on cloud computing, including its basic concepts, the cloud's evolution throughout the years, and the benefits of cloud computing. Additionally, this chapter discussed various deployment models, including public, private, and hybrid clouds, as well as various service models such as IaaS, PaaS, and SaaS.

Understanding cloud computing is crucial for incident response professionals, as it has become an essential part of modern technology, and many organizations have adopted cloud-based solutions to store and process their data. It is therefore a complex infrastructure and having a sound understanding of how a cloud tenant can be set up in various forms and its complexities can help incident responders to effectively respond to security incidents and investigate in a forensically sound manner.

In the next chapter, we will learn about legal complexities and DFIR impacts as we learn about how to navigate jurisdiction and privacy regulations.

Further reading

- *Introduction to Cloud*: https://www.coursera.org/learn/introduction-to-cloud
- Bank of Canada Government skills program: https://customers.microsoft.com/en-ca/story/1560503487084546279-bankofcanada-government-canada-skills-program
- *What is cloud computing?* https://azure.microsoft.com/en-ca/resources/cloud-computing-dictionary/what-is-cloud-computing#:~:text=Simply%20put%2C%20cloud%20computing%20is,resources%2C%20and%20economies%20of%20scale.
- *What is cloud computing?* https://aws.amazon.com/what-is-cloud-computing/
- What is cloud computing? https://www.ibm.com/topics/cloud-computing
- What is Platform as a Service? PaaS examples + SaaS versus PaaS versus IaaS https://www.zendesk.com/blog/what-is-paas/

2
Trends in Cyber and Privacy Laws and Their Impact on DFIR

When considering the cloud, organizations must factor in the legal risks associated with their data being hosted off-premises by a third-party cloud service provider. As a result, there is also a direct implication for the availability of forensic artifacts, what artifacts can be acquired or accessed outside of a particular country, and so on. Jurisdiction plays a key role in cloud forensics. This chapter aims to uncover the legal, privacy, and contractual risks that typically arise out of cloud usage and its impact on forensic investigations.

The role of a breach counselor (breach coach)

A breach counselor (also known as a breach coach) is an attorney with expertise in cybersecurity and related legal frameworks. A breach counselor's responsibility is to understand the data hosted by an affected organization and develop an understanding of the respective legal implications for the organization because of the cybersecurity incident or breach. Typically, breach coaches are retained when there is a risk of litigation due to the impact of the security incident or breach (for example, unauthorized disclosure of private and sensitive data leading to identity fraud against customers) and as a result, breach coaches provide recommendations and legal advice to the affected organization as they navigate and respond to the incident.

Breach coaches can also represent the organization in a court of law should the matter go to court, but in most cases, an organization retains breach coaches to identify the organization's legal obligations to report the incident in due course and to limit the chances of litigation.

For breach coaches to provide legal advice to the affected organization, breach coaches work with DFIR teams to identify the nature and cause of the cybersecurity incident, the extent of private or sensitive data disclosure, and any additional insights in relation to the cyber incident itself. To ensure all the parties in a cybersecurity incident (the breach coach, the organization, and the DFIR team) can freely communicate with each other about the cyber incident without the risk of such communications being disclosed, breach coaches exercise something called **solicitor-client privilege** or **litigation**

privilege. Solicitor-client privilege or attorney-client privilege protects the communication between the organization, lawyer, and DFIR team. Where the communication is intended to be privileged and confidential, it is protected from disclosure, unless the communication is deemed to be factual in nature, in which case the privilege may not be exercised in certain jurisdictions.

Litigation privilege preserves the documents and communications specifically drafted for the purpose of litigation, for example, a cybersecurity forensic report prepared at the instruction of legal counsel.

There can be one or more breach coaches retained by an organization, depending upon the countries/jurisdictions in which the organization does business.

> **Important note**
>
> It is very important that digital forensic investigators familiarize themselves with the various legal regulations and frameworks that are applicable across jurisdictions, along with the role of a breach coach. Where required, DFIR teams should consult breach coaches/counselors to ensure appropriate legal compliance when collecting, analyzing, or handling forensic artifacts that may contain sensitive information.

General legal considerations for cloud adoption

The legal framework for the cloud and its adoption varies from one country to another, but at a high level, here are some of the common concepts that are typically considered with respect to a legal framework:

- **Data protection and privacy**: As of 2023, the majority of organizations will have to consider the concerns around securing their data hosted in the cloud. Regulations such as, but not limited to, the **General Data Protection Regulation (GDPR)** in the **European Union (EU)** and the **California Consumer Privacy Act (CCPA)** in the **United States (US)** outline how personal data must be handled and protected in the cloud. Some of these data protection and privacy laws may also restrict digital forensic investigators from transferring artifacts outside of respective jurisdictions:

  - GDPR in the EU sets out specific rules for the protection of personal data, which also include instructions that the processing of personal information shall be done lawfully, fairly, and transparently within the EU, and that individuals have the right to access, rectify, and erase their personal information. This means that you cannot transfer any artifacts as part of an investigation outside of the EU (GDPR enforcement) zone, and will be required to set up and conduct your forensic investigation locally within the EU region. Investigators may also be required to work with their EU counterparts instead, to comply with GDPR requirements. Even if you can access the artifacts from anywhere in the world, GDPR requires that any artifacts that may contain personal information are physically located/stored within the EU.

- CCPA also outlines some of the considerations for incident investigations where personal information is involved. It is similar to GDPR in stating that artifacts must be collected lawfully, meaning there should be a legal basis on which to collect these artifacts (which may contain personal information, health information, and so on), and investigate. CCPA also requires investigators to comply with deletion requests for personal information that may be collected as part of investigations, and investigators are required to apply the necessary security controls to prevent the unauthorized access to, or destruction or modification of, artifacts during investigations.

- **Cyber risk management**: As the cloud is always available (online), it constantly poses a security risk, including the risk of data breaches and cyber-attacks. Legal frameworks and guidelines often require **Cloud Service Providers (CSPs)** to implement security measures and risk management strategies to protect against risk. These typically include CSPs having appropriate risk management documentation, including incident response plans, to ensure CSPs are familiar with the procedures for detecting, containing, and recovering from an incident.

  Businesses or cloud service consumers are also required to establish their own risk management program prior to embarking on cloud adoption. This also means that businesses work with CSPs to define an appropriate incident response plan (clearly outlining the roles and responsibilities between the CSP and business), deploy specialized tooling to protect, detect, and support investigations in the cloud (for example, an **Endpoint Detection and Response (EDR)** tool) in the event of a cyber incident, and develop in-house or outsourced (on a retainer) experts who are familiar with cloud infrastructure.

- **Compliance**: Cloud computing must comply with a range of regulations, such as industry-specific regulations (GDPR for protecting EU citizens' private information), financial regulations (**Payment Card Industry Data Security Standard (PCI DSS)**), and healthcare regulations (**Health Insurance Portability and Accountability Act (HIPAA)** or **Health Information Trust Alliance (HITRUST)**). Legal frameworks and guidelines may set requirements for CSPs to comply with these regulations.

  Furthermore, if your services are offered to US government agencies, then your cloud infrastructure must be shown to comply with the **Federal Risk and Authorization Management Program (FedRAMP)**. The FedRAMP program provides a standardized approach and framework for security assessments, access control and authorizations, and the continuous monitoring of cloud infrastructure services, to ensure CSPs achieve the necessary security compliance prior to offering services to US government agencies. Compliance with FedRAMP ensures digital forensic investigators access to any necessary logs and artifacts, as FedRAMP outlines requirements for CSPs to maintain logs and artifacts, preserve evidence for forensic analysis, and comply with the appropriate legal and regulatory mandates. However, it is important to note that CSPs do not need to show FedRAMP compliance for all their service offerings (entire cloud products).

Cloud services/products are typically a subset of specialized and curated cloud service offerings that comply with FedRAMP and are specifically designed to cater to US government agencies who would like to leverage cloud services. It is therefore important for investigators to recognize whether the cloud service or product offering that is the subject of an investigation is compliant with FedRAMP or not, as the availability of artifacts and logs for investigation may vary significantly as a result.

- **Applicable jurisdiction**: Cloud computing can involve data processing and storage in multiple jurisdictions, which can raise questions about jurisdictional authority and legal requirements. Legal frameworks and guidelines may address these issues and set requirements for cross-border data transfers.

- **Contractual considerations**: Cloud computing often involves contractual agreements between CSPs and their customers. Legal frameworks and guidelines may set requirements for these agreements, such as the inclusion of specific provisions related to data protection, security, and liability.

In summary, organizations must recognize the legal guardrails to protect the privacy of the information stored within their systems as they transition to the cloud. It is important that they safeguard and implement appropriate controls to prevent the accidental or unauthorized disclosure of private and sensitive information. For DFIR teams, it is important that they understand the compliance requirements to support the organization's cloud transition. Similarly, as part of the investigation into a cybersecurity incident, understanding the legal requirements and their goals will enable the DFIR teams to focus their investigation on identifying the root cause and impact of the breach of private or sensitive information, and to plan appropriate mitigation to prevent reoccurrence of security incidents.

eDiscovery considerations and legal guidance

eDiscovery, or **electronic discovery**, refers to identifying, collecting, preserving, and producing data stored in digital formats or electronic storage as part of a legal or regulatory investigation. This includes searching for **electronically stored information** (**ESI**) such as emails, documents, datasets, and any other digital content with specialized tools and software. The legal framework and guidelines for eDiscovery are constantly evolving, but there are several key standards and guidelines that are widely recognized and used in the industry. In digital forensics, ESI plays a key role in investigating digital crimes or intellectual property theft. Digital forensic investigators rely on ESI for reconstructing the activities of a threat actor, determining the source of the breach, or identifying any suspects. eDiscovery is a critical component of this process as it requires investigators to collect, preserve, and analyze in a forensically sound and legally defensible manner. Outlined in the following bullet list are some of the most accepted standards for ESI:

- **International Organization for Standardization/International Electrotechnical Commission (ISO/IEC) 27050: ISO/IEC 27050**: This standard provides a comprehensive framework for managing ESI during eDiscovery processes. It is designed to help organizations ensure that they are complying with legal and regulatory requirements related to eDiscovery, while also protecting the confidentiality, integrity, and availability of sensitive data. Some of the key elements of ISO/IEC 27050 include the following:

- **Identification**: This phase involves identifying the relevant ESI that may be subject to a legal request or investigation. This includes data that is stored on servers, in emails, on mobile devices, or in other digital formats.

- **Preservation**: Once the relevant ESI has been identified, it must be preserved to ensure that it is not altered or destroyed. This may involve making copies of data prior to any review or investigation, implementing legal holds, or restricting access to certain data, ensuring the data cannot be destroyed by anyone.

- **Collection**: After the ESI has been preserved, it must be collected and analyzed to determine its relevance to the legal request or investigation. This may involve searching for specific keywords or phrases, reviewing metadata, or using forensic tools to extract data from digital devices.

- **Analysis**: Once the ESI has been collected, it must be analyzed to determine its significance and relevance to the legal request or investigation. This may involve reviewing the data to identify patterns or trends or using analytics tools to extract insights from large datasets.

- **Production**: The relevant ESI must be produced for the requesting party or authority. This may involve providing copies of data, producing reports or summaries of data, or testifying in court as an expert witness.

- **Cloud Security Alliance (CSA) guidance**: The CSA provides a range of guidance documents related to cloud computing, including guidance on eDiscovery in cloud environments. The CSA's guidance is designed to help organizations manage the unique challenges of eDiscovery in the cloud, such as data privacy, security, and legal and regulatory compliance:

  - **Data privacy**: The CSA recommends that organizations implement strong data privacy controls to protect sensitive data during eDiscovery processes. This may involve using encryption to protect data at rest and in transit, implementing access controls to limit who can access data, or using data masking to obfuscate sensitive information.

  - **Security**: The CSA recommends that organizations implement appropriate controls to protect against breaches and incidents during eDiscovery processes. This may involve using security monitoring tools to detect and respond to threats, implementing multi-factor authentication to protect against unauthorized access, or using intrusion detection and prevention systems to detect and block malicious activity.

  - **Legal and regulatory compliance**: The CSA recommends that organizations ensure that they are complying with legal and regulatory requirements related to eDiscovery. This may involve conducting regular risk assessments, implementing policies and procedures for eDiscovery, or engaging legal counsel to provide guidance on legal and regulatory issues.

- **Federal Rules of Civil Procedure (FRCP)**: The FRCP is a set of rules that oversee civil proceedings in US federal courts. These rules have been amended several times to address eDiscovery issues. For example, the rules require parties to implement appropriate procedures to preserve any relevant digital content that contains relevant information when litigation is expected. The rules also establish the scope of eDiscovery, which includes any supporting information, such as working papers, that could lead to the discovery of admissible evidence.

- **Sedona Conference**: The Sedona Conference is a nonprofit legal research and educational organization that provides legal guidance on a range of issues, including eDiscovery. It produces publications that cover a variety of eDiscovery principles, such as proportionality, data privacy, and the use of technology-assisted review, preservations, records management within eDiscovery processes, multi-jurisdictional eDiscovery, and cost and liabilities management because of eDiscovery. The Sedona Conference's publications are often cited by courts in eDiscovery cases and are widely regarded as one of the authoritative sources of guidance on eDiscovery issues.

- **Electronic Discovery Reference Model (EDRM)**: The EDRM is a framework that outlines the stages of the eDiscovery process, from information management to production. The framework is designed to provide a common language and structure for eDiscovery activities, which can help parties to a legal matter understand and manage the eDiscovery process more effectively. The EDRM framework includes nine steps, including information management, identification, preservation, collection, processing, review, analysis, production, and presentation. Each stage is designed to build on the previous one, with the goal of producing accurate, complete, and defensible evidence that can be used in legal proceedings.

In summary, irrespective of the choice of eDiscovery framework that investigators may follow, the underlying procedures for discovery, collection, preservation, and presentation of electronically stored information are generally similar. Legal courts around the world expect that ESI is collected in a forensically sound and legally defensible manner.

Digital forensics challenges

The cloud has brought significant benefits to organizations, including increased flexibility, scalability, and cost savings. However, it has also introduced new challenges when it comes to eDiscovery and forensics. Outlined in the following list are some of the common challenges an investigator could encounter. Each cloud forensic case may present a unique challenge; however, these are some of the common themes:

- **Data complexity and volume**: The cloud provides organizations with virtually unlimited storage capacity, which means that the amount of data that needs to be searched, collected, and analyzed during eDiscovery and forensic investigations can be overwhelming.

- **Data security**: CSPs are responsible for securing the data stored in their systems, but organizations also have a responsibility to ensure that their data is protected during eDiscovery and forensic investigations. This can be particularly challenging in multi-tenant cloud environments, where data from multiple organizations is stored on the same servers.

- **Jurisdictional issues**: Cloud data can be stored in multiple jurisdictions, which can make it difficult to determine which laws and regulations apply to eDiscovery and forensic investigations. This is particularly challenging when data is stored in countries with strict data protection laws, as organizations may need to navigate complex legal frameworks to access and process data. Forensic investigators would have to work through breach coaches (legal counsel) to obtain subpoenas to allow them to search and access data that may be hosted by CSPs in another jurisdiction. CSPs may also have policies and procedures in place, which may be a further hindrance in obtaining necessary information. This obviously requires multi-party cooperation (organization, investigator, CSP, breach coach) to allow access to the artifacts that are the subject of the investigation.

- **Lack of transparency**: CSPs often use proprietary technologies and processes to manage their cloud infrastructure, which can make it difficult for organizations to understand how their data is being stored, accessed, and protected. This lack of transparency can make it challenging for organizations to conduct effective eDiscovery and forensic investigations.

- **Technical challenges**: Conducting eDiscovery and forensic investigations in the cloud requires specialized technical skills and tools. This includes the ability to collect and analyze data from a variety of sources in the cloud, including structured and unstructured datasets, as well as the ability to ensure that data is preserved in a forensically sound manner.

- **Data location and access**: CSPs often spread data between various locations or zones (even if it is in the same country, data is spread between various volumes to ensure availability). This makes it difficult for investigators to locate and access relevant data. CSPs may also have their own access control that prevents or restricts certain datasets.

In summary, DFIR teams are expected to encounter these challenges when dealing with a cloud investigation case. In the real world, this is often complicated by multi-jurisdictional legal requirements, eDiscovery requirements, and adhering to various legal requirements to ensure the investigation is acceptable in a court of law. Nevertheless, it is important that you familiarize yourself with these challenges ahead of time and plan your investigations around them.

Legal frameworks for private data

In general terms, private data is any data that is personal or sensitive in nature and is not intended for public dissemination. Examples include your name, date of birth, address, and **Social Security Number** (**SSN**) as these are typically classified as **Personally Identifiable Information** (**PII**), meaning these datasets can be used to identify someone. **Payment Card Information** (**PCI**) is a group of confidential datasets that includes bank account, credit card number, card validation number, and the expiration month and year of the card. Finally, you have data such as medical records, diagnosis and assessment reports, X-ray reports, and psychological assessment reports, which are referred to as **Personal Health Information (PHI)**, which is sensitive in nature.

The sensitivity of the information also presents a challenge for incident responders and digital forensic investigators. Private data is often protected by laws and regulations governing data privacy and security (GDPR, CCPA, and so on), and therefore companies and incident responders are responsible for acting appropriately to safeguard private data and prevent unauthorized access, use, or disclosure. This also means that companies must address the necessary contractual obligations to ensure private data remains private. From a cloud forensics point of view, it is important for a forensic investigator to understand the nuances of various datasets that may be hosted in the cloud. Indicated in the next sections are some of the legal considerations.

Contractual private data

Any information that is shared between parties in a contractual agreement is considered confidential and not meant for public distribution. This type of data is typically protected by the terms of the contract itself, as well as applicable laws and regulations governing data privacy and security. Examples include trade secrets, financial information, personal information of employees or customers, and proprietary information about products or services. The parties to a contract may be required to sign a **non-disclosure agreement (NDA)** or confidentiality clause that specifically outlines the types of information that are considered confidential and the obligations of the parties with respect to safeguarding that information.

Regulated private data

This refers to any information that is regulated or protected under regulatory laws and compliance requirements. For example, medical records, financial records, and PII. There are financial penalties and sanctions if companies fail to protect these regulated datasets. From an incident response standpoint, the following are some of the considerations the organizations should take into account:

- **Regulatory compliance**: Organizations that collect, process, or store regulated private data must follow regulations, such as HIPAA or GDPR. DFIR teams must be familiar with these regulations and ensure that their actions do not violate any compliance requirements.

- **Privacy laws**: Privacy laws dictate how regulated private data should be collected, processed, and stored. DFIR teams must consider these privacy laws to ensure that their actions do not violate the privacy rights of individuals or organizations involved.

- **Data retention policies**: Organizations that collect regulated private data often have specific data retention policies that dictate how long the data should be stored. This can typically range from 1 to 10 years. DFIR teams must take note of these policies to ensure that they do not destroy any data that should be preserved.

- **Chain of custody**: DFIR teams must maintain a proper chain of custody for all data they collect during an investigation. This is especially crucial for regulated private data, as any mishandling or unauthorized disclosure can result in significant legal and financial consequences, including financial penalties for the company and DFIR teams.

- **Notification requirements**: Many regulations require organizations to notify affected individuals or regulatory authorities, including the Office of Privacy Commissioner (if applicable), in the event of a data breach within a specified time from the time the breach is discovered or identified. DFIR teams must be aware of these notification requirements and ensure they work with breach coaches to address notification requirements. Breach coaches will provide guidance on breach notification requirements to the DFIR teams to prioritize certain investigative areas and be compliant with the notification requirements.

Jurisdictional requirements in relation to private data

Private data could be subject to specific legal requirements and protections in different jurisdictions, and it is critical to comply with those requirements when handling incidents involving private data. This also includes notification requirements set out by these jurisdictions. For example, GDPR in the EU requires organizations to notify relevant authorities and individuals within 72 hours of a data breach that affects private data. CCPA requires businesses to notify affected parties/customers immediately upon personal information disclosure or breach.

When it comes to DFIR, these jurisdictional requirements can impact the collection, handling, and sharing of private data. For example, data may need to be collected and processed in a specific way to comply with local privacy laws. Similarly, the sharing of data with law enforcement agencies or other third parties may require legal approval or specific contractual agreements. It is critical for DFIR professionals to be familiar with the relevant jurisdictional requirements and to work closely with legal teams and breach coaches to ensure that all legal and regulatory requirements are met when handling incidents involving private data. Failure to comply with these requirements can result in significant legal and financial consequences for the organization and potentially for individuals involved in the investigation.

The following regulations affect a lot of industries and organizations, and DFIR teams should be familiar with these depending on what type of data is investigated and analyzed:

- **Health Insurance Portability and Accountability Act (HIPAA)**: Beyond GDPR and CCPA, in the US there are other privacy laws that exist, some at the federal level, such as HIPAA, which is designed to safeguard the privacy of an individual's health information and enforces healthcare providers to ensure private and sensitive information is protected while breaches are reported.

- **Fair Credit Reporting Act (FCRA)**: This law regulates the collection, use, and disclosure of credit information by consumer reporting agencies, employers, and other entities. It also gives consumers the right to access and correct their credit information.

- **Family Educational Rights and Privacy Act (FERPA)**: This law protects the privacy of students' educational records and gives parents and students the right to access and correct these records.

- **Gramm-Leach-Bliley Act (GLBA)**: This federal law regulates what personal information is collected, used, and disclosed by financial institutions. It requires these institutions to safeguard this information and provide consumers with notice of their privacy policies.

- **Electronic Communications Privacy Act (ECPA)**: This law regulates the interception of electronic communications and sets out rules for obtaining and disclosing electronic communications stored by third-party service providers.

- **Children's Online Privacy Protection Act (COPPA)**: This law outlines guidelines for online service providers on the collection of personal information from children, specifically those under the age of 13. It requires online service providers to seek consent from their parents prior to collecting personal information from children.

- **Video Privacy Protection Act (VPPA)**: This law regulates the collection, use, and disclosure of personal video viewing information by video rental and streaming services. It requires these services to obtain consent before disclosing this information.

- **International Organization for Standardization/International Electrotechnical Commission (ISO/IEC) 27018**: First published in 2014, ISO/IEC 27018 is a standard for providing guidelines for the protection of PII in public cloud environments. DFIR teams should note that this is a standard and not a regulation to comply with. However, the standard provides a framework for implementing controls to protect PII and to help customers and regulators assess the level of security implemented by a CSP. The guidance domains include the following:

  - **Consent and notice for data processing**: The standard requires CSPs to obtain consent from customers prior to collection, use, and disclosure of their personal information, and to provide notice about how their information will be used.

  - **Transparency regarding sub-contractors**: The standard requires CSPs to disclose the use of subcontractors that may have access to customers' personal information.

  - **Limitations on data use**: The standard requires CSPs to limit the use of customers' PII to that for which it was collected, and to obtain additional consent if the information is to be used for other purposes.

  - **Security and confidentiality controls**: The standard requires CSPs to implement security and confidentiality controls to protect customers' personal information, such as encryption including data tokenization, access controls, and incident response procedures.

- **Data retention and disposal**: The standard outlines CSPs must establish policies and procedures for the retention and disposal of customers' PII, and ensure that data is securely destroyed when it is no longer needed.

- **Generally Accepted Privacy Principles (GAPP)**: A framework developed by the **American Institute of Certified Public Accountants (AICPA)** and the **Canadian Institute of Chartered Accountants (CICA)** to address privacy concerns. GAPP is based on 10 fundamental privacy principles developed based on **Fair Information Practices (FIP)** for maintaining privacy. These include the following:

  - **Management**: An organization must assign information governance responsibility to an individual or team within the organization and implement appropriate policies and procedures complying with relevant privacy laws.

  - **Notice**: An organization must notify and detail what personal information is collected, used, retained, and disclosed to individuals.

  - **Choice and consent**: Individuals or customers are given the opportunity to opt out of sharing private data if they choose to do so. This includes opting-out choices on collection, usage, and disclosure of personal information.

  - **Collection**: An organization must clearly outline and collect data on specific personal information necessary for its business purposes.

  - **Use, retention, and disposal**: An organization must only use and retain personal information for its business purposes and dispose of it in a secure manner.

  - **Access**: An organization must provide individuals/customers with access to their personal information allowing the option to change, update, or clarify any inaccuracies.

  - **Disclosure to third parties**: An organization must only disclose or share personal information with third parties after they have received an individual's consent or as required by law.

  - **Security for privacy**: An organization must implement safeguards and ensure personal or private information is secured from unauthorized access, processing, disclosure, or destruction.

  - **Quality**: Like access, an organization must ensure personal or private information that is collected is correct and up to date.

  - **Monitoring and enforcement**: An organization must monitor and ensure compliance against the outlined principles and take appropriate action to address any violations.

- **General Data Protection Regulation (GDPR)**: A privacy regulation in the EU that requires organizations to comply with how personal data is managed. GDPR applies to any organization, irrespective of location, that collects and processes the PII of EU residents and citizens. GDPR outlines the key requirements for data controllers and processors:

  - **Consent**: Organizations must request permission from individuals prior to processing their personal data, for example, they should use **customer relationship management software (CRM)** that has a consent management tool that documents the users consenting to the collection, storage, and processing of information of its users.

  - **Transparency**: Organizations must provide individuals with clear information on the purposes of the collection and processing of their personal data.

  - **Data subject rights**: Individuals have the right to access, manage the accuracy of, or remove their personal data.

  - **Data minimization**: Organizations must only collect and process personal data that is necessary for their business.

  - **Security**: Organizations must implement appropriate controls to ensure the security of personal data.

  - **Accountability**: Organizations must be able to demonstrate compliance with GDPR, including implementing appropriate data protection policies and procedures.

> **Note**
>
> GDPR also includes strict requirements for data breach notification, with organizations required to report any breaches to the regulatory authority within 72 hours of becoming aware of the breach. Non-compliance with GDPR can result in significant fines and reputational damage, making it imperative for organizations to ensure that they are following the regulation.

- **Privacy Impact Assessment (PIA)**: PIA provides detailed steps to allow organizations to review, address, and identify any privacy risks associated with a project. It provides a comprehensive evaluation criterion to validate how personal information is collected, used, stored, and processed. The PIA process helps organizations to identify and mitigate privacy risks before they arise, as well as to ensure that privacy considerations are integrated into the design and implementation of the project or initiative. This can help to build trust with stakeholders, including customers and employees, and to avoid legal and reputational risks associated with privacy breaches.

> **Note**
>
> In some jurisdictions, such as the EU under GDPR, PIAs may be mandatory for certain types of data processing activities, such as those involving sensitive personal data or the large-scale processing of personal data.

- In Canada, some of the key privacy laws include the following:

  - **Personal Information Protection and Electronic Documents Act** (**PIPEDA**), which provides the framework for the management and processing of personal information by businesses and organizations.

  - For federal-government-led institutions, there is the **Privacy Act**, which defines the rules for the collection, use, and disclosure of personal information.

  - The **Canadian Anti-Spam Legislation** (**CASL**) regulates the sending of electronic messages (emails) and requires prior consent before sending these messages.

  - **Freedom of Information and Protection of Privacy Act** (**FIPPA**) is applicable to British Columbia public organizations and sets out guidelines for the collection, use, and disclosure of personal information. It requires these organizations to protect personal information and to provide individuals with the ability to access their own personal information.

  - **Personal Information Protection Act** (**PIPA**), which is applicable only to businesses in the province of Alberta, Canada. This law requires organizations to obtain consent prior to the collection, usage, or disclosure of personal information during commercial activities in the province of Alberta, Canada.

  - **Law 25 in Quebec, Canada**, is a law that is aimed at modernizing legal requirements to protect personal information. Under Law 25, private sector organizations must obtain consent from individuals or customers when it comes to the collection, processing, or disclosing of their personal information. Law 25 also requires organizations to take steps to place guardrails to protect personal information and to report any data breaches. Quebec has its own privacy regulator, the **Commission d'accès à l'information** (**CAI**), which oversees and enforces privacy laws in the province. DFIR teams should be aware of the role of the CAI in investigating and enforcing privacy breaches in the province of Quebec and should work closely with breach coaches to ensure compliance with these laws.

In summary, it's all about organizations obtaining consent prior to the collection and usage of information and clearly outlining the business purpose for such collection of personal information. Organizations are ultimately responsible for deploying appropriate controls to safeguard personal information. Similarly, for DFIR teams it is important to be aware of these privacy laws and jurisdictional requirements, as breach coaches will rely upon DFIR teams to provide appropriate recommendations based on applicable jurisdiction and regulatory requirements.

The following table outlines a summarized view of various privacy laws, their applicable jurisdiction, focus areas, and notification requirements.

Applicable Law	Applicable Jurisdiction(s)	Area(s)	Requirements for notifying affected individuals
General Data Protection Regulation (GDPR)	EU	Personal data protection, data subject rights, data processing by data controllers and processors, cross-border data transfers, data breaches	Notification to supervisory authorities **within 72 hours of becoming aware of the breach**; notification of affected individuals when possible.
California Consumer Privacy Act (CCPA)	California, US	Personal data protection, data subject rights, consumer privacy, sale of personal information	Notification of personal data breaches to **affected individuals and the California Attorney General without undue delay and within 45 days of discovering the breach.**
Personal Information Protection and Electronic Documents Act (PIPEDA)	Canada (applies to federally regulated organizations)	Personal data protection, consent, data subject rights, data retention and disposal, data transfers	Notification to affected individuals and the Office of the Privacy Commissioner of Canada as soon as the breach has occurred.
Health Insurance Portability and Accountability Act (HIPAA)	US	Protection of personal health information, data security and confidentiality, data subject rights	Notification of breaches of health information to affected individuals, the US Department of Health, and Human Services, and the media (if required), within 60 days of discovering the breach.
Personal Data Protection Act (PDPA)	Singapore	Personal data protection, data subject rights, data processing by data controllers and processors, cross-border data transfers, data breaches	Notification of personal data breaches to affected individuals and the Personal Data Protection Commission **within 72 hours** of discovering the breach.

Applicable Law	Applicable Jurisdiction(s)	Area(s)	Requirements for notifying affected individuals
Privacy Shield Framework	US, EU	Cross-border data transfers	Notification of personal data breaches to affected individuals and the relevant authority as soon as possible **and within 72 hours** of the discovery of the breach.
Personal Information Protection Act (PIPA)	South Korea	Personal data protection, data subject rights, data processing by data controllers and processors, cross-border data transfers, data breaches	Notification of personal data breaches to affected individuals and the Korea Communications Commission as soon as possible and **within 24 hours** of discovering the breach.
Data Protection Act 2018	United Kingdom	Personal data protection, data subject rights, data processing by data controllers and processors, and cross-border data transfers.	Notification of breaches including details of the breach **within 72 hours** of discovering the breach.
Personal Information Protection Act (PIPA)	British Columbia, Canada	Personal data protection, consent, data subject rights, data retention and disposal, data transfers	Notification of personal information breaches to affected individuals and the Office of the Information and Privacy Commissioner for B.C. Canada **as soon as possible** after discovering the breach.
Personal Information Protection Act (PIPA)	Alberta, Canada	Personal data protection, consent, data subject rights, data retention and disposal, data transfers	Notification of personal data breaches to affected individuals and the Office of the Information and Privacy Commissioner for Alberta **as soon as possible** once the organization has determined the breach.

Applicable Law	Applicable Jurisdiction(s)	Area(s)	Requirements for notifying affected individuals
Act respecting the protection of personal information in the private sector (P-39.1)	Quebec, Canada	Personal data protection, consent, data subject rights, data retention and disposal, data transfers	Notification of personal data breaches to affected individuals and the Commission d'accès à l'information **without undue delay and as soon as possible** and once the organization has ascertained that the breach of personal information has occurred.
Personal Information Protection Act (PIPA)	Ontario, Canada	Personal data protection, consent, data subject rights, data retention and disposal, data transfers	Notification of personal data breaches to affected individuals and the Office of the Information and Privacy Commissioner of Ontario **as soon as possible** after the organization confirms that the breach has occurred.
Biometric Information Privacy Act (BIPA)	Illinois, US	Biometric data protection, consent, data subject rights	Notification of data breaches to affected individuals, the Illinois Attorney General, and the Illinois Department of Innovation and Technology **without unreasonable delay and within 30 days** of discovering the breach.
California Privacy Rights Act (CPRA)	California, US	Personal data protection, data subject rights, consumer privacy, sale of personal information	Notification of personal data breaches to affected individuals and the California Attorney General **without undue delay and within 45 days** of discovering the breach.
Stop Hacks and Improve Electronic Data Security (SHIELD) Act	New York, US	Personal data protection, data security, data breach notification	Notification of data breaches to affected individuals and the New York State Attorney General **without unreasonable delay and within a reasonable period.**

Table 2.1 – Summary view of privacy laws and associated notification requirements for breaches

Legal implications for data retention and deletion

Storing and retaining data, including in a multi-tenant cloud setup, can have significant legal implications for organizations. These implications may vary depending on the type of data being stored, the jurisdiction in which the data is stored, and the applicable laws and regulations. Specifically, these include the following:

- **Data retention requirements**: Depending on the type of data and the jurisdiction in which it is stored, there may be legal requirements for organizations to retain data for a certain period. Failure to comply with these requirements can result in fines and penalties.

- **Data privacy laws**: Data privacy laws, such as GDPR in the EU, place strict requirements on how personal data is collected, used, and disclosed. Organizations that store and retain personal data must comply with these laws, including implementing appropriate security measures to protect the data.

- **Data breach notification laws**: Many jurisdictions have data breach notification laws that require organizations to notify affected individuals and regulatory authorities in the event of a data breach. Organizations that store and retain data must have appropriate breach notification policies and procedures in place to comply with these laws.

- **Intellectual property laws**: Storing and retaining data, particularly in a cloud setup, may implicate intellectual property laws related to ownership and control of the data.

> **Property laws**
>
> Set of laws enforced to protect creations of human intellect such as inventions, literacy, artistic works, symbols, names, and images. These laws are designed to protect the inventors and encourage creative freedom.

- **eDiscovery requirements**: Organizations may be required to produce data in response to legal requests, such as during litigation or government investigations. Failure to retain data that may be relevant to these requests can result in legal sanctions.

On the other hand, data deletion has a very significant impact from a legal compliance standpoint and from a digital forensic standpoint, especially where legal and regulatory guidelines are enforced on data retention. In some jurisdictions, failure to comply with retention requirements can attract financial penalties as regulators will perceive this as mishandling data. From a forensic standpoint, if data is deleted that contains sensitive data or evidence of wrongdoing, there can be a significant reputational impact on the organization along with forensic investigation impacts.

Responsibilities and liabilities of the cloud and their implications for incident response

With the cloud, DIFR has become a little more complicated. As such, it has significant implications for the assigning of liabilities and responsibilities for data breaches and other security incidents. In cloud computing, there are several different parties involved, including the CSPs, the cloud customer, and any third-party providers that may be involved. Each of these parties may have different roles and therefore different levels of liability and responsibility exposures in the event of a security incident.

CSPs generally have a higher level of liability and responsibility for security incidents because they are responsible for the overall security and availability of the cloud infrastructure. This includes maintaining the physical security of the data centers, securing the network infrastructure, and implementing security controls to protect customer data.

Cloud customers have the responsibility for security incidents because they are responsible for configuring and securing their own applications and data within the cloud environment. This includes implementing appropriate access controls, encrypting sensitive data, and monitoring their own systems for security incidents. It is important for DFIR teams to understand that threat actors will always attempt to exploit what is exposed to the internet. So, if a customer web application is internet-facing, threat actors will attempt to exploit the vulnerabilities in the applications owned and hosted by the customer, rather than the underlying cloud infrastructure.

In terms of DFIR, the implications of liability and responsibility in cloud computing are significant. DFIR investigations may require access to data that is stored within the cloud environment, which can be challenging to obtain if the data is encrypted or if access controls are not properly configured. CSPs may also have their own incident response processes that need to be followed in the event of a security incident, which can impact the ability of DFIR teams to conduct investigations in a timely and effective manner.

Ultimately, liability and responsibility in cloud computing can significantly differ and can affect DFIR investigations. It is important for organizations to understand their own responsibilities and to work closely with CSPs to ensure that proper security controls are in place and that incident response processes are well defined and understood.

Jurisdiction and cross-border data transfers

When data is transferred across borders, it may be subject to different legal frameworks and regulations. This can include data privacy laws, data localization requirements, and government surveillance laws. For example, GDPR in the EU has strict requirements for cross-border data transfers, which can impact the ability of organizations to transfer data to CSPs located outside of the EU.

As incident responders, it is important to be aware of the legal implications of cross-border data transfers, especially when conducting DFIR investigations. Depending on the regional and global legal framework in place, access to data stored in the cloud may be restricted, or additional legal requirements may need to be met before data can be accessed.

Therefore, as incident responders, it is important to stay informed about the legal framework in place and to develop appropriate incident response plans that consider the unique challenges presented by cloud computing. By doing so, we can help ensure that investigations are conducted in a forensically sound manner and that the privacy and security of data is protected.

Summary

This chapter provided various legal and privacy aspects for DFIR teams to consider prior to embarking upon a forensic investigation of a case where the cloud may be involved. A basic understanding of legal requirements will certainly help DFIR teams in making sure all the incident response sets adhere to legal and regulatory requirements. Some of the key learnings from this chapter include the following:

- **It is all about jurisdiction**: Where is the data located? Is it on a cloud system or a physical server? It is very important for DFIR teams to understand the location of the data being stored and whether there are any legal requirements to adhere to prior to collecting or transferring data for investigations.

- **Private data**: It's critically important for DFIR teams to recognize the type of data that is hosted on these affected systems. It could be PII, PHI, PCI, any other sensitive data, or all of them. However, it is important that they consider the legal requirements in each of the jurisdictions prior to collecting and analyzing the data. Keep in mind, DFIR teams are expected to ensure they clearly obtain consent from the organization prior to analyzing any sensitive information, and DFIR teams are expected to apply necessary security controls so that only authorized and qualified members of the team can analyze sensitive data. Once the analysis is completed, DFIR teams should make considerations to securely delete the data.

- **Various legal regulations**: DFIR teams obviously face a tough challenge keeping up to date with various laws, legal frameworks, guidance notifications, and so on. It therefore becomes imperative that the legal counsel or breach coach becomes your best friend, specifically, to advise DFIR teams on various legal requirements, notification requirements, and consent prior to the collection, storage, and maintenance of such sensitive data.

Through previous chapters, we learned about data being available in the cloud and elsewhere. Collecting and processing personal information poses a great responsibility for organizations and an even greater responsibility for DFIR teams to identify the root cause of any breaches that contain personal information. Given the various laws enforcing strong response and breach notifications, it becomes imperative that DFIR teams are well aware of how to investigate breaches, specifically if the data is being stored on the cloud.

In the next few chapters, we will focus on introducing the cloud for novices, and where logs can be found that can be crucial from an investigation point of view. We will also look at various CSPs and their relative capabilities to support DFIR teams in their investigative journey.

Further reading

- *Data breach – Frequently asked questions*: https://www.siskinds.com/data-breach-frequently-asked-questions/

- *Legal Issues Surrounding Cloud Computing*: https://www.opengrowth.com/resources/legal-issues-surrounding-cloud-computing

- *The Legal Issues of Cloud-based Computing Services*: https://www.bennettjones.com/Publications-Section/Updates/The-Legal-Issues-of-Cloud-based-Computing-Services

- *Legal Concerns and Challenges In Cloud Computing*: https://www.linkedin.com/pulse/legal-concerns-challenges-cloud-computing-leandro-valente/

- *Guidelines for the Discovery of Electronic Documents in Ontario*: http://www.oba.org/en/pdf_newsletter/e-discoveryguidelines.pdf

- *The Basics Of eDiscovery*: https://www.exterro.com/basics-of-e-discovery

- *eDiscovery Considerations for International Litigation*: https://www.law.com/legaltechnews/2022/12/12/e-discovery-considerations-for-international-litigation/?slreturn=20230408095421

- *6 Things to Know About Cloud eDiscovery*: https://www.cloudficient.com/blog/6-things-to-know-about-cloud-ediscovery

- *On-Premise vs. Cloud Considerations for eDiscovery*: https://www.lawtechnologytoday.org/2018/09/cloud-considerations-for-e-discovery/

- *Summary of privacy laws in Canada*: https://www.priv.gc.ca/en/privacy-topics/privacy-laws-in-canada/02_05_d_15/

- *Data protection and privacy laws*: https://id4d.worldbank.org/guide/data-protection-and-privacy-laws

- *U.S. Privacy Laws: The Complete Guide*: https://www.varonis.com/blog/us-privacy-laws

- *Privacy Act of 1974*: https://www.justice.gov/opcl/privacy-act-1974

- *U.S. data privacy laws to enter new era in 2023*: https://www.reuters.com/legal/legalindustry/us-data-privacy-laws-enter-new-era-2023-2023-01-12/

- *Guidelines for processing personal data across borders*: https://www.priv.gc.ca/en/privacy-topics/airports-and-borders/gl_dab_090127/

- *Managing Privacy Compliance in Multiple Jurisdictions*: https://www.truevault.com/resources/essentials/managing-privacy-compliance-in-multiple-jurisdictions

- *Navigating data privacy laws in multi-jurisdictional investigations*: https://www.lexology.com/library/detail.aspx?g=8f442946-a6ae-47d2-a25c-d04fd1e7a088

3

Exploring the
Major Cloud Providers

As discussed in *Chapter 1*, cloud computing has become the preferred choice for many organizations looking to modernize their IT infrastructure and take advantage of the benefits of cloud adoption. As incident responders, it is important to focus on the digital forensics of popular cloud service providers due to their widespread adoption by organizations. Among the top cloud service providers on the market, you will most likely encounter three main cloud providers in your next cloud forensics project: **Amazon Web Services (AWS)**, **Microsoft Azure**, and **Google Cloud Platform (GCP)**.

Understanding how these providers work, their security measures, and where forensic artifacts may be stored is crucial for organizations looking to ensure the security of their data and applications, as well as being crucial for incident responders looking to respond to security incidents. Each cloud service provider has its own architecture and security controls, which must be understood to ensure that forensic investigations are conducted effectively. For example, AWS, Azure, and GCP all have different approaches to data storage, access control, and logging, which can impact forensic investigations.

In this chapter, we will explore the importance of knowing about these three most common cloud service providers and their most common services. By understanding the cloud service providers, organizations can be better prepared to respond to security incidents and conduct forensic investigations in the cloud.

> **Note**
>
> The purpose of this chapter is to gain a high-level familiarity with the industry's leading cloud providers and their products—we will dive deeper into log resources and responding to incidents for each cloud provider in *Parts 2* and *3* of this book.

Amazon Web Services (AWS)

Introduced in 2006, AWS is a cloud computing platform that provides a wide range of services to help organizations build and deploy their applications and infrastructure. AWS offers infrastructure and computing resources at scale and allows organizations to virtualize their entire IT infrastructure in the cloud, making AWS a critical tool for many organizations. Incident responders, in particular, need to have a solid understanding of AWS as it has become one of the most popular platforms for hosting critical systems and services.

AWS offers a vast array of services, each designed to meet the specific needs of organizations and developers. With over 200 services available, it can be overwhelming to navigate the platform, especially for those new to AWS. In this section, we will focus on the core services that are commonly used by organizations of all sizes. These include compute services such as Amazon **Elastic Compute Cloud (EC2)**, storage services such as Amazon **Simple Storage Service (S3)**, database services such as Amazon **Relational Database Service (RDS)**, networking services such as Amazon **Virtual Private Cloud (VPC)**, and security services such as AWS **Identity and Access Management (IAM)**.

We will explore the key AWS services that incident responders should be familiar with, and explain why knowing about AWS is important for effective incident response in modern IT environments.

Amazon Elastic Compute Cloud (EC2)

Amazon EC2 is a web service provided by AWS that allows organizations to create virtualized infrastructure or servers (also known as virtual machines) and run them in the cloud. EC2 enables organizations to have complete control over their computing resources and provides a scalable and flexible infrastructure for building applications. With EC2, organizations can launch and manage virtual servers called instances, which can be configured with different computing capabilities, storage capacities, and networking features. It is important to note, for DFIR teams, that AWS refers to these virtual machines as *instances* and each virtual machine is identified using an instance identifier.

EC2 provides several benefits that make it an important tool for organizations of all sizes. First, it offers on-demand scalability, which means organizations can easily adjust their computing resources as their needs change. EC2 also provides a high level of availability, with multiple Availability Zones and automatic failover capabilities. Additionally, EC2 is highly customizable, allowing organizations to choose from a wide range of instance types, operating systems, and software configurations.

The following screenshot demonstrates Amazon EC2 instance creation through the web GUI, including options to customize the virtual machine operating system, hardware, networking, and storage capabilities.

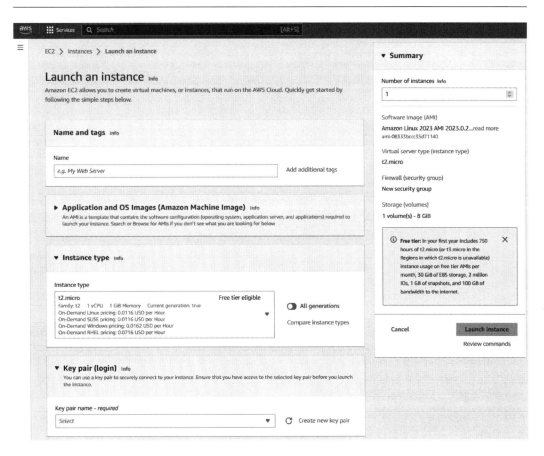

Figure 3.1 – Launching an instance in Amazon EC2

Organizations can also utilize AWS's CLI to create instances and other AWS resources. The AWS CLI is a powerful tool provided by AWS that allows organizations to manage their AWS resources and services through a CLI. As an example, organizations can create an instance by running a specific command, such as `aws ec2 run-instances`, followed by the necessary parameters you would normally define through the GUI, such as instance type, security groups, and key pairs. This enables organizations to automate the process of instance creation and provisioning in AWS, enhancing efficiency and scalability.

For incident responders, EC2 is particularly important because it provides a flexible and scalable infrastructure for responding to security incidents. EC2 instances can be quickly spun up (i.e., through the creation of new virtual machines) to handle increased workloads during an incident. EC2 instances can be easily isolated and quarantined, allowing incident responders to contain the incident and prevent it from spreading to other parts of the organization.

Amazon Virtual Private Cloud (VPC)

Amazon VPC is a cloud-based networking service that enables organizations to create and manage their own private virtual network in the AWS cloud. With VPC, organizations can create isolated sections of the AWS cloud, called subnets, and control access to these subnets through custom network **Access Control Lists** (**ACLs**) and security groups. Note that, by default, AWS will create a VPC instance when you create a new instance in AWS. The VPC comes with a default configuration but allows you to customize it per your needs. Similar to AWS EC2 instances, each VPC is identified through a VPC ID by AWS. VPCs can be created as needed or any existing VPCs can be accessed within your AWS VPC dashboard. An example of a VPC is shown in the following diagram:

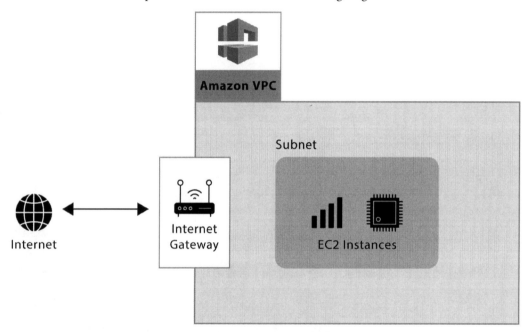

Figure 3.2 – Amazon VPC example

From a digital forensics and incident response perspective, VPC provides several key benefits. First, it enables organizations to create an isolated and secure environment for their computing resources, reducing the risk of unauthorized access or data breaches. Second, it provides granular control over network traffic, allowing organizations to monitor and restrict access to specific resources and subnets. Finally, it enables organizations to create a centralized logging and monitoring solution, making it easier to detect and respond to security incidents.

To respond to incidents in a VPC, responders must first identify the affected resources and isolate them within the VPC. They can then use AWS tools, such as AWS CloudTrail and AWS CloudWatch, to monitor network traffic and identify any suspicious activity. Incident responders can also leverage the VPC's custom network ACLs and security groups to restrict access to the affected resources and limit the spread of the incident. Responding to incidents in AWS will be discussed in *Part 2* of this book.

Amazon Simple Storage Service (S3)

Amazon S3 is a cloud-based object storage service offered by AWS. S3 enables organizations to store, retrieve, and manage large amounts of data in a highly scalable, secure, and cost-effective manner. S3 is a crucial component of many organizations' data storage and backup strategies, and it is used for a wide range of use cases, including data lakes, web and mobile applications, backups, and disaster recovery. AWS refers to each S3 instance as a **bucket** and, by default, when an organization creates an S3 bucket, it is not publicly available on the internet. You will need to make necessary changes to allow public accessibility over the internet. However, do note, misconfigurations in S3 buckets will allow data on S3 to be available on the internet (even if it was not intended to be). So, it is important that S3 buckets are configured appropriately.

From a digital forensics and incident response perspective, S3 provides several key benefits. First, it enables organizations to store large amounts of data in a secure and scalable manner, making it easier for investigators and responders to access and analyze data. Second, S3 provides a range of security and compliance features, including encryption, access control, and audit logging, which help organizations protect their data and comply with applicable regulations. Finally, S3 enables organizations to quickly and easily recover from data loss or corruption, reducing the impact of incidents on their operations.

Digital forensics investigators can use S3 to analyze data in a secure and scalable environment. By accessing an organization's S3 buckets, investigators can examine the data stored within them, identify patterns and anomalies, and extract relevant evidence. They can also use S3's audit logging features to track changes to the buckets and identify any suspicious activity.

The following screenshot demonstrates the creation process for an AWS S3 bucket. Buckets will require a name as well as an AWS Region as the general configuration, ownership/access configuration, as well as server-side encryption.

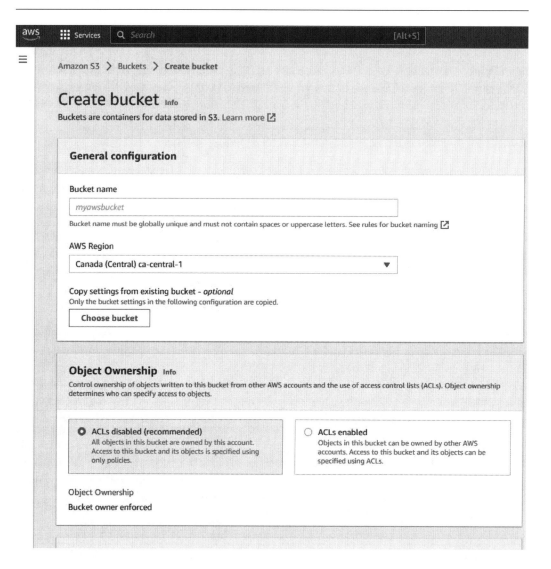

Figure 3.3 – Creating an S3 bucket

AWS Identity and Access Management (IAM)

AWS IAM is a web service offered by AWS that provides a secure and centralized way to manage user identities and access to AWS resources. IAM allows organizations to control who can access AWS resources, and what actions they can perform on those resources. This enables organizations to enforce security policies, maintain compliance, and reduce the risk of unauthorized access or data breaches.

IAM is important because it enables organizations to manage user access to AWS resources in a granular and scalable way. With IAM, organizations can create and manage organizations, groups, and roles, and assign specific permissions to each one. This helps to ensure that only authorized organizations can access AWS resources and that they can only perform the actions that are necessary for their job responsibilities. The IAM module allows organizations to set up granular access to controls for relevant AWS resources.

From a digital forensics and incident response perspective, IAM provides several key benefits. First, it enables investigators and responders to identify and track user activity within AWS resources. By analyzing IAM logs, investigators can identify which users were granted access to specific resources, and when they accessed them. This information can help investigators identify potential security breaches, data exfiltration attempts, or other suspicious activity.

Second, IAM enables organizations to respond quickly to security incidents by revoking access to AWS resources for specific organizations or groups. This can help to contain the impact of an incident and prevent further unauthorized access or data breaches. IAM also provides the ability to create temporary access keys for specific use cases, which can help to limit the scope of potential damage in the event of a compromised key.

To use an organization's IAM for digital forensics and incident response purposes, investigators and responders must have the appropriate permissions to access and analyze IAM logs. IAM logs provide a detailed record of user activity within AWS resources, including who accessed them, when they were accessed, and what actions were performed. By analyzing these logs, investigators can identify patterns of suspicious activity, track user behavior, and correlate events across different AWS services. The following screenshot shows the IAM dashboard containing a list of all users, roles, policies, and access reports (Access Analyzer reports, credential reports, and organization activities in relation to IAM):

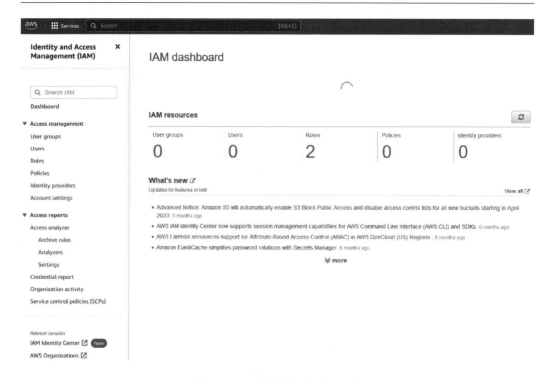

Figure 3.4 – AWS IAM dashboard

Amazon Relational Database Service (RDS)

Amazon RDS is a managed service offered by AWS that enables organizations to create, operate, and scale relational databases in the cloud. With RDS, organizations can choose from popular database engines such as MySQL, PostgreSQL, Oracle, and Microsoft SQL Server and easily manage their databases without worrying about infrastructure management. RDS automates time-consuming database administration tasks, such as patching, backups, and software upgrades, allowing organizations to focus on their core business.

RDS is an essential service for organizations that require a scalable, reliable, and cost-effective way to manage their relational databases in the cloud. With RDS, organizations can easily create and manage multiple database instances, each with their own database engine, storage capacity, and performance metrics. RDS also supports high availability and disaster recovery options, such as multi-Availability-Zone deployments, automatic failover, and backups, ensuring that organizations' data is always accessible and protected. Amazon RDS database instances can be accessed through any database client for the specific database engine (e.g., MariaDB, Microsoft SQL Server, MySQL, Oracle, PostgreSQL, etc.). To find the database instance connection information (i.e., host, port, and user) for a created database instance, organizations can use the AWS RDS console, found in the AWS Management Console, and navigate to their database instance's **Connectivity** and **Security** tab. Other methods to find connection information include the AWS CLI or the RDS API.

Digital forensics and incident responders can use an organization's RDS to investigate and respond to security incidents and data breaches. RDS provides audit logging, which allows organizations to monitor database activity, such as user logins, SQL statements, and modifications to database objects. Audit logs can be exported to Amazon S3 for long-term retention and analysis.

In the event of a security incident or data breach, incident responders can use RDS to perform forensic analysis, such as identifying the source of the attack, determining the extent of the compromise, and assessing the impact on the organization's data. Incident responders can use RDS snapshots to create a point-in-time copy of the database instance before the incident occurred, allowing them to analyze the database contents and activity leading up to the incident. Incident responders can also restore the snapshot to a new RDS instance for further analysis.

Microsoft Azure

Microsoft Azure is a cloud computing platform and service offered by Microsoft that provides a range of cloud services, including compute, storage, networking, and analytics. It allows organizations to build, deploy, and manage applications and services through a global network of data centers, providing the ability to scale up or down as needed without the need for on-premises infrastructure. Azure offers a variety of services, including virtual machines, databases, app services, IoT, and machine learning, and can integrate with other Microsoft productivity suites, such as Microsoft 365 (we will discuss productivity suites in *Chapter 7* of this book). Azure also provides a range of security features, including IAM, network security, and threat protection, to help keep data and applications secure.

We will explore the key Azure services that incident responders should be familiar with, and explain why knowing about Azure is important for effective incident response in modern IT environments.

Microsoft Azure virtual machines

Microsoft Azure's equivalent of Amazon EC2 is Azure virtual machines, which organizations can deploy and run on Microsoft's cloud infrastructure. Azure virtual machines support a wide range of operating systems and provide a high level of control. With Azure virtual machines, organizations can choose from a wide range of preconfigured virtual machine images or create custom virtual machine images and then run them in the cloud.

Azure virtual machines are important for organizations that require a scalable and flexible way to run their applications in the cloud. Organizations can easily provision and deploy Azure virtual machines, scale up or down their computing resources, and pay only for the resources that they use. Azure virtual machines support a wide range of operating systems, including Windows, Linux, and FreeBSD, as well as a wide range of virtual machine sizes, from small to large. The following screenshot shows

Microsoft Azure's virtual machine creation page, including options to customize the virtual machine operating system, hardware, and storage capabilities. Azure virtual machines have a similar element to AWS EC2 and other cloud provider virtualizations—that is, options to customize the hardware, operating system, storage, and networking configurations for your virtual machines.

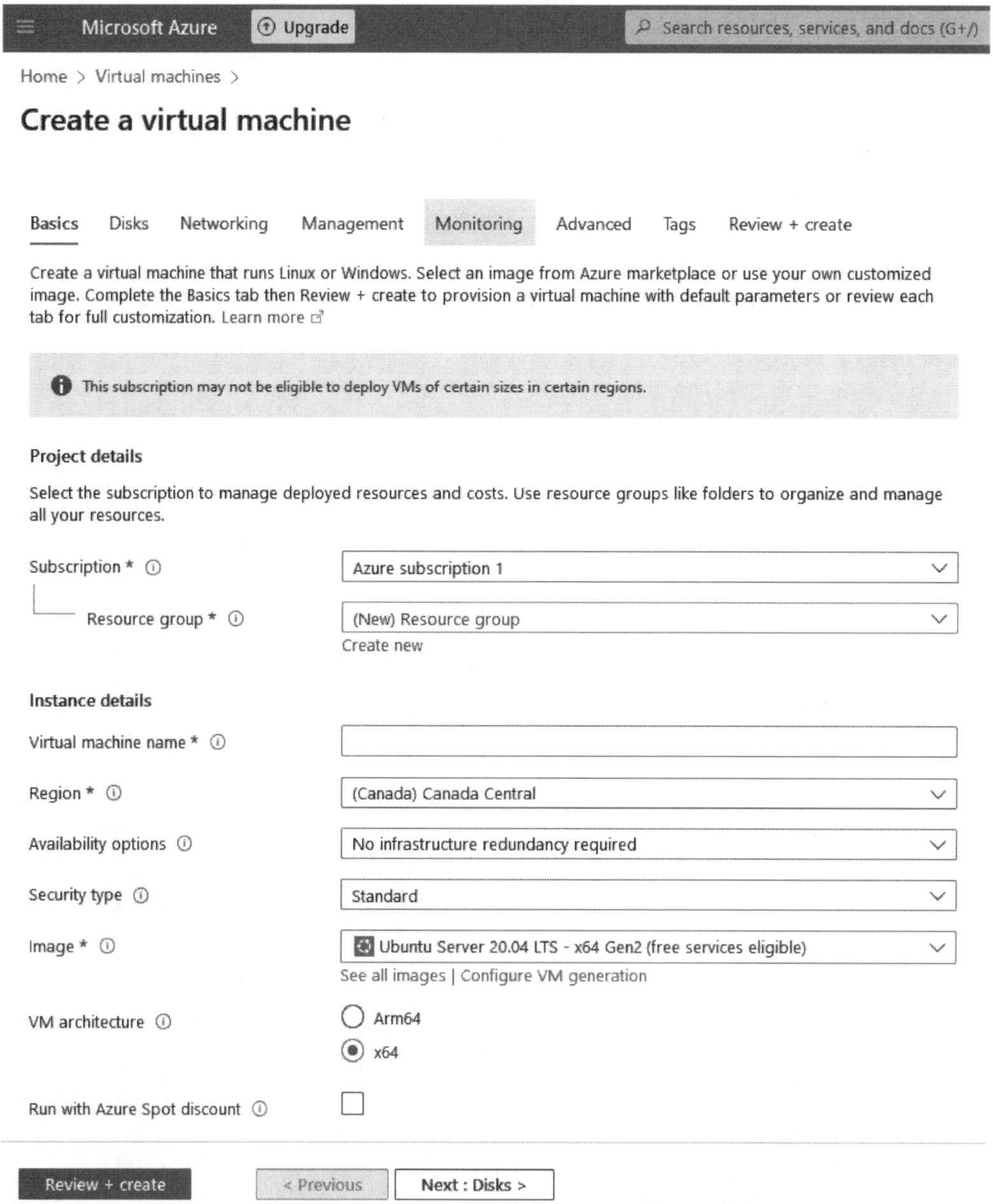

Figure 3.5 – Launching a virtual machine instance in Azure

Digital forensics and incident responders can use an organization's Azure virtual machines to investigate and respond to security incidents and data breaches. Azure virtual machines provide logging and monitoring capabilities that allow organizations to track and analyze the execution of their virtual machines. Azure virtual machine logs can be exported to one of Microsoft Azure's native security tools, Azure Monitor, for long-term retention and analysis or forwarded to Microsoft's **Security Information and Event Management** (**SIEM**) tool, Microsoft Sentinel.

> **Azure Monitor**
>
> Azure Monitor is a comprehensive monitoring solution for collecting, analyzing, and responding to telemetry from the Microsoft Azure cloud.

Microsoft Azure Virtual Network

Microsoft Azure Virtual Network is a cloud-based service that allows organizations to create, configure, and manage **Virtual Private Networks** (**VPNs**) on the Microsoft Azure cloud platform. Azure Virtual Network provides a secure and private connection between resources deployed in the cloud and on-premises resources, enabling organizations to extend their network infrastructure into the cloud. With Azure Virtual Network, organizations can create virtual networks, subnets, and network security groups to control access to resources and protect them from unauthorized access.

Azure Virtual Network is important for organizations that require a secure and private network infrastructure in the cloud. With Azure Virtual Network, organizations can create a virtual network that is isolated from the public internet, enabling them to secure their applications and data in the cloud. Azure Virtual Network supports a wide range of connectivity options, including site-to-site VPN, point-to-site VPN, and ExpressRoute, allowing organizations to choose the connectivity option that best meets their needs. An example of an Azure Virtual Network setup is shown in the following diagram. Note the similar role of Azure Virtual Network to that of an AWS VPC, that is, to manage virtualized resources such as a virtual machine in a virtual network.

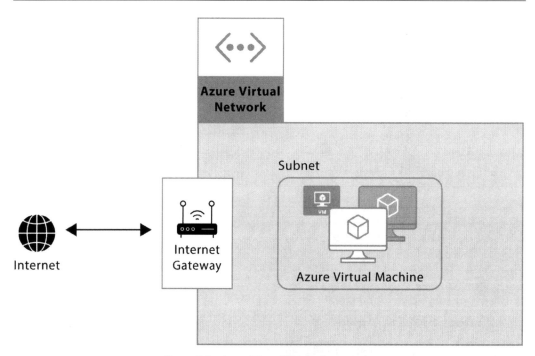

Figure 3.6 – Azure Virtual Network example

Digital forensics and incident responders can use an organization's Azure Virtual Network to investigate and respond to security incidents and data breaches. Azure Virtual Network provides logging and monitoring capabilities that allow organizations to track and analyze network traffic between resources deployed in the cloud and on-premises resources. Azure Virtual Network logs can be exported to Azure Monitor for long-term retention and analysis.

In the event of a security incident or data breach, incident responders can also use Azure Virtual Network to identify potential attack vectors and investigate the extent of the compromise. Incident responders can analyze Azure Virtual Network logs to identify anomalous network traffic, such as unauthorized access attempts or data exfiltration attempts. Incident responders can also use Azure Virtual Network security features, such as network security groups, to control access to resources and prevent unauthorized access.

Microsoft Azure Blob Storage

Microsoft Azure Blob Storage is a cloud-based object storage solution that enables organizations to store large amounts of unstructured data, such as text, images, videos, and audio files, in a cost-effective and highly scalable manner. Azure Blob Storage is a key component of the Azure platform, and it provides a number of features and benefits that make it an important tool for organizations of all sizes.

One of the key benefits of Azure Blob Storage is its scalability. Organizations can store virtually unlimited amounts of data in Blob Storage, and the storage capacity can be easily scaled up or down as needed. This makes it an ideal solution for organizations that need to store large amounts of data but don't want to invest in expensive hardware or infrastructure.

Another benefit of Azure Blob Storage is its durability. Azure Blob Storage uses redundant storage to ensure that data is always available, even in the event of hardware failures or other types of disruptions. This means that organizations can rely on Azure Blob Storage to store their critical data, without worrying about data loss or downtime.

Azure Blob Storage also provides a number of features that make it easy to manage data stored in the cloud. Organizations can easily access and manage data through a web-based interface, and Blob Storage provides a range of security features, such as encryption, access controls, and audit logs, to help protect data from unauthorized access and ensure compliance with industry regulations.

Digital forensics and incident responders can use an organization's Azure Blob Storage to store and analyze data related to cyber incidents, such as malware infections, data breaches, or ransomware attacks. By storing data in Azure Blob Storage, responders can easily access and analyze large amounts of data, without the need for specialized hardware or infrastructure. They can also use Blob Storage's built-in security features to ensure that data is protected and secure.

In the event of an incident in Azure Blob Storage, responders should follow established incident response procedures to quickly identify and contain the incident. This may involve isolating the affected Blob Storage containers or accounts, preserving data for forensic analysis, and identifying the root cause of the incident. Once the incident has been contained, responders can use Azure Blob Storage's audit logs and other data analysis tools to investigate the incident and identify any additional threats or vulnerabilities that may need to be addressed.

The creation of a Blob Storage instance requires three Azure resources:

- Storage account
- Container
- Storage blobs

The storage account acts as a unique zone in Azure for your data. A container is created within your storage account and organizes a set of blobs inside. Blobs contain your files for storage. *Figure 3.7* shows an example of a Microsoft Azure Storage account.

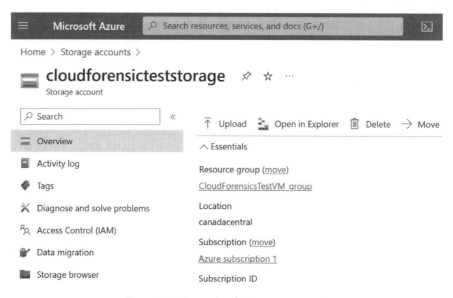

Figure 3.7 – Example of a Storage account

Microsoft Azure Active Directory (Azure AD)

Microsoft **Azure Active Directory (Azure AD)** is a cloud-based IAM solution that allows organizations to manage access to their resources across the Microsoft Azure platform. Azure AD is Microsoft's equivalent to AWS IAM. Azure AD is a core component of Microsoft's cloud offerings, providing authentication and authorization services to a range of Microsoft cloud services, such as Microsoft 365, Azure, and Dynamics 365. Azure AD is an essential tool for organizations that want to manage access to their resources in the cloud, enabling them to enforce security policies, streamline user management, and improve overall security.

Azure AD also provides a range of identity management features, including **Multi-Factor Authentication (MFA)**, Conditional Access policies, and **Role-Based Access Control (RBAC)**. These features allow organizations to control access to their resources based on user roles, device health, and other contextual factors.

Digital forensics and incident responders can use an organization's Azure AD to investigate security incidents related to IAM. By analyzing Azure AD logs and audit trails, responders can identify anomalous behavior, such as unauthorized access attempts, account compromise, or credential theft.

Microsoft Azure SQL Database

The Microsoft Azure equivalent of Amazon RDS is Azure SQL Database, which provides a fully managed RDS for Microsoft Azure. It serves as a flexible platform for storing and organizing SQL data within the cloud environment, allowing access to your data without the worry of system and database administrative tasks associated with machines that may be hosting your database. Azure SQL Database is based on the Microsoft SQL Server database engine and provides organizations with a wide range of features and capabilities for managing their data, including automatic tuning, high availability, and built-in security features.

Azure SQL Database is important for organizations that need a scalable and secure platform for managing their data in the cloud. With Azure SQL Database, organizations can easily provision and manage their databases in the cloud, without the need for costly hardware and infrastructure investments. Azure SQL Database provides organizations with a high degree of flexibility and scalability, allowing them to scale their database resources up or down as needed.

Digital forensics and incident responders can use an organization's Azure SQL Database to investigate and respond to security incidents and data breaches. Azure SQL Database provides a range of logging and auditing capabilities that allow organizations to track and analyze database activity, including user activity, schema changes, and data modifications. Azure SQL Database also provides built-in security features, such as transparent data encryption and row-level security, that can help protect data against unauthorized access.

In the event of a security incident or data breach, incident responders can use Azure SQL Database to identify potential attack vectors and investigate the extent of the compromise. Incident responders can analyze Azure SQL Database logs to identify anomalous database activity, such as unauthorized access attempts or data modifications. Incident responders can also use Azure SQL Database security features, such as auditing and row-level security, to investigate and mitigate the impact of a security incident.

Google Cloud Platform (GCP)

GCP is a suite of cloud computing services provided by Google. Similar to both AWS and Azure, GCP provides organizations with a wide range of cloud services that can be used to build, deploy, and manage applications and services.

Google Compute Engine (GCE)

Google Compute Engine (**GCE**) is a cloud computing service offered by GCP that provides organizations with virtual machine instances on demand. With GCE, organizations can launch virtual machine instances quickly and easily, configure them to their specifications, and scale them up or down as needed. The following screenshot shows GCE's dashboard, where you can create virtual machine instances. All created virtual machine instances will appear on this page.

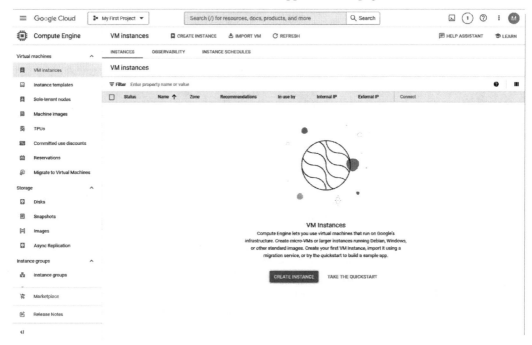

Figure 3.8 – GCE dashboard

GCE supports a range of operating systems, including Linux and Windows, and provides organizations with a range of machine types optimized for different workloads. Similar to AWS and Azure, you can configure your Google virtual machines with different computing capabilities, storage capacities, and networking features. *Figure 3.9* depicts the GCE virtual machine instance creation page.

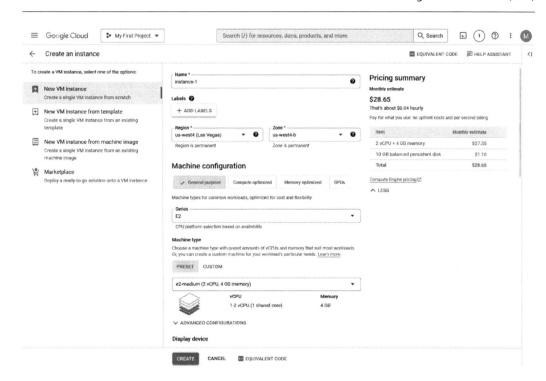

Figure 3.9 – Launching a virtual machine instance in GCE

GCE differs from AWS EC2 and Microsoft Azure virtual machines in several ways. First, GCE provides organizations with a range of custom machine types optimized for different workloads, allowing organizations to choose the optimal configuration for their applications and services. Second, GCE provides organizations with access to Google's global network infrastructure and data centers, which can provide faster network performance and lower latency than other cloud providers. Finally, GCE provides organizations with integrated monitoring and logging tools, such as Google's operations suite (formerly known as Stackdriver), which can simplify the process of managing and monitoring virtual machine instances. Incident responders can use monitoring and logging tools such as Google's operations suite to look for any indicators of compromise in the context of a security incident.

Google's operations suite

Google's operations suite is a monitoring, logging, and diagnostics platform offered by GCP, used to collect and analyze metrics, logs, and traces from Google cloud resources and applications.

Google Virtual Private Cloud (VPC)

Google VPC is a networking service that enables organizations to create and manage their private, software-defined network on GCP. Google VPC provides a secure and scalable way to host cloud resources by allowing organizations to isolate resources within their network, control access to them, and configure network settings according to their business needs.

Google VPC allows organizations to create their virtual network within the GCP environment. This virtual network is logically isolated from other networks, providing a secure and private environment for cloud resources. Organizations can customize network settings such as IP addresses, subnets, firewall rules, and routes, according to their business requirements. This way, organizations can control the flow of traffic between resources and ensure that only authorized users can access the resources. An example of a Google VPC network is shown in the following diagram. Note the similar role of Google VPC to that of AWS VPC and Azure Virtual Network, that is, to manage virtualized resources such as a virtual machine in a virtual network.

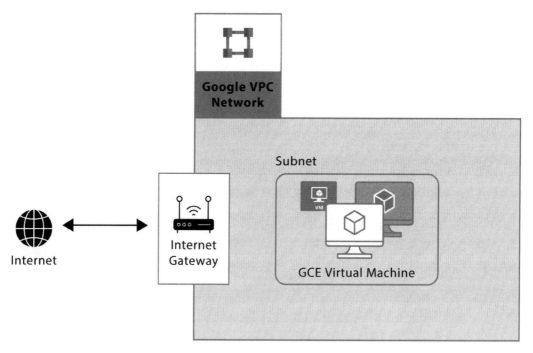

Figure 3.10 – Google VPC network example

Google Cloud Storage (GCS)

Google Cloud Storage (**GCS**) is Google's equivalent to Amazon S3 and Azure Blob Storage, providing users with a scalable and highly available object storage service. GCS enables users to store and retrieve any amount of data from anywhere in the world, and provides a range of storage classes to suit different data types and access patterns. The following screenshot demonstrates the creation process for a GCS object. GCS also organizes storage objects into buckets, as shown.

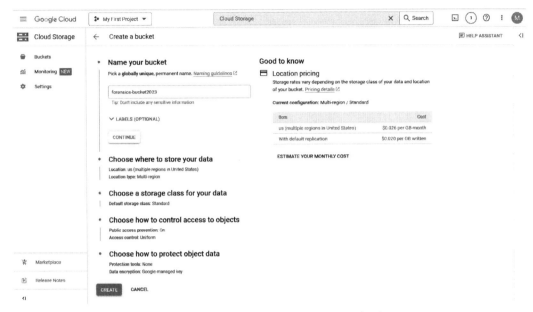

Figure 3.11 – Using GCS to create a storage bucket

Google storage buckets require the following:

- A unique naming convention
- A location (Google data center region) to store your data
- Access control configuration (through ACLs)
- Server-side encryption/protection

Google Cloud SQL

Google Cloud SQL is Google Cloud's equivalent to AWS RDS and Azure SQL Database, providing a fully managed RDS hosted by Google cloud. Cloud SQL supports MySQL, PostgreSQL, and SQL Server databases, and provides automatic backups, replication, and failover capabilities. Google Cloud SQL is a fully managed RDS that provides organizations with a solution to store and manage their databases on GCP. This service allows users to deploy, manage, and scale their databases with ease, freeing them from the overhead of managing infrastructure, backups, and software updates. With Google Cloud SQL, users can choose between MySQL, PostgreSQL, and SQL Server to power their applications and services.

Other cloud service providers

While AWS, Microsoft Azure, and GCP dominate the cloud service provider market, there are also other options available for organizations. Oracle Cloud, IBM Cloud, Alibaba Cloud, Rackspace, and DigitalOcean are some examples of less common cloud service providers. Each provider offers essential cloud services, such as creating virtual images and virtual networks, cloud storage, and database services—these are the same services we discussed previously for AWS, Azure, and GCP. Oracle Cloud, for instance, provides comprehensive cloud computing solutions, including IaaS, PaaS, and SaaS, while IBM Cloud offers a hybrid cloud platform that integrates with private and public clouds. Alibaba Cloud is the largest cloud provider in China, while Rackspace provides managed cloud services, and DigitalOcean focuses on simple cloud infrastructure for developers.

Summary

This chapter on cloud service providers provided an overview of three major players in the industry: AWS, Microsoft Azure, and GCP. It emphasized the importance of gaining a general understanding of these providers' products and services. Each of these platforms has a range of offerings, but most organizations commonly utilize cloud provider solutions related to virtual machine creation, virtual network services, storage, and database services. Having a general understanding of these fundamental aspects is essential to effectively respond to incidents in the cloud and conduct forensics.

In the event of an incident or security breach in the cloud, knowledge of how these providers handle virtual machine creation, networking, and storage enables a quick and informed incident response. Understanding their respective capabilities and configurations allows for more efficient incident management and forensic analysis. In the next chapter, we will take a deep dive into responding to AWS incidents—specifically where various logs for AWS products are stored and how they can be utilized for conducting your forensic analysis in the context of a security incident.

Further reading

- Oracle Cloud: `https://www.oracle.com/ca-en/cloud/`

- IBM Cloud: `https://www.ibm.com/cloud`

- Alibaba Cloud: `https://in.alibabacloud.com/en`

- Rackspace: `https://www.rackspace.com/cloud`

- DigitalOcean: `https://www.digitalocean.com/`

- Amazon AWS security best practices: `https://docs.aws.amazon.com/AmazonS3/latest/userguide/security-best-practices.html`

- Connecting to AWS RDS DB instances: `https://docs.aws.amazon.com/AmazonRDS/latest/UserGuide/CHAP_CommonTasks.Connect.html#CHAP_CommonTasks.Connect.EndpointAndPort`

- Overview of Azure Monitor: `https://learn.microsoft.com/en-us/azure/azure-monitor/overview`

- Overview of Azure Sentinel SIEM: `https://learn.microsoft.com/en-us/azure/sentinel/overview`

- Overview of Google Cloud's operation suite: `https://cloud.google.com/products/operations`

4

DFIR Investigations – Logs in AWS

Through *Chapters 1* to *3*, you may have recognized the importance of the cloud in today's technological landscape, and with any technological innovation comes threats against it. As organizations use more cloud products and host and store personal or sensitive information, it is prone to unauthorized disclosure, accidentally or by threat actors exploiting a vulnerability in the configuration of the systems. This chapter will focus on how to handle incidents that have occurred within **Amazon Web Services (AWS)**. We will discuss various log sources that are available for investigators and how investigators can make use of these log sources.

Before we can begin our investigation, we will need to understand which logs are available by default versus which log sources must be explicitly turned on; something organizations should consider for ensuring breaches can be investigated thoroughly. We will focus on configuring these logs and look at utilizing some of the native features of AWS for investigation. Specifically, we will discuss the following AWS data sources:

- **Virtual Private Cloud** (**VPC**) flow logs
- **Simple Storage Service** (**S3**) access logs
- AWS CloudTrail
- AWS CloudWatch
- Amazon GuardDuty
- Amazon Detective

VPC flow logs

We briefly introduced VPC in *Chapter 3*. VPC is the core of the network configuration for every instance within AWS. Each AWS instance (**Elastic Compute Cloud (EC2)**) is assigned a VPC and uniquely identified using a VPC ID. VPC allows users complete control of the network environment, including defining specific IP addresses (non-public routable IPs), subnets, and security groups. Users can also configure a **virtual private network** (**VPN**) through their VPC connection. In default configurations, AWS will automatically create a VPC for every new instance of EC2. Users can also connect their EC2 instance to an existing preconfigured VPC instead.

All VPCs have a **VPC identifier** (**VPC ID**). The VPC ID is the single reference point for all network-related configuration items. For each instance, if you want to configure any network properties within AWS, you must look into each VPC specifically. In the next example, for a specific EC2 instance, certain details are captured for VPC.

> **Note**
>
> Before we dive into details, it is essential to note that VPC flow logs are similar to network flow logs. These logs only capture header information of the network traffic; for example, source IP, destination IP, protocols, port, and if the connection was accepted or rejected (depending upon the inbound and outbound connection rules).

VPC basics

In the following screenshot, you will notice a few configurational information under the **Networking** tab, which is specifically helpful for **digital forensics and incident response** (**DFIR**) teams:

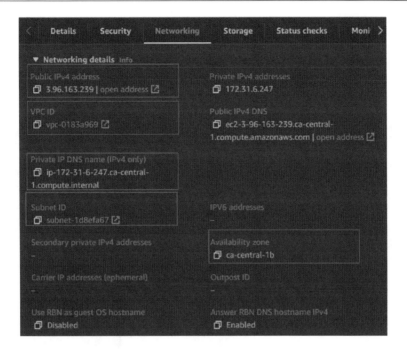

Figure 4.1 – Default VPC setup

This includes the following:

- **Public IPv4 address**: The publicly routable IP address scheme for this EC2 instance.

- **VPC ID**: A unique identifier that connects all network configuration items to this VPC setup.

- **Private IP DNS name (IPv4 only)**: Non-publicly routable IP assigned to the EC2 instance on a network interface. AWS typically uses this to provide backend communications or EC2 instance-to-EC2 instance communications.

- **Subnet ID**: The IP subnet that the VPC hosts.

- **Availability zone**: The AWS region where the VPC is configured initially.

DFIR teams can use this core information set to filter events and perform their analysis. In the *AWS CloudWatch* section of the chapter, we will look into how to tie this all together for investigation.

As illustrated in the preceding screenshot, each VPC is provided with one or more subnet(s) responsible for assigning IPs and managing the network segment. You may assign multiple subnets under the same VPC to various EC2 instances:

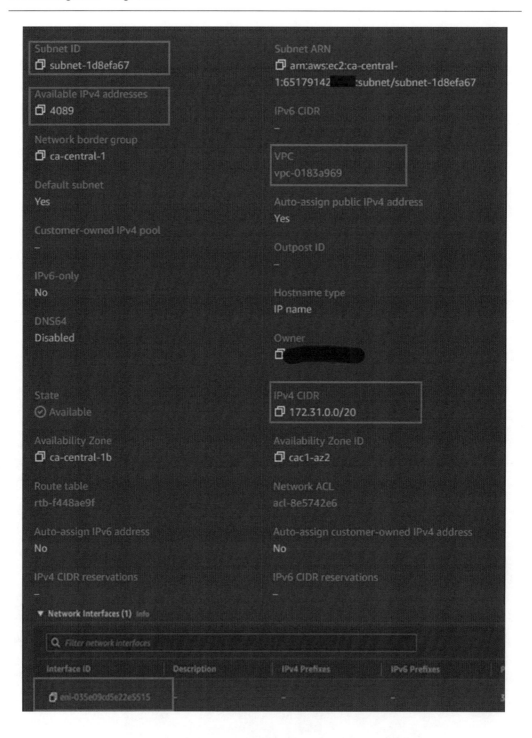

Figure 4.2 – A default subnet configuration and network interface

Similar to a VPC configuration, the preceding screenshot illustrates some of the default properties of a subnet assigned to a VPC. These include the following:

- **Subnet ID**: A unique identifier to identify the subnet assigned to the VPC.

- **Available IPv4 addresses**: Number of IPs assigned under this subnet. While AWS reserves IPs for administrative purposes, the total available IPs under this configuration are 4089.

- **Network border group**: An assigned internet edge location. A network border group is a collection of AWS edge locations and **points of presence** (**PoPs**) that are geographically distributed and designed to provide a secure and reliable connection between a VPC and the public internet.

- **Route table**: A unique identifier that points to a specific routing information schema assigned to this subnet.

- **Subnet ARN**: A subnet **Amazon Resource Name** (**ARN**) is a unique identifier that can reference the subnet in various AWS services and APIs, such as AWS CloudFormation templates, AWS **Identity and Access Management** (**IAM**) policies, and AWS Lambda functions.

- **VPC**: The VPC that this subnet is assigned to. Note that this subnet is assigned to the VPC referenced in *Figure 4.1*.

- **Owner**: Unique identifier of the account under which the instance, VPC and subnet are assigned. For privacy purposes, this is masked.

- **IPv4 CIDR**: A **Classless Inter-Domain Routing** (**CIDR**) notation scheme for the IPs assigned under this subnet. In *Figure 4.2*, /20 indicates that the first 20 bits of the IP address are used for the network address, and the remaining 12 bits for the host address.

- **Availability Zone ID**: A unique identifier assigned to each availability zone. This EC2 instance and subnet are assigned to Canada (ca-central); however, if required, you may place the subnet in another availability zone to provide **fault tolerance** (**FT**) and resilience.

- **Network ACL**: Another unique identifier to precisely identify the **access control lists** (**ACLs**) configured for this subnet. ACLs will enforce what is allowed versus restricted for network resources. This can also include inbound and outbound network filters.

- eni-035e09cd5e22e5515: The network interface ID.

While the preceding screenshot specifies essential configurational elements, each property can be adjusted per organizational requirements. However, DFIR teams need to note that the aforementioned aspects will play a role in your investigation and the nature of the threat you are observing as part of the investigation.

For DFIR teams, the following tabs offer additional detailed insights into the network configuration:

- **Flow logs** indicates how the network is logged. This VPC/subnet is logged in CloudWatch, which allows DFIR teams to query the network logs. We will investigate and query logs in a later part of the chapter:

Figure 4.3 – VPC flow logs

> **Note**
> Note that VPC flow logs are not enabled by default and require explicit setup.

- The next screenshot offers a deeper insight into **route tables** configured to connect to the internet. Note the **Target** internet gateway identifier (unique identifier) this subnet connects to. The route table defines how routing will perform for all instances related to this subnet. In organizations where a custom VPC is set up, this route table may look different or point to another network resource within AWS. It may not expose the instance directly to the internet. DFIR teams need to make a note of the gateway and the route table that the resources are assigned to for the investigation:

Figure 4.4 – Routing table

- The following screenshot shows details of inbound and outbound **network ACL (NACL)** lists that will define the network activity expected by the subnet. The ACLs operate at Layer 3 of the **Open Systems Interconnection (OSI)** model and filter traffic. In the next screenshot, you may notice two rules. A network rule number determines the order in which rules are enforced. Rule numbers are integers; lower numbers have higher priority, and rules are evaluated in ascending order. Specifically, in *Figure 4.5*, you will notice ⋆ in the **Rule number** column, which means this rule will be evaluated last once any rule numbers are assessed. Based on inbound and outbound ACLs, this resource is available online. It can access any part of the internet, presently the least secure setup and a default setup offered by AWS:

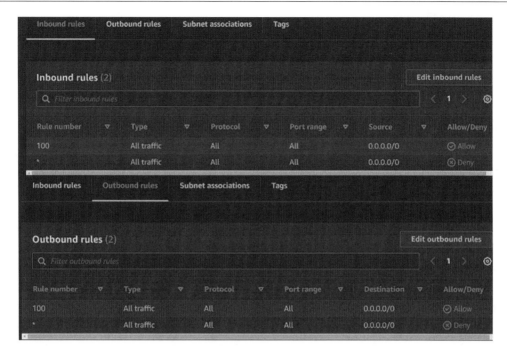

Figure 4.5 – NACLs configured for subnet

Now that we have reviewed various configuration items under the VPC, here is the summary dashboard that AWS offers for each of the VPCs, which outlines the VPC configuration properties and assignments along with additional information:

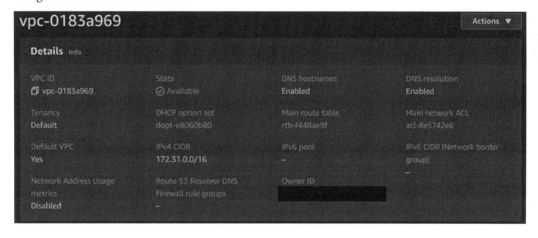

Figure 4.6 – VPC summary dashboard

The VPC summary dashboard page will also provide additional information regarding the subnets associated with this VPC and the flow logs configured. VPC flow logs are not enabled by default and require specific AWS resource access configured within AWS's IAM module. We will be looking into how to set up flow logs to enable DFIR teams to investigate network activity on AWS and query them.

The following screenshot outlines AWS's diagrammatic representation or resource map of how the network is configured from an internal AWS perspective connecting to the internet. The resource map displays the connections among the resources in a VPC, outlining the traffic path from subnets to **network address translation** (**NAT**) gateways, internet gateways, and gateway endpoints. Using the resource map, DFIR teams can comprehend the VPC's design, determine the number of subnets, identify which subnets correspond with route tables, and discern which route tables contain routes to NAT gateways, internet gateways, and gateway endpoints:

Figure 4.7 – Resource map for vpc-0183a969 VPC

Moreover, the resource map can assist you in identifying unsuitable or inaccurate setups, such as private subnets separated from NAT gateways or private subnets with direct routes to the internet gateway. You can select specific resources from the **Resource map** screen, such as route tables, and modify their settings. This functionality is presently under development.

Sample VPC flow log

Here is a sample VPC flow log and the properties captured by the flow log. It is essential to understand the elements captured within each flow log.

Flow logs are recorded between time intervals where it aggregates network traffic into a log:

```
2 65179142xxxx eni-035e09cd5e22e5515 45.79.132.41 172.31.5.217 41340
636 6 1 44 1682678411 1682678469 REJECT OK
```

Let us look into the details of each element of the flow log:

- 2: This field indicates the version of the VPC flow log's format.

- 65179142xxxx: This is the ID of the AWS account that owns the network interface. This is currently masked for privacy reasons.

- eni-035e09cd5e22e5515: This is the ID of the network interface (**elastic network interface (ENI)**). Notice this log matches the *Figure 4.2* configuration, which reflects the network connection of an EC2 resource.

- 45.79.132.41: This is the source IP address of the traffic.

- 172.31.5.217: This is the destination IP address of the traffic.

- 41340: This is the source port number.

- 636: This is the destination port number.

- 6: This is the protocol number. In this case, it is TCP (6). Port 6 is currently unassigned.

- 1: This is the number of packets transferred during the flow.

- 44: This is the number of bytes transferred during the flow. Note the bytes transferred during this flow session.

- 1682678411: This is the start time of the flow in epoch time (seconds since January 1, 1970).

- 1682678469: This is the end time of the flow in epoch time.

- REJECT: Action taken on traffic by a security group or NACL. Actions include ACCEPT/ REJECT/NO DATA/SKIPDATA. NO DATA and SKIPDATA are edge cases where NO DATA is recorded to indicate the flow log event is empty. In contrast, SKIPDATA is recorded when flow capture cannot capture the log during network aggregation intervals due to capacity limitations. SKIPDATA log entry means multiple network logs could not be captured due to internal configurational errors.

- OK: This is the status of the action.

DFIR use cases for VPC flow logging

There are several reasons why DFIR teams should utilize VPC flow logs in their incident investigation when investigating an AWS resource. Here are some use cases where VPC flow logs can play a crucial role for DFIR teams:

- **Threat detection and monitoring**: VPC flow logs can be used to detect suspicious or malicious network traffic. DFIR teams can identify traffic patterns that indicate known threats or potential intrusions by analyzing the flow logs. For example, they can use flow logs to detect port scanning, brute-force attacks, command-and-control traffic, and data exfiltration by reviewing flow logs' activity spikes.

- **IR**: DFIR teams can use VPC flow logs to reconstruct an event's timeline and identify an attack's source in a security incident. By analyzing the flow logs, they can determine the systems and applications that were affected, the duration of the attack, and the IP addresses and ports used by the attacker.

- **Forensic analysis**: VPC flow logs can also be used in digital forensic investigations to identify the source of an attack and trace the path of data access through the network. DFIR teams can use the flow logs to determine the source IP address, the destination IP address, and the protocols used during the network connection. This information can help them identify the source of a data breach or other security incident.

- **Compliance monitoring**: VPC flow logs can be utilized to monitor compliance with security policies and regulations. DFIR teams or the **Security Operations Center** (**SOC**) can use the flow logs to detect unauthorized access to sensitive data and security violations. This information can be used to generate reports for compliance auditors or to support legal investigations.

- **Anomaly detection**: Finally, VPC flow logs can be used to detect abnormal network traffic. DFIR teams can use **machine learning** (**ML**) techniques to identify patterns of traffic that deviate from the expected behavior of the network. This can help them detect potential security incidents or system failures before they become more serious.

S3 access logs

Amazon S3 is a very popular cloud storage service that is highly scalable and dependable for data storage and retrieval. S3 provides **high availability** (**HA**), storage performance, and accessibility of any amount of data from around the world.

In AWS, S3 operates on *buckets*, which contain *objects*. Objects are any files, documents, images, and videos. Each object is identified using a unique identifier known as the key that serves within a bucket. A bucket can be visualized as a folder that contains all the objects.

Logging options

Access logs record information about the requests made to an Amazon S3 bucket, including details such as request information, specific resource requests, and the time and date of the request. Amazon S3 uses a specific internal account to write server access logs, which requires AWS account owners to configure explicit permission within their IAM modules to allow S3 to log server access requests.

> **Note**
> Note that S3 access logs are not enabled by default and require explicit setup.

DFIR use cases for S3 monitoring

Since S3 storage is used for moving and hosting data, most DFIR use cases revolve around data analysis and movement. Some specific DFIR use cases include:

- **Data leakage**: Data leakage or data exposure can occur due to misconfiguration of an S3 bucket. Through access logs, you can help identify unauthorized access to data stored in S3 buckets. By monitoring bucket access logs and performing anomaly detection, you can identify suspicious activities such as large data transfers, unexpected access patterns, or unauthorized attempts to access specific objects.

- **Malware and ransomware detection**: S3 buckets can be targeted by attackers to store and distribute malware or ransomware. DFIR teams can monitor S3 for file integrity changes, unexpected file types, or suspicious behavior that can help identify such malicious files. Integration with **threat intelligence** (**TI**) can enhance detection capabilities.

- **IR and forensic investigation**: S3 monitoring can provide insights during IR and forensic investigations. Through access logs, DFIR teams can help reconstruct events, identify the source of an incident, and understand the scope of the compromise. Monitoring access logs, object metadata, and versioning can aid in analyzing activities leading to a security incident.

- **Data exfiltration detection**: Attackers may attempt to exfiltrate sensitive data by copying or downloading it from S3 buckets. Monitoring S3 access logs and performing content analysis can help identify large or unexpected data transfers that may indicate data exfiltration attempts. This can also be done through integrations with CloudTrail and CloudWatch and the development of a log pattern insight that allows DFIR teams to determine deviations in file access and identify exfiltration activities.

AWS CloudTrail

AWS CloudTrail records activities performed on the management console of AWS accessing any AWS resource—for example, an EC2 instance created or terminated, changes to the VPC settings, and so on. Any activity on the management console of AWS is recorded as an event within CloudTrail.

CloudTrail consolidates detailed action log events in a centralized location and provides a comprehensive and unified view of account's activity, making it easier to search, analyze, download, and respond to account activity across your AWS infrastructure. It also identifies what actions were performed by which user and any other details that help DFIR teams analyze and respond to an incident in AWS.

CloudTrail logs can be integrated into CloudWatch to query activities and perform further analysis. We will discuss CloudWatch in the next section.

The following screenshot demonstrates an example of a CloudWatch dashboard:

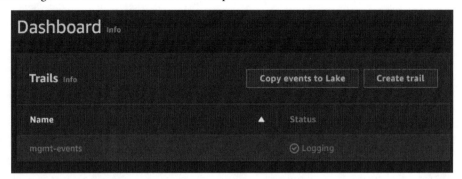

Figure 4.8 – CloudWatch dashboard

At the time of writing, we see that events are recorded under the mgmt-event trail. It aggregates all management activities performed under each AWS account. Events are recorded in CloudTrail **JavaScript Object Notation (JSON)** log format.

There are three types of events that CloudTrail can record: management events, data events, and CloudTrail data insight events. Let's take a closer look at these:

- **Management events**: As the name suggests, these record AWS account management-level activities, including operations performed on the AWS account. AWS refers to these as **control-plane operations**. Examples are **application programming interface (API)** operations, **AWS IAM**, creating new EC2 instances, editing VPC configurations, configuring routing operations, creating subnets, and creating new trails under CloudTrail.

- **Data events**: Records information regarding operations performed on the resource. AWS refers to these as **data-plane operations**. Usually, data events are voluminous, and you will have to configure them to ensure that AWS resources can provide them.

> **Note**
> Data event logging is not enabled by default and requires administrators to allow it explicitly.

Here is a list of AWS resources that provide these data events:

Data Event	Resources	Specific Events
DynamoDB	AWS::DynamoDB::Table	API-level activities, including PutItem, DeleteItem, and UpdateItem
DynamoDB Streams	AWS::DynamoDB::Stream	Dynamo API calls on streams

Data Event	Resources	Specific Events
Lambda	`AWS::Lambda::Function`	Lambda function execution activities, including `Invoke` API calls
S3	`AWS::S3:Object`	S3 object-level activity, including `GetObject`, `DeleteObject`, and `PutObject` API calls on S3 buckets
S3 Access Points	`AWS::S3::AccessPoint`	Amazon S3 API activity on **access points (APs)**
S3 Object Lambda	`AWS::S3ObjectLambda::AccessPoint`	S3 Object Lambda APs' API activity, such as calls to `CompleteMultipartUpload` and `GetObject`
CloudTrail	`AWS::CloudTrail::Channel`	`PutAuditEvents` on CloudTrail Lake for logging events outside of AWS
Cognito	`AWS::Cognito::IdentityPool`	Cognito API activity on identity pools
Amazon **Elastic Block Store (EBS)** direct APIs	`AWS::EC2::Snapshot`	Direct APIs, such as `PutSnapshotBlock`, `GetSnapshotBlock`, and `ListChangedBlocks`, on Amazon EBS snapshots
GuardDuty	`AWS::GuardDuty::Detector`	`GuardDuty` API activity for a detector

Table 4.1 – AWS data event collectors

- **CloudTrail data insight events**: CloudTrail Insights provides insights into abnormal activities such as large volumes or spikes of API calls or high error rates within an AWS account. Insights are logged when CloudTrail notices deviations within API usage and error rates within the AWS account.

Creating a trail

CloudTrail is not automatically enabled when an account is created within AWS. Security teams must define a trail to collect all the necessary information/activities within the AWS account for audit, compliance, and investigation purposes.

You will first have to define a trail and uniquely identify it for it to be integrated with other AWS resources such as **CloudWatch**. As described earlier, a trail is similar to an audit trail that tracks the activities of a user within an AWS account. In the following screenshot, we identify the trail as mgmt-events to signify what types of events are collected within this trail. We then select the location where this trail is stored. You can create a new S3 bucket; however, if your security operations team owns an S3 bucket, you can also place your trail there. We have masked the account number associated with this trail for security reasons:

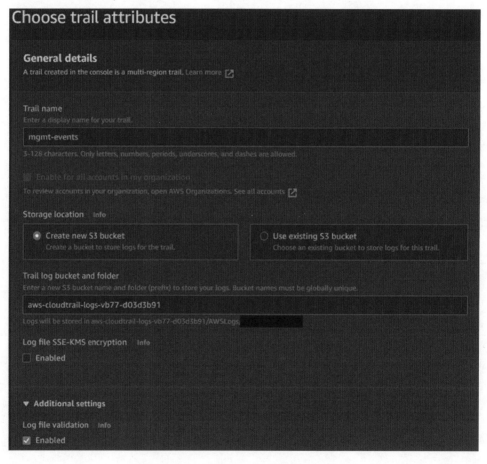

Figure 4.9 – Setting up CloudTrail logging

When configuring CloudTrail logs, you can enable it to feed into CloudWatch automatically. We will discuss more about CloudWatch in a later part of the chapter. Essentially, providing CloudTrail logs to CloudWatch allows DFIR teams to focus their investigation and log reviews on a single console, giving them a **single-pane-of-glass (SPOG)** view of the logs:

Figure 4.10 – AWS CloudWatch for AWS CloudTrail

When defining a CloudTrail log, you should also configure what types of data events are collected within CloudTrail. Earlier in this section, we referred to three types of data events: management events, data events, and data insight events.

The following screenshot defines the configurations enabled for the trail to collect records. As you can see in the screenshot, CloudTrail will collect events associated with the management of AWS resources itself, such as accessing/querying, creating, modifying, or deleting resources. For example, an AWS IAM administrator creating another account with privileges triggers a management event recorded under this trail:

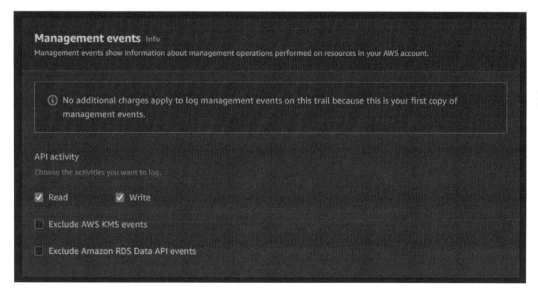

Figure 4.11 – CloudTrail management events' configuration

On the other hand, a data event specifically collects events associated with data-level activities within an AWS resource, such as tracking changes to the files stored on an S3 bucket. Monitoring data events allows DFIR teams to confirm if the data was accessed, modified, or deleted within these AWS services. The next screenshot indicates the configuration required to enable data events. It reflects the options for DFIR teams to configure and allow appropriate CloudTrail logging:

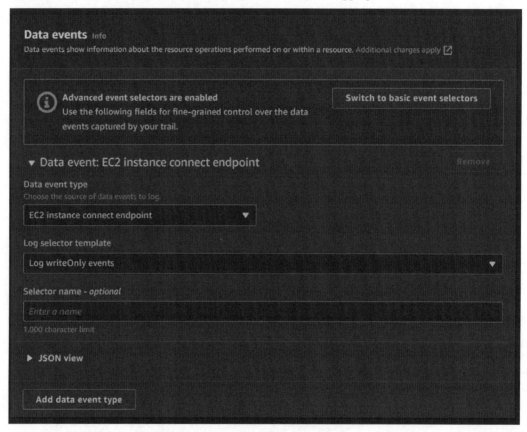

Figure 4.12 – CloudTrail data events' configuration

Log file validations

When you create a trail, you also want to protect its integrity so that there are no unauthorized changes. Hence, we also enable a log file validation checkmark to enforce integrity checks on the trail as it is generated to ensure the course is not altered and is accurate for investigation. Integrity checks results are delivered to the same S3 buckets as digests. DFIR teams can utilize the log file digests to validate the integrity of log files. Each log file is hashed and digitally signed. CloudTrail log data digest files are signed using RSA, where a private key is generated for each region, and SHA-256 data is used to sign using the private key, resulting in a digital signature. The SHA-256 data is generated from the **Universal Time Coordinated** (**UTC**) timestamp of the log file, S3 path, SHA-256 hash of the current digest file (in hex format), and signature of the previous digest file (in hex format). These elements together form a hashing string, which is used to generate a SHA-256 hash of the data, which is then signed.

Once a signature is generated, it is further encoded in a hex format. Hexadecimal signatures are then recorded within the `x-amz-met-signature` tag of the digest files stored on S3.

DFIR teams can choose to enable log file validation later through the AWS Management Console, API, or AWS command line:

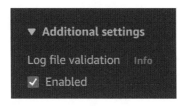

Figure 4.13 – Log file validation is enabled

Event data stores

Since CloudTrail is an auditing tool that documents events/changes within an AWS account, security teams must indicate the data lake where these events are filtered and stored once a trail is created. AWS refers to this data lake of events as an **event store**. You can create one or more event stores to store management or data events based on filters across various regions within the AWS account. Event stores offer long-term retention of up to 7 years. Organizations can send these logs to a centrally managed **security information and event management** (**SIEM**) solution.

Once an event store is created, it effectively allows DFIR teams to immediately use it and query the store for associated activities on a specific AWS resource (module/service) and details about the event.

The following screenshot demonstrates the steps required to configure an event store and apply a filter. We select all management and data events in the same event store in this example:

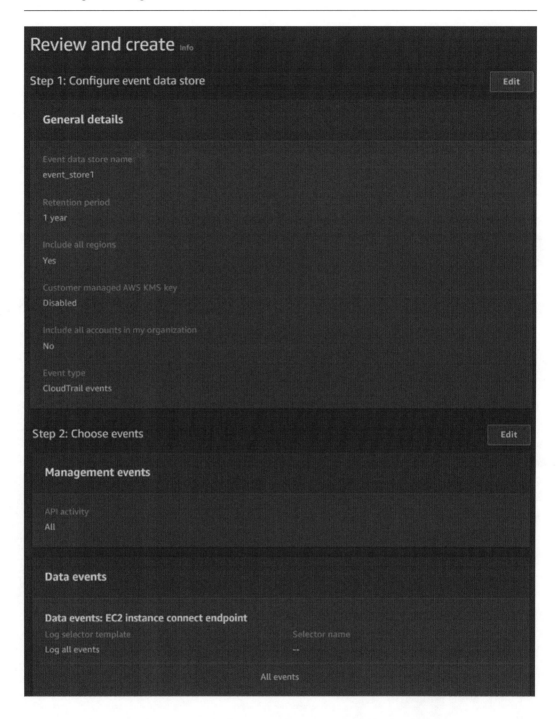

Figure 4.14 – Configuring event stores in AWS CloudTrail

Querying CloudTrail event stores

CloudTrail allows DFIR teams to query event stores, where all management and data events are stored as with any logging tool. In simplistic terms, CloudTrail events can be queried using **SQL**.

Note that within CloudTrail, given that the events are immutable, only SQL SELECT statements are allowed. You can apply filters using WHERE clauses. However, CloudTrail does not allow users to manipulate data within event stores.

While event stores can be named, DFIR teams must note the unique event data store ID generated by AWS to run SQL queries. The following screenshot demonstrates a SQL query and associated query results. In this example, we are querying to return entire values stored in the event store. However, once comfortable, DFIR specialists can directly query the event store to obtain the necessary information from the store:

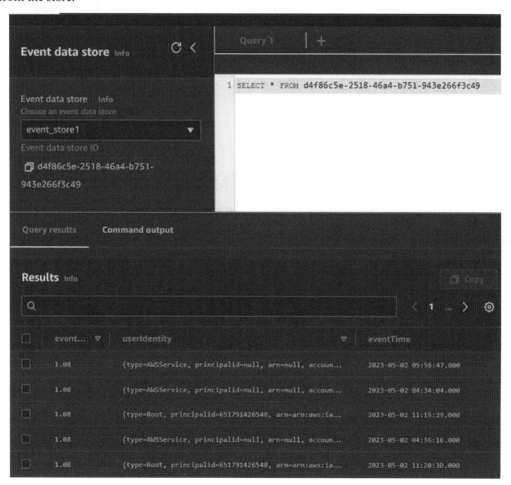

Figure 4.15 – Simple SQL query and results on AWS CloudTrail

Another example is where you query event stores to identify the top active users. In DFIR cases, this can be a needle in a haystack, with multiple users and interaction points. However, you are looking for one particular outlier where you can start your investigation into this case.

Investigating CloudTrail events

Any DFIR specialist would love to access an event store full of logs that provide invaluable information for an investigation. This section will examine some investigative strategies that DFIR specialists can adopt to investigate CloudTrail events. Note that any queries performed on the CloudTrail event store are also recorded within the same event store.

Investigating directly within the event store

DFIR teams can directly choose to investigate the logs available in the event store. For example, we will investigate event stores to identify users who most frequently accessed AWS resources from the console.

By default, when you log in to CloudTrail, CloudTrail will automatically provide a summary of events in its dashboard, which includes some recent user activities. It will also record any API calls performed by other AWS resources. It consists of any API calls a resource made internally to another within AWS and user interaction via the AWS web browser.

For example, the following screenshot demonstrates some recent events in this demo lab. This dashboard also allows DFIR teams to click and obtain more specific information about a particular event entry. Each entry in the dashboard is reflective of each event:

Figure 4.16 – Dashboard view of events ordered by time in descending order

For example, in the first event, the `cf_user1` user interacted with an AWS EC2 resource. We know from *Chapter 3* of this book that each EC2 instance is uniquely identified using an instance ID within AWS. It is, therefore, more accessible for DFIR teams to track back and remember which instance the user interacted with and gather specific configurations. Through the summary view, we can understand that the `cf_user1` user stopped an EC2 instance identified by `i-09c02a7e1ff652c13` on May 10, 2023, 05:55:49 (UTC-04:00). Should DFIR teams need additional information, this can be obtained by clicking on the link under the **Event name** field. The following screenshot shows the details of the captured event:

Figure 4.17 – Additional information about the event recorded in CloudTrail

It is important to note that additional information captures the source IP address, which records the IP address of the threat actor who may have compromised and accessed this AWS account to stop this instance. DFIR teams can further dig into the IP address and identify what other activities were performed by this user or from this source IP address, giving a timeline of events. In the additional information section, DFIR teams also have the opportunity to capture a raw event record in JSON format. AWS refers to this as an **event payload**. Usually, this is available within the dropdown under **Event history**. An event payload allows DFIR teams to review the raw log and determine more specific actions a user or attacker may have performed on the affected resource. Specifically, it also identifies other metadata that may be useful for further investigation. Here is a raw event log or event payload for stopping an instance, as indicated in the preceding screenshot:

```
{
    "eventVersion": "1.08",
    "userIdentity": {
        "type": "IAMUser",
        "principalId": "AIDAZPQOL4P2OUQxxxxx",
        "arn": "arn:aws:iam::xxxxxxxx6548:user/cf_user1",
        "accountId": "xxxxxxxx6548",
        "accessKeyId": "xxxxxxxxxxxxMBCSD6",
        "userName": "cf_user1",
        "sessionContext": {
            "sessionIssuer": {},
```

```
                "webIdFederationData": {},
            "attributes": {
                "creationDate": "2023-05-10T09:55:05Z",
                "mfaAuthenticated": "true"
            }
        }
    }
},
"eventTime": "2023-05-10T09:55:49Z",
"eventSource": "ec2.amazonaws.com",
"eventName": "StopInstances",
"awsRegion": "ca-central-1",
"sourceIPAddress": "184.147.70.116",
"userAgent": "AWS Internal",
"requestParameters": {
    "instancesSet": {
        "items": [
            {
                "instanceId": "i-09c02a7e1ff652c13"
            }
        ]
    },
    "force": false
},
"responseElements": {
    "requestId": "1497712b-d47d-462a-a3a0-048d82463a96",
    "instancesSet": {
        "items": [
            {
                "instanceId": "i-09c02a7e1ff652c13",
                "currentState": {
                    "code": 64,
                    "name": "stopping"
                },
                "previousState": {
                    "code": 16,
                    "name": "running"
                }
            }
        ]
    }
},
"requestID": "1497712b-d47d-462a-a3a0-048d82463a96",
"eventID": "5ecd20de-1c37-41f1-b200-8660fe5d5eed",
```

```
    "readOnly": false,
    "eventType": "AwsApiCall",
    "managementEvent": true,
    "recipientAccountId": "xxxxxxxx6548",
    "eventCategory": "Management",
    "sessionCredentialFromConsole": "true"
}
```

In the preceding raw event payload, we have highlighted essential elements or attributes of the log that DFIR teams should typically make a note of:

- **Account used for logging in to the AWS console and type of account** ({`"arn"`: `"arn:aws:iam::xxxxxxxx6548:user/cf_user1"`}): In this instance, we have an IAM regular user logging in to an AWS account with a unique identifier (`xxxxxxxx6548`). We have tokenized the account number for security reasons.

- **Username field** ({`userName`: `"cf_user1"`}: The actual username that was used to authenticate to this session.

- **Session creation date and time** (`"attributes"`: {`"creationDate"`: `"2023-05-10T09:55:05Z"`,`"mfaAuthenticated"`: `"true"`}: The time of the session that was created after authenticating the user to an AWS session. This entry demonstrates that the user successfully logged in to the AWS console and verified its two-factor token to complete the authentication process.

- **Event time** ({`"eventTime"`: `"2023-05-10T09:55:49Z"`}: The actual date and time of the event that was recorded in UTC time.

- **Source IP address** ({`"sourceIPAddress"`: `"184[.]147[.]70[.]116"`}: Source IP address of the user or threat actor who performed this event. For security reasons, IP addresses are defanged.

- **Instance information** (`"instanceId"`: `"i-09c02a7e1ff652c13"`,`"currentState"`: {`"code"`: 64, `"name"`: `"stopping"`},`"previousState"`: {`"code"`: 16, `"name"`: `"running"`}): Specific event entries reflecting current and previous states of the instances that confirm what specific actions were performed. In this example, we have a running instance that the user logged in to and stopped the instance.

Putting this in the perspective of a DFIR investigation, one can deduce and summarize the activities performed in this case and identify the next steps concerning the investigation.

Downloading and investigating event store results offline

Since CloudTrail event logs are in JSON format and you can query, filter, and extract results accordingly for investigation, we can always query the event store and download the logs for offline review. This is specifically useful where DFIR teams do not have access to AWS. However, investigation into CloudTrail events is imperative from an investigation point of view.

Using the source IP address captured in the previous example, we will query the event data store to identify activities from this IP address. For this, we will perform the following query:

```
SELECT * FROM d4f86c5e-2518-46a4-b751-943e266f3c49 WHERE eventTime >
'2023-04-30 00:00:00' AND sourceIPAddress='184.147.70.116'
```

Remember—event data stores are uniquely identified using an event data store ID; we filter dates based on our incident investigation, and further filtering is applied to the `sourceIPAddress` attribute.

While query results are displayed in a tabulated format, you can copy entire raw records using the **Copy** option. You do have to select event records or everything you would like to copy:

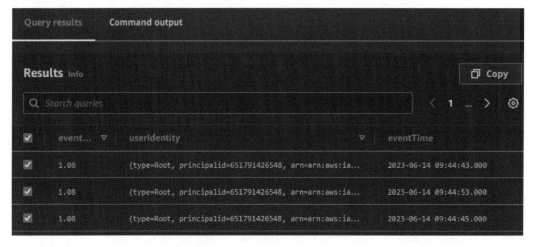

Figure 4.18 – Search query result

Using any third-party tools such as CyberChef, you can parse this JSON log for further investigation. Alternatively, you may use any log parsing tool to parse and further investigate the logs.

Alternatively, you can download the whole set of logs directly from the associated Amazon S3 bucket. You can find the location for this S3 bucket by simply navigating to the CloudTrail dashboard and selecting the relevant trail name. See the next screenshot for an example:

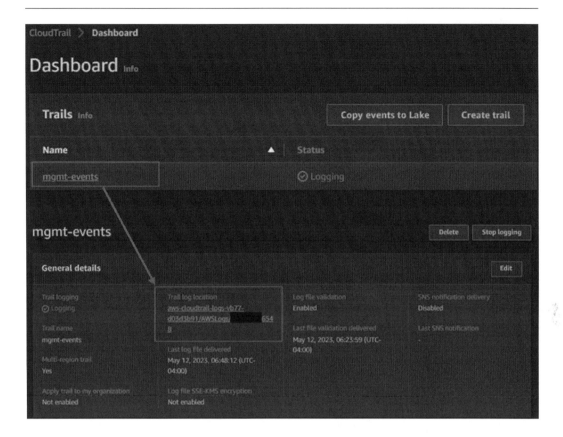

Figure 4.19 – Navigating to CloudTrail S3 bucket

When you navigate to the S3 bucket, you will notice that CloudTrail details are stored in two different object repositories; one contains the digest (which we discussed in the earlier sections of the chapter), which includes information to verify the integrity of the logs, while the other object repository is where actual logs are stored.

The logs are further stored per region, based on each AWS region the resources are operating from and sending logs to CloudTrail. DFIR teams need to understand that AWS breaks down the storage of logs per calendar day. When downloading S3 logs, you will need this information before your log collection from S3. Downloading all the data hosted on S3 may be huge and not beneficial from an investigation standpoint. However, it depends upon the circumstances of the investigation. The next screenshot provides an overview of a sample set of logs available for May 1, 2023, located under the ca-central-1 region, and how AWS stores CloudTrail logs:

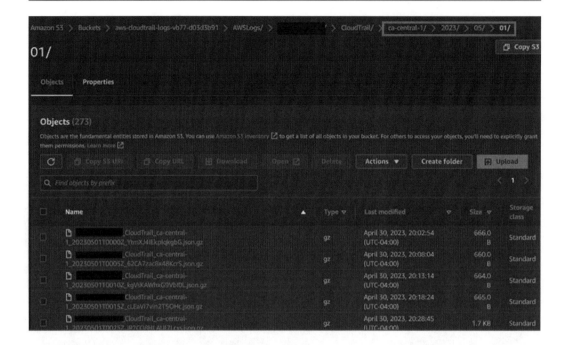

Figure 4.20 – Obtaining CloudTrail logs from the CA-Canada Central region

You may download multiple files simultaneously if you have API access to AWS. However, AWS limits downloads to one file at a time from the web console, which may make it time-consuming.

While CloudTrail stores its logs in gzip format to preserve storage, AWS will serve you an unzipped log format while downloading.

DFIR use cases for CloudTrail logging

Next are some use cases for enabling CloudTrail and how it can support DFIR teams:

- **Incident investigation**: CloudTrail can support your incident investigations. Some common investigation themes can be looked into, such as AWS account takeovers, where an attacker creates an unauthorized account to create/modify resources within AWS. You can use CloudTrail logs to determine the username, source IP address, and how they authenticated themselves into AWS. CloudTrail logs also provide vital information about whether the attacker performed specific modifications and the configuration previously set. Other investigation areas include the following:

  - **Looking for malicious or rogue EC2 instances**: Through CloudTrail logs, you can determine if the attacker created an EC2 **virtual machine** (**VM**) to access specific production environments. CloudTrail can provide information on the instance type, instance ID – which can be used for further investigative hunting – and the date and time of the creation of such rogue EC2 instances. Because CloudTrail logs activities across multiple regions under the organization, DFIR teams can also use the CloudTrail logs to determine attacker lateral movements across various AWS resources in various regions.

- **Unauthorized API calls**: Since CloudTrail tracks all the API calls made by AWS internally from one resource to another, as well as API calls made by users, CloudTrail logs can be used to determine any unauthorized use of API resources. For example, a sudden surge of API calls using a specific access token can allow DFIR teams to quickly determine if the associated account was compromised, allowing unauthorized access to the attackers.

- **Security and compliance auditing**: Given a large portion of CloudTrail's purpose is to create an audit trail of all activities, CloudTrail can be used for monitoring compliance with security policies and regulations. For example, in healthcare, where user access must be closely monitored and provided on a least-privileged basis, CloudTrail logs can be valuable for fine-tuning these privileges based on the activities recorded, thus ensuring compliance.

- **Infrastructure monitoring and troubleshooting**: Outside of DFIR, CloudTrail can benefit developers and application testers to ensure their applications operate effectively. CloudTrail will allow developers to review API calls and determine the cause of any unintended consequences.

AWS CloudWatch

AWS **CloudWatch** monitors your AWS resources in near real time. You can collect and monitor resource usage and key metrics in a SPOG view. CloudWatch presents every resource metric on its dashboard for quick view. However, for DFIR teams, CloudWatch can query certain logs to support an investigation.

From a security perspective, CloudWatch is a log management solution that can centrally collect and monitor logs from systems, applications, and resources. It offers log analytics on top to allow interactive searching and analysis capabilities. Similar to CloudTrail, CloudWatch offers log exports via S3 buckets. Note that logs in CloudWatch never expire and are retained indefinitely. Administrators can change the retention policy and choose between a log retention of a day or up to 10 years. Alternatively, organizations can send CloudWatch logs to an SIEM solution via an API for centralized monitoring and management of logs.

CloudWatch is a service that allows you to search and analyze log data interactively. You can monitor logs from Amazon EC2 instances and CloudTrail logged events, create alarms, and receive notifications for specific API activity to perform troubleshooting. Additionally, you can audit and mask sensitive data, adjust log retention, and archive log data. CloudWatch Logs can also log information about DNS queries that Route 53 receives. It uses a purpose-built query language with sample queries, command descriptions, query autocompletion, and log field discovery to help you get started.

You can access CloudWatch using any of the following methods:

- **AWS CloudWatch console**: Direct access to CloudWatch dashboards and logs

- **AWS Command Line Interface (CLI)**: Using modules provided by Amazon to connect to AWS via commonly available terminals or command-line consoles within popular operating systems

- **CloudWatch APIs**: Using your technologies to publish or monitor AWS CloudWatch logs via APIs

- **AWS SDKs**: Build applications that publish logs into CloudWatch

> **Note**
>
> From a DFIR perspective, it is essential to note that CloudWatch logs, when enabled, only record activities performed on an AWS account and do not capture what specific actions were performed within each resource. (For example, CloudWatch will not capture events/records of activities performed by a user/threat actor within an EC2 instance. It will, however, record if the threat actor logged in to the AWS console and made changes, deleted EC2 instances, and so on.)

The following diagram illustrates a typical configuration of logs that are recoded into CloudWatch:

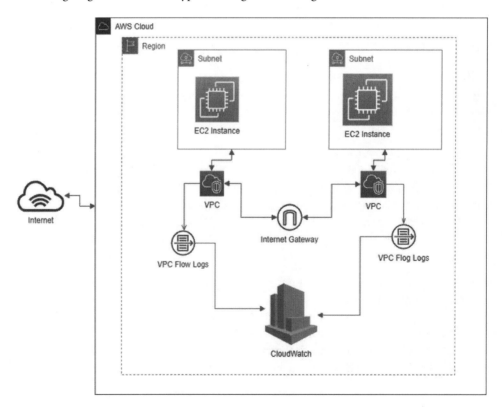

Figure 4.21 – Sample CloudWatch logging architecture of an EC2 instance with a VPC

The following sections will review the difference between CloudWatch and CloudTrail and how DFIR teams can set it up for incident investigation.

CloudWatch versus CloudTrail

So, let us look at some key differences between CloudWatch and CloudTrail. DFIR teams need to realize the difference in the features and how they can complement an incident investigation:

- **CloudWatch is a log management tool**: CloudWatch offers monitoring and observability capabilities, explicitly collecting and displaying resource usage and metrics from various AWS products. It provides an *as-it-happens* view of the logs.

- **CloudTrail records API interactions**: CloudTrail records API interactions between users and internal AWS resources, which makes a record of all activities within an AWS account. Unlike CloudWatch, CloudTrail only records API-related activities and allows specific querying for application troubleshooting or security investigations.

Since CloudWatch is a log management tool at its core, CloudWatch can ingest CloudTrail events and, therefore, offers a single console view into various log sources. DFIR teams can use the CloudWatch API to pull logs into their local SIEM solution for further monitoring and investigation.

Setting up CloudWatch logging

Once the organization establishes its AWS account, you can turn on CloudWatch logging. However, doing so requires a few steps, including configuring privileges for other AWS resources to allow them to send logs to CloudWatch. CloudWatch is regional; therefore, the best approach is to create a CloudWatch setup where most AWS resources are hosted. It is important to note for DFIR teams that enabling CloudWatch speeds up the incident investigation process. So, if an organization does not have CloudWatch, setting up an appropriate policy can allow flow logs to be immediately available, which is crucial for investigations.

Configuring VPC flow logging

Every category of logs is recorded in CloudWatch as a log group. A log group is a collection of similar types of logs. For example, all VPC flow logs will be under a single log group for CloudWatch; similarly, all CloudTrail events will be under a separate log group. In the next example, two log groups were created, with specific logging enabled for each. Each AWS resource will publish its flow logs within each log group as a log stream. For example, let us say you have five EC2 instances running, and you later create another five EC2 instances. At the end, when you log in to the CloudWatch console, you will see one log group that has multiple log streams uniquely identifying each EC2 resource using its network interface ID.

Note that a log stream is a stream of network flow logs that only captures specific elements within the stream. We discussed what a flow log contains in an earlier part of this chapter in the *VPC flow logs* section. Each log stream contains multiple entries of flow logs associated with the network interface, which can then be queried or analyzed to obtain further insights. The following screenshot describes how CloudWatch groups all flow logs based on categories. In the screenshot, you will see VPC flow logs are grouped under `vpcgrp1`, while CloudTrail logs are grouped under `aws-cloudtrail-logs-vb77-569383a0`:

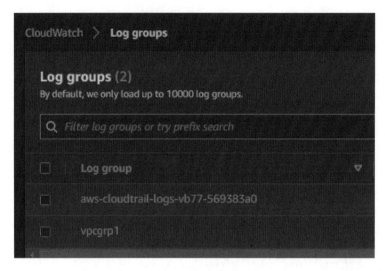

Figure 4.22 – CloudWatch log groups

VPC flow log access requirements

Since AWS is publishing flow logs originating per EC2 instance to be published or sent to another AWS resource, AWS requires the account to have appropriate IAM configurations to allow services to interact. By default, AWS does not automatically enable logs to be published to CloudWatch (given it is a separate subscription). Rights associated with flow logs must have appropriate permissions to allow VPC to post them on CloudWatch.

At a high level, the following permissions are typically required:

- `CreateLogGroup`: Remember, as indicated in *Figure 4.22*, that logs are grouped per category. This allows write permissions to create new log groups with a specific name.

- `CreateLogStream`: Each EC2 resource will publish its VPC logs within the log group as a log stream. This allows write permission to create a new log stream per resource.

- `PutLogEvents`: Allows permissions to write log events in batches within each stream.

- `DescribeLogGroups`: Describe or list log groups associated with the AWS account.

- `DescribeLogStream`: Similar to log groups, this allows listing all log streams within a specific log group associated with the account.

- `GetLogRecord`: Allows the ability to read all fields within a single log event.
- `GetQueryResults`: Allows the ability to read/return query results from specific queries.

There are additional permissions that are assigned to the CloudWatch role:

- `DescribeQueries`: Allows listing of CloudWatch Logs Insights queries that were recently executed
- `StopQuery`: Allows permissions to stop a CloudWatch Logs Insights query from execution
- `DeleteQueryDefinition`: Ability to delete a saved CloudWatch query
- `PutQueryDefinition`: Ability to create and update a query
- `GetLogDelivery`: Allows the ability to read log delivery information for specific logs
- `ListLogDeliveries`: Similar to `GetLogDelivery`, this allows log information to be listed for all log deliveries associated with an AWS account
- `CreateLogDelivery`: Allows permissions to create a new log delivery
- `UpdateLogDelivery`: Allows the ability to edit log delivery configurations

In addition to the IAM permissions, you must configure policies to allow flow logs to assume specific roles within your AWS account. For this case, we explicitly set up a policy to enable VPC flow logs to take roles within the AWS account. Policies group roles and resource assignments along with specific resource access conditions. Policies are how IAM manages permissions by attaching them to specific IAM users or identity profiles. A policy defines its permissions when associated with an identity, a user, or a resource.

Next is an example of an IAM policy specifically created using a visual tool provided by AWS to allow VPC flow logs to be published and for users to access and query the logs:

```
{
    "Version": "2022-10-17",
    "Statement": [
        {
            "Sid": "VisualEditor0",
            "Effect": "Allow",
            «Action»: [
                "logs:DescribeQueries",
                "logs:GetLogRecord",
                "logs:StopQuery",
                "logs:TestMetricFilter",
                "logs:DeleteQueryDefinition",
                "logs:PutQueryDefinition",
                "logs:GetLogDelivery",
                "logs:ListLogDeliveries",
```

```
                    "logs:Link",
                    "logs:CreateLogDelivery",
                    "logs:DeleteResourcePolicy",
                    "logs:PutResourcePolicy",
                    "logs:DescribeExportTasks",
                    "logs:GetQueryResults",
                    "logs:UpdateLogDelivery",
                    "logs:CancelExportTask",
                    "logs:DeleteLogDelivery",
                    "logs:DescribeQueryDefinitions",
                    "logs:DescribeResourcePolicies",
                    "logs:DescribeDestinations"
                ],
                "Resource": "*"
            },
            {

                "Sid": "VisualEditor1",
                "Effect": "Allow",
                "Action": "logs:*",
                "Resource": "arn:aws:logs:*:xxxxxxxx6548:log-group:*"
            },
            {

                "Sid": "VisualEditor2",
                "Effect": "Allow",
                "Action": "logs:*",
                "Resource": [
                    "arn:aws:logs:*:xxxxxxxx6548:destination:*",
                    "arn:aws:logs:*:xxxxxxxx6548:log-group:*:log-stream:*"
                ]
            }
        ]
}
```

At a high level, here is a breakdown of the policy. The policy has three statements in the form of array entries:

- **Statement 1**: A list of CloudWatch Logs actions that are allowed. These actions include various management and data retrieval operations for CloudWatch Logs.

- **Statement 2**: Allow logs:* instances (CloudWatch Logs actions) within a specific AWS account. This will include all log groups associated with the AWS account.

- **Statement 3**: Allow actions on all logs:* instances associated with a specific AWS account and all log streams specified within the AWS account.

Remember—policies allow users to access, edit, or query CloudWatch logs. You will, however, need to set up trust relationships between AWS resources for it to share/publish logs in the first place. This is typically done automatically when you first set up and enable CloudWatch. However, you can make granular trust policies for specific trust relationships between resources. Here is an example of a trust relation configured within the IAM module:

```
{
    "Version": "2012-10-17",
    "Statement": [
        {
            "Effect": "Allow",
            "Principal": {
                "Service": "vpc-flow-logs.amazonaws.com"
            },
            "Action": "sts:AssumeRole"
        }
    ]
}
```

The preceding JSON represents an IAM role trust policy that allows the Amazon VPC flow logs service (vpc-flow-logs.amazonaws.com) to assume the role. This trust policy is used when establishing a trust relationship between an IAM role and a trusted entity (in this case, the VPC flow logs service). The AssumeRole security token allows the relevant AWS resource a temporary set of security credentials that, in this case, the VPC service can use to communicate with other AWS services (CloudWatch) to pass the flow logs. AssumeRole allows for cross-account access and can be used for making API calls to any AWS service.

Querying CloudWatch logs on the AWS console

For manually querying CloudWatch within AWS, DFIR teams can utilize Logs Insights to construct specific queries for investigation. Logs Insights enables interactive querying capabilities to search and analyze log data. CloudWatch automatically identifies relevant fields from various log sources, including any custom logs sent to CloudWatch in JSON format. You can also create visual outputs, including graphs, as part of Logs Insights queries.

In the next example, we are looking at VPC flow logs. However, when querying, you may choose all log groups. The following screenshot demonstrates an example of querying within CloudWatch Logs Insights. The query targets the vpcgrp1 log group to identify the **timestamp** of the log, **message** (complete log information), LogStream (the source network identifier from where flow logs are generated), and the **log** (the account and the log group where the log was identified, useful when querying multiple log groups). Select the appropriate time range for CloudWatch to look up the logs:

Figure 4.23 – Sample query on CloudWatch

When you query within Logs Insights, CloudWatch will generate results and a histogram to allow investigators to drag and select timelines based on identified anomalies within the histogram. The next screenshot is an example of such a query result, with a histogram that outlines the events based on timestamp and number of records per date and time entries:

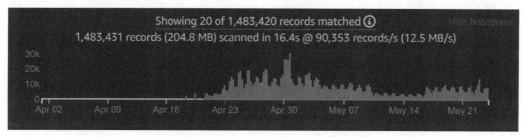

Figure 4.24 – Sample visualization generated by CloudWatch for VPC traffic

By just utilizing a sample query to determine traffic patterns observed by all VPC logs, you can further begin to filter down for the investigation. You filter on dates (through a selection option) and specific VPC log streams if the subject of investigation is nailed down to an EC2 instance connected with a particular log stream. Each query will also provide you with summary details of the log (as a simple string), along with a visualization, as indicated in *Figure 4.24*.

CloudTrail also provides pre-canned queries to get DFIR teams started; they can use these base queries to modify and apply necessary filters to obtain results for their investigation.

We used a sample query to determine all network traffic that was tagged as ACCEPT, meaning allowed by VPC and EC2 (configured via security groups,) and examine the traffic volume of each of those sessions:

```
filter action="ACCEPT" | filter bytesTransferred > 100 | stats
sum(bytes) as bytesTransferred by srcAddr, srcPort, dstAddr, dstPort,
action
```

The preceding query is run against all VPC log streams; however, AWS will limit the results to 1,000 records if we do not specify the *limit* result option. This is to avoid resource constraints to pull the results.

The next screenshot outlines the results we obtain once we run the previous query:

#	srcAddr	srcPort	dstAddr	dstPort	action	bytesTransferred
▶ 1	172.31.4.234	22	72.142.26.…	27599	ACCEPT	6605
▶ 2	45.61.49.156	123	172.31.5.2…	60309	ACCEPT	152
▶ 3	172.31.5.217	60309	45.61.49.1…	123	ACCEPT	152
▶ 4	172.31.4.234	22	99.248.72.…	57666	ACCEPT	17853
▶ 5	172.31.4.234	22	99.248.72.…	57667	ACCEPT	14077
▶ 6	99.248.72.244	57667	172.31.4.2…	22	ACCEPT	12531
▶ 7	99.248.72.244	57666	172.31.4.2…	22	ACCEPT	12515
▶ 8	72.142.26.182	34180	172.31.4.2…	22	ACCEPT	4947
▶ 9	172.31.4.234	22	72.142.26.…	34180	ACCEPT	6261

Figure 4.25 – CloudWatch query results

Let us look at an example of data exfiltration over SSH. We want to determine the overall network traffic on where there was outbound network traffic from the AWS EC2 instance to a remote threat actor-controlled server. You can use a CloudWatch query to filter to a specific IP address or just the source port (srcPort) to identify which other EC2 instance was accessed from this IP address. In the next example, we specifically look at all outbound network connections. If you are interested in inbound network activity on a specific port, you can set the destination port (dstPort) on the filter:

```
filter action="ACCEPT" | filter bytesTransferred > 100 | filter
srcPort=22 |stats sum(bytes) as bytesTransferred by srcAddr, srcPort,
dstAddr, dstPort, action
```

We can look into network spikes through the results and associated visualizations provided by CloudWatch. As indicated earlier, since CloudWatch offers interactive querying capabilities, you can click and select specific traffic spikes to filter down the time range associated with those network outbound spikes. In the next screenshot, we drill down into the network spikes identified by CloudWatch:

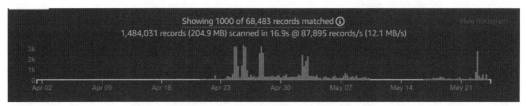

Figure 4.26 – Initial query results

To continue with the routine investigation, we choose a date/time by interactively selecting the spikes, which provides more granular visualizations. Note that the date/time in the filter is now converted to hours:

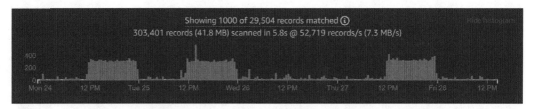

Figure 4.27 – Granular view of outbound network traffic

Through this deep dive, we can boil down the network traffic to three large spikes attributed to outbound network activity. Note that the traffic patterns still indicate multiple IP addresses; some of them can still be legitimate. To nail down potential threat actor IP addresses, at the same time, on the same screen with applicable time filters, we will edit the query to identify IP addresses with the largest to fewest data transfers. In a data exfiltration scenario, threat actors would exfiltrate large volumes of information from the servers. For this example, we filter outbound network traffic to anything above 1,000,000 bytes (approximately 1 MB) transferred and sort them in descending order:

```
filter action="ACCEPT" | filter bytesTransferred > 1000000 | filter
srcPort=22 |stats sum(bytes) as bytesTransferred by srcAddr, srcPort,
dstAddr, dstPort, action | sort bytesTransferred desc
```

As a result, we get about 19 data transfer events across the 3 instances of network spikes that can be potentially attributed to data exfiltration activity. Since we filtered the results down, DFIR teams can now use the destination IP address field to perform some form of **open source intelligence** (**OSINT**) to determine the legitimacy of the IP addresses to nail down further or apply necessary filters:

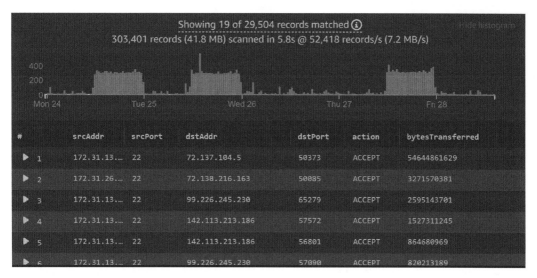

Figure 4.28 – Query result on data exfiltration of over 1 MB

As we can see in the descending order of bytes transferred results, we can immediately start looking at those spikes to determine and correlate them with the rest of the investigation. Here is just an example of an IP address filter to identify a network activity to a specific IP address:

```
filter action="ACCEPT" | filter bytesTransferred > 1000000 | filter
srcPort=22  | filter dstAddr="72.137.104.5" |stats sum(bytes) as
bytesTransferred by srcAddr, srcPort, dstAddr, dstPort, action | sort
bytesTransferred desc
```

We see in the next screenshot the results of the query:

#	srcAddr	srcPort	dstAddr	dstPort	action	bytesTransferred
▶ 1	172.31.13...	22	72.137.104.5	50373	ACCEPT	54644861629
▶ 2	172.31.13...	22	72.137.104.5	50277	ACCEPT	569864849
▶ 3	172.31.13...	22	72.137.104.5	54704	ACCEPT	16733737

Figure 4.29 – IP address-based network activity

As we know, VPC flow logs are similar to NetFlow logs; we can use the results we extracted and further query to determine the source of the network traffic—that is, which EC2 instance the traffic originates from. You can do that by correlating the source IP address field (`srcAddr`) and mapping it back to which EC2 instance was assigned this IP during the incident. We edit this query to yield the following fields:

- `timestamp`: Date and time of the event

- `message`: A NetFlow summary in message format

- `logStream`: The VPC log stream responsible for this message

The next query aims to obtain the exfiltration activity's entire message and log stream information:

```
filter action="ACCEPT"      | filter srcPort=22    | filter
dstAddr="72.137.104.5"      | fields @timestamp, @message, @logStream
```

Based on the query indicated previously, we can see the details of each event in the screenshot. This allows DFIR teams to obtain specific information about the network flow log and additional metadata:

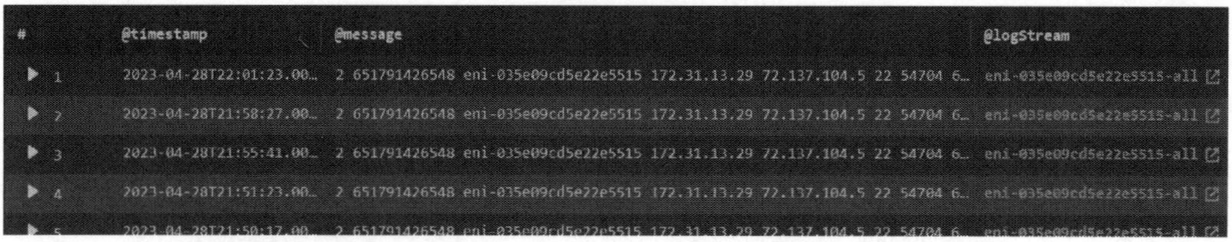

Figure 4.30 – Screenshot of the results from the preceding query

The preceding results provide a hyperlink to the log information for each row while presenting other critical data. Through the drop-down option against each row, the following additional information is presented for further investigation. In the next screenshot, we expand an example log event to highlight the fields captured by the VPC flow log:

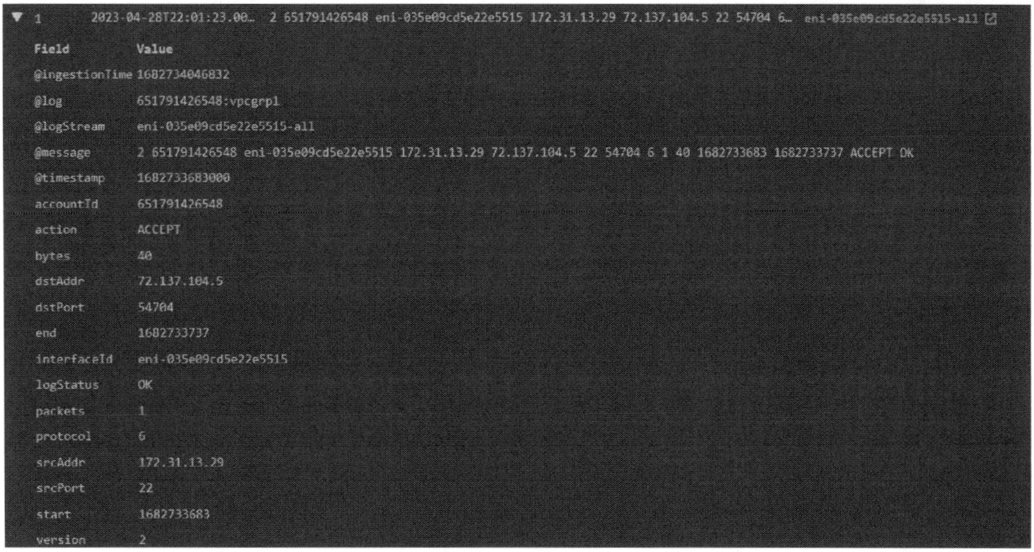

Figure 4.31 – Additional VPC flow log information

You can use pre-canned CloudWatch queries to add extra filters to further your investigation. Through the additional information reflected in the preceding screenshot, we can nail down to which EC2 instance the outbound network traffic originated by correlating the ENI ID to the EC2 instance. In summary, we started from 89,827 records to just 3 with the highest data exfiltration within the applicable time filter. As DFIR teams, you must slice and dice further on other IP addresses; this demonstrates how CloudWatch can contribute to an investigation.

DFIR use cases for CloudWatch

Through this chapter's sections, we now know why CloudWatch is vital from a DFIR perspective. Next are some use cases on how CloudWatch can be used for forensic investigation and anomaly detection:

- **Log review**: CloudWatch, as we all know, offers a centralized repository for logs, including CloudTrail logs. Therefore, it provides a SPOG where DFIR teams can query all logs quickly and yield investigative results. You can leverage CloudWatch to detect abnormal activity and unauthorized access and correlate events across various log sources ingested into CloudWatch.

- **Anomaly detection**: DFIR teams can define thresholds and alarms based on specific metrics (for example, CPU utilization, network traffic, or storage) to identify unusual patterns or deviations from normal behavior. Anomalous metrics can serve as early indicators of security breaches or compromised instances.

- **IR automation**: CloudWatch natively integrates with other workflow-based services, including AWS Lambda and AWS Systems Manager Automation, for automatic orchestration of isolation, snapshot creation, and user account changes upon a specific event alert. Workflows are based on triggers that allow automated remediation and containment actions.

- **Compliance and auditing**: Since CloudWatch offers centralized logging and monitoring capabilities, this also allows compliance monitoring and supporting audits. DFIR teams can leverage CloudWatch logs and metrics to demonstrate adherence to security policies, track user activity, and generate reports for compliance audits.

Amazon GuardDuty

GuardDuty is a threat detection service designed to help protect AWS resources and workloads by continuously monitoring for malicious activity and unauthorized behavior. Note that this is a detection service and not a response service. It detects and notifies the user of a potential threat within an AWS resource. However, integration with automated services such as Lambda will enhance GuardDuty's capabilities to respond to threats based on established playbooks for each threat detected. GuardDuty uses ML, anomaly detection, and integrated TI to identify potential security threats within your AWS environment.

Some DFIR use cases are as follows:

- **Threat detection**: GuardDuty analyzes CloudTrail logs, VPC flow logs, and DNS logs to detect **indicators of compromise (IOCs)** and potential threats. It applies ML algorithms to identify patterns and anomalies that might indicate malicious activities, such as unauthorized access attempts, reconnaissance, or instances exhibiting behavior associated with malware or botnets. These IOCs are collected through AWS's TI partners and third-party vendor tools offered to their clients. DFIR teams do not have control or the ability to manage these IOCs.

- **TI**: GuardDuty leverages TI feeds from AWS, partner organizations, and OSINT to enhance its threat detection capabilities. It compares network activity within your AWS environment against known malicious IPs, domains, and other indicators to identify potential security risks.

- **Centralized security monitoring**: GuardDuty provides a centralized view of security findings across your AWS accounts and regions. It aggregates and prioritizes security alerts, allowing security teams to focus on the most critical threats. The consolidated dashboard and event stream enable quick detection and response to potential security incidents.

- **Automated remediation**: GuardDuty integrates with other AWS services, such as AWS Lambda and AWS Systems Manager, to facilitate automated responses to security events. You can orchestrate customized actions or use pre-built response playbooks to automate remediation actions, such as isolating compromised instances, blocking malicious IPs, or updating security groups.

- **Security operations and IR**: GuardDuty is crucial in security operations and IR workflows. It provides real-time alerts and findings, enabling security teams to investigate and respond to potential security incidents quickly. Integrating with AWS services such as Amazon CloudWatch and AWS Lambda enables automated IR and security teams to take immediate action.

Permissions and trust

To leverage the capabilities of GuardDuty, DFIR teams must ensure that, at a minimum, the following permissions must be allowed:

- `ec2:DescribeInstances`: Describe EC2 instances
- `ec2:DescribeImages`: Describe EC2 instances' images
- `ec2:DescribeVpcEndpoints`: Identify the VPC endpoint name
- `ec2:DescribeSubnets`: Identify VPC subnet information
- `ec2:DescribeVpcPeeringConnections`: Identify and enumerate VPC peering information
- `ec2:DescribeTransitGatewayAttachments`: Identify VPC transit gateway, if any
- `organizations:ListAccounts`: List user accounts configured under the AWS account (organization)
- `organizations:DescribeAccount`: Describe the AWS account type (user/root)
- `s3:GetBucketPublicAccessBlock`: Check for an S3 public access block on the bucket
- `s3:GetEncryptionConfiguration`: Obtain S3 data encryption information
- `s3:GetBucketTagging`: Obtain S3 bucket tags
- `s3:GetAccountPublicAccessBlock`: Check for an S3 public access block on the AWS account
- `s3:ListAllMyBuckets`: Enumerate S3 buckets owned by an AWS account
- `s3:GetBucketAcl`: Enumerate S3 bucket ACLs
- `s3:GetBucketPolicy`: Enumerate S3 bucket policy
- `s3:GetBucketPolicyStatus`: Obtain current bucket policy status

Furthermore, the Amazon GuardDuty service requires it to assume a specific IAM role. The roles can have additional policies configured, which may be attached. Amazon GuardDuty typically requires the `sts:AssumeRole` role to delegate access. Allowing GuardDuty to assume this role enables the service to act on behalf of the role and perform authorized actions based on the permissions assigned.

Amazon GuardDuty malware scan

Enabling malware scans on EC2 instances and other resources is a great way to begin hunting for malware. GuardDuty provides a built-in service for altering or modifying an existing EC2 instance to natively scan the EC2 endpoints for evidence of compromise or malware. It examines data storage such as Amazon EBS volumes and other storage forms attached to a particular EC2 instance. It also provides the ability to obtain snapshots of relevant storage volumes should it detect evidence of malware.

Depending upon the AWS account and its operating regions, Amazon GuardDuty offers malware scanning capabilities through the following vendors: Bitdefender, CloudHesive, CrowdStrike, Fortinet, Palo Alto Networks, Rapid7, Sophos, Sysdig, Trellix. For DFIR teams, this means that they do not have to integrate or deploy software on affected AWS resources (such as EC2); instead, they enable GuardDuty on specific AWS accounts and activate malware scans, which offer these solutions automatically and allow scanning of EBS for the presence of malware.

> **Note**
>
> Amazon GuardDuty is specifically beneficial in cases where the installed antivirus configured within the EC2 instance may have been potentially disabled or tampered with by a threat actor. GuardDuty malware scans on EC2 instances allow insights into any malicious activities or malware downloaded by a threat actor for performing any nefarious actions without any additional security tooling deployments. This is beneficial as threat actors do not typically go after disabling GuardDuty.

GuardDuty also integrates with CloudWatch without specific configurations so that DFIR teams can query additional telemetry based on the malware scan. The following screenshot demonstrates an example of GuardDuty's integration with CloudWatch, specifically malware scan events:

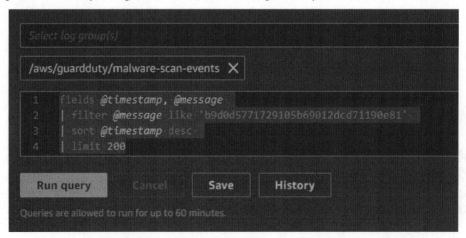

Figure 4.32 – Example of CloudWatch query for Amazon GuardDuty malware scan

Besides malware scans, GuardDuty offers insights into threats based on TI and detections of activities performed by various resources within the AWS account. Here is a sample set generated by GuardDuty to illustrate different detections. Note that each of the detections is rated by GuardDuty and is tagged as high, medium, or low-risk:

Finding type	Resource
[SAMPLE] Impact:Kubernetes/MaliciousIPCaller.Custom	EKSCluster: GeneratedFindingEKSClusterName
[SAMPLE] Discovery:RDS/TorIPCaller	RDSDBInstance: GeneratedFindingDBInstanceId
[SAMPLE] UnauthorizedAccess:Runtime/TorClient	EKSCluster: GeneratedFindingEKSClusterName
[SAMPLE] UnauthorizedAccess:EC2/MetadataDNSRebind	Instance: i-99999999
[SAMPLE] Recon:EC2/PortProbeEMRUnprotectedPort	Instance: i-99999999
[SAMPLE] UnauthorizedAccess:EC2/SSHBruteForce	Instance: i-99999999
[SAMPLE] Recon:IAMUser/TorIPCaller	GeneratedFindingUserName: GeneratedFindingAccessKeyId

Figure 4.33 – Sample threat detections within Amazon GuardDuty

Once a malware scan is initiated, GuardDuty generates a unique detector ID to identify each scan uniquely. We started a scan on one of the EC2 instances to determine if there was any evidence of malware. Next is the JSON output of the malware scan on one of the EC2 instances, demonstrating an example of an ongoing scan:

```
{
  "DetectorId": "26c440764b66ddeb7ff50f0881fc5e52",
  "AdminDetectorId": "26c440764b66ddeb7ff50f0881fc5e52",
  "ScanId": "b9d0d5771729105b69012dcd71190e81",
  "ScanStatus": "RUNNING",
  "ScanStartTime": "2023-06-03T11:53:24.000Z",
  "TriggerDetails": {},
  "ResourceDetails": {
    "InstanceArn": "arn:aws:ec2:ca-central-1:xxxxxxx6548:instance/i-
00229ce2dd123a2e6"
  },
  "ScanResultDetails": {},
  "AccountId": "xxxxxxxx6548",
  "AttachedVolumes": [
    {
      "VolumeArn": "arn:aws:ec2:ca-central-1:xxxxxxxx6548:volume/vol-
061392d9abebf9433",
      "VolumeType": "gp2",
      "DeviceName": "/dev/sda1",
```

```
        "VolumeSizeInGB": 30,
        "EncryptionType": "UNENCRYPTED"
    },
    {
        "VolumeArn": "arn:aws:ec2:ca-central-1:xxxxxxxx6548:volume/vol-
06c47b3cf15b2d6ae",
        "VolumeType": "gp3",
        "DeviceName": "xvdb",
        "VolumeSizeInGB": 30,
        "EncryptionType": "UNENCRYPTED"
    }
    ],
    "ScanType": "ON_DEMAND"
}
```

Once the scan is completed, GuardDuty generates a scan report accessible via the **Malware scans** page, accessing the unique GuardDuty malware scanning detection ID. The next screenshot demonstrates that Amazon GuardDuty identified potential malware on the disk (Amazon EBS storage):

Figure 4.34 – Amazon GuardDuty malware scan detections

This allows DFIR teams to confirm the presence of malware and hunt for threats further. Next are examples of the results of the detections. We see the scan has picked up eight threats on the disk, and here is a sample detection summary of one of the threats:

Threats detected (8)

1. Backdoor.Generic.671372

Name	Backdoor.Generic.671372
Severity	HIGH
Hash	021a24e99694ff7d91a6864e1b443c8e8df5c9a41...
File path	/Users/Administrator/Downloads/093640a69c8eafbc603...
File name	093640a69c8eafbc60343bf9cd1d3ad3
Volume ARN	arn:aws:ec2:ca-central-1:▮▮▮▮▮6548:volume/vol-061...

Figure 4.35 – Amazon GuardDuty malware scan detections

As you can see, the malware scan identifies the name of the sample detected, which is typically assigned by the vendor that scanned this binary. The SHA-256 hash of the file identified on the disk can be handy for DFIR teams for further threat hunting and detection. The file path and name identify the file's location and allow DFIR teams to manually collect artifacts and AWS volume information on where this file was identified. For AWS purposes, this is recognized as part of AWS resource naming conventions that determine the account owner and information on which volume this detection occurred (`arn:aws:ec2:ca-central-1:xxxxxxxx6548:volume/vol-061392d9abebf9433`).

DFIR teams can also identify the scanning partner that scanned this instance through the summary page. In our example, Bitdefender scanned this detection:

Figure 4.36 – Amazon GuardDuty scanner

Once Amazon GuardDuty completes the scans, it allows DFIR teams to also pivot into the Amazon Detective service:

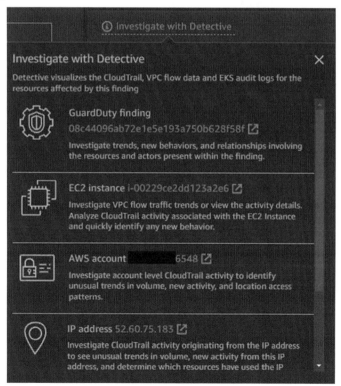

Figure 4.37 – Amazon Detective playbook on Amazon GuardDuty detections

Amazon Detective

Amazon Detective helps DFIR teams analyze, investigate, and visualize security data from various AWS services. It automatically collects and analyzes log data from AWS CloudTrail, Amazon VPC flow logs, and Amazon GuardDuty to provide insights into potential security vulnerabilities and suspicious activities within an AWS environment. Some of the capabilities of Amazon Detective are as follows:

- **Security graph**: Amazon Detective uses a graph-based approach to visualize and analyze security-related data by creating a graphical representation of AWS resources, accounts, and their relationships, allowing DFIR teams to identify patterns, anomalies, and potential security threats quickly.

- **Automated data ingestion**: Amazon Detective automatically collects and ingests data from AWS CloudTrail, Amazon VPC flow logs, and Amazon GuardDuty for aggregating and processing to provide insights and recommendations.

- **Threat hunting**: Amazon Detective enables DFIR teams with pre-built queries and analytics to proactively hunt for security threats and anomalies. These queries leverage ML algorithms and statistical models to identify suspicious activities and potential security issues.

- **Security findings**: Amazon Detective presents security findings based on its analysis of the collected data. These findings are prioritized and include details about accounts, resources, activities, and potential threats. It also includes supporting evidence and artifacts to allow further investigations.

> **Note**
> Note that to enable Amazon Detective, having Amazon GuardDuty is a pre-requisite.

Summary

To summarize, AWS offers integration of API logs and generic event logs and provides a SPOG to determine threat actor activity or an insider threat within an AWS account. With CloudWatch and CloudTrail, DFIR teams can natively investigate AWS using AWS's tools and identify activities an unauthorized user performs at a granular level. Furthermore, resources such as EC2 and S3 offer additional information concerning the configuration that allows DFIR teams to deduce and obtain further information for investigations. Remember that some security solutions, such as VPC flow logs, are not enabled by default and require the account owner or administrator to allow them explicitly. Integrating CloudTrail logs with CloudWatch and enabling Amazon GuardDuty offers DFIR teams a deep insight into threats within an AWS account and resources without explicitly going through deployments of security tools. Enabling GuardDuty and, subsequently, Amazon Detective allows telemetric information and the ability of the DFIR team to pinpoint the threat and perform additional threat hunting. Organizations and DFIR teams must be aware that enabling any security features is separately priced by AWS and will be reflected in your next bill.

In the following few chapters, we will similarly explore native capabilities for investigations on Microsoft Azure and Google Cloud, and we will eventually tie them together with other open source and commercial tools for extracting forensic artifacts from these cloud instances for purposes of offline investigation. Overall, the goal is to ensure DFIR teams have enough information at hand and from multiple sources of logs that validate threat actor activities and enable the teams to confirm unauthorized activities beyond a reasonable doubt using these tools.

Further reading

- *CIDR/VLSM Calculator*: https://www.subnet-calculator.com/cidr.php

- Port number assignments: https://www.iana.org/assignments/service-names-port-numbers/service-names-port-numbers.txt

- *CloudTrail concepts*: https://docs.aws.amazon.com/awscloudtrail/latest/userguide/cloudtrail-concepts.html#cloudtrail-concepts-data-events

- The cyber Swiss Army knife – a web app for encryption, encoding, compression, and data analysis: https://gchq.github.io/CyberChef/

- Amazon GuardDuty – malware protection for Amazon EBS volumes: https://aws.amazon.com/blogs/aws/new-for-amazon-guardduty-malware-detection-for-amazon-ebs-volumes/

- *Bitdefender and Amazon Web Services Strengthen Cloud Security*: https://businessinsights.bitdefender.com/bitdefender-and-amazon-web-services-strengthen-cloud-security

- Introduction to GuardDuty malware protection: https://www.cloudhesive.com/blog-posts/new-guardduty-malware-protection/

- *Prisma Cloud Supports Amazon GuardDuty Malware Protection*: https://www.paloaltonetworks.com/blog/prisma-cloud/amazon-guardduty-malware-protection/

- *Hunting malware with Amazon GuardDuty and Sysdig*: https://sysdig.com/blog/hunting-malware-with-amazon-guardduty-and-sysdig/

- *Trellix leverages Amazon GuardDuty Malware Protection for Extended Detection and Response (XDR)*: https://www.trellix.com/en-us/about/newsroom/stories/xdr/trellix-leverages-amazon-guardduty-malware-protection.html

- *Unauthorized IAM Credential Use Simulation and Detection*: https://catalog.workshops.aws/aws-cirt-unauthorized-iam-credential-use/en-US

- *Ransomware on S3 - Simulation and Detection*: https://catalog.workshops.aws/aws-cirt-ransomware-simulation-and-detection/en-US

- *Cryptominer Based Security Events - Simulation and Detection*: https://catalog.workshops.aws/aws-cirt-cryptominer-simulation-and-detection/en-US

- *SSRF on IMDSv1 - Simulation and Detection*: https://catalog.workshops.aws/aws-cirt-ssrf-imdsv1-simulation-and-detection/en-US

- *AWS CIRT Toolkit for Incident Response Preparedness*: https://catalog.workshops.aws/aws-cirt-toolkit-for-incident-response-preparedness/en-US

- *Logging IP traffic using VPC Flow Logs*: https://docs.aws.amazon.com/vpc/latest/userguide/flow-logs.html

- *What is VPC Flow Logs, and how can you publish flow logs to CloudWatch and S3?*: https://www.manageengine.com/log-management/amazon-vpc-publishing-flow-logs-to-cloudwatch-and-s3.html

- *Publish flow logs to CloudWatch Logs*: https://docs.aws.amazon.com/vpc/latest/userguide/flow-logs-cwl.html

- *Least-privilege Cloudwatch Logs policy for API Gateway*: https://repost.aws/questions/QUUWdk2GyPRKeTadZ9EpO3aQ/least-privilege-cloudwatch-logs-policy-for-api-gateway

- *AWS Security Incident Response Guide*: https://docs.aws.amazon.com/whitepapers/latest/aws-security-incident-response-guide/aws-security-incident-response-guide.html

- *Threat Hunting AWS CloudTrail with Sentinel: Part 1*: https://www.binarydefense.com/resources/blog/threat-hunting-aws-cloudtrail-with-sentinel-part-1/

- *Threat Hunting AWS CloudTrail with Sentinel: Part 2*: https://www.binarydefense.com/resources/blog/threat-hunting-aws-cloudtrail-with-sentinel-part-2/

- AWS security products: https://aws.amazon.com/products/security/

Part 2:
Forensic Readiness: Tools, Techniques, and Preparation for Cloud Forensics

In this part, we will investigate incidents in the cloud, specifically utilizing cloud-native tools to investigate threats and analyze artifacts. We will establish prerequisites for cloud investigations, identify a scenario, and investigate using cloud-native tools.

This part has the following chapters:

- *Chapter 4, DFIR Investigations – Logs in AWS*
- *Chapter 5, DFIR Investigations – Logs in Azure*
- *Chapter 6, DFIR Investigations – Logs in GCP*
- *Chapter 7, Cloud Productivity Suites*

5

DFIR Investigations – Logs in Azure

In the previous chapter, we discussed responding to incidents in **Amazon Web Services** (**AWS**). This chapter will focus on responding to incidents in Microsoft Azure, the second most popular cloud computing product. One critical aspect of incident response in Azure is analyzing log data from different Azure services. In this chapter, we will explore the various log sources available in Azure, how to acquire them, and best practices for analyzing this data to detect, contain, and resolve security incidents in Azure. By understanding the tools and techniques available for incident response in Azure, incident response professionals can better protect and respond to an organization's cloud infrastructure in the context of a security incident.

Following a similar pattern to AWS, understanding which logs within Azure are available by default versus what defenders and investigators may have to enable is critical to cloud forensics. This chapter outlines the various logs available for some of the important Azure services and products discussed in *Chapter 3*, and also looks at utilizing these sources in the context of an investigation. Specifically, we will discuss the following Azure data sources:

- Azure Log Analytics
- Azure Virtual Network
- Azure Storage
- Azure Virtual Machines
- Microsoft Sentinel

Azure Log Analytics

Azure Log Analytics is a cloud-based service offered by Azure that allows organizations to collect, analyze, and gain insights from their log and operational data. It provides a centralized platform for monitoring, troubleshooting, and detecting anomalies across various cloud and on-premises environments. With Azure Log Analytics, organizations can gain visibility into their systems and applications, enabling them to make informed decisions and take proactive action to maintain optimal performance and security.

Azure Log Analytics can be considered the equivalent of AWS CloudTrail (discussed in *Chapter 4*) when it comes to collecting and analyzing logs from various Azure services. By collecting logs from these services, organizations can gain insights into their performance, availability, and security. It provides a unified platform for monitoring and troubleshooting Azure resources.

Azure Log Analytics is of paramount importance as it serves as the backbone for logging within the Azure ecosystem, providing comprehensive insights into Virtual Network environments, storage services, and EC2 instances. For that reason, we'll briefly introduce the Azure Log Analytics role for the main Azure products and services here, then demonstrate how to integrate Log Analytics in the Azure product section of this chapter.

To effectively manage and optimize cloud operations, organizations rely on Azure Log Analytics for comprehensive insights across various Azure services:

- **Azure Virtual Networks**: Azure Log Analytics integrates with Azure Network Watcher, which provides insights into Virtual Network traffic, network security groups, and flow logs. By analyzing these logs, organizations can monitor network activity, detect suspicious behavior, and ensure compliance with security policies.

- **Azure Storage**: Azure Log Analytics can collect logs from Azure Storage services, such as Blob storage and Table storage. This enables organizations to monitor and analyze storage-related activities, such as read and write operations, access patterns, and storage capacity utilization.

- **Azure instances**: Azure Log Analytics agents can be installed on Azure VMs to collect log data from these instances. This includes logs related to operating system events, application logs, and custom log files.

The idea with Log Analytics is to have telemetry from all your Azure resources available to query and/or visualize. Incident responders can then query these logs for any indicators of compromise. The following screenshot shows an example of log queries in Azure Monitor. We will discuss Azure Monitor later in this chapter:

Figure 4.1 – Example of log queries

The query language in Azure is based on **Kusto Query Language** (**KQL**). KQL provides a syntax and set of operators that enable incident responders to retrieve, analyze, and visualize large volumes of data stored in Azure. Understanding KQL is critical for incident responders.

While Azure Log Analytics, with its KQL, offers robust capabilities to parse vast datasets and retrieve essential insights, it becomes even more pivotal when considering the network infrastructure it monitors. Azure Virtual Networks, a cornerstone of Microsoft's cloud environment, presents its own set of complexities. Understanding these networks and their interactions is paramount, and Log Analytics provides the tools to keep a keen eye on them.

Azure Virtual Networks

A virtual network is very similar to the traditional network that you would operate and stand up in your own organization's data center. Similar to how networking allows your organization's assets and resources to communicate with each other, Azure's Virtual Network service allows you to build a network for your Azure resources and services to communicate with each other, the public internet, or any of an organization's on-premise networks and resources.

Similar to AWS's VPC, when you create a virtual machine resource in Azure, you can create an Azure Virtual Network or use an existing one (if it has been created already). Your virtual network is just like any other entity managed by Azure (known as an Azure Resource), such as a virtual machine, data store, database, or any other service we had previously discussed in *Chapter 3*.

For demonstration purposes and the purpose of this section, we have a created virtual network in Azure called `CloudForensicsTestVM-vnet`. All virtual networks can be accessed directly from the **Virtual networks** service on Azure's **Home** page:

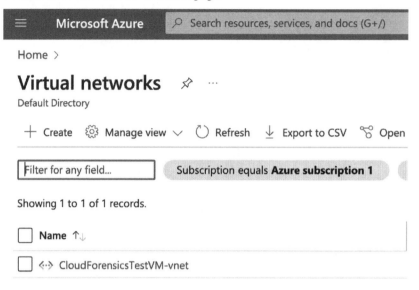

Figure 4.2 – Example of a virtual network

Depending on the size of an organization, there will likely be unused virtual networks that have been created for testing and development – incident responders should consider starting with investigating virtual networks containing production servers/services or critical jewels or investigating a virtual network based on whether any VMs contained have been reported compromised.

Investigators can expand into a virtual network and determine its network properties and configurations, as shown here:

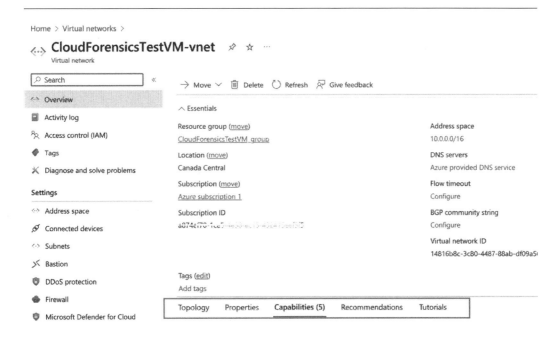

Figure 4.3 – Example of virtual network properties

All virtual networks within Azure contain five key tabs:

- **Topology**: This is your virtual network topology. Think of this as a network diagram that's auto-generated by Azure. This is especially useful for investigators to gain an understanding of an organization's cloud infrastructure without dependence on whether the IT team has maintained networking diagrams and documentation. The following screenshot shows an example network topology containing a network interface and a single VM instance – the outline surrounding the interface and VM represents the virtual network and default subnet:

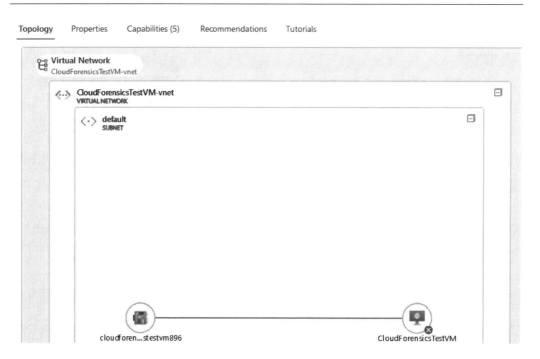

Figure 4.4 – Example of a virtual network topology

- **Properties**: This tab will include all networking configuration properties for your virtual network. This includes your IP address space, subnets, and Virtual Network ID. Investigators should take note of the address space and subnet IPs as understanding the network's IP address range and subnet allows responders to identify and trace the origin of suspicious activities or malicious traffic. Further, knowing your address space allows you to correlate with other log sources that may capture resource IPs (for example, EDR logs):

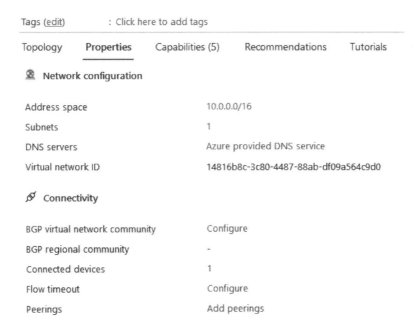

Figure 4.5 – Example of network properties

- **Capabilities**: This tab contains Azure products and services that may be utilized to further enhance the virtual network. For example, organizations may enable Azure's DDoS protection or Azure Firewall as opposed to configuring their own load balancer or firewall. These capabilities not only provide additional security protection for Azure resources and assets but also act as additional log sources in an incident. For example, enabling Microsoft Defender for Cloud will provide threat protection for your VMs, containers, databases, storage app services, and more. Cloud Defender will generate additional security alerts/logs for any malicious activity detected in your Azure resource. We will dive deeper into Microsoft Defender for Cloud later in this chapter:

Figure 4.6 – Example of virtual network capabilities

- **Recommendations**: The **Recommendations** tab provides a list of Azure recommendations based on cost, security, reliability, performance, and operational excellence. Threat management teams can utilize the **Recommendations** tab to enable any security posture and reliability quick wins based on personalized best practices defined by Microsoft's automated advisor engine. Further, incident responders could utilize this tab for any recommendations to determine any gaps that may exist at the time of the incident and provide this in their recommendations report for threat management teams to action:

Figure 4.7 – Example of Microsoft's virtual network recommendations

- **Tutorials**: This tab provides a list of free training from Microsoft. Microsoft, Amazon, and Google all continuously update features and products within their cloud offering. As a result, incident responders can utilize this tab to gain a quick understanding of any newly added features.

One essential tool that complements these properties and ensures the robustness of the network's security posture is Azure's **Network Security Group** (**NSG**) flow logs. These logs provide granular visibility into network traffic, bridging the gap between network configuration and actual network activity.

NSG flow logs

In Azure, an NSG and a virtual network are two different concepts that play distinct roles in network security and network infrastructure management. An NSG is a fundamental component of Azure's network security architecture. It acts as a virtual firewall for controlling inbound and outbound traffic to VMs, subnets, or network interfaces within an Azure virtual network. NSGs allow you to define inbound and outbound security rules to filter network traffic based on protocols, ports, source IP addresses, and destination IP addresses. They provide a fine-grained level of network security control by allowing or denying traffic based on rule configurations.

An Azure virtual network is a foundational construct in Azure networking that represents an isolated network environment in the Azure cloud. As we have seen previously in this chapter, Azure Virtual Network allows organizations to define IP address ranges, subnets, and network topology to build their network infrastructure.

Defining **access control lists** (**ACLs**) for an NSG in Azure involves configuring rules that control inbound and outbound network traffic for associated resources within a virtual network. ACLs act as virtual firewalls and provide granular control over network communication. Through NSG rules, you can specify allowed or denied traffic based on source/destination IP addresses, ports, and protocols.

These rules help enforce security policies and restrict unauthorized access to VMs or subnets, allowing administrators to define and manage network traffic flow effectively. An example of an NSG is shown in the following screenshot:

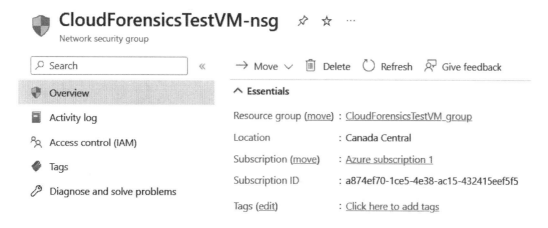

Figure 4.8 – Example of an NSG

Defining ACLs in Azure and AWS have similarities in terms of their purpose and functionality. Both platforms allow users to create rules that control inbound and outbound network traffic based on source/destination IP addresses, ports, and protocols. An example of ACL rules for Azure NSGs is shown in the following screenshot. In this instance, the network only allows incoming (inbound) connections to port 22 (SSH) from a public source IP that has been redacted for security reasons:

Priority ↑↓	Name ↑↓	Port ↑↓	Protocol ↑↓	Source ↑↓	Destination ↑↓	Action ↑↓
⌄ Inbound Security Rules						
100	AllowMyIpAddressSS...	22	TCP	▬▬▬▬▬	Any	✓ Allow
65000	AllowVnetInBound	Any	Any	VirtualNetwork	VirtualNetwork	✓ Allow
65001	AllowAzureLoadBalan···	Any	Any	AzureLoadBalancer	Any	✓ Allow
65500	DenyAllInBound	Any	Any	Any	Any	✗ Deny
⌄ Outbound Security Rules						
65000	AllowVnetOutBound	Any	Any	VirtualNetwork	VirtualNetwork	✓ Allow
65001	AllowInternetOutBound	Any	Any	Any	Internet	✓ Allow
65500	DenyAllOutBound	Any	Any	Any	Any	✗ Deny

Figure 4.9 – ACLs

Incident responders can analyze ACLs to identify any unauthorized inbound connection rules (for example, RDP port open, allowing incoming connections from any IP address) or create new ACL rules to block any network-based indicators of compromise (for example, command and control IPs).

As discussed in *Chapter 4*, a (network) flow log is a record of network traffic flow information, capturing details such as source and destination IP addresses, ports, protocols, and other relevant metadata related to network traffic. In the context of Azure, NSG flow logs specifically refer to the flow logs generated by NSGs in Azure. NSG flow logs provide visibility into the network traffic flowing through NSGs within a virtual network.

By enabling NSG flow logs, organizations gain insights into network communication patterns, allowing them to monitor and analyze traffic behavior, detect anomalies, troubleshoot connectivity issues, and enhance network security analysis. These logs can be leveraged for forensic analysis, providing a valuable resource for understanding the full extent of a security breach and securing Azure network environments.

Similar to AWS's VPC flow logs, NSG flow logs are not enabled by default in Azure. As a result, they require explicit setup. To enable NSG flow logging, you must create an NSG flow log resource in Azure. Next, Azure gives you the option to download NSG logs locally, forward them to another tool (for example, a **security information and event management** (**SIEM**) system), or use Microsoft's Azure Network Watcher Traffic Analytics solution. Traffic Analytics analyzes your Azure NSG flow logs within Azure, allowing organizations to visualize and query network activity and identify threats and areas of concern (open ports, unusual network traffic, and so on). The following three sequential steps are required to enable and view NSG flow logs:

1. **Create an Azure storage account**: To enable and create NSG flow logging, you must create and allocate storage to hold these logs in Azure. This can be done while you're creating the flow log in Azure. Refer to the following screenshot to gain a visual understanding of an example storage account being set up in Azure, particularly during the NSG flow log creation process:

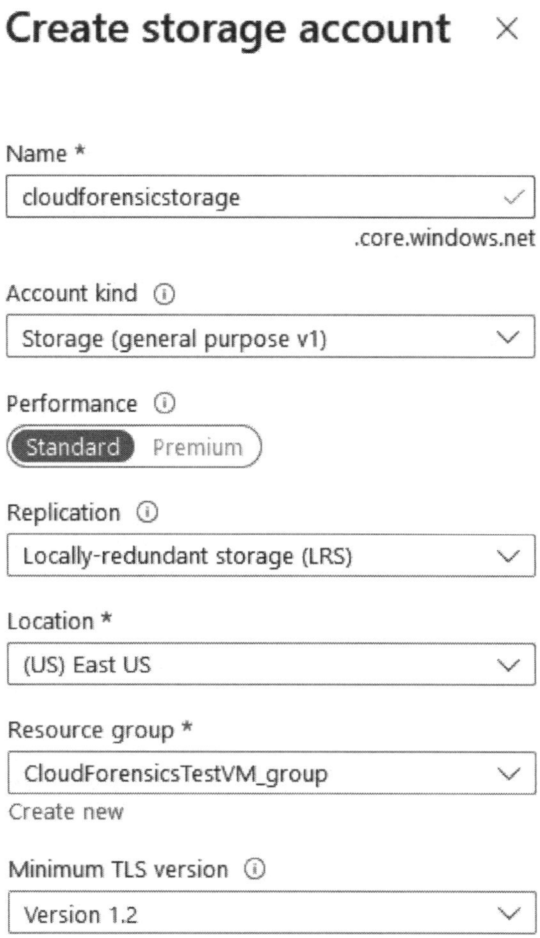

Create storage account ×

Name *

cloudforensicstorage   ✓

.core.windows.net

Account kind ⓘ

Storage (general purpose v1)   ∨

Performance ⓘ

(Standard) Premium

Replication ⓘ

Locally-redundant storage (LRS)   ∨

Location *

(US) East US   ∨

Resource group *

CloudForensicsTestVM_group   ∨

Create new

Minimum TLS version ⓘ

Version 1.2   ∨

Figure 4.10 – Creating a storage account

The following screenshot demonstrates the creation of a flow log in Azure:

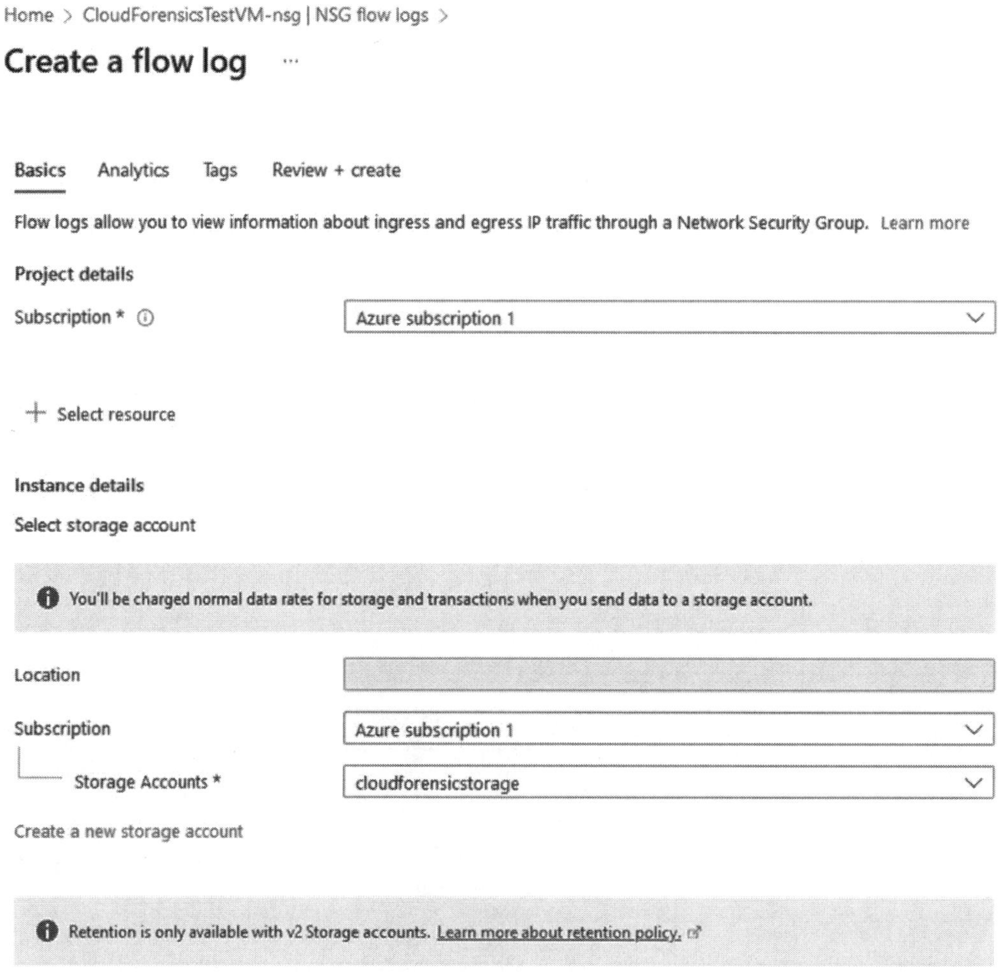

Home > CloudForensicsTestVM-nsg | NSG flow logs >

Create a flow log   ...

Basics   Analytics   Tags   Review + create

Flow logs allow you to view information about ingress and egress IP traffic through a Network Security Group. Learn more

Project details

Subscription * ⓘ | Azure subscription 1   ⌄ |

╋ Select resource

Instance details

Select storage account

> ⓘ You'll be charged normal data rates for storage and transactions when you send data to a storage account.

Location | |

Subscription | Azure subscription 1   ⌄ |

└── Storage Accounts * | cloudforensicsstorage   ⌄ |

Create a new storage account

> ⓘ Retention is only available with v2 Storage accounts. Learn more about retention policy. ↗

Figure 4.11 – Creating a flow log

2. **Create an NSG flow log**: This includes populating resources as well as other properties related to flow logging. You can export, process, analyze, and visualize NSG flow logs by using tools such as Microsoft's Traffic Analytics, Splunk, Grafana, or any other SIEM tool. In this example, we will enable Microsoft's Traffic Analytics as it is already integrated into Microsoft and allows quick and easy ingestion of the logs. The following screenshot demonstrates how to enable Traffic Analytics and send your network traffic to an Azure Log Analytics workspace:

Home > CloudForensicsTestVM-nsg | NSG flow logs >

Create a flow log ...

Basics   **Analytics**   Tags   Review + create

Version 1 logs ingress and egress IP traffic flows for both allowed and denied traffic. Version 2 provides additional throughput information (bytes and packets) per flow. Learn more. ⤢

Flow Logs Version   ◯ Version 1
                                    ⦿ Version 2

Traffic Analytics

Traffic Analytics provides rich analytics and visualization derived from flow logs and other Azure resources' data. Drill through geo-map, easily figure out traffic hotspots and get insights into optimization possibilities. Learn about all features ⤢

☑ Enable Traffic Analytics

Traffic Analytics processing interval ⓘ	Every 10 mins ⌄
Subscription	Azure subscription 1 ⌄
└── Log Analytics Workspace * ⓘ	DefaultWorkspace-a874ef70-1ce5-4e38-ac15-432415eef5f5-CCA ⌄

Figure 4.12 – Creating a flow log and enabling Traffic Analytics

3. Navigate to the Traffic Analytics workspace you created in *step 2* to view and query the NSG flow log that was created in *steps 1* and *2*.

Microsoft provides the following pre-built query to query NSG flow logs:

```
AzureNetworkAnalytics_CL
| where SubType_s == "FlowLog"
| extend FlowDirection = iff(FlowDirection_s == 'O', 'Outbound',
'Inbound')
| extend AllowedOrDenied = iff(FlowStatus_s == 'A', 'Allowed',
'Denied')
| extend SourceIP = iff(isempty(SrcIP_s), extract_all(@"(\
d{1,3}\.\d{1,3}\.\d{1,3}\.\d{1,3})", SrcPublicIPs_s), SrcIP_s)
| extend DestinationIP = iff(isempty(DestIP_s), extract_all(@"(\
d{1,3}\.\d{1,3}\.\d{1,3}\.\d{1,3})", DestPublicIPs_s), DestIP_s)
| extend Protocol = case(L4Protocol_s == 'T', "TCP",
L4Protocol_s == 'U', "UDP", L4Protocol_s)
| project-rename NSGFL_Version = FASchemaVersion_s
| project TimeGenerated, FlowDirection, AllowedOrDenied,
SourceIP, DestinationIP, DestPort_d, Protocol, L7Protocol_s,
NSGList_s, NSGRule_s, NSGFL_Version
| limit 100
```

Here is a breakdown of the KQL query:

- Table selection: `AzureNetworkAnalytics_CL` specifies the data table from which the query fetches the data – in this case, the Azure Network Analytics logs

- Filtering: `| where SubType_s == "FlowLog"` filters the data so that it only includes where the `SubType` column has a value of `FlowLog`

- Data transformation with `extend`: The `extend` command is used multiple times to add new columns to the data:

    - `FlowDirection = iff(FlowDirection_s == 'O', 'Outbound', 'Inbound')`: This adds a new column, `FlowDirection`, that classifies the flow direction as `'Outbound'` or `'Inbound'` based on the value in `FlowDirection_s`

    - `AllowedOrDenied = iff(FlowStatus_s == 'A', 'Allowed', 'Denied')`: This determines whether the flow was allowed or denied

    - `SourceIP` and `DestinationIP`: These lines handle IP address extraction and formatting

    - `Protocol = case(...)`: This sets the protocol as TCP or UDP or retains the original value based on the condition

- Renaming a column: `| project-rename NSGFL_Version = FASchemaVersion_s` renames the `FASchemaVersion_s` column to `NSGFL_Version`

- Selecting specific columns: The `project` command is used to select specific columns to be included in the final output

- Limiting results: `| limit 100` limits the output to the first 100 records

In general, a KQL query will have the following general structure:

- **Table selection**: Queries start by specifying a data table (for example, network events)

- **Pipes** (`|`): This is used to chain different commands, where the output of one command is passed as input to the next

- **Filtering (where)**: This is used to include only those records that meet certain criteria

- **Data transformation (extend)**: This adds new columns or modifies existing ones

- **Aggregation and grouping**: Functions such as `sum`, `count`, `avg`, and `group by` are used for data aggregation

- **Projection (project)**: This specifies which columns to include in the final output

- **Sorting and limiting**: Commands such as `sort by` and `limit` control the order and the number of records in the output

The query results are shown in the following screenshot. As you can see, all allowed and denied inbound/ outbound traffic is captured and displayed in tabular format. In this case, the entry containing an allowed inbound connection is our SSH connection into the VM resource (**SourceIP** has been redacted for privacy reasons) and signifies a potential point of entry and unauthorized access into the VM:

	TimeGenerated [UTC]	FlowDirection	AllowedOrDenied ↑↓	SourceIP	DestinationIP
>	5/11/2023, 7:35:02.012 PM	Outbound	Allowed	10.0.0.4	["13.71.172.130","13.71.172.132","20.38.146.156","20
>	5/11/2023, 7:35:02.012 PM	Outbound	Allowed	10.0.0.4	["20.42.65.84","20.42.65.85","20.42.65.88","20.48.201
>	5/11/2023, 7:35:02.012 PM	Outbound	Allowed	10.0.0.4	["40.112.243.50"]
>	5/11/2023, 7:45:25.579 PM	Inbound	Allowed	▬▬▬▬▬	10.0.0.4
>	5/11/2023, 7:45:25.579 PM	Outbound	Allowed	10.0.0.4	["20.88.109.28","20.189.173.3","20.189.173.10","20.18
>	5/11/2023, 7:45:25.579 PM	Outbound	Allowed	10.0.0.4	["13.71.172.130","20.38.146.158","52.246.155.145"]
>	5/11/2023, 7:45:25.579 PM	Outbound	Allowed	10.0.0.4	["185.125.190.18"]
>	5/11/2023, 7:25:29.259 PM	Outbound	Allowed	10.0.0.4	["13.90.21.104","20.42.65.90","20.42.73.27","20.48.20
>	5/11/2023, 7:25:29.259 PM	Outbound	Allowed	10.0.0.4	["13.71.172.130","20.38.146.158","52.246.155.145"]
>	5/11/2023, 7:25:29.259 PM	Outbound	Allowed	10.0.0.4	["185.125.190.24"]
>	5/11/2023, 7:25:29.259 PM	Outbound	Allowed	10.0.0.4	["20.81.7.118"]
>	5/11/2023, 7:25:29.259 PM	Outbound	Allowed	10.0.0.4	["20.39.140.162"]
>	5/11/2023, 7:35:00.342 PM	Inbound	Denied	103.239.221.142	10.0.0.4
>	5/11/2023, 7:35:00.342 PM	Inbound	Denied	185.35.184.34	10.0.0.4
>	5/11/2023, 7:35:02.012 PM	Inbound	Denied	["1.202.117.76"]	10.0.0.4

Figure 4.13 – Flow log query results

Digital forensic and incident response use cases do not significantly change when transitioning from AWS flow logs to Azure flow logs due to their underlying purpose of capturing network traffic data. While there might be differences in the log format, user interface, and naming convention, both solutions offer valuable insights into network activity, facilitating investigations, threat detection, and incident response, regardless of the cloud provider.

Within the realm of Azure Virtual Network, we've delved into creating a flow log and its subsequent querying, shedding light on the dynamic interplay of network data. Our next focus will be Azure Storage – a vital piece of the Azure ecosystem that not only stores such logs but offers extensive capabilities for managing and accessing vast volumes of data seamlessly.

Azure Storage

Azure Storage is a cloud-based storage service provided by Azure. Azure Storage provides different storage options, one of which is Azure Blob storage.

Azure Blobs, or Azure Binary Large Objects, are specific storage types within Azure Storage that are designed for storing unstructured data such as documents, images, videos, and other file types. It offers a simple and cost-effective way to store large amounts of data and provides features such as high availability, durability, and scalability. Azure Blobs are commonly used for backup and restore, content distribution, media streaming, and as a data source for applications running in the cloud.

Within an Azure storage account, incident responders may want to start by reviewing the level of access for a given storage account (and by extension, the data it holds). This can be accomplished by navigating to the storage account's **Access Control (IAM)** page and checking all users with access to the data:

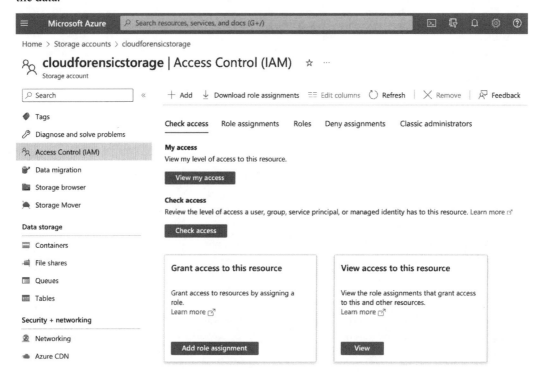

Figure 4.14 – The Access Control (IAM) pane

Next, investigators can utilize the **Activity log** page in the storage account – this can be found in the left pane. **Activity log** will show Azure tenant-wide activity at a subscription/Azure tenant level (for example, we can determine when a storage account was created in Azure and by whom). Turning to the following screenshot, we are presented with illustrative examples of an activity log:

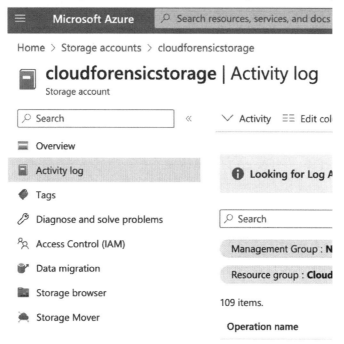

Figure 4.15 – Activity log

While the preceding screenshot provides an initial overview of the storage activity log, capturing its inherent structure and key data points, the following screenshot delves deeper, showcasing the results of a specific query, offering you insights into the type of information that can be extracted and analyzed from such logs:

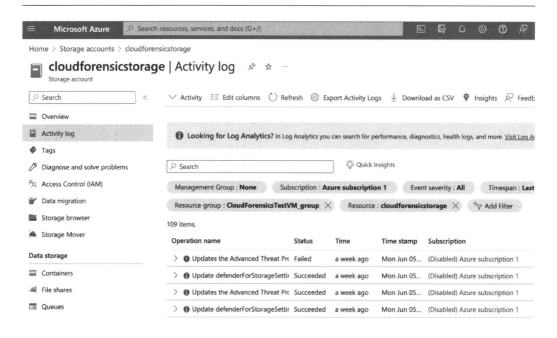

Figure 4.16 – Activity log (continued...)

Investigators can export the log in the log format of their choice (for example, JSON, CSV, and so on) and analyze for any unusual activity – for example, which accounts modified your Azure resources (including storage resources) and what actions took place. The activity log contains all activity and therefore captures any new features or capabilities that have been turned on and/or updated.

Azure Monitor

Azure Monitor is a comprehensive monitoring solution offered by Azure that allows organizations to collect, analyze, and act on telemetry data from various Azure resources, including Azure Storage and Azure Blobs. It provides insights into the performance, availability, and health of these resources, helping organizations gain visibility and make informed decisions.

Incident responders can utilize the data produced from Azure Monitor for forensic investigation. For example, in the context of Azure Storage, incident responders can use Azure Monitor to chart egress (outgoing) data from an Azure storage account or blob. Incident responders can then use the egress data visualization to narrow down any spikes of egress data – that is, at which point in time there was an unusual amount of data leaving the organization's cloud storage. This is particularly useful for security incidents involving data exfiltration as it allows incident responders to not only narrow down on dates/times of interest but also gain an understanding of the quantity of data that may have been stolen by bad actors. The following screenshot demonstrates an example of Azure Monitor being used to visualize and chart egress data over 30 days:

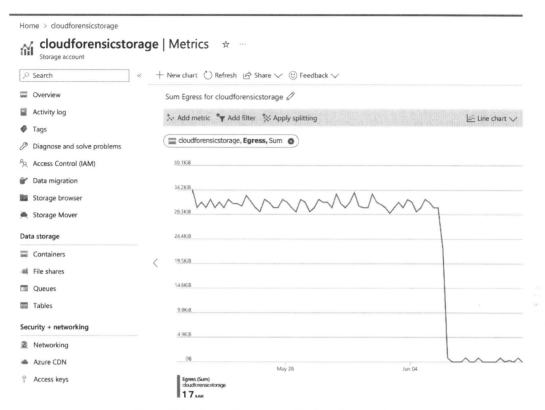

Figure 4.17 – Azure Monitor visualization of egress data

Similar to the virtual network logs we discussed previously, an organization's resource logs (including a storage account and Storage Blob), must also be connected to an Azure Log Analytics workspace to enable the features of the Azure Monitor log, as well as run queries against this data. We had previously connected VPC logs to a Traffic Analytics workspace, which meant sending the VPC network data to a Log Analytics workspace in the backend to read and write traffic logs to. The following is a screenshot from Microsoft's Azure portal on how to get set up with enabling Log Analytics for all your Storage-related resources:

Get started with Log Analytics

Log Analytics collects data from a variety of sources and uses a powerful query language to give you insights into the operation of your applications and resources. Use Azure Monitor to access the complete set of tools for monitoring all of your Azure resources.

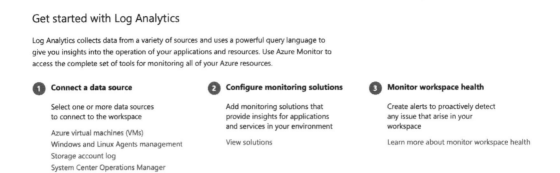

1 Connect a data source

Select one or more data sources to connect to the workspace

Azure virtual machines (VMs)
Windows and Linux Agents management
Storage account log
System Center Operations Manager

2 Configure monitoring solutions

Add monitoring solutions that provide insights for applications and services in your environment

View solutions

3 Monitor workspace health

Create alerts to proactively detect any issue that arise in your workspace

Learn more about monitor workspace health

Figure 4.18 – Getting started with Log Analytics

The following screenshot shows how to connect an Azure storage account (and its resources) to a Log Analytics workspace. From the left pane, navigate to **Diagnostic settings** to enable logs being sent to Log Analytics:

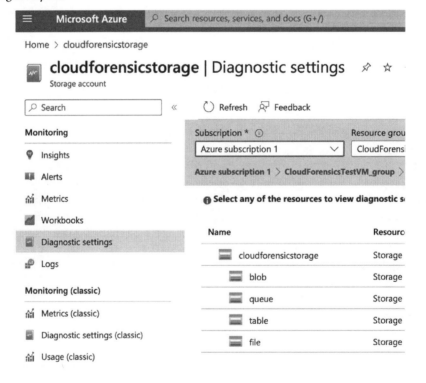

Figure 4.19 – Connecting Log Analytics to storage resources

Next, you should see all associated resources under your storage accounts. To enable Log Analytics, click on the storage account or any other resource:

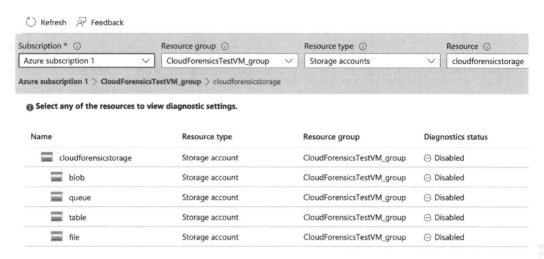

Figure 4.20 – Connecting Log Analytics to storage resources (continued…)

Transitioning to the following screenshot, we're zooming into the nuanced procedure of connecting log analytics, this time specifically focusing on the diagnostic settings of a particular storage account:

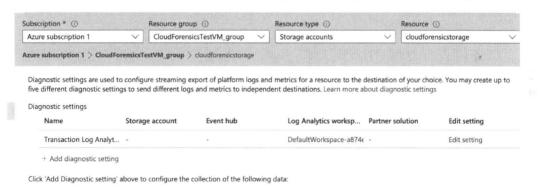

Figure 4.21 – Connecting Log Analytics to storage resources (continued…)

Finally, the following screenshot provides a detailed look into these diagnostic settings, highlighting the intricacies and parameters that users can leverage and configure:

Figure 4.22 – Connecting Log Analytics to storage resources (continued…)

A similar process can be applied to the Azure Blob level, sending all read/write/delete and transaction logs to the Log Analytics workspace:

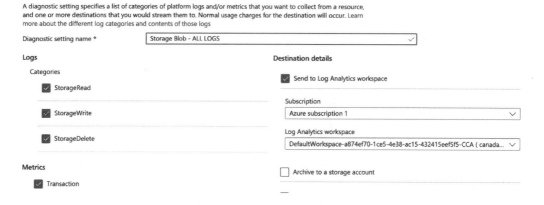

Figure 4.23 – Connecting Log Analytics to storage resources (continued…)

The final **Diagnostics settings** pane should look as follows, with **Diagnostics status** set to **Enabled**:

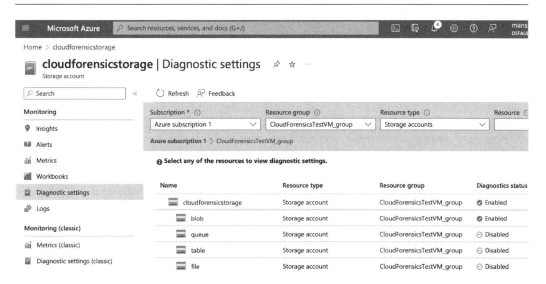

Figure 4.24 – Connecting Log Analytics to storage resources (continued…)

Incident responders can now query Azure Storage logs using the **Logs** functionality under **Monitoring**, which opens the query panel in Azure. See the following sample query to get all operations on Blobs within an Azure storage account:

```
StorageBlobLogs
| where TimeGenerated > ago(7d)
| project TimeGenerated, OperationName, AuthenticationType, Uri, _
ResourceId, CallerIpAddress
```

The preceding query can be utilized to display additional columns/fields from the storage accounts' tables (that is, `AzureMetrics` and `StorageBlobLogs`) as well as narrow down on events of interest (that is, anonymous logins, operations of interest, and so on). The following screenshot demonstrates the query results of all a storage account's blob activity:

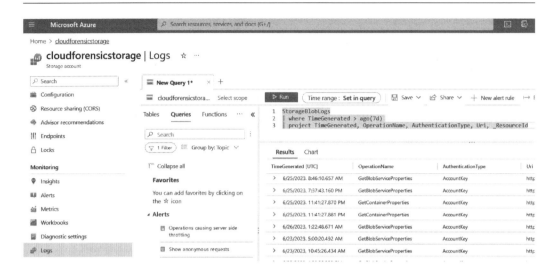

Figure 4.25 – Query results of blob storage activity

Now that we understand the nuances of Azure Storage and the intricacies of querying Blob Storage Activity, it's clear that Azure's capacity for data management and analytics is vast. Moving forward, we'll delve into another integral component of Azure's infrastructure: Azure Virtual Machines. This not only complements the storage solutions but also empowers them by providing dynamic compute resources for diverse workloads.

Azure Virtual Machines log analysis

We discussed Azure Virtual Machines in *Chapter 3*. In Azure, VMs are widely used to deploy and run various applications and services. To ensure the security and stability of these VMs, incident responders and administrators must analyze the logs generated by the VMs. These logs provide valuable insights into the system's activities, performance, security incidents, and potential vulnerabilities. In this section, we will explore the different log sources within Azure that incident responders can analyze for effective VM log analysis.

- **Azure Log Analytics**: Azure Log Analytics is a powerful tool that centralizes log data from various sources, including Azure VMs. It provides a comprehensive log management solution and offers advanced querying and visualization capabilities. By integrating Azure VMs with Log Analytics, incident responders can collect and analyze logs from multiple VMs in a unified manner. The logs that are collected can include performance data, system events, security events, and custom application logs. Incident responders can utilize Log Analytics by leveraging its powerful querying capabilities using KQL. By constructing KQL queries targeted toward your VMs, incident responders can search through logs and telemetry data collected by Azure Monitor to identify potential **indicators of compromise (IoCs)** such as suspicious IP addresses, unusual network traffic patterns, or specific event logs associated with known threats.

These queries can be tailored to filter and correlate relevant data sources, enabling proactive threat hunting and rapid identification of compromised systems or malicious activities within an Azure environment.

- **Windows Event Logs**: Azure VMs running on Windows operating systems generate Windows Event Logs, which capture important system events and errors. Incident responders can analyze these logs to identify system crashes, application failures, login attempts, and other critical events. Windows Event Logs are categorized into different event log channels, such as System, Security, Application, and more, making it easier to filter and analyze specific types of events.

- **Azure Activity Logs**: Azure Activity Logs provides an audit trail of operations performed on Azure resources, including VMs. These logs capture information about resource creation, updates, and deletions, as well as administrative actions taken by users and Azure services. Incident responders can leverage Azure Activity Logs to track changes made to VM configurations, identify potential misconfigurations, and investigate suspicious activities.

- **Azure Monitor**: Azure Monitor can also be utilized to capture VM performance metrics, diagnostic logs, and even custom application logs. Incident responders can utilize Azure Monitor to visualize anomalies in the VM, such as unusual CPU usage or disk bandwidth, which may suggest unauthorized access. Azure Monitor also integrates with **Azure Kubernetes Service** (**AKS**) to provide monitoring and logging capabilities for any AKS containers. You can enable monitoring when you create an AKS cluster or add it to an existing cluster. Additionally, Azure Monitor extends its capabilities to serverless computing resources in Azure, such as Azure Functions and Azure Logic Apps. By leveraging Application Insights, a feature of Azure Monitor, incident responders can gain in-depth insights into serverless components.

- **Windows Defender Logs**: For VMs running Windows Defender, incident responders can analyze the logs generated by the antivirus software. These logs contain information about detected threats, blocked malware, and other security-related events. By analyzing Windows Defender logs, responders can identify potential security breaches, investigate malware infections, and take appropriate actions to mitigate risks. Windows Defender is the endpoint security antivirus tool at the endpoint level (that is, installed on your VMs).

- **Azure Linux VMs and Linux Logs**: For Linux-based VMs in Microsoft Azure, incident responders can analyze logs generated by the system's syslog service and Microsoft security tools. Incident responders can utilize Azure's integration with Linux VMs, which provides system events through syslog, such as system alerts, errors, user login activities, and other system-level messages. These logs are instrumental in tracing system anomalies, security incidents, and potential unauthorized access. In addition to the basic syslog capabilities, Azure offers integration with its suite of security tools, such as Microsoft Defender, which can be used to enhance the security monitoring of Linux VMs. Microsoft Defender provides advanced threat protection features, detecting and analyzing potential threats and vulnerabilities for Linux resources.

Having explored the diverse range of log sources available on Azure Virtual Machines, from Azure Log Analytics to Windows Defender Logs, it's evident that Azure provides comprehensive tools for incident responders to track and analyze VM activities. With this foundation in place, we can now shift our focus to an even more integrated security solution within the Azure ecosystem: Microsoft Defender for Cloud. This solution synergistically utilizes these logs to offer holistic security insights and proactive threat protection.

Microsoft Defender for Cloud

Previously called Azure Security Center, Microsoft Defender for Cloud provides advanced threat detection and security monitoring for Azure resources, including VMs. It analyzes security-related events, performs behavioral analysis, and provides security recommendations. Incident responders can leverage Microsoft Defender for Cloud to identify potential security vulnerabilities, investigate security incidents, and respond to threats effectively. The following screenshot demonstrates an example of security alerts being reported by Microsoft Defender for Cloud. In this example, we can observe that Mimikatz's credential theft tool was detected on a VM resource. Incident responders can utilize these alerts in the larger context of their investigation to determine attack tactics utilized by bad actors:

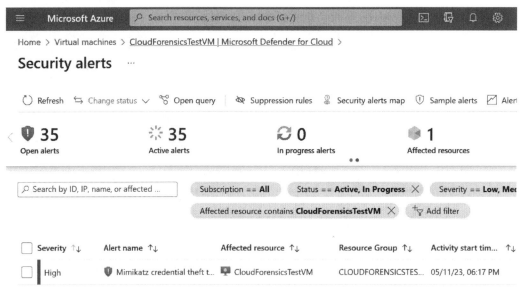

Figure 4.26 – Microsoft Defender for Cloud alerts

Microsoft Defender for Cloud also provides configuration recommendations based on continuous monitoring, which can help incident responders identify any outstanding security vulnerabilities. The following screenshot shows an example of the **Recommendations** pane in Microsoft Defender for Cloud:

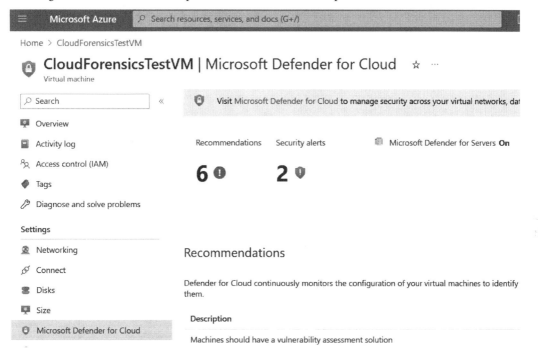

Figure 4.27 – Microsoft Defender for Cloud – Recommendations

While Microsoft Defender for Cloud offers comprehensive monitoring and security recommendations, Azure also provides tools for in-depth network traffic analysis for your VMs. One of the most valuable tools for this purpose is NSG flow logs. This feature gives administrators granular insights into network activities, complementing the protections provided by Microsoft Defender for Cloud.

NSG flow logs

NSG flow logs capture information about network traffic flowing through NSGs associated with Azure VMs. These logs provide insights into allowed and denied network connections, including source and destination IP addresses, ports, and protocols. Incident responders can analyze NSG flow logs to detect suspicious network activities, identify potential attacks, and enforce network security policies effectively. We discussed NSG flow logs earlier in this chapter.

> **Important note**
>
> Products and services such as Virtual Network, Storage, and Virtual Machines in Azure share common monitoring and logging capabilities through services such as Azure Log Analytics, Azure Monitor, and Azure Activity. These services provide comprehensive insights into the health, performance, and activity of the resources deployed in Azure.
>
> Regardless of whether you are monitoring a virtual network, storage, or VMs, the fundamental approach remains similar. Azure Log Analytics allows you to collect, centralize, and analyze logs and metrics from various sources. Azure Monitor provides a unified monitoring experience, offering alerts, dashboards, and visualizations to gain real-time insights into resource performance and availability. Azure Activity Logs captures subscription-level events and actions for auditing and tracking purposes.

After delving into the intricacies of logging information of Azure Virtual Machines, specifically the capabilities of Microsoft Defender for Cloud and NSG flow logs, it's clear that Azure offers robust tools for security and traffic analysis. However, Azure's suite doesn't stop there. Transitioning to our next section, we'll explore the comprehensive threat intelligence capabilities of Microsoft Sentinel.

Microsoft Sentinel

Microsoft Sentinel is a powerful cloud-native SIEM solution offered by Azure. It enables organizations to detect, investigate, and respond to security threats by collecting, analyzing, and visualizing vast amounts of security data from various sources in real time.

A SIEM is a comprehensive software solution that combines **security information management (SIM)** and **security event management (SEM)** capabilities. It serves as a central hub for ingesting and correlating logs and events from diverse sources, providing a unified view of an organization's security landscape.

During a security incident, incident responders can leverage Microsoft Sentinel's advanced features to effectively respond and mitigate threats. Here are specific ways incident responders can utilize Microsoft Sentinel:

- **Log collection and integration**: Microsoft Sentinel supports the ingestion of data from a wide range of sources, including Azure services, on-premises infrastructure, security solutions, and third-party tools. Incident responders can configure data connectors to collect logs and events, ensuring comprehensive visibility across the entire environment.

- **Threat detection and analytics**: Microsoft Sentinel employs machine learning algorithms and advanced analytics to detect and prioritize potential security threats. Its built-in analytics templates and detection rules help identify suspicious activities, anomalous behavior, or known attack patterns. Incident responders can leverage these capabilities to identify IoCs and detect emerging threats.

- **Real-time monitoring and alerting**: Microsoft Sentinel provides real-time monitoring of security events and generates alerts based on predefined rules and analytics. Incident responders can configure alert rules to trigger notifications when specific conditions or behaviors indicative of a security incident occur. These alerts can be customized to prioritize critical events and be integrated with other incident response systems.

- **Investigation and hunting**: Microsoft Sentinel offers powerful search and query capabilities to investigate security incidents thoroughly. Incident responders can query and explore large volumes of data, filter results based on various attributes, and pivot between different data dimensions. The interactive workspace in Sentinel allows responders to visualize and correlate data, enabling in-depth investigations and proactive threat hunting.

- **Automated response and orchestration**: Microsoft Sentinel provides playbooks, which are pre-defined automated workflows, to facilitate incident response actions. Incident responders can create playbooks to automate repetitive and manual tasks, such as enriching alerts with additional context, blocking suspicious IP addresses, or quarantining compromised assets. This feature helps streamline incident response processes and reduce response times.

- **Integration with security solutions**: Microsoft Sentinel integrates seamlessly with various Microsoft security solutions and third-party tools. Incident responders can leverage these integrations to enrich investigations, gather additional context, and orchestrate response actions across the security ecosystem, providing a unified and coordinated approach to incident response.

The following screenshot shows Microsoft Sentinel with active alerts and data connected:

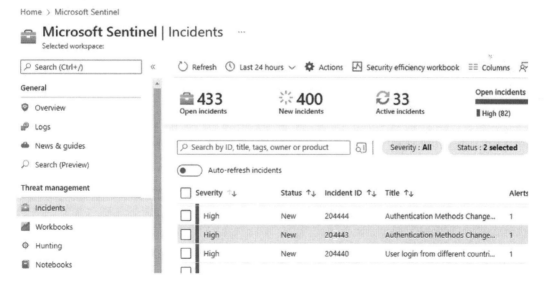

Figure 4.28 – Microsoft Sentinel – Incidents

Microsoft Sentinel is not automatically activated for customers; it requires manual setup and configuration. Organizations must actively choose to implement and configure Microsoft Sentinel in their Azure environment to utilize its security analytics and threat intelligence capabilities. As we conclude our exploration of Microsoft Sentinel, it's evident that its advanced threat intelligence and security analytics capabilities play a pivotal role in fortifying Azure's cloud ecosystem. By utilizing Microsoft Sentinel as a SIEM, security analysts and incident responders can harness the full potential of Sentinel to safeguard their digital environments in an ever-evolving threat landscape.

Summary

This chapter delved into the crucial role of log analysis in incident response within the Azure environment. It emphasized the significance of understanding the available log sources in Azure, how to obtain them, and best practices for analyzing the data to effectively detect, contain, and resolve security incidents. By familiarizing incident response professionals with the tools and techniques specific to Azure, they can enhance their ability to safeguard and respond to security incidents in a cloud infrastructure context.

This chapter highlighted the importance of differentiating between default log availability and the need to enable certain logs, drawing parallels to AWS. Then, it outlined the diverse logs provided by essential Azure services and products, as previously discussed in *Chapter 3*, and examined their utilization for investigative purposes. In particular, this chapter explored Azure Log Analytics, Azure Virtual Network flow logs, Azure Storage, Azure Virtual Machines, and other Azure tools, such as Microsoft Sentinel, as valuable data sources for incident response.

In the next chapter, we will shift our focus to **Google Cloud Platform** (**GCP**) and explore the various log sources that can be enabled and utilized during incidents.

Further reading

To learn more about the topics that were covered in this chapter, take a look at the following resources:

- *Azure Monitor*: https://learn.microsoft.com/en-us/azure/virtual-machines/monitor-vm

- *Microsoft Defender for Cloud*: https://learn.microsoft.com/en-us/azure/defender-for-cloud/defender-for-cloud-introduction

- *Log Analytics*: https://learn.microsoft.com/en-us/azure/azure-monitor/logs/log-analytics-tutorial

- *NSG flow logs*: https://learn.microsoft.com/en-us/azure/network-watcher/network-watcher-nsg-flow-logging-overview

- *Azure Virtual Networks*: https://learn.microsoft.com/en-us/azure/virtual-network/virtual-networks-overview

- *Traffic Analytics*: `https://learn.microsoft.com/en-us/azure/network-watcher/traffic-analytics`

- *Microsoft Defender for Endpoint*: `https://learn.microsoft.com/en-us/microsoft-365/security/defender-endpoint/microsoft-defender-endpoint?view=o365-worldwide`

- *Microsoft Sentinel*: `https://learn.microsoft.com/en-us/azure/sentinel/overview`

6

DFIR Investigations – Logs in GCP

You must have noticed each cloud service provider's common resources and elements by now. In this chapter, we will dive straight into the security capabilities of **Google Cloud Platform** (**GCP**), what log sources are available, and how we can conduct our investigation. Note that cloud providers may use common terminologies. However, the applications and availability of logs may differ for each cloud service provider. Therefore, it is essential to understand which logs will be available during an incident investigation.

In *Chapter 3*, we briefly introduced specific cloud service offerings within GCP; in this chapter, we will dig deep into some of its core components and digital forensics. This chapter outlines the logs available for some of the critical GCP services and products discussed in *Chapter 3* and looks at utilizing these sources in the context of an investigation.

Specifically, we will discuss the following topics in this chapter:

- GCP core services
- GCP identity and access management
- Policy Analyzer
- GCP Logs Explorer
- VPC Flow Logs
- Packet Mirroring
- Compute Engine logs
- Logging Dataflow pipelines
- GCP storage logs

- Cloud Security Command Center
- GCP Cloud Shell

We will discuss Google Workspace in *Chapter 7*, along with Microsoft 365 (M365), as these relate to email and cloud-hosted collaboration services.

GCP core services

GCP is a suite of cloud computing services provided by Google. It offers a wide range of tools and services to build, deploy, and manage applications and infrastructure in the cloud. It provides services similar to cloud providers, such as AWS and Microsoft Azure.

Here are some of the critical service offerings from GCP:

- **Compute services**: GCP offers several compute options, including **Google Compute Engine (GCE)** (**virtual machines [VMs]**), **Google Kubernetes Engine (GKE)** (managed Kubernetes), and **App Engine** (managed platform for applications)

- **Storage services**: GCP provides various storage options such as **Google Cloud Storage (GCS)** (object storage), **Cloud SQL** (relational database service), **Cloud Bigtable** (NoSQL database), and **Cloud Firestore** (document database)

- **Networking**: GCP offers networking services such as **Virtual Private Cloud (VPC)** for creating private networks, **Cloud Load Balancing** for distributing traffic, and **Cloud CDN** for content delivery

- **Big data and machine learning**: GCP includes services such as **BigQuery** (serverless data warehouse), **Cloud Dataflow** (data processing), **Cloud Pub/Sub** (messaging and event streaming), and **Cloud Machine Learning Engine** (managed machine learning)

- **Identity and access management (IAM)**: IAM allows you to manage access to GCP resources and services, defining roles and permissions for users and groups

- **Management and monitoring**: GCP provides tools for managing and monitoring your resources, such as **Cloud Console** (web-based management interface), **Cloud Logging** (centralized log management), **Cloud Monitoring** (performance and health monitoring), and **Cloud Trace** (request latency analysis)

- **Security and compliance**: GCP incorporates various security features, including encryption at rest and in transit, IAM roles and policies, VPC Service Controls, and compliance certifications to meet industry standards

- **Developer tools**: GCP offers developer tools such as **Cloud SDK** (command-line tools), **Cloud Build** (continuous integration and delivery), and **Cloud Source Repositories** (version control system)

- **AI and ML services**: GCP provides pre-trained AI models and APIs through services such as **Cloud Vision API**, **Cloud Natural Language API**, and **Cloud Translation API**, enabling developers to integrate AI capabilities into their applications

- **Serverless computing**: GCP offers serverless services such as **Cloud Functions** (event-driven functions), **Cloud Run** (serverless containers), and **Cloud Scheduler** (cron job scheduler)

Now that we have looked at the core services GCP offers, we can dive deeper into specific services that investigators would be interested in. The focus will be on specific GCP services that form the backbone of any investigations, including identities, logs from the Compute Engine, and so on. We will start with GCP's IAM console that is core to allowing users access to the GCP resources.

GCP IAM

IAM provides a framework for controlling resource access within the GCP realm by defining the relationships between identities, roles, and the corresponding resources. Within this system, the concept of resources extends to include a wide array of entities, such as GCE VM instances, GKE clusters, **Cloud Storage buckets**, and the organizational structure consisting of organizations, folders, and projects.

IAM operates on the principle that direct access permissions are not granted to end users; instead, permissions are organized into roles, which are subsequently assigned to authenticated principals or members (Google account, service account, Google group, authenticated users, cloud identity domain, etc.).

Central to IAM's functioning is the **allow policy**, or **IAM policy**, which serves as the mechanism for specifying and enforcing the assignment of roles to principals. Each allow policy is linked to a specific resource. When an authenticated principal attempts to access a resource, IAM examines the associated allow policy, thereby ascertaining the permissibility of the intended action based on its stipulations. While the allow policy lets you set guidelines to allow access to specific resources, GCP will also enable you to set up a **deny policy** that specifies what users or roles do not have access to. A deny policy lets you set up a deny rule based on specific conditions that determine the permissibility of the resource. Deny policy examples include setting restrictions on defining new API keys or deleting or editing GCE resources or configurations.

By embracing IAM within the GCP ecosystem, organizations can establish granular control over access privileges, ensuring that identities are assigned only the necessary roles to interact with designated resources. This approach to access management enables increased security and effective governance over the GCP environment.

GCP's IAM roles and identities

From the perspective of incident response and forensics, it is essential to understand how cloud service providers organize and provision identities and privileges to these identities. Note that handling identities is generally different for each cloud service provider.

In the case of GCP, end users do not directly get assigned privileges. Instead, privileges are assigned to **roles**. You can imagine roles as a group or a collection of privileges that grant access to various services within GCP's environment. Users or API services needing to access these resources are termed **principals** by GCP. Therefore, privileges are assigned to roles, and roles are attached to principals. A policy is a collection of roles that can be attached to one or more principals.

The following figure summarizes how IAM policies are defined, assigned, enforced, and ultimately managed through GCP's IAM module:

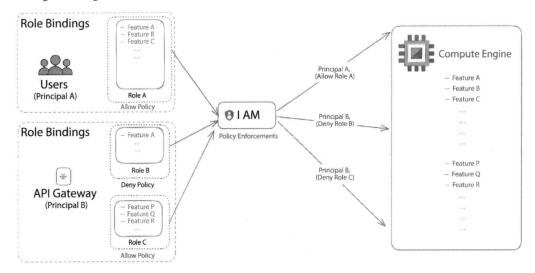

Figure 6.1 – GCP's IAM enforcement architecture

While the preceding figure just illustrates a generic version of how permissions can be assigned to each GCP resource, GCP also offers federated integration to active directories to manage access to GCP resources. This, however, uses a similar concept to enforce IAM policies. You can create granular allow and deny policies to enforce specific resource elements. For example, you can allow access to an instance within GCE while restricting access to other instances.

Policy Analyzer

Given that IAM assignments occur over roles where principals are assigned access permissions to a resource using roles, GCP offers additional tools for troubleshooting and investigating IAM policy configurations. Policy Analyzer allows DFIR teams to analyze excess privileges assigned to users or roles that may have resulted in abuse. Policy Analyzer can also determine whether a user has the necessary permissions to perform specific actions, such as deleting a table, a GCE resource, and so on.

The following is an example of Policy Analyzer's output. We can see in the query result what roles and permissions were configured for a user under a GCP resource. Note that resources are allocated toward a project, and GCP tags them as resources:

Resource	Principal ↑	Role grant	Permission grant	Inheritance	
My First Project	gr@xoreaxeax.ca	Owner	appengine.applications.get	My First Project	VIEW BINDING ▾
My First Project	gr@xoreaxeax.ca	Owner	cloudasset.assets.exportIamPolicy	My First Project	VIEW BINDING ▾
My First Project	gr@xoreaxeax.ca	Owner	cloudasset.assets.exportOSInventories	My First Project	VIEW BINDING ▾
My First Project	gr@xoreaxeax.ca	Owner	cloudasset.assets.exportResource	My First Project	VIEW BINDING ▾
My First Project	gr@xoreaxeax.ca	Owner	cloudasset.assets.queryAccessPolicy	My First Project	VIEW BINDING ▾
My First Project	gr@xoreaxeax.ca	Owner	cloudasset.assets.queryIamPolicy	My First Project	VIEW BINDING ▾
My First Project	gr@xoreaxeax.ca	Owner	cloudasset.assets.queryOSInventories	My First Project	VIEW BINDING ▾
My First Project	gr@xoreaxeax.ca	Owner	cloudasset.assets.queryResource	My First Project	VIEW BINDING ▾
My First Project	gr@xoreaxeax.ca	Owner	cloudasset.assets.searchAllIamPolicies	My First Project	VIEW BINDING ▾
My First Project	gr@xoreaxeax.ca	Owner	cloudasset.assets.searchAllResources	My First Project	VIEW BINDING ▾

Figure 6.2 – Policy Analyzer query results and list of permissions per role

DFIR use cases for Policy Analyzer

Using a policy analyzer in the context of DFIR within GCP enables organizations to evaluate compliance and security across various GCP resources. Here are some use cases for GCP Policy Analyzer:

- **IAM policies**: Analyzing IAM policies includes assessing roles assigned to users, service accounts, and groups, as well as identifying potential misconfigurations or overly permissive access.

- **Network security policies**: Review firewalls, network configurations, and routing policies to ensure proper network segmentation and secure connectivity and protection against unauthorized access.

- **Data encryption and key management policies**: Verify that data encryption policies are enforced for sensitive information at rest and in transit. This involves assessing the usage of encryption keys, key rotation practices, and compliance with encryption standards.

- **Logging and monitoring policies**: Assess logging configurations and monitoring practices to ensure that appropriate logs are generated and retained and that log analysis tools are properly configured to detect security incidents and abnormal activities.

- **Service account and API access policies**: Verify the security of service accounts and API access configurations. This includes assessing permissions granted to service accounts, auditing the usage of service accounts, and ensuring proper management and revocation of API access credentials.

As you can see, GCP Policy Analyzer helps identify policy violations and non-compliant resources. However, it does not provide information on the activity performed due to policy deviations; we need Logs Explorer to identify specific actions performed. We will look at GCP Logs Explorer, which ingests and hosts detailed logs and has advanced filtering options and real-time log streaming capabilities, making it essential for any investigator to use.

GCP Logs Explorer

GCP designed **Logs Explorer** to troubleshoot performance issues with applications and systems by reviewing the logs. The user interface for Logs Explorer features a histogram that displays log rates and associated spikes. Nevertheless, where there are logs, you can always use them to investigate their incident. Google also offers the Logs Explorer API, which allows automation or query logs via a Python program or any other medium through an API key. The following screenshot is an example of GCP's histogram on Logs Explorer that highlights activities by time:

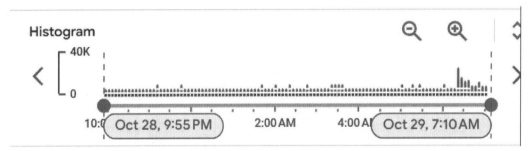

Figure 6.3 – GCP's Logs Explorer histogram

However, Logs Explorer only displays logs per period; it does not quantify or correlate the logs against other activities within the system. You can set the time range for which you want to see the logs, with a default log retention of 30 days. For this, GCP offers **Log Analytics**, a separate service that allows real-time analytics on the roles to allow log aggregation and quantification of the logs collected. This is a separate service and requires you to explicitly upgrade your log bucket to allow GCP to perform log analytics. GCP Log Analytics enables users to use **BigQuery** on the logs. BigQuery is a data warehouse where users can perform queries on massive datasets and perform analytics on them. GCP offers BigQuery as a separate service, which is not available by default. For example, you can run BigQuery to query your logs against known malicious domains from a threat intelligence source.

For DFIR teams to access Logs Explorer, teams must be assigned the following roles:

- `roles/logging.viewer`: For viewing all logs under the_Required and _Default buckets.

- `roles/logging.privateLogViewer`: For viewing all logs, including data access logs.

- `roles/logging.viewAccessor`: Condition-based log view that grants access to user-defined logs. This role grants access to logs within a user-defined bucket if no condition is specified.

- `Roles/logging.fieldAccessor`: For viewing restricted fields within a log entry bucket. You will need to configure field-level access.

Overview of log buckets

Every log a resource generates is ingested by a Cloud Logging infrastructure that determines the conditions and criteria for the bucket assignments for log storage, known as log **sinks**. Log sinks are part of GCP's logging infrastructure that determines how logs are routed to relevant log buckets. GCP also allows you to export these logs to a third-party log aggregation tool through a Pub/Sub topic that helps third-party log aggregation tools subscribe to Pub/Sub to authorize and import the logs.

GCP offers two pre-defined log buckets, `_Required` and `_Default`. Buckets are independent of each other and serve as a default destination per GCP account for logging required logs. Users/administrators can also create their sinks/buckets, which are classified as user-defined buckets. As log entries are passed to logging infrastructure, log routing is initiated, in which, based upon the configured filters for inclusion and exclusion of the log entry, logs are routed to appropriate sinks or redirected to Pub/Sub topics for external consumption, or the logs are dropped altogether. Logs can also be redirected to the BigQuery dataset, allowing users to run Log Analytics for correlation and further analysis.

As indicated previously, cloud log entries are, by default, routed to one of these log buckets:

- `_Required`: The `_Required` log buckets collect the following types of logs:

  - **Admin Activity logs**: These contain log entries for API calls for reading resource metadata or configuration. For example, an API call to read GCE configurations is recorded under this sub-category.

  - **System Event logs**: Any changes to a cloud resource, for example, GCE, are recorded under this sub-category. Users/administrators cannot turn off logging this type of log by creating an exclusion filter; it is always recorded.

  - **Access Transparency logs**: Any actions performed by Google Cloud members within a GCP account are recorded under this log. This allows a transparent view into any actions the cloud service provider performs – in this case, Google.

- **_Default**: Any logs that do not satisfy the conditions of the _Required bucket are routed to _Default buckets. The following types of logs are automatically redirected:

  - **Data Access logs**: These are log entries that include what API calls were made to access metadata or configuration information about a GCP resource. Data Access logs are typically voluminous and are disabled by default. If you run BigQuery, then Data Access logs are enabled. Therefore, it is essential to understand the operating resources and whether the logs are enabled.

  - **Policy Denied logs**: As the name suggests, log entries are categorized as Policy Denied logs when GCP denies access to a resource based on a defined set of conditions or policies. Policy Denied logs are enabled by default and cannot be disabled. However, you can configure an exclusion filter not to record these logs.

- **User-defined bucket**: These are log buckets created by users to collect a subset of logs produced by GCP resources. You can create your user-defined bucket in any cloud project. When you create a log bucket, you do have to specify the region in which the log bucket will be stored.

DFIR use cases for using Logs Explorer

The following are some of the DFIR use cases for utilizing GCP's native Logs Explorer:

- **Incident investigation**: During an incident, Logs Explorer enables you to search and analyze logs across various GCP services. You can correlate events from different logs to reconstruct the timeline of an incident, identify the root cause, and determine the extent of the impact.

- **Threat hunting**: Logs Explorer allows you to query and filter logs based on specific criteria or patterns related to known threats or **indicators of compromise (IOCs)**. By analyzing logs from GCP services such as Cloud Storage, Cloud Functions, or Cloud Pub/Sub, you can proactively search for suspicious activities or abnormal behavior.

- **User activity monitoring**: Logs Explorer provides visibility into user activities within GCP services. You can track user logins, administrative actions, API calls, and resource access to identify unauthorized or suspicious actions. This information can help detect insider threats or compromised user accounts.

- **Data leak and exposure detection**: Logs Explorer can be employed to identify potential data leaks or exfiltration attempts. By analyzing logs from relevant services, such as Cloud Storage or BigQuery, you can search for patterns indicative of unauthorized data access, large data transfers, or unusual data egress.

- **Forensic analysis**: Logs Explorer can serve as a valuable source of evidence during forensic investigations. By querying and analyzing logs, you can reconstruct events, identify the actions taken by an attacker, or track the movement of an adversary within your GCP environment.

Familiarizing with Logs Explorer

We'll look at an example of querying Logs Explorer. Logs Explorer has handy features allowing investigators to click and filter relevant artifacts. Let's familiarize ourselves with multiple areas of Logs Explorer:

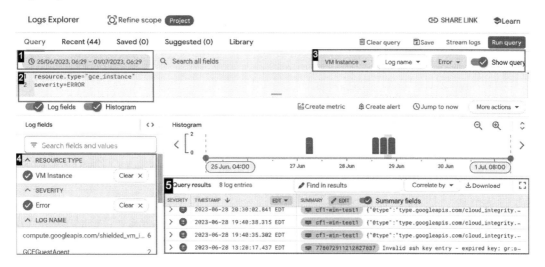

Figure 6.4 – Logs Explorer overview

As we can see in the Logs Explorer dashboard, a few key elements will be helpful to security teams. We have numbered them for your easier reference:

1. **Date/time filter**: This allows the teams to nail down specific events and activities that may have occurred within a time range.

2. **Query pane**: This text bar allows the team to search queries manually. Note that this search query term will automatically be updated when you click and update the filter.

3. **Query filter fields**: This enables the teams to filter specific GCP resources, objects or logs, and types of logs. Note that we have filtered records associated with a VM instance, with severity as an error in this example.

4. **Log fields pane**: This view gives the user a more granular view into the number of events per type of logs filter or severity rating. As indicated earlier, every record is categorized before it is routed to relevant log storage destinations.

5. **Query results pane**: This view lets the user look into the logs more thoroughly. Each entry allows the user to expand and view all the fields within a log entry and perform additional filtering based on investigative leads.

Our next section will look into a sample investigation using Logs Explorer, but first, let us look at VPC Flow Logs.

VPC Flow Logs

Like AWS, VPC Flow Logs are not enabled for GCE by default. Turning on VPC Flow Logs is relatively easy and requires minimal effort. It's important to note that VPC Flow Logs are aggregated by time in minutes and summarized in a dashboard that includes relevant information. VPC Flow Logs are enabled at the subnet level, meaning every flow log is associated with a subnet that your GCE is part of. This typically refers to GCP's internal subnet architecture. Turning on VPC Flow Logs for a noisy server may generate many logs, ultimately impacting costs.

Enabling VPC Flow Logs

To analyze traffic, you must first enable VPC Flow Logs within GCE. As GCEs are created by default, a regional VPC acts as the network gateway for the virtual server to access the internet or other GCP resources. Alternatively, if a custom VPC node is created, you must ensure that the VPC Flow Log option is turned on for the GCE to send logs to Logs Explorer. We'll look at an example for one of the GCEs under network details.

Like AWS, VPC Flow Logs are not automatically enabled and require manual activation. GCP provides a range of customizable network settings, including the ability to create subnets, establish firewall rules, and set up VPC connections. The following figure displays the VPC network configured for one of the regions with a custom VPC network called `test-lab1`:

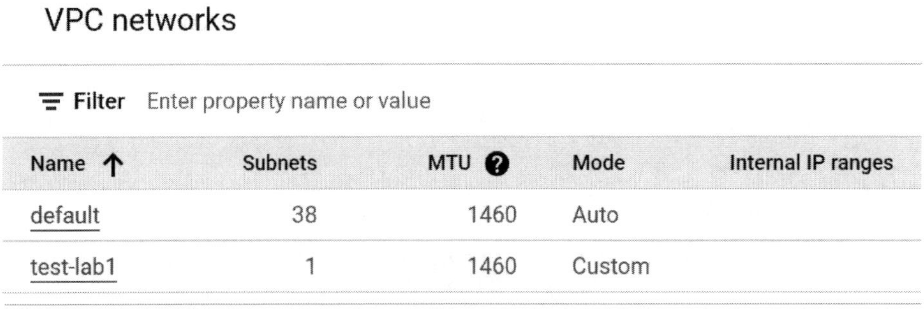

VPC networks

Filter	Enter property name or value			
Name ↑	**Subnets**	**MTU** ❓	**Mode**	**Internal IP ranges**
default	38	1460	Auto	
test-lab1	1	1460	Custom	

Figure 6.5 – Network subnet details for a GCE

VPC Flow Logs are subnet-specific; therefore, it is essential to note that when enabling VPC Flow Logs, you must make changes to the VPC subnet and allow the flow logs to be collected. If the GCE has more than one VPC connected to the instance, you must verify and enable each VPC subnet to collect flow logs. In the following figure, we look at the sample customized VPC we created named `test-lab1` with a VPC subnet named `subnet-lab1`:

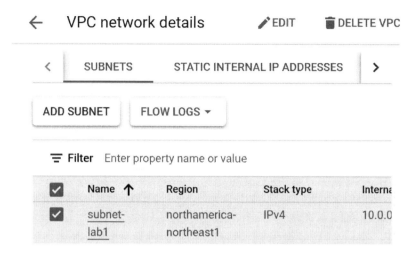

Figure 6.6 – VPC subnet information

Click and edit the subnet name and select the option for turning **FLOW LOGS** on or off. Once enabled, specify the frequency of aggregation of network packets. Remember that VPC Flow Logs only collect header information, not full packet details. As a result, it is essential to weigh the aggregation frequency and identify the most suitable time interval for aggregation. Packet aggregation can occur at 5-second, 30-second, 1-minute, 5-minute, 10-minute, and 15-minute intervals.

Suppose GCP resources produce a lot of network traffic throughout the day; in that case, a higher frequency flow log aggregation can be set to allow granular network traffic visibility. Low-frequency flow log aggregation is suitable for those who do not have a lot of network traffic activity. The following figure demonstrates the option for setting flow logs:

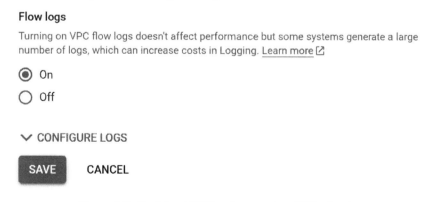

Figure 6.7 – Enabling VPC Flow Logs under a VPC subnet

While setting up the flow logs, select the sample rate of the packets that will be aggregated into the flow logs and reported to Logs Explorer, ideally at 100%. This means that 100% of observed traffic is sent to Logs Explorer and not downsized to a specific percentage of traffic activity. The following figure demonstrates the subnet configuration with a sample rate of 100% of the observed network traffic with an aggregation interval of 5 seconds:

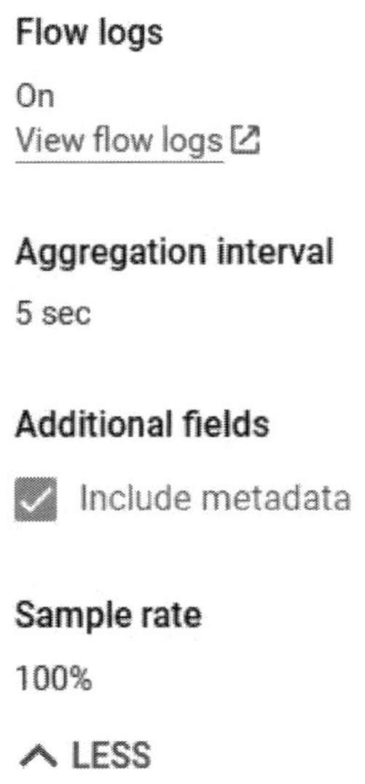

Flow logs

On
View flow logs ☑

Aggregation interval

5 sec

Additional fields

☑   Include metadata

Sample rate

100%

∧ LESS

Figure 6.8 – Flow log network aggregation configuration

Once the VPC is configured, flow logs are automatically sent to Logs Explorer, where investigators can begin threat hunting. The following section will demonstrate an example use case for using Logs Explorer and hunting VPC Flow Logs for malicious activities.

Hunting VPC Flow Logs for malicious activities

In this scenario, we have a GCP Cloud Storage bucket named `app-data1` with a few backups critical for the organization. The infrastructure setup is such that any internal GCP resource or application can access GCP Cloud Storage but is not publicly available to users or on the internet. The following figure indicates a list of Cloud Storage objects stored within the `app-data1` bucket:

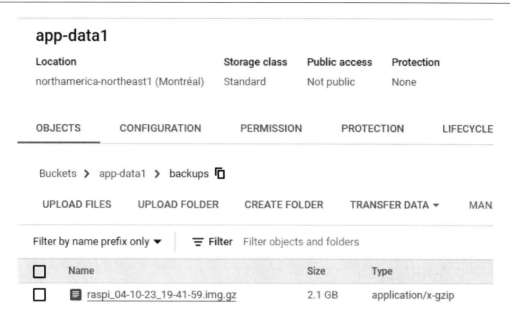

Figure 6.9 – Cloud Storage view

We have a threat actor who is using a GCE VM, `cf1-ta-vm`, (with an internal IP address of `10.0.0.15` and an external IP of `34.152.3.1`) to grab these files from Cloud Storage and ultimately exfiltrate the data to a threat actor-controlled remote server at `3.98.136.11`.

We will now look into using Logs Explorer to hunt for threat actor activity concerning this GCE resource:

1. As a first step, we begin by selecting appropriate event times within the Logs Explorer dashboard to capture the most relevant events.

2. We then look for the associated log entry when this file was uploaded to the GCS bucket. Investigators must pay attention to the `methodName` attribute with the `storage.objects. create` value, indicating that the object was created within a specific bucket. The following figure illustrates the log record created when uploaded to the bucket and the full file path identified within the `resourceName` attribute:

```
∨  ⓘ    2023-07-27 07:07:08.090 EDT       storage.googleapis.com    storage.objects.create    _s/backups
                                          "gr@xoreaxeax.ca"

▼  {
     insertId: "1rjfp3ze7uh9u"
     logName: "projects/vaulted-timing-390314/logs/cloudaudit.googleapis.com%2Fdata_access"
  ▼  protoPayload: {
       @type: "type.googleapis.com/google.cloud.audit.AuditLog"
     ▸  authenticationInfo: {1}
     ▸  authorizationInfo: [2]
       methodName: "storage.objects.create"
     ▸  requestMetadata: {4}
     ▸  resourceLocation: {1}
       resourceName: "projects/_/buckets/app-data1/objects/backups/raspi_04-10-23_19-41-59.img.gz"
     ▸  serviceData: {2}
       serviceName: "storage.googleapis.com"
     ▸  status: {0}
     }
     receiveTimestamp: "2023-07-27T11:07:08.996818240Z"
  ▸  resource: {2}
     severity: "INFO"
     timestamp: "2023-07-27T11:07:08.090421700Z"
  }
```

Figure 6.10 – Log entry for object uploaded to GCS bucket

3. The next step is to look for any GCE VMs accessing this resource. Using the log fields pane (as described in *Figure 6.4*), we will filter the logs relevant to the purpose of the investigation. As logs are filtered, the **Query** pane is automatically updated. Using the result query within the **Query results** pane, tag the JSON formatted results for src_ip (source IP), dest_ip (destination IP), and bytes_sent (bytes sent) to be visualized within the log entry summaries. Right-click and access these options for tagging fields. Notice that the following figure demonstrates tagging key fields for easier visualization and investigation:

Figure 6.11 – Logs Explorer field filters

4. Once relevant filters are applied to support the investigation, we can review the log entries within Logs Explorer and identify threat actor activities. From the Logs Explorer view, we can see that the threat actor first copied the files from GCS to the GCE VM with the `cf1-ta-vm` hostname and associated IP address (`10.0.0.15`) as the destination IP. Given that the transfer is within GCP's infrastructure, the transfers occur through GCP's backend network infrastructure. Notice the bytes sent size within the following snippet with the order of tags as `src_ip` followed by `dest_ip` and `bytes_sent`:

	Query results	174 log entries					Find in results	
SEVERITY	TIMESTAMP ↑		EDT ▼	SUMMARY	✎ EDIT	✅ Summary fields		
> ✳	2023-07-27 07:25:23.464 EDT			3.98.136.11	10.0.0.15	144	{"bytes_sent":"144", "col	
> ✳	2023-07-27 07:25:23.464 EDT			216.239.32.174	10.0.0.15	7084	{"bytes_sent":"7084",	
> ✳	2023-07-27 07:25:29.541 EDT			3.98.136.11	10.0.0.15	720	{"bytes_sent":"720", "col	
> ✳	2023-07-27 07:25:34.534 EDT			3.98.136.11	10.0.0.15	240	{"bytes_sent":"240", "col	
> ✳	2023-07-27 07:26:10.978 EDT			3.98.136.11	10.0.0.15	24672	{"bytes_sent":"24672",	
> ✳	2023-07-27 07:26:18.210 EDT			172.217.13.138	10.0.0.15	300	{"bytes_sent":"300", '	
> ✳	2023-07-27 07:26:18.210 EDT			3.98.136.11	10.0.0.15	87608	{"bytes_sent":"87608",	
> ✳	2023-07-27 07:26:24.209 EDT			3.98.136.11	10.0.0.15	43344	{"bytes_sent":"43344",	
> ✳	2023-07-27 07:26:30.636 EDT			3.98.136.11	10.0.0.15	48800	{"bytes_sent":"48800",	
> ✳	2023-07-27 07:26:35.642 EDT			172.217.13.138	10.0.0.15	300	{"bytes_sent":"300", '	
> ✳	2023-07-27 07:26:35.642 EDT			3.98.136.11	10.0.0.15	69840	{"bytes_sent":"69840",	
> ✳	2023-07-27 07:26:42.512 EDT			3.98.136.11	10.0.0.15	53136	{"bytes_sent":"53136",	

Figure 6.12 – Query result for GCS data transfer to GCE

5. Putting the pieces together, we have determined that GCS storage objects were copied to a local GCE host. We now flip the destination IP and identify whether that GCE host was responsible for outbound connections. We apply filters on the source IP address as `10.0.0.15` and immediately see the outbound connection to a remote server along with the `bytes_sent` values, which we attribute to a threat actor-controlled server.

> ✱	2023-07-27 07:26:18.210 EDT	cf1-ta-vm	10.0.0.15	3.98.136.11	382332640	{"bytes_sent":"382332640",
> ✱	2023-07-27 07:26:24.209 EDT	cf1-ta-vm	10.0.0.15	3.98.136.11	321387200	{"bytes_sent":"321387200",
> ✱	2023-07-27 07:26:30.636 EDT	cf1-ta-vm	10.0.0.15	3.98.136.11	386827392	{"bytes_sent":"386827392",
> ✱	2023-07-27 07:26:35.642 EDT	cf1-ta-vm	10.0.0.15	172.217.13.138	52256	{"bytes_sent":"52256", "con
> ✱	2023-07-27 07:26:35.642 EDT	cf1-ta-vm	10.0.0.15	3.98.136.11	382801376	{"bytes_sent":"382801376",
> ✱	2023-07-27 07:26:42.512 EDT	cf1-ta-vm	10.0.0.15	3.98.136.11	376155552	{"bytes_sent":"376155552",
> ✱	2023-07-27 07:26:48.132 EDT	cf1-ta-vm	10.0.0.15	3.98.136.11	361400576	{"bytes_sent":"361400576",
> ✱	2023-07-27 07:27:06.615 EDT	cf1-ta-vm	10.0.0.15	34.75.254.221	144	{"bytes_sent":"144", "connectic
> ✱	2023-07-27 07:27:22.972 EDT	cf1-ta-vm	10.0.0.15	216.239.36.174	8344	{"bytes_sent":"8344", "conne
> ✱	2023-07-27 07:27:36.324 EDT	cf1-ta-vm	10.0.0.15	172.217.13.138	11264	{"bytes_sent":"11264", "con
> ✱	2023-07-27 07:28:36.411 EDT	cf1-ta-vm	10.0.0.15	172.217.13.138	43580	{"bytes_sent":"43580", "con
> ✱	2023-07-27 07:29:41.513 EDT	cf1-ta-vm	10.0.0.15	172.217.13.138	552	{"bytes_sent":"552", "connect:

Figure 6.13 – Logs Explorer hunting for outbound connections

As we can see through the sequence of steps illustrated, investigators can extract relevant event logs attributed to threat actor activities through interactive filtering capabilities and click-through filters to the log fields. There is always the option of extracting all the logs, performing an offline analysis, and slicing-and-dicing them further to determine specific actions the threat actor performs. There are various ways, however, for command-line entries to be extracted. Investigation teams can use this information to obtain a complete snapshot of the GCE. We will explore this mechanism in *Chapter 10*.

> **Note**
>
> Logs Explorer has limitations on recording commands entered within the GCE; any commands entered by the user or the threat actor are not recorded within Logs Explorer.

Expanding on network monitoring capabilities, let us delve into GCP's Packet Mirroring feature, which complements the insights provided by VPC Flow Logs.

Packet Mirroring

GCP's Packet Mirroring feature allows security teams to collect network packets from VMs and identify security threats or activities associated with the VMs. GCP's Packet Mirroring only mirrors traffic between VMs and external interfaces and does not mirror traffic between cluster nodes such as GKE. We will learn more about containers, including **Docker** and **Kubernetes**, in *Chapter 11*.

To mirror packets, ensure the principals are attached with the compute.packetMirrorUser and compute.packetMirroringAdmin roles.

An internal load balancer must be deployed with **network passthrough** capabilities that pass the traffic to the **collector** instances to enable packet mirroring. The load balancer must be pointed to a **managed instance group** in the backend with pre-configured instance templates, allowing GCP to create collector instances automatically. The collector instance can be a VM with tools for capturing and receiving network packets via the internal load balancer.

When setting up an internal load balancer, ensure that it is created within the same region as the instance being mirrored, **Session affinity** is set to **None**, and **backend subsetting** is not enabled. Also, ensure that packet forwarding rules are created on the load balancers to forward all the mirrored packets while configuring the load balancer. This setting cannot be changed once configured.

When creating an internal load balancer, a managed instance group must be created and assigned VMs within that group. GCP will then determine this VM as part of the collector instance for packet mirroring and capture.

The following figure demonstrates a simple configuration for an internal network load balancer. We created a sample load balancer, `lb2`, and configured it on `subnet-lab1` under the `test-lab1` VPC. We also created a managed instance group, `instance-group1`, that automatically makes the collector VMs for receiving network packets:

lb2

Frontend

Protocol ↑	IP version	Scope	Subnetwork	IP:Ports	DNS name
UDP	IPv4	northamerica-northeast1	subnet-lab1	10.0.0.8:all	

Backend

Region	Network	Endpoint protocol	Session affinity	Health check	Logging
northamerica-northeast1	test-lab1	UDP	None	lb1-healthck	Enabled (sample rate: 1) All optional fields excluded

Instance group ↑	IP stack type	Scope	Healthy	Auto-scaling	Use as failover group
instance-group-1	IPv4	northamerica-northeast1-a	✅ 0 of 0	No configuration	No

Figure 6.14 – Internal load balancer configuration

Once a load balancer is created, configure the **packet mirroring policy** and specify the target VPC and subnet for the source of packet capture. Alternatively, select a suspect GCE from where the network packets will be collected. Note that the target VPC and collector instance must be created within the same network region for successfully mirroring packets.

In the following screenshot, we configure the packet mirroring policy (pkt-mirror1) that defines the collector VM or VPC network (in this case, test-lab1) and the load balancers (specified in the form of a forwarding rule, lb2-forwarding-rule) the policy will be attached to. **Policy enforcement** must be turned on to enable packet mirroring.

Figure 6.15 – Packet mirroring policy

The packet mirroring policy is also configured to forward and mirror packets associated with the test-lab1 VPC, with the suspect VM attached to subnet-lab1.

Now, in the collector VM, we begin collecting network packets by running tcpdump. Note the IP address of the suspect VM before initiating network packet capture:

```
$ sudo tcpdump -i INTERFACE_NAME -f "host IP_ADDRESS" -w dump.pcap
```

The following parameters are supplied when running tcpdump:

- -i INTERFACE_NAME: Collector instance network interface name that will listen to network packets (ens33, enp03, etc.)

- `-f  "IP_ADDRESS"`: Filter flag to apply a packet capture based on a specific IP address of the suspect VM

Outputs from `tcpdump` can also be written to a file. In the example, we dump the packets using the `-w` flag and provide the file location.

Investigators prefer to capture full packets recording all threat actor activities across multiple VMs via the VPC network before focusing on specific GCP services for investigation.

Once the packets are written to the disk, the following GCP command-line options can be used to access GCP storage and upload artifacts:

```
$ gcloud auth login
```

It is assumed that the investigation team will have its own identities and associated roles attached to those identities (principals). First, you must log in by entering the preceding command and following the on-screen instructions.

Once completed, you can access Google Cloud Storage and copy the artifacts using the following command:

```
$ gsutil cp [SOURCE_FILE] gs://[BUCKET_NAME]/[DESTINATION_PATH]
```

The following are the key parameters that are required to upload artifacts successfully:

- `SOURCE_FILE`: The source artifacts that the team would like to investigate
- `BUCKET_NAME`: The Google Cloud Storage bucket name
- `DESTINATION_PATH`: The destination folder path within the storage bucket

As we can see, the VPC Flow Logs offered by GCP present substantial data related to network traffic patterns, which can significantly enhance security and troubleshooting efforts. Packet mirroring amplifies the potential for monitoring and analyzing network traffic but also enables the identification of potential security threats in real time.

The following section will examine more granular GCE logs, offering profound insights into activities and enabling correlation capabilities via Logs Explorer.

Compute Engine logs

GCE is a service offered by GCP that allows users to create VMs within GCP's infrastructure. These VMs can be hosted across any part of the world where GCP operates. It provides flexibility and scalability options, making various preconfigured VM instances available. It can create on demand or resize a VM based on requirements. Users can create a VM instance or a group of VMs through **GCE Instance Group Manager**, which manages the deployment and configuration of VMs.

GCP's logging platform

GCP's Cloud Logging platform automatically collects and aggregates logs from various GCP resources via Logs Explorer. It offers a single-pane view of all the logs and filters, allowing investigators to hunt for specific alerts or threats and use them for monitoring. Some of the types of logs it collects are as follows:

- **Platform logs**: Generated through GCP's services, these logs are used for debugging and troubleshooting. Examples of platform logs include VPC Flow Logs.

- **Component logs**: Similar to platform logs, these are generated by GCP's software-based components, such as Kubernetes clusters. GKE logs are classified as component logs.

- **Security logs**: Two forms of security logs are collected within GCP; the first is **Cloud Audit logs**, which provide administrative information and activities performed by the administrator, supporting cloud audit and compliance requirements. Secondly, **Access Transparency logs** log any actions performed by Google's staff directly on a Google Cloud tenant to allow for transparency and compliance.

- **User-written logs**: As the name suggests, they log any custom application logging, which can be sent to Cloud Logging through the OpsAgent, Logging Agent, Cloud Logging API, and other libraries. We will learn about the OpsAgent in a later part of this chapter.

- **Multi-cloud and hybrid logs**: These include logs from other cloud providers such as Microsoft Azure and on-premises infrastructure. They can be collected alongside GCP logs; however, there may be cost implications based on the number of logs.

GCP's default logging

Every VM within GCP is preconfigured to send default logs to the **Cloud Logging platform**. These include CPU utilization, memory utilization, network bandwidth consumption, and so on. While the telemetry collected is rudimentary, it is vital in determining whether any abnormal activities are detected within the monitoring console for deep-dive investigation.

Specifically speaking of logging agents, Google primarily relies on the **OpsAgent**, legacy agents, and custom logging packages.

OpsAgent

GCP uses OpsAgent as the primary source for monitoring and collecting telemetric data from Windows and Linux-based systems. The OpsAgent is based on FluentBit, a third-party but lightweight logging and telemetry data provider that allows metrics collection in the **Prometheus** format. FluentBit (**fluentd**) handles automatic tagging and metrics parsing before sending it to the logging platform.

Google also relies on **OpenTelemetry Collector**, another open source service, for specific metrics.

GCP users can also configure their fluentd configuration for specific application-level logging that will be automatically sent to Google's Cloud Logging platform.

By using the OpsAgent and deploying custom configuration files (fluentd configurations), investigators can collect metrics and logs from various third-party applications such as Microsoft Active Directory, Apache Tomcat, **Internet Information Services (IIS)**, MySQL, MariaDB, and many more. The OpsAgent also allows log collections from GKE.

The following are some of the log sources that the OpsAgent collects by default:

- **Files**: Logs written to disk, such as `/var/log/syslog` and `/var/log/messages` in Linux
- **Journald** daemon and **Systemd** logs
- **TCP port**: Listen to a TCP port and collect logs
- **Windows event logs**: Logs from Windows operating systems
- **Fluentd Forward**: Logs collected via Fluentd Forward over TCP

The following metrics are reported by the OpsAgent by default without any additional configuration on the host VM. These metrics help identify deviations from the baseline and, if a breach occurs, allow the security team to respond immediately:

- **CPU metrics**: CPU states (idle, interrupt, system, and user), CPU load, CPU usage time, and CPU utilization
- **Disk metrics**: Disk used (bytes), disk I/O time, disk operations, disk pending operations, disk utilization (percent), disk bytes read, and disk bytes written
- **IIS metrics (Windows)**: IIS open connections, IIS transferred bytes, IIS connections, and IIS requests
- **Network interface metrics**: Network errors, packets, and traffic (bytes)
- **Memory metrics**: Memory usage, memory states (buffered, cached, free, slab, and used), and memory utilization (percent)
- **MSSQL metrics**: SQL server open connections, SQL server transaction rate, and SQL server write transaction rate
- **Swap metrics (Linux only)**: Swap usage, swap I/O operations, and swap utilization (percent)
- **Network metrics**: TCP connections

- **Process metrics**: Process count by states (running, sleeping, and zombie), process CPU time, process disk read I/O, process disk writes I/O, fork count, process resident memory (allocations), and process virtual memory (usage)

- **Agent self metrics**: Agent API request count, agent log entry count, agent memory usage, agent metric point count, agent enabled receiver count, and agent uptime

Legacy logging agent

Google has currently deprecated the legacy logging agent. However, there are still VMs that require legacy agents, so they continue to be supported by Google. While fluentd is still being used here, the application utilizes older methodologies for collecting the metrics and routing them to Logs Explorer.

Logging Dataflow pipelines

Dataflow pipelines provide a stream of data or batch processing capabilities at scale. GCP's Dataflow pipeline is based on **Apache Beam**. Logs can be streamed at variable volumes in near real time using Dataflow applications.

Any actions performed on GCP Dataflow are recorded by default in Logs Explorer. Through Logs Explorer, investigators can detect any changes to the Dataflow parameters or whether unauthorized users altered the pipeline.

Note that a Docker instance forms the base of any Dataflow pipeline's operations. Therefore, investigators must also investigate the logs emitted by the GKE cluster and GCE Instance Group Manager. GCP relies on Instance Group Manager to create multiple managed VMs that run the containers (GKE) to handle instance resourcing and deploying VMs automatically.

The following figure outlines some sample resources required for successful Dataflow pipeline execution. Like **Syslog**, Dataflow events are tagged with a severity rating; it also generates the exact name of the job that emitted the log entry. Using the filters within Logs Explorer, relevant logs can be specifically targeted and investigated in a Dataflow job or pipeline:

Figure 6.16 – Resource types for Dataflow pipeline execution

The following figure is a snippet of a log stream that outlines the sequence and flow of the logs emitted by the Dataflow service that triggers other resources such as Kubernetes, GCE Instance Group Manager, and so on:

```
>  i   2023-07-21 06:59:43.547 EDT    dataflow.googleapis.com   dataflow.jobs.create   ../locations/northamerica-northeast2/jobs/   gr8x@resxexx.ca   audit_log, method: "dataflow.jobs.create", principal_email: "gr8x...
>  i   2023-07-21 06:59:46.968 EDT    The workflow name is not a valid Cloud Label. Labels applied to Cloud resources (such as GCE Instances) for monitoring will be labeled with this modified job name: my_first_job-...
>  i   2023-07-21 06:59:58.128 EDT    compute.googleapis.com   ..ute.regionInstanceGroupManagers.get   ..ataflow-myfirstjob-07210359-79zs-harness   service-5831437516398dataf...   The resource 'projects/vaulted-timing-3-...
>  i   2023-07-21 06:59:58.314 EDT    compute.googleapis.com   beta.compute.instanceTemplates.get   ..ataflow-myfirstjob-07210359-79zs-harness   service-5831437516398dataf...   The resource 'projects/vaulted-timing-398-...
>  i   2023-07-21 06:59:58.723 EDT    compute.googleapis.com   ..ta.compute.instanceTemplates.insert   ..ataflow-myfirstjob-07210359-79zs-harness   service-5831437516398dataf...   audit_log, method: "beta.compute.instan...
>  i   2023-07-21 07:00:00.168 EDT    compute.googleapis.com   ..ta.compute.instanceTemplates.insert   ..ataflow-myfirstjob-07210359-79zs-harness   service-5831437516398dataf...   audit_log, method: "beta.compute.instan...
```

Figure 6.17 – Log streams emitted by GCP Dataflow

To summarize, monitoring and investigating Dataflow logs is no different from analyzing any other activity logs emitted by relevant GCP resources. It is essential to understand that when a resource is accessed, GCP in the backend may access other associated resources or dependencies to deliver the service, impacting the number of logs or the logs emitted by relevant dependent services.

GCP storage logs

Like AWS's S3 buckets, GCP Storage also refers to storage containers as buckets. Each bucket can contain any file format, referred to as an **object**. Principals can be assigned granular permissions and access to each bucket or object. Storage buckets can also be made publicly accessible on the internet, depending on the use case. Storage metadata is recorded in the key/value pair format at the bucket level to manage the object life cycle. Values assigned to keys can be a bucket name string or an array of object life cycle management configurations.

Once a storage bucket is created, you cannot change the bucket name, the location (where the bucket is hosted), the project associated with the storage bucket, or the metadata generation number, uniquely identifying the bucket state.

Storage permissions

Similar to IAM permissions, specific permissions are required for accessing objects by a resource or a principal. In GCP's IAM realm, permissions are assigned to roles and roles are attached to principals.

The following table outlines the list of permissions required for accessing storage objects:

Permission name	Description
storage.buckets.create	Creates a storage bucket within a project
storage.buckets.delete	Deletes a storage bucket from a project
storage.buckets.get	Reads metadata associated with the bucket, including bucket configurations
storage.buckets.list	Lists buckets in a project
storage.buckets.update	Updates metadata associated with the bucket and configuration of the bucket
storage.buckets.getObjectInsights	Reads metadata associated with the object within the bucket

Table 6.1 – Minimum IAM permissions required to create and manage buckets

Storage object logging

Like all the resources within GCP, activities on storage buckets emit logs and are recorded within Logs Explorer; storage logs or access logs associated with the objects are also recorded within Logs Explorer. Investigators should, therefore, consider reviewing storage-related logs to determine evidence of data exfiltration and any threats against GCP's storage buckets.

Investigating GCP Cloud storage logs

When setting up GCP Cloud Storage, ensure that it has appropriate permissions set. This also includes public access prevention policies that must be turned on or off, depending on the use case.

The following example will examine the logs to determine privilege escalation attempts to GCP's Cloud Storage. For this purpose, we created a temporary storage folder, `test_cf1_test1`, and set it for non-public access to the folder; we have not enabled any fine-grained access control for this purpose:

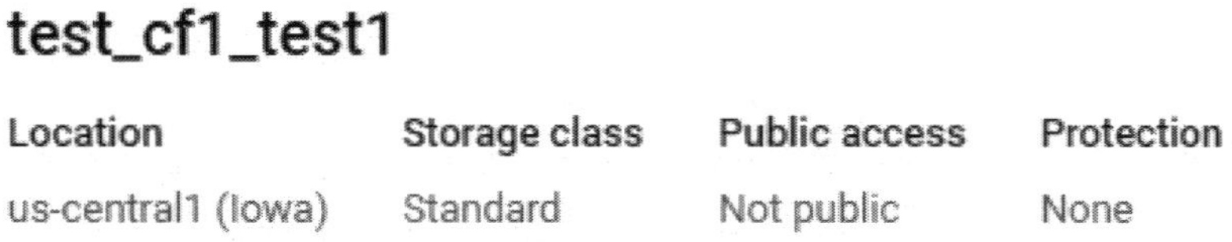

test_cf1_test1

Location	Storage class	Public access	Protection
us-central1 (Iowa)	Standard	Not public	None

Figure 6.18 – GCP Cloud Storage configuration summary example

We will examine the storage logs within Logs Explorer. We evaluate the IAM policies configured using GCP's **command-line interface** (**CLI**) in the following figure, using the `gsutil iam get gs://test_cf1_test1` command and requesting IAM policies configured for this bucket. This is equivalent to making a GET request to `https://storage.googleapis.com/storage/v1/b/<bucket>/iam`, but as an authenticated user:

```
gr@cloudshell:~ (vaulted-timing-390314)$ gsutil iam get gs://test_cf1_test1
{
  "bindings": [
    {
      "members": [
        "projectEditor:vaulted-timing-390314",
        "projectOwner:vaulted-timing-390314"
      ],
      "role": "roles/storage.legacyBucketOwner"
    },
    {
      "members": [
        "projectViewer:vaulted-timing-390314"
      ],
      "role": "roles/storage.legacyBucketReader"
    },
    {

      "members": [
        "projectEditor:vaulted-timing-390314",
        "projectOwner:vaulted-timing-390314"
      ],
      "role": "roles/storage.legacyObjectOwner"
    },
    {
      "members": [
        "projectViewer:vaulted-timing-390314"
      ],
      "role": "roles/storage.legacyObjectReader"
    }
  ],
  "etag": "CAI="
}
```

Figure 6.19 – IAM policies on a Cloud Storage folder example

Note that the following primary roles are configured for the storage folder. GCP automatically applies legacy roles to buckets when owners create a **uniform bucket-level access** (meaning all objects within the bucket have similar access permissions enabled):

- `roles/storage.legacyBucketOwner`: Principals with `roles/editor` or `roles/owner` are granted this access

- `roles/storage.legacyBucketReader`: Principals with `roles/viewer` are granted this access

- `roles/storage.legacyObjectOwner`: Principals with `roles/editor` or `roles/owner` are granted this access

- `roles/storage.legacyObjectReader`: Principals with `roles/viewer` are granted this access

Now we know that access to this folder is only limited to those users or principals with `roles/editor` access or `roles/owner` access. In summary, any other principals or general public access are not allowed for this folder.

We will review Logs Explorer to determine the access requests made when an authenticated user or principal attempts to access the bucket using non-standard methods, such as accessing Cloud Storage buckets through a Python program.

We will look at a log entry for an authenticated user attempting to access the bucket. Within the `authorizationInfo` section, we look specifically at the highlighted areas: `CallerIP`, which refers to the user's IP address that is trying to access the bucket, and `callerSuppliedUserAgent` (**user-agent** string), which is reflective of the browser and operating system variant that the user is using to attempt to access the storage. Finally, we also look at what resource is being requested along with the assigned permission tagged to this bucket and object, and whether IAM granted this access:

```
{
  [...]
    "requestMetadata": {
      "callerIp": "184.147.94.133",
      "callerSuppliedUserAgent": "Mozilla/5.0 (Windows NT 10.0;
Win64; x64) AppleWebKit/537.36 (KHTML, like Gecko) Chrome/114.0.0.0
Safari/537.36,gzip(gfe),gzip(gfe)",
      [...]
      [...]
      {
        "resource": "projects/_/buckets/test_cf1_test1",
        "permission": "storage.buckets.getIamPolicy",
        "granted": true, }
```

Let us look at a situation where an unauthenticated user tries to gain access to GCP's Cloud Storage buckets and objects outside of GCP's Cloud console. Similar to the previous example, we'll look at a similar form of log entry and look for the `authorizationInfo` section. The request is for accessing the `test_cf1_test1` bucket. In this case, note the user-agent string and IP address. Given that the user attempted to authenticate as the owner/principal, and since the access attempt was via a Python command-line application instead of a browser accessing the bucket, this permission was denied as there is no public access to the folder outside of the GCP console, GCP CLI, or GCP API:

```
{
  [...]
    "status": {
      "code": 7,
      "message": "PERMISSION_DENIED"
    },
    [...]
    "requestMetadata": {
```

```
    "callerIp": "12.47.194.133",
    "callerSuppliedUserAgent": "python-requests/2.25.1,gzip(gfe)"}
    [...]
  "authorizationInfo": [
    {
      "resource": "projects/_/buckets/test_cf1_test1",
      "permission": "storage.buckets.get",
      [...]
  "severity": "ERROR",
  [...]
    }
```

The following figure outlines the series of attempts while allowing access to GCP API tools:

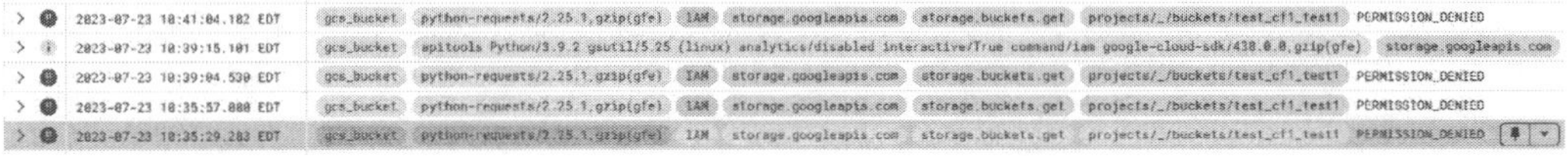

Figure 6.20 – Multiple denied access attempts to non-GCP applications while only allowing API access

As we can see, Logs Explorer forms the basis of most of the investigative insights into activities performed by the user or external resources.

Next, we will look into some of GCP's dashboards that offer insight into the security status of the resources configured within GCP.

Cloud Security Command Center (Cloud SCC)

Cloud SCC is like a dashboard for notifying organizations and security teams about possible threats or vulnerabilities. Cloud SCC is only available when a GCP account is set up as an organization. Individual GCP users do not have access to Cloud SCC. When an anomaly is identified, it creates a report of a particular threat or misconfiguration in GCP's realm, called a **finding**. Cloud SCC provides a consolidated view of all the findings and anomalies detected within a cloud service, such as a GCE.

Note that there are two activation levels; by default, organizations, when they sign up, are assigned the **Standard service tier**, which has limited functionality and includes looking at the general security health of GCEs and their configurations. It also includes features such as error reporting, continuous exports to Pub/Sub, and access to other integration points, including Cloud Data Loss Prevention, Cloud Armor, and so on.

Google also offers a **Premium service tier**, which comes at a price that includes additional capabilities, as outlined in the following screenshot, such as **Event Threat Detection**, **Web Security Scanner**, **Container Threat Detection**, **Virtual Machine Threat Detection**, **Security Health Analytics**, and **Rapid vulnerability detection**:

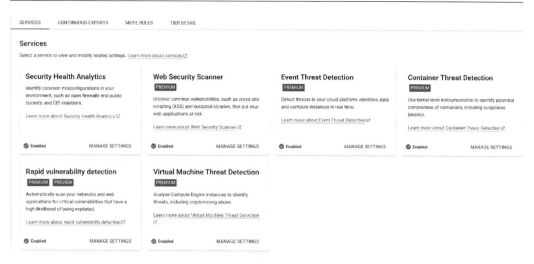

Figure 6.21 – Cloud SCC Premium subscriptions

The following sections will examine some of the Cloud SCC capabilities in more depth.

IAM roles

Now that we know GCP uses IAM roles to assign access to principals, it is vital to understand the various access privileges required for teams to have access to Cloud SCC dashboards and other details.

From a DFIR perspective, the following roles are required for accessing the Cloud SCC console:

- `roles/resourcemanager.organizationAdmin`: Provides admin access at the organization level. An organization can have multiple projects.

- `roles/securitycenter.admin`: Administrative or superuser access to Cloud SCC and other resources within Cloud SCC. It provides access to project-level detections.

- `roles/securitycenter.adminViewer`: Admin read-only access to the security center. Users can view scan results and see threat detections. No changes are allowed. It provides access to project-level detections.

- `roles/securitycenter.findingsViewer`: Provides restrictive access to view only the findings generated within Cloud SCC for a specific project.

- `roles/cloudsecurityscanner.editor`: Provides project-level access, with administrative controls (read-write controls) to run cloud web scanning. Access to all the resources within the web scanner module is provided.

Threats and Findings dashboards

The GCP **Threats** and **Findings** dashboards provide visibility into potential threats and security incidents, allowing organizations to manage security threats and findings within their GCP environment. They are a central hub for monitoring and analyzing security events and proactively detecting and responding to threats by aggregating data from various services and tools within GCP.

The **Threats** dashboard displays threats per VM instance and threats identified within the overall GCP environment. This includes any potential misconfigurations and features that, as a result, introduced a vulnerability within the GCP environment. The following figure is a sample dashboard with identified threats:

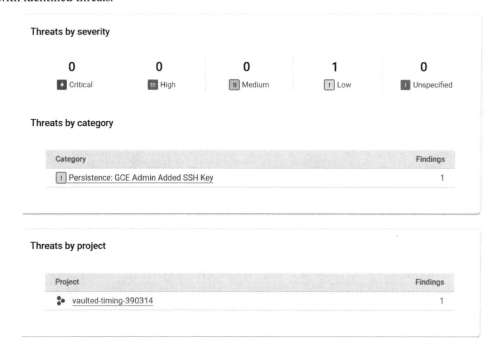

Figure 6.22 – Threats dashboard

Details of identified threats are documented on the **Findings** page. Findings provide detailed information on the threat, severity, event detection time (event time), event reporting time (create time), GCP resource, GCP project, and resource type. Findings also allow investigators to utilize filters to investigate the identified findings further and gain an understanding of the threat. The following is the drill-down screenshot of an identified threat within the **Findings** section:

Figure 6.23 – Findings dashboard

Note that findings are classified into **Threat**, **Misconfiguration**, or **Vulnerability**. By default, if investigators navigate to the **Findings** page, it will display all the findings that are not muted and have been active for the previous seven days.

On the **Findings** page, within the **Quick filters** pane, investigators can quickly filter down the types of findings that they are interested in and are relevant to the investigation:

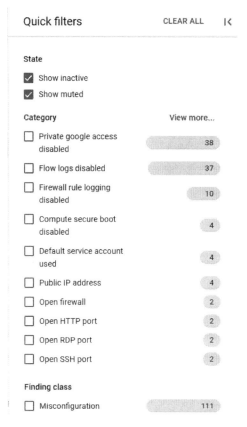

Figure 6.24 – Findings quick filters

Once filters are applied, the findings are available for review and investigators can determine more information. In the following screenshot, we have filtered down **Open RDP port** and identified two findings concerning the exposed RDP port. GCP has classified this detection as a high-severity finding:

Figure 6.25 – Findings based on quick filters

Each finding provides a link to get more details about the results that indicate what was detected, including **Artificial Intelligence (AI) Generated Summary**, **Description**, **Affected Resource**, **Security Marks**, suggested next steps, and related links to various standards and detection services. It also allows investigators to mute this detection to ensure that findings do not report on similar exposures.

As we delve into the intricacies of Cloud SCC Assets, we will explore how this feature empowers investigators and security teams with a detailed inventory of GCP resources, identifying vulnerabilities, misconfigurations, and potential threats. This visibility lays the foundation for practical risk assessment and proactive security measures, ultimately fostering a more resilient and secure cloud infrastructure. Let us now navigate the key functionalities that Cloud SCC Assets brings to the cloud security journey.

Cloud SCC Assets

Investigators always appreciate seeing all the assets and knowing what is configured within an environment. Similarly, GCP's Cloud SCC offers something called Cloud SCC Assets that provides a high-level view of all the categories of assets, their details, and the configurational information set for these assets. Getting the lay of the land is vital when investigating a complex case. Investigators can use this asset management page to obtain relevant information and potentially identify the next steps in their investigation.

The following figure outlines the asset summary configured within our sample GCP instance and the relevant resource types:

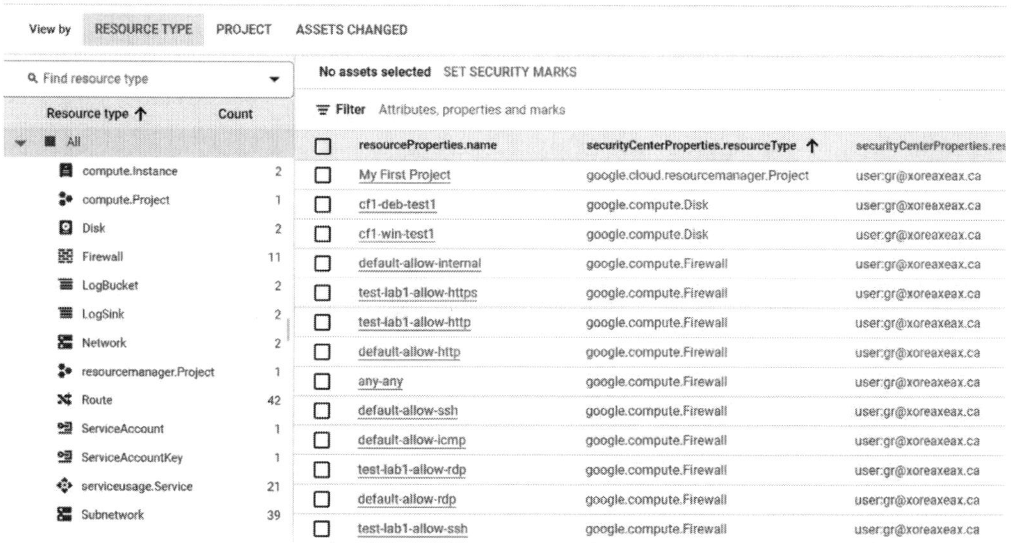

Figure 6.26 – Cloud SCC Assets view

Only assets associated with the current project or resources are visible in the asset view. More information is presented within each asset under the `resourceProperties.name` field. For example, we can select the `compute.Instance` resource type in the filters, then click on the first item. The following figure summarizes what kind of resource is configured and its various configurational elements (or attributes). It also presents resource properties in the JSON format and includes any additional metadata for this asset. Finally, this page also provides any findings about this particular asset:

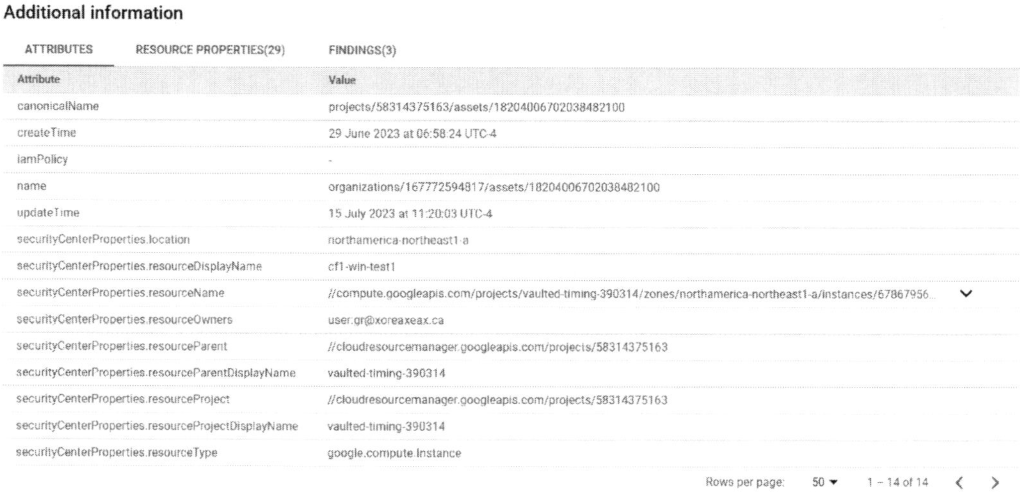

Figure 6.27 – Asset detail view

Configurational vulnerabilities

Platform configurational vulnerabilities is a GCP feature that natively scans the configurations of various GCP services and GCP VMs and identifies vulnerabilities within the infrastructure. Although very simplistic, this dashboard provides detailed findings for each configurational vulnerability. GCP deems something a vulnerability or a threat if it sees a deviation from acceptable standards. Since each organization differs, some variations would be permissible for the business.

From an investigation point of view, the vulnerability findings feature offers historical insights into when GCP observed the vulnerability or the deviation, the severity of the associated findings, and the number of services or endpoints impacted, and provides a mapping to various commonly accepted security standards.

> **Note**
>
> GCP's vulnerability findings can be used to determine potential root causes and, through digital forensics, confirm whether the threat actor exploited any of these vulnerabilities.

The following figure illustrates the list of vulnerabilities, including third-party application vulnerabilities. Each finding will also provide detailed descriptions of where this deviation was identified:

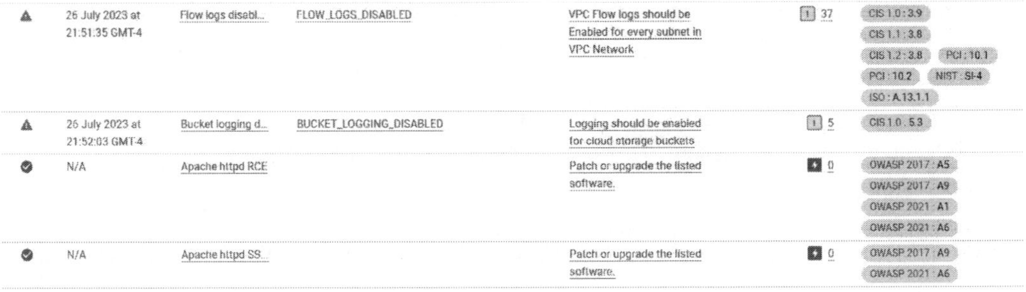

Figure 6.28 – List of vulnerabilities

From a digital forensics standpoint, configurational vulnerabilities can provide investigators with clues about potential gaps within an infrastructure and indicate whether any of the gaps could have been the root cause of an incident.

In the next section, we venture into the command-line environment, which allows access to various GCP resources. GCP Cloud Shell is helpful for incident responders who are very comfortable with command-line tools. It can be useful for quick access and investigative insights into a GCP resource.

GCP Cloud Shell

Cloud Shell is GCP's native command-line tool that allows access to various GCP services over a command-line interface. GCP Cloud Shell, a browser-based shell environment, can be used to investigate and identify potential security incidents for threat-hunting activities. Investigators can also use Cloud Shell to turn a service such as packet mirroring on or off. It also has an interactive code editor for users or investigators who want to import custom code, enabling Cloud Shell to perform certain activities. GCP's Cloud Shell can also be accessed locally through the Google Cloud SDK or an in-browser session.

GCP offers essential command-line tools, specifically `gcloud` and `gsutil`. `gcloud` provides access to general GCP services such as **GCE**, **BigQuery**, and so on. In comparison, `gsutil` is a specific utility tool to access storage buckets.

Through `gcloud`, investigators can access Logs Explorer and collect all the associated logs for offline analysis. Investigators can also list the services a user has subscribed to or all VPC policies:

Figure 6.29 – GCP Cloud Shell

GCP Cloud Shell offers investigators a browser-based command-line interface for investigating incidents. It allows access to GCP resources for tasks such as log analysis, memory examination, and malware assessment. Cloud Shell aids in artifact preservation, collaboration, and automation, enabling efficient, scalable, and secure digital forensics and incident response operations.

Summary

After diving deep into GCP, we know the GCP infrastructure is very similar to other popular cloud providers. We highlighted the importance of understanding the varying verbosity of logs emitted by GCP services, emphasizing the need for investigators to seek corroborating evidence to confirm events. GCP's centralized logging system, which flows into Logs Explorer, is a powerful tool for administrators to troubleshoot routine issues and for investigators to delve into event correlations across the GCP ecosystem.

We learned about similarities between how GCP organizes its buckets and objects, which is conceptually similar to AWS. Cloud SCC offers a dashboard or a security scorecard on infrastructure for administrators. At the same time, for investigators, it is a goldmine of findings, with detailed information on where to look when kicking off an investigation. Cloud SCC offers unique insights into vulnerabilities without deploying specific agents within the hosts. Finally, we looked at Cloud Shell, which provides more freedom for investigators to perform investigative activities from the command line.

In the next chapter, we will dive deep into email workspaces, especially Microsoft 365 and Google Workspaces, and identify methodologies for investigating cloud email workspaces.

Further reading

- Google Access Transparency policy: `https://cloud.google.com/privacy`

- Cloud Audit Logs overview: `https://cloud.google.com/logging/docs/audit#system-event`

- Enabling logging: `https://cloud.google.com/logging/docs/audit/configure-data-access`

- Cloud SCC IAM, access control with IAM: `https://cloud.google.com/security-command-center/docs/access-control`

- IAM for organization-level activations: `https://cloud.google.com/security-command-center/docs/access-control-org`

- Exporting Security Command Center data: `https://cloud.google.com/security-command-center/docs/how-to-export-data?authuser=2`

- Investigating and responding to threats: `https://cloud.google.com/security-command-center/docs/how-to-investigate-threats#defense_evasion_breakglass_workload_deployment`

- Using event threat detection: `https://cloud.google.com/security-command-center/docs/how-to-use-event-threat-detection`

- How Security Command Center helps you detect and stop cyber attacks: `https://cloud.google.com/security-command-center/docs/concepts-how-scc-determines-env-under-attack`

- Compute Engine IAM roles and permissions: `https://cloud.google.com/compute/docs/access/iam`

- FluentBit: `https://github.com/fluent/fluent-bit`

- Install Google CLI: `https://cloud.google.com/sdk/docs/install#linux`

- Live forensics to analyze a cyber-attack: `https://cloud.google.com/blog/products/identity-security/how-to-use-live-forensics-to-analyze-a-cyberattack`

7
Cloud Productivity Suites

By this point in the book, you are well acquainted with the core components and log sources that are integral to **Cloud Service Providers** (**CSPs**) such as **Amazon Web Services** (**AWS**), Azure, and **Google Cloud Platform** (**GCP**). As we pivot to productivity suites, it's crucial to recognize that these platforms—namely Microsoft 365 and Google Workspace—are often the epicenter of organizational data and activity. The investigation of incidents in these environments comes with its own unique challenges and possibilities, as these services offer not just computing and storage but also extensive collaborative tools, all available through a **Software as a Service** (**SaaS**) model. The SaaS model, though convenient for organizations, means analysis will be dependent on which log sources are made available for investigators by the products.

It's important to note that AWS does not have a cloud productivity suite akin to Microsoft 365 or Google Workspace. While AWS offers a vast array of cloud infrastructure and platform services, it has not ventured deeply into the cloud-based office productivity market. Microsoft and Google, on the other hand, have a longstanding presence in productivity software and have naturally extended their offerings into the cloud. AWS has focused more on backend infrastructure (**Infrastructure as a Service**, or **IaaS**) and hasn't prioritized creating a competing suite in this space. In this chapter, we will delve deeper into the features of Microsoft 365 and Google Workspace, examining their integral components and the kinds of logs and data that are pertinent in a forensic investigation.

Specifically, we will discuss the following topics in this chapter:

- Overview of Microsoft 365 and Google Workspace core services
- **Identity and Access Management** (**IAM**) in Microsoft 365 and Google Workspace
- Auditing and compliance features in Microsoft 365 and Google Workspace
- Google Workspace Admin console and security features

Understanding these productivity suites is critical for a thorough and effective investigation. While they share some similarities with more traditional cloud services, the depth and breadth of user activity necessitate a specialized approach to forensics. By the end of this chapter, you will have an understanding of the forensic capabilities and limitations of Microsoft 365 and Google Workspace, arming you with the knowledge to conduct more effective investigations in these environments.

> **Important note**
>
> This chapter will focus on core services, auditing, and compliance features of Microsoft 365 and Google Workspace. *Chapter 12* will focus on details of responding to compromised cloud productivity suites, including the collection and analysis of the various services and logs discussed in this chapter.

In *Chapter 12*, we will discuss how to collect and analyze unified audit logs in a Microsoft 365 investigation.

Overview of Microsoft 365 and Google Workspace core services

Microsoft 365 and Google Workspace are robust cloud productivity suites that provide a wide range of services designed to enable collaboration, communication, and seamless data management for businesses. These productivity suites are directly associated with their parent cloud platforms – Azure for Microsoft and GCP for Google – which makes them particularly relevant in the context of cloud forensics. Understanding their core services and how they relate to their respective cloud platforms will provide you with a comprehensive view necessary for forensic investigations.

Microsoft 365

Microsoft 365 is an integrated suite of cloud-based productivity tools, including Office applications such as Word and Excel, as well as advanced services for collaboration and secure data management such as SharePoint, Teams, and OneDrive. For **Digital Forensics and Incident Response** (**DFIR**) professionals, understanding Microsoft 365 is crucial. Its ubiquitous use in modern enterprises means that critical evidence and data trails often reside within its ecosystem, and mastering its architecture and security features is key to conducting effective investigations and ensuring cyber resilience. Let's take a closer look at the platform and its features:

- **Licensing**: Microsoft 365 licensing is crucial in the context of organizational security as different license levels offer varying security capabilities. For example, an E5 license offers advanced threat protection features such as **Threat Intelligence** (**TI**) and **Advanced Threat Analytics** (**ATA**), which are not available in lower-tier licenses such as E3 or E1. Licenses are assigned at the user level, meaning that each employee can be granted access to different suites of tools and security features depending on their role within the organization. This granular approach allows companies to optimize costs while ensuring that employees have the appropriate level of security measures in place. For instance, an IT administrator might need an E5 license for its robust security features, while a sales representative might only need an E3 license. Choosing the right Microsoft 365 license is therefore not just a matter of functionality but also a vital consideration for implementing a layered security posture.

Security professionals should consider allocating a higher-tier license such as E5 to take advantage of all of Microsoft's advanced security and eDiscovery tools.

- **Office applications**: Microsoft 365 includes industry-standard office applications such as Word, Excel, and PowerPoint, which have moved from being standalone software to being deeply integrated into the cloud ecosystem. These apps now offer real-time collaboration and cloud storage capabilities.

- **Microsoft Teams**: Teams is a collaboration hub where chat, video meetings, and file storage happen. It's integrated with other Microsoft services and offers robust auditing and logging features valuable for forensics.

- **SharePoint and OneDrive**: SharePoint is used for creating websites and portals and is deeply ingrained with OneDrive, Microsoft's cloud storage solution. These services offer detailed access and modification logs.

- **Exchange Online**: This is Microsoft's cloud-based email solution that integrates with Outlook and provides extensive logging and auditing features that are critical during forensic investigations.

- **Advanced security and compliance**: Microsoft 365 offers an array of advanced security measures, including threat protection, **Data Loss Prevention** (**DLP**), and more. The Security and Compliance Center is a unified interface for managing and auditing these features.

> **Important note**
> Microsoft Compliance Center is now known as Microsoft Purview. It can be accessed through `https://compliance.microsoft.com/homepage`.

The following screenshot displays the Microsoft 365 portal and some of the core services offered in 365. This can be accessed through `https://www.microsoft365.com/` after logging in:

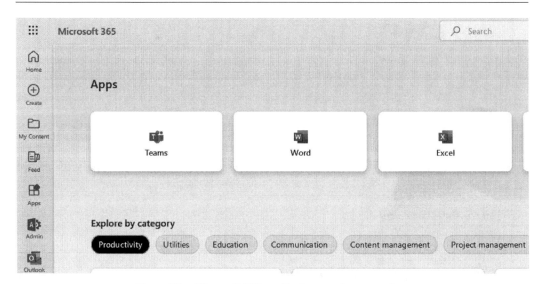

Figure 7.1 – Microsoft 365 applications and core services

Google Workspace

Google Workspace is a collection of cloud computing, productivity, and collaboration tools, software, and products developed by Google. Similar to Microsoft 365, it has become a go-to solution for businesses and organizations of all sizes for its ease of use, scalability, and the collaborative nature of its services. For anyone involved in IT management, cybersecurity, or DFIR, gaining a thorough understanding of Google Workspace is essential due to its widespread adoption and unique architecture—especially in small-medium businesses. Here's an overview of the platform and its features:

- **Licensing**: Google Workspace operates on a subscription-based model similar to Microsoft 365, but there are key differences in how licensing works between the two. Google Workspace licenses are generally simpler and more straightforward. Google offers various licensing tiers such as Business Starter, Business Standard, Business Plus, and Enterprise, each with varying levels of features and storage capacities.

    Microsoft, on the other hand, offers different enterprise licenses denoted by E1, E3, and E5, with an array of options within each category that includes various Microsoft products and services. While Google Workspace licensing focuses mainly on scaling the core set of Google services, Microsoft's E# licensing can include a broader range of products such as advanced security and compliance packages, telephony capabilities, and more. Therefore, when choosing between Google Workspace and Microsoft 365, organizations need to carefully assess their specific needs in terms of features, security, and compliance requirements.

- **Google Drive**: Similar to Microsoft's OneDrive, Google Drive is a cloud storage service where users can store files online and access them from any device. Google Drive integrates seamlessly with other Google services and allows for easy sharing and collaboration.

- **Google Docs, Sheets, and Slides**: These are the Google equivalents of Microsoft Word, Excel, and PowerPoint, respectively. They provide the essential functions you would expect from productivity software and emphasize real-time collaboration among team members.

- **Google Meet**: As a counterpart to Microsoft Teams, Google Meet offers video conferencing services that are tightly integrated with other Google Workspace applications. It allows for easy scheduling and screen sharing and provides robust security features.

- **Gmail**: While Microsoft has Exchange Online, Gmail is Google's email platform. With an enterprise subscription to Google Workspace, organizations get business email addresses and additional administrative controls.

- **Google Calendar**: This is Google's time-management and scheduling tool, which can be compared to Microsoft's Outlook Calendar. It integrates tightly with Gmail and Meet to streamline scheduling and event planning.

- **Google Chat**: This is Google's instant messaging platform, a counterpart to Microsoft Teams' chat feature. It offers direct messages and team chat rooms, alongside file sharing and task management functionalities.

- **Google Forms and Google Sites**: While not direct counterparts to any single Microsoft application, Google Forms and Sites offer easy form creation and website building, respectively, integrated within the Google ecosystem. These can be valuable tools for internal or external engagement.

- **Advanced security and compliance**: Google Workspace offers a range of security features designed to keep data safe, such as **Two-Factor Authentication (2FA)**, **Single Sign-On (SSO)**, and admin controls for user access. It also has its Vault service for eDiscovery, which is important for legal and compliance reasons.

  DLP and endpoint management are other advanced security features in Google Workspace that allow for the enforcement of rules on data sharing and manage how data is accessed on mobile devices.

The following screenshot showcases some of the applications and core services offered by Google Workspace:

Figure 7.2 – Google applications and core services

After delving into an overview of the features and services offered by Microsoft 365 and Google Workspace, it's crucial to understand how these platforms ensure the security and integrity of user data. The subsequent section, focused on IAM in both Microsoft 365 and Google Workspace, will explore the mechanisms these suites employ to authenticate, authorize, and manage user identities, ensuring that only the right individuals have access to specific resources.

IAM in Microsoft 365 and Google Workspace

IAM serves as the cornerstone of any organization's cybersecurity strategy. It controls who has access to which resources, and how securely that access is granted and tracked. In the realms of Microsoft 365 and Google Workspace, IAM takes on a critical role due to the cloud-based nature of these platforms and the sheer volume of data they manage.

Microsoft 365

Understanding the IAM features of **Azure Active Directory (Azure AD)** is essential for cloud security, particularly within the Microsoft 365 suite. Azure AD allows for detailed **Role-Based Access Control (RBAC)** and **Multi-Factor Authentication (MFA)**. It also supports **Conditional Access (CA)** policies that adapt security based on user location, device state, and risk profile, effectively blocking potentially unsafe access attempts. Furthermore, Azure AD's auditing, through log entries for various activities such as sign-ins and password changes, and integration with tools such as Azure Sentinel for log aggregation, provides critical data for incident responders. This comprehensive approach to access and audit management is a fundamental aspect of maintaining security and conducting forensic investigations in cloud environments. Here's an overview of Microsoft 365's IAM features:

- **Azure AD**: The heart of Microsoft 365's IAM is Azure AD, an enterprise-level **Identity Service Provider (IDSP)**. Azure AD allows for complex RBAC to Microsoft's suite of services and any integrated third-party or internal apps. Security professionals can create custom roles, define access permissions at granular levels, and enforce MFA.

- **CA policies**: Azure AD also supports CA policies that can enforce security protocols based on the user's location, device state, and risk profile. For example, a policy can be set to block access from logins outside of the organization's internal network.

- **Audit logs and alerts**: Incident responders can benefit from Azure AD's robust auditing capabilities. Log entries are generated for a wide variety of events such as user sign-ins, password resets, and privilege escalations. Azure Sentinel can be used to aggregate logs from Azure AD and other sources for more comprehensive **Threat Detection and Response (TDR)**. Login activity will also be captured in Microsoft Unified Audit logs, discussed later in this chapter.

Google Workspace

Diving deeper into the authentication features of Google Workspace, let's explore its approach to IAM, ensuring that data access is both seamless for users and secure against unauthorized access:

- **Google Identity Platform**: Google Workspace's IAM centers on Google's Identity Platform, which includes basic identity services such as SSO and MFA. While not as extensive as Azure AD, Google Identity still offers essential features for securing access.

- **Context-Aware Access**: As with Microsoft's CA, Google Workspace provides Context-Aware Access features. These can enforce access policies based on factors such as the user's device and location, allowing security professionals to create granular, situation-based rules.

- **Work Insights and Alert Center**: Google Workspace has the Work Insights tool and an Alert Center API, which provide monitoring and alerting services. Work Insights can be configured to track various metrics that can be useful for spotting abnormal patterns indicative of a security incident. The Alert Center API provides real-time alerts for suspicious activity, and it can be integrated with **Security Information and Event Management (SIEM)** solutions for centralized monitoring.

- **OAuth apps whitelisting**: Google Workspace allows admins to whitelist or block OAuth 2.0-based apps, preventing unauthorized data access. This is particularly useful for mitigating risks associated with third-party apps that request broad permissions but are not vetted.

For security professionals and incident responders, understanding the IAM capabilities of these platforms is crucial for safeguarding organizational data and swiftly responding to security incidents.

Auditing and compliance features in Microsoft 365 and Google Workspace

Ensuring the security and compliance of organizational data is a top priority for security professionals and incident responders. Both Microsoft 365 and Google Workspace offer robust sets of features designed to monitor, audit, and secure data while helping organizations meet compliance requirements. Next, we discuss their respective capabilities.

Microsoft 365's Security and Compliance Center (Microsoft Purview)

Moving forward, we will discuss the core of Microsoft 365's security mechanisms, focusing on the Security and Compliance Center (now known as Microsoft Purview). Purview is rich in features such as eDiscovery, DLP, and audit logs, all important features that can be leveraged in a digital forensic investigation. Let's take a closer look at these features:

- **eDiscovery**: Microsoft 365 comes with eDiscovery Manager, a feature that enables organizations to search, hold, analyze, and export content from its ecosystem, such as emails, documents, and chats. This is particularly useful during investigations and litigation, where specific datasets need to be isolated and examined. A screenshot of Microsoft **eDiscovery (Standard)** is shown next:

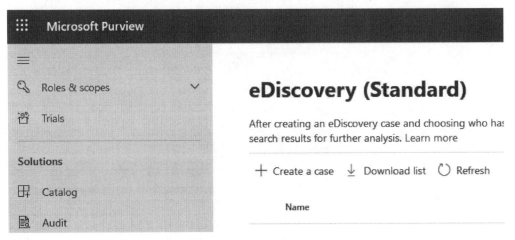

Figure 7.3 – Microsoft eDiscovery

- **DLP**: Microsoft 365's DLP feature allows admins to identify sensitive information such as credit card numbers or **Social Insurance Numbers (SINs)/Social Security Numbers (SSNs)** across services and set up policies to detect, control, and block data sharing.

- **Audit logs**: Detailed audit logs in Microsoft 365 can be configured to track various activities, including file and folder access, modifications, and user behavior. These are known as Microsoft Unified Audit logs. Microsoft Unified Audit logs are a key feature within Microsoft Purview, designed to provide a consolidated and comprehensive record of activities across various Microsoft 365 services such as SharePoint Online, Exchange Online, OneDrive, Azure AD, Microsoft Teams, and more. These logs serve as a rich repository of data that is invaluable for both security professionals and incident responders.

Unified audit logs capture a wide array of activities. These can range from file accesses and modifications in SharePoint and OneDrive to user sign-in activities in Azure AD, and from administrative actions such as adding or removing users to specific data-sharing events in Teams and Outlook. The unified nature of these logs means that organizations don't have to navigate to each separate service for logging. In *Chapter 12*, we will discuss how to collect and analyze unified audit logs in a Microsoft 365 investigation.

> **Important note**
>
> Unified audit logs can be found under the **Audit** tab in Microsoft Purview. Audit logs must be enabled by the organization to start recording user and admin activity. They are not enabled by default.

The following screenshot shows the default audit search pane:

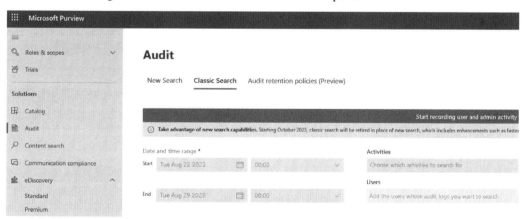

Figure 7.4 – Audit search pane in Microsoft 365 Compliance Center (Microsoft Purview)

- **Threat protection features**: Microsoft's Threat Protection suite integrates with the Microsoft Purview, offering advanced threat analytics and **Artificial Intelligence (AI)**-powered insights. For incident responders, these tools can automate the detection and remediation of a wide range of threats. Microsoft has rebranded this product to Microsoft 365 Defender. In the future, Microsoft may enhance this suite with the integration of technologies such as Microsoft Security Copilot. Microsoft Security Copilot is envisioned as an advanced AI tool, part of Microsoft's broader AI (Microsoft Copilot) initiatives, designed to augment an organization's security expertise and response to security incidents.

> **Important note**
>
> Microsoft 365 Defender can be accessed through `security.microsoft.com`.

- **Compliance Manager**: This tool helps organizations assess and manage their compliance posture by offering a compliance score, assessments, and recommendations. It helps security professionals align organizational processes with industry standards and regulations.

Google Workspace Admin console and security features

Shifting to the administrative hub of Google Workspace, the upcoming section will provide a look at the Admin console. This central dashboard doesn't merely serve as a control panel for administrators but houses pivotal features such as the Alert Center API, Google Vault, DLP, and audit logs, which collectively play a critical role in monitoring, preserving, forensics, and securing the environment as incident responders. Let's take a closer look:

- **Alert Center**: Google Workspace's Alert Center API provides security alerts in real time, enabling admins to act quickly on potential issues such as phishing attacks or suspicious login attempts. Alert Center can be integrated with third-party SIEM solutions for better **Incident Response (IR)**.

- **Vault**: Google Vault allows for the retention, archiving, and eDiscovery of emails, chats, and files, much like Microsoft's eDiscovery. This tool is critical for compliance, litigation, or internal investigations.

- **DLP**: Similar to Microsoft 365, Google Workspace also has a DLP feature that can be configured to detect sensitive data and either warn the user or block transactions entirely.

- **Audit logs**: Google Workspace provides detailed logs for various services such as Gmail, Drive, and mobile devices. These logs can be exported to BigQuery or third-party SIEM systems for advanced analysis and reporting, enabling a quicker response to incidents. These logs are accessible through the Google Admin console under the **Reporting** section.

> **Important note**
>
> Reports are accessed through the Google Admin console menu by going to **Reporting | Reports | User Reports**.

- **Security Health**: The Security Health feature in Google Workspace gives an overview of security settings and how they match with recommended best practices. It provides a dashboard view of potential vulnerabilities, enabling admins to tighten security measures as necessary.

The following screenshot shows the central Google Workspace Admin console where the Workspace administrator can access the various features discussed previously:

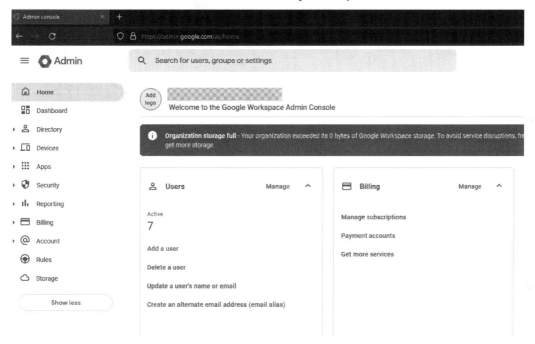

Figure 7.5 – Google Workspace Admin console

Both Microsoft 365 and Google Workspace offer a range of features aimed at auditing, compliance, and security. Microsoft 365 generally offers more advanced and granular controls via its Microsoft Purview, particularly useful for larger enterprises with complex needs. Google Workspace, on the other hand, offers a simpler but still robust set of features via its Admin console. For security professionals and incident responders, understanding the capabilities of these platforms is essential for effective **Incident Management** (**IM**), auditing, and ensuring compliance.

Summary

You have gained an understanding of core services and IAM features, as well as the auditing and compliance capabilities within Microsoft 365 and Google Workspace. These aren't just your run-of-the-mill cloud services; they are the backbone of organizational data and activity, featuring extensive collaborative tools under a SaaS model. The SaaS architecture amplifies the complexity of conducting investigations, given that you are reliant on log sources provided by these platforms.

You've learned the importance of features such as Microsoft's Unified Audit logs and Google Workspace's Alert Center API, which are indispensable tools for incident responders. We delved into IAM, discussing how Azure AD and Google Identity Platform can be leveraged for more secure and monitored environments. Finally, we touched upon the security and compliance features in both suites, equipping you with the knowledge to ensure your organization remains compliant with various legal frameworks.

In the next chapter, we will pivot our focus toward the DFIR process in cloud environments. While this chapter equipped you with an understanding of the two most common productivity suites, the next chapter will deepen your insight into critical aspects of the DFIR process. We'll jump into how the DFIR process is applied in cloud infrastructures, providing you with the knowledge to effectively manage, analyze, and respond to security incidents for organizations with a larger cloud presence.

Further reading

- Microsoft 365 licensing: `https://learn.microsoft.com/en-us/microsoft-365/commerce/licenses/subscriptions-and-licenses?view=o365-worldwide`

- Microsoft Enterprise licensing guide: `https://download.microsoft.com/download/3/D/4/3D42BDC2-6725-4B29-B75A-A5B04179958B/Licensing_guide_Microsoft_365_Enterprise.pdf`

- Microsoft Purview eDiscovery solutions: `https://learn.microsoft.com/en-us/purview/ediscovery`

- Microsoft Security Copilot: `https://www.microsoft.com/en-ca/security/business/ai-machine-learning/microsoft-security-copilot#overview`

Part 3:
Cloud Forensic Analysis – Responding to an Incident in the Cloud

In this part, we take one step forward in debunking the complexities of forensically acquiring cloud artifacts, including memory and disk artifacts, understanding network logs, and obtaining them for offline analysis and investigation. We will also look at fundamental forensic artifacts and their importance in investigations. This section will investigate containers hosted in the cloud, along with cloud productivity suites.

This part has the following chapters:

- *Chapter 8, The Digital Forensics and Incident Response Process*

- *Chapter 9, Common Attack Vectors and TTPs*

- *Chapter 10, Cloud Evidence Acquisition*

- *Chapter 11, Analyzing Compromised Containers*

- *Chapter 12, Analyzing Compromised Cloud Productivity Suites*

The Digital Forensics and Incident Response Process

So far, we have mostly looked at cloud-native tools for investigators to review logs and perform analysis. In the subsequent chapters, we will be looking at some of the third-party tools that complement cloud-native tools – tools that can aid in collecting and analyzing forensic artifacts, marrying cloud-native and third-party toolsets every investigator should be familiar with before embarking upon a cloud forensic case. Specifically, this chapter will revisit the basics of digital forensics and the incident response process. We will also identify some core concepts and introduce tools we have typically used in cloud forensic cases.

In this chapter, we will learn about the following:

- The basics of the incident response process
- Commonly used tools and techniques for host and memory forensics
- Options to conduct live forensics
- Network forensics
- A refresher on malware analysis
- Traditional forensics versus cloud forensics

This chapter assumes you are familiar with most of these topics; this is just a refresher on commonly accepted incident response techniques and tools utilized in cases.

The basics of the incident response process

The incident response process is an overarching process that allows investigators to approach incident response cases in a structured manner. The seven stages within the incident response process enable investigators to understand the actions required to satisfy the conditions in each stage. The following diagram outlines the critical steps of the incident response process:

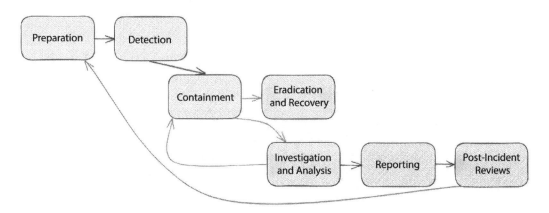

Figure 8.1 – The incident response process

Here are the key stages:

- **Preparation**: This is the pre-incident stage, where organizations work with the incident response teams to document and plan activities in the event of an incident. Typically, organizations will establish their objectives for handling an incident and how to address critical cybersecurity issues arising from incidents in the form of an **incident response plan**.

  The incident response plan will typically include the roles and responsibilities of various actions during an incident, key stakeholders who are notified, and so on. The incident response plan will also include organizations' objectives for handling multiple incidents. Once the plans have been documented, organizations conduct periodic exercises to train, test, and update their plans regularly.

- **Detection**: This phase refers explicitly to the process where security teams are armed with tools to identify an incident. Typically, this will be the organization's **security incident and event monitoring (SIEM)** tool or their **endpoint detection and response (EDR)** tool. These tools are monitored by a dedicated group of teams who provide an early warning about an incident occurring. Organizations set up routine security monitoring and alerting to identify breaches or incidents immediately. This is also the stage where security teams must triage the incident as soon as they are notified. **Triage** is a concept where **Digital Forensic and Incident Response (DFIR)** teams evaluate the breach, the scope of the breach, and the impact as a result of this breach and decide if further investigation is necessary. This is the step where the security team identifies the breach as an **incident**.

> **Note**
> Security teams need to scope the incident correctly, identify how many systems are impacted, how big or small the spread of the breach is, and so on; otherwise, key elements can be missing from investigations.

- **Containment**: Right after the security teams call an incident and regroup various security teams, the typical first step is to contain the incident. Imagine an example of a burst pipeline with water gushing out; your first action would be to stop the leak before you can fix it. In similar teams in a cyber incident situation, the first action is, in this case, always about stopping the leak or a breach, then determining what has happened, how this incident occurred, and so on. Security teams can deploy specific security tools to contain the incident or use what is already deployed within an organization's IT environment.

  Examples include disconnecting the host from the network, network quarantining the host using an EDR tool, and shutting certain services down (not allowing access to users). This stage is also where security teams must preserve any evidence before they are eliminated. We learned about evidence preservation in *Chapter 2* and its importance in investigations and potential legal actions. In most situations, organizations that do not have the skills or capabilities to preserve evidence usually rely on third-party professionals who offer DFIR services.

- **Eradication and recovery**: In our view, the eradication and recovery and investigation and analysis phases occur in parallel, provided necessary forensic evidence is preserved. In the eradication and recovery stage, incident response teams work with other security teams within the organizations or authorized third parties to remediate the incident. This can include configurational changes, patching, or a complete system rebuild from backup or scratch. Once remediation is completed, these systems are restored to normal operations.

- **Investigation and analysis**: Once you have stopped the incident from escalating further, investigation teams take over the case. Investigation teams are responsible for analyzing what happened; this includes a review of logs and forensic artifacts and understanding how the incident occurred, what data was impacted, the extent of the damage, and so on. This stage also provides input to the detection, eradication, and recovery stages to detect any associated incidents and apply additional remediations or security hardening that are required for recovery activities. Often, this is the stage where investigation teams identify the incident's root cause. In incident response jargon, we call it **patient zero**. The investigation team will leverage threat intelligence to identify the threat actor, their motives, and potential **indicators of compromise** (**IoCs**) that may locate any additional investigative avenues.

- **Reporting**: Once the investigation has been wrapped up, key facts have been determined, and the root cause has been identified, the investigation team moves to the reporting stage. Ideally, the incident report will include all the aspects of the incidents, artifacts reviewed, a timeline of the incident's occurrence, actions performed, and so on. Once the report has been developed, it is circulated to various relevant stakeholders. Depending on the nature and severity of the incident, the incident reports may only be shared with a limited group, including, in some cases, a breach coach (external legal counsel) to support and prepare the organizations for any potential litigation risks resulting from the incident.

- **Post-incident reviews**: Once everything has been wrapped up and the organization has moved back to the business-as-usual phase, organizations and security teams typically conduct a debrief, or what is known as a post-incident review. Security teams review documentation and investigative notes that were prepared during and after the incident and identify procedural gaps on how to improve in detecting or mitigating this incident from reoccurring. Security teams update their incident response plan using the knowledge they've gained from handling this incident.

Having established the fundamental aspects of the incident response process, let's jump into the practical tools and techniques that are utilized in digital forensics investigations. These tools play a critical role in uncovering digital evidence, analyzing volatile memory, dissecting filesystems, and piecing together timelines of events.

Tools and techniques for digital forensic investigations

One of the challenges in any incident investigation is acquiring artifacts quickly and in a forensically sound manner. In some cases, investigators may collect artifacts to investigate the incident further and identify the root cause. Moving swiftly to collect artifacts and evidence is crucial to investigations. This section will explore some valuable host and memory artifacts for investigations.

Prerequisites

Before investigators can begin collecting their logs from the cloud console, we can utilize some of the prerequisites that were explored in previous chapters (enabling logs, audit trails, and so on), along with the ones listed here. These prerequisites will help investigators conduct their incident response activities much more smoothly:

- **Instance protection**: Some CSPs will allow instance protection once an incident is declared. For example, in AWS, you can configure your instance to prevent it from termination. This will ensure you are not terminating or deleting the instance once it shuts down and that all the artifacts and associated volumes are preserved for investigation. Investigators can even apply tags as a visual marker for security administrators not to change or update their configuration.

- **Decommission**: Deregister and decommission the instance from auto-scaling groups where possible.

- **Isolate instance**: Wherever possible, and if necessary, investigators should update the host firewall (the CSP's firewall) to limit traffic to external IPs and ports. Investigators can access the instance from the cloud console and not connect from the internet.

- **Inventory-associated volumes**: When an incident is declared, and investigators have identified the instance, inventory the volumes attached to the host as snapshots may be required for all the connected volumes.

- **Recreate in an isolated lab**: If the situation warrants, based on the investigative leads, then investigators should consider making a copy or snapshot of the instance and then using that to re-launch in a dedicated and isolated forensics lab hosted on the cloud to capture the necessary artifacts.

Cloud host forensics

Host forensics or digital forensics involves collecting, processing, analyzing, and preserving digital host-based evidence. It requires discovering artifacts, traces, and information not generally available to security tools and often hidden from general users. Host forensics plays a crucial role in cybersecurity and law enforcement investigations, providing insights into some of the actions taken by attackers or users, a timeline of activities, and so on. It is helpful in cases of intellectual property theft, data breaches, malware infections, and insider threats, and it is commonly used in ransomware cases.

Recognizing that this book is intended for DFIR professionals, we will look at various forensic elements that investigators can perform at a high level. We will also spend time identifying key artifact sources that can be useful in the event of investigations. Collecting artifacts from cloud instances is similar; the artifacts and event logs are consistent across the deployment model. So, there is no difference between a physical host deployed in a data center versus a host running on the cloud.

Key artifact sources

We want to learn about key sources of artifacts that can sometimes be referred to for investigation. These sources often provide evidence that pinpoints what activity a user or threat actor (subject of the investigation) could have done in a system. By querying these artifact repositories, you will learn about threat actors and the vast depth of information operating systems generally retain when a user operates a computing system.

However, note that with every iteration of Windows, Linux, or any other operating system, the information that's collected by the artifact or the artifact repository itself could change or may no longer be available. It is essential to note the version of the operating system, including major and minor versions, to prepare investigators on what artifacts would be available for a given version.

In the next subsection, we'll look at two prominent and commonly used operating systems that are deployed for servers and IT infrastructural environments. You will also see similar deployments in the cloud (irrespective of the cloud provider).

Windows operating system

One of the most popular operating systems is Windows; it collects tons of artifacts that can be very helpful for investigations. The following is a list of artifact repositories that Windows typically records. However, as indicated earlier, depending on the operating system's major and minor versions, some artifacts may be available in a different folder path or no longer available. Note that the following logs are not an exhaustive list, and third-party tools may collect additional records and artifacts that can be crucial for investigation:

- **Core Windows logs**:

  - `C:\Windows\System32\Tasks\*`: Contains XML files associated with Task Scheduler and contains information such as task definitions, task author, trigger criteria, and any task customizations. These are automated processes that trigger under specific conditions or at certain times. Threat actors use Task Scheduler to hide and evade detection while maintaining persistence. You may also see files associated with Task Scheduler created under `C:\Windows\Tasks\*` for some legacy systems.

  - `C:\Windows\Prefetch\*`: Prefetch is a Windows feature that allows the application to optimize loading times by preloading data files and libraries that it frequently uses. It provides forensic evidence or proof that an application was executed, including if any code or script was injected within an application (for example, code execution via PowerShell). When an application is executed for the first time, it creates a prefetch file that documents all the files and libraries that can be pre-loaded into memory from the disk before execution. Prefetch includes information such as executable name, execution times, and count.

  - `C:\Windows\System32\winevt\Logs\*`: Windows Event Logs are the most critical log sources every investigator will want to look into. Various categories of logs have dedicated log files that record associated events. Some of the important ones to look for are as follows:

    - `Security.evtx`: Login/logouts, destination hostname and IP address, alternate username, logon session ID, and logon type.

    - `System.evtx`: Windows system startup/shutdown time, service installs, driver failure/ installations, hardware changes, and any system-related activities.

    - `Windows PowerShell.evtx`: PowerShell script executions and cmdlet invocation, often corroborated with `Microsoft-Windows-WinRM%4Operational.evtx` for information on remote session authentication and session information and `Microsoft-Windows-PowerShell%4Operational.evtx` for script block logs.

    - `Microsoft-Windows-PowerShell%4Operational.evtx`: Records details of PowerShell executions, including script blocks, module loads, and script policies.

    - `Microsoft-Windows-TerminalServices-RDPClient%4Operational.evtx`: **Remote Desktop Connections** (**RDP**) activity and destination RDP connections including IP address and hostname (evidence of lateral movement initiation). It can be corroborated with `Security.evtx`.

- `Microsoft-Windows-TerminalServices-RemoteConnectionManager%4 Operational.evtx`: Evidence of the RDP source IP address and username (evidence of where lateral movement occurred). This can be corroborated with `Microsoft-Windows-Terminal Services-LocalSessionManager%4Operational.evtx`, `Microsoft-Windows-RemoteDesktopServices-RdpCoreTS%4Operational.evtx`, and `Security.evtx`.

- `Microsoft-Windows-TaskScheduler%4Operational.evtx`: Information about scheduled task execution, creation, and registration and corroborated with `Security.evtx` for evidence of administrator privilege usage.

- `Microsoft-Windows-WMI-Activity%4Operational.evtx`: **Windows Management Instrumentation** (**WMI**)-related activities, including WMI queries, WMI method invocations, and WMI provider operations.

- `Microsoft-Windows-WinRM%4Operational.evtx`: **Windows Remote Management** (**WinRM**) is used for remote administrations and provides information about remote sessions and authentications.

- `C:\Windows\System32\Logfiles\W3SVC1\*`: Contains information about **Internet Information Services** (**IIS**) activities, including incoming HTTP requests and responses, requested URLs, user agent strings, response codes, error codes, and descriptions. The log files also include server-side errors, application crashes, or issues. Investigators can use this information to perform traffic analysis, such as the number of requests and data transferred.

- `C:\Windows\appcompat\Programs\Amcache.hve`: **Application Compatibility** (**AppCompat**) is a cache or database that stores information about application compatibility. AppCompat is used to track application executions, including the full file path, last modification of an executable, and so on. In older Windows systems, this cache also records when the application was last executed. `Amcache.hve` records application installations and executions. It includes full application metadata and the SHA1 hash of the executable file.

- `C:\Windows\System32\config\SAM`: The Windows **Security Accounts Manager** (**SAM**) database that is responsible for storing local user account information and their unique **security identifier** (**SID**), password hashes, and account policies, such as password strength, account lockout policy, and so on. It also plays a crucial role in Window's authentication process. Irrespective of the Windows operating system version, Windows will automatically maintain the relevant SAM database and any local accounts created within the host machine. Access to the SAM database requires elevated privileges, and threat actors often try to attack the SAM database to compromise credentials and use it to perform other forms of attack.

- `C:\Windows\System32\config\SOFTWARE`: This is one of the critical registry hives that collects information about the system state, installed software, and various other configurational elements of Windows. Investigators can use the SOFTWARE registry hive to investigate if unauthorized software was installed, modified, or deleted. Investigators can also identify if any core elements were modified, such as startup programs (for maintaining persistence), system configurations (to lower defenses), and more.

- `C:\Windows\System32\config\SECURITY`: The `SECURITY` registry hive is responsible for recording all the configurations related to the operating system's security. This includes user accounts, associated account groups, password hashes, permissions in registry entries, and security policies. Investigators can analyze this registry hive to reconstruct threat actors, unauthorized user activity, and security policy violations. Like the `SAM` database, the `SECURITY` hive is also protected by the Windows operating system kernel and requires elevated privileges to modify.

- `C:\Windows\System32\config\*.LOG1`: The `LOG1` file is a transaction log file that ensures the integrity of relevant registry hives (including `SOFTWARE`, `SAM`, and `SECURITY`). When changes are made to system configurations, changes are written to the relevant transaction log `LOG1` file, and when the changes are committed to the hive, the transaction log is marked as complete.

- **User profiles**:

  - `C:\Users\*\AppData\Roaming\Microsoft\Windows\PowerShell\PSReadline\ConsoleHost_history.txt`: Provides command history for PowerShell console executions by a user.

  - `C:\Users\*\NTUser.DAT`: For every user, an `NTUSser.DAT` file is created automatically by Windows that contains information about user-specific configurations or preferences, user interactions with various applications, actions taken, and most recently accessed resources.

  - `C:\Users\*\NTUser.DAT.LOG1`: Similar to registry hives, this transaction log file records all the transactions (changes) before committing the changes within the `NTUser.DAT` file. Investigators can use this for further correlation of user activities.

- **Root drive (C:\, D;\, …)**:

  - `%SYSTEMDRIVE%\$Recycle.Bin\**`: `%SYSTEMDRIVE%` refers to the root drive partition nomenclature, which contains the `RecycleBin` folder. This folder, in turn, contains all the files and subfolders that are tagged for deletion. Investigators can use this to identify if any files were attempted to be deleted by the user or the threat actor.

  - `%SYSTEMDRIVE%\$LogFile`: `$LogFile` is a special Windows file associated with the filesystem, specifically the **New Technology File System** (**NTFS**). `$LogFile` records metadata and directory and file creations, modifications, and deletions. Investigators can parse `$LogFile` to identify system changes over time and obtain information that allows information to be recovered from file storage that's relevant to the investigation.

- `%SYSTEMDRIVE%\$MFT`: This refers to the **Master File Table (MFT)** of the NTFS filesystem. It provides metadata associated with files and directories, including timestamps, file sizes, and directory-to-file relationships. Investigators can use MFT to reconstruct the sequence of events concerning filesystem changes.

Linux operating systems

Given that most of the Linux ecosystem is open sourced and used in various industry sectors, including its application in the cloud, Linux provides investigators with much forensic value. When collecting forensic artifacts from Linux or performing live forensics, you should prioritize the following artifacts:

- `/etc/passwd`: A plaintext file that contains information such as the **username**, **User ID (UID)**, **Group ID (GID)**, **home path**, and **default shell** application.

- `/etc/group`: Similar to the `/etc/passwd` file, it stores information related to user groups on the system.

- `/etc/crontab`: Cron is a job scheduler that automates the execution of commands or scripts per a predefined schedule. Threat actors can use cron jobs to maintain persistence within an environment.

- `/etc/fstab`: Contains information about the filesystem, drives, and partitions, including how devices are mounted at startup.

- `/etc/rc.d/**`: Contains startup and shutdown scripts for services. Threat actors can use this directory to maintain persistence and evade detection.

- `/etc/init.d/**`: Similar to `/etc/rc.d/**`, this directory contains **init scripts** or initialization scripts for system services. Threat actors can use this directory to inject malicious scripts during system initialization.

- `/etc/systemd.d/**`: Contains additional configurations for init scripts. It also allows you to override or extend script scope and services.

- `/var/log/**`: This directory contains valuable event logs stored in files generated by system processes and applications.

- `/home/<username>/*`: The home directory is the user's directory (defined within `/etc/passwd`), allowing the user to store files, configurations, and user-specific data.

- `/home/*/.ssh/known_hosts`: Contains a list of public keys for remote servers that the user has previously used. It provides evidence of attempts of SSH-based connection to these remote servers.

- `/home/*/.ssh/autorized_keys`: It contains a list of public keys allowed to authenticate as the user for remote access. When a user wants to log into a remote server using SSH key-based authentication, their public key is added to the `authorized_keys` file on the server.

Other artifacts/metadata

Once we have collected host-specific artifacts, investigators investigating the cloud instance should also collect **instance metadata**, including instance configuration, IP address allocations, VPC Subnet assignments, policy configurations, and more.

As we can see, host forensics involves meticulously examining a computer or device's storage, operating system, and files to identify and gather critical digital evidence. This process uncovers artifacts such as log files, user profiles, registry entries, and system logs, aiding in reconstructing events, user activities, and potential security breaches.

Shifting our focus from host forensics, let's jump into memory forensics. Memory forensics uncovers vital insights by examining the volatile memory of a system, providing a deeper understanding of ongoing processes, active applications, and potentially concealed artifacts.

Fast forensic collection tools

Fast forensics refers to using streamlined and efficient methodologies and tools in digital forensics investigations. Traditional forensic processes can be time-consuming, leading to delays in investigations. Fast forensics aims to address this issue by prioritizing speed without compromising the integrity of the investigation. Investigators should consider fast forensics approaches to enhance their response times, allowing them to identify and mitigate cyber threats quickly, respond to incidents promptly, and minimize the impact of the incident.

Several tools have been developed to support fast forensics. Fast forensics is typically practical when dealing with a large organization with endpoints spread geographically. Some of the notable fast forensic tools are as follows:

- **CyLR**: CyLR is a live response tool that collects artifacts from various sources and creates a package that can be utilized in offline analysis. CyLR packages can be analyzed using Magnet Axiom or Sleutkit Autopsy tools. CyLR can be deployed via EDR or popular script deployment techniques for automated collections. It can be used to collect from Windows and Linux operating systems.

- **KAPE**: Developed by Eric Zimmerman, **Kroll Artifact Parser and Extractor** (**KAPE**) is known for its modular and extensible framework, making it highly adaptable to various digital forensic scenarios. The tool is particularly valued for its ability to collect artifacts from various sources within an operating system, helping investigators efficiently extract crucial evidence. KAPE utilizes a configuration file to define specific artifacts and locations of interest, allowing forensic practitioners to customize their data collection based on the requirements of a particular investigation.

- **PowerForensics**: PowerForensics, on the other hand, is a specific PowerShell module focused on forensics. It provides a set of cmdlets that enable users to interact with the NTFS filesystem, allowing for valuable forensic information to be extracted from Windows machines. PowerForensics can be used to analyze artifacts such as file metadata, file content, and other filesystem structures.

- **Kansa**: Kansa is an open source incident response and threat-hunting framework written in PowerShell. It facilitates collecting and analyzing artifacts from Windows systems to aid in security investigations. Kansa provides a set of PowerShell scripts and modules that can automate various aspects of the incident response process. The framework allows security professionals and incident responders to run predefined or custom PowerShell scripts across multiple endpoints in a network.

We have included more details in the *Further reading* section.

Memory forensics

Memory forensics is an advanced digital investigation technique that analyzes a computer or device's volatile memory (**random access memory – RAM**). Unlike traditional host forensics, which examines storage and files, memory forensics dives into the live state of a system, revealing active processes, running applications, and hidden artifacts that can provide valuable insights into cyberattacks, malicious activities, and volatile data that might not be stored on disk. Everything that's executed within the operating system of the host has to go through the host's memory. This approach offers a unique perspective on the digital landscape, enabling investigators to uncover crucial evidence that might otherwise remain concealed.

Memory forensics captures information such as running processes and threads, malware or rootkits, open file handles, caches and clipboard contents, encryption keys, hardware and software configuration, registry keys, websites visited, and commands entered on the console.

Memory forensics in cloud environments presents a unique set of challenges and opportunities. As organizations increasingly migrate their systems to cloud platforms, understanding and analyzing volatile memory becomes crucial for detecting security breaches, insider threats, and unauthorized access.

Especially in the cloud, memory forensics faces challenges due to the shared nature of resources, dynamic provisioning, and limited access to physical hardware. Virtualization and containerization add layers of complexity, making it essential to adapt traditional memory forensics methodologies. However, the cloud also offers advantages such as centralization of logs, ease of scalability, and the potential to capture memory snapshots across various instances simultaneously. This can aid in identifying sophisticated attacks that might target multiple instances or users within the cloud environment.

Let's look at some primary artifacts investigators should typically collect and analyze. These artifacts resemble the Windows operating system running in the cloud or on a server. Given that memory forensics is worthy of a separate book, we assume you are familiar with the basics of computer memory and its various elements and functionalities.

Memory acquisition tools

In the context of cloud forensics, there are a few options for investigators: collect and analyze the memory images of a live system or collect and analyze the memory artifacts written to the disk in an offline host. The following figure illustrates the distinction between live and dead systems and the tools available for collecting memory images from them:

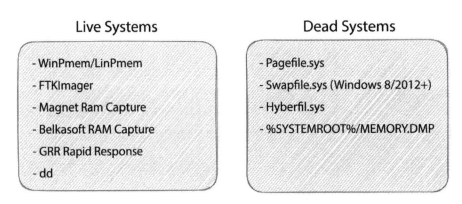

Figure 8.2 – Memory acquisition sources/tools

Let's look at some of the toolsets that can acquire memory in a live system while looking at memory remnants of a dead system that can be collected for forensic investigations:

- **Live systems**: Live system memory acquisition tools are essential components of memory forensics, allowing investigators to capture and analyze the volatile memory of a running host system. Here are a few live system memory acquisition tools:

  - **WinPmem**: **WinPmem** is a memory acquisition tool for **Windows** operating systems. It operates as a kernel module to ensure reliable memory captures without disrupting the system's operation. It provides forensically sound memory dumps for subsequent analysis using compatible tools such as **Volatility**.

  - **FTKImager**: This is one of the most popular and easy-to-use tools for memory capture for Windows-based operating systems. Designed primarily for disk imaging and data acquisitions, it can capture live memory images, including collecting pagefiles and memory dumps if required.

  - **Magnet RAM Capture**: Magnet RAM Capture is a tool designed for quickly capturing live memory from Windows systems. It's known for its simplicity and efficiency, making it suitable for experienced analysts and those new to memory forensics.

- **Belkasoft RAM Capture**: **Belkasoft RAM Capture** is a memory acquisition tool designed to capture the live memory (RAM) of Windows computers. It was developed by Belkasoft, a digital forensics and incident response software company. Like other memory acquisition tools, Belkasoft RAM Capture is utilized in digital investigations to gather volatile data from running systems for subsequent analysis.

- **GRR Rapid Response**: **GRR Rapid Response** (**GRR**) is an open source incident response platform created by Google. It allows security teams to perform remote live forensics and investigations across many endpoints in a networked environment. GRR offers real-time data collection, remote memory acquisition, filesystem analysis, and process monitoring. Its client-server architecture allows administrators and analysts to manage and control agents deployed on target systems centrally.

- **dd**: In Linux systems, dd is a command that's commonly used on Linux/Unix platforms for low-level copying and conversion of data. In the context of digital forensics, dd is used in Linux/Unix systems for acquiring a copy of the memory or RAM. Note that it's not typically recommended due to the potential risks and challenges involved. Improper use of dd for memory acquisition can result in inaccurate or incomplete memory captures and disrupt the target system's operation.

- **Offline systems**: Also known as dead systems, these are the systems that investigators cannot access remotely or connect to. In offline systems, investigators look for memory remnants left on the disk when a host was pulled offline. These affect what information can be gathered by investigators. Some of the most common artifacts are as follows:

  - **Page files (pagefile.sys and hiberfil.sys)**: In Windows-based operating systems, a page file (pagefile.sys) is a virtual memory extension, allowing the memory to use this storage to store data temporarily. In older Windows versions, this file is known as swapfile.sys. Typically, this is performed when physical RAM space is at capacity and applications are queued for execution; Windows will automatically offload memory pages into disk via pagefile.sys. From a forensic perspective, pagefile.sys can contain remnants of sensitive or valuable information, including fragments of files, registry data, and even passwords. These remnants might not be present in the main memory or traditional disk storage, making the page file a potential source of evidence. Note that the page file is volatile, meaning its contents are not retained after a system shutdown or reboot. However, if a system is hibernated, the contents of the page file can persist in the hibernation file (hiberfil.sys) for potential recovery. It's a good practice to capture page files during memory acquisition.

  - **Crash dumps**: Crash dumps are also an excellent source for memory analysis. Typically, crash dumps are stored as MEMORY.DMP in the %SystemRoot% folder of your Windows operating system. Based on the size of the dump file, investigators can identify if it's a complete memory dump (also known as **Kernal Memory Dump**) or a snapshot of a memory page that was dumped during a crash (**Active Memory Dump**). In any case, existing memory analysis tools should allow investigators to parse and analyze these crash dumps. Note that in Linux systems, memory pages written to disk are known as **swap files** and are only utilized when the allocated memory is insufficient. Investigators can only collect the swap files. Swap files are not retained on the disk when rebooting a Linux system. Note that investigators may see swap files on disk if a Linux system is hibernated. However, this is rare; Linux systems are not commonly hibernated.

While there are plenty of options for collecting memory images (live or dead systems), it is essential to note that from a cloud forensics standpoint, it is no different from collecting memory swap files or pages from the disk as that of a dead box system. Investigators must collect the correct disk copies associated with the respective cloud instances. Now that we have a memory snapshot or an image, let's explore the tools to analyze them.

Memory analysis tools

In this section, we'll look at some of the tools that are commonly used during an investigation, especially for analyzing system memory artifacts. Once memory images have been collected, there are special tools that carve information off memory:

- **Volatility**: Volatility is one of the most popular open source memory forensics frameworks and a preferred choice by investigators for memory analysis. Written entirely in Python, it allows you to analyze memory snapshots and supports various operating systems. It provides multiple plugins for extracting information about running processes, network activity, registry data, and more. Volatility supports multiple memory dump formats and is extensively used by professionals in the field. Volatility can also natively analyze older Windows versions of **hiberfil.sys** and **pagefile.sys**. However, various other specific tools are developed to address challenges and handle changes to hibernate files with changes to Windows operating systems in a much better way.

- **Velociraptor**: Velociraptor is an open source endpoint monitoring and digital forensics platform designed to provide high-fidelity data collection and analysis capabilities across a network of endpoints. One of the critical features of Velociraptor is its ability to perform live memory analysis on endpoints to uncover insights, detect anomalies, and gather evidence for incident response and forensic investigations. Analysts can tailor memory analysis tasks to their specific investigation needs with support for customizable queries and plugins. Beyond memory analysis, Velociraptor facilitates proactive threat detection through predefined indicators and patterns. Its centralized management, workflow automation, scalability, and active user community contribute to its effectiveness in various environments (physical, virtual, and the cloud).

- **Rekall**: Rekall is a fork on Volatility and enhanced it by enabling live memory forensics. Like Volatility, Rekall includes most of the features of Volatility and can analyze **hiberfil.sys**, **pagefile. sys**, and swap files in different operating systems.

- **GRR**: GRR is another open source incident response platform that is agent-based. Investigators must deploy an agent to capture telemetry or perform live memory forensics. Although more powerful memory analysis tools are available, such as Velociraptor and Volatility, GRR remains a valuable tool in any organization's DFIR arsenal due to its unique strengths and capabilities. GRR is designed explicitly for collecting endpoint data, including real-time analysis of memory files, making it a versatile tool for any cybersecurity team.

- **Magnet AXIOM**: Designed to assist law enforcement agencies, corporate investigators, and DFIR professionals, Magnet AXIOM is a license-based commercial tool developed by Magnet Forensics that focuses on efficiently collecting, analyzing, and presenting digital evidence from various sources. It supports data acquisition from diverse sources such as computers, smartphones, and cloud services. Magnet AXIOM also supports the analysis of artifacts such as files, emails, and chat messages. It supports memory images captured from various operating systems, including **hiberfil.sys**, **pagefile.sys**, and swap files. It can also parse quick forensics packages collected through multiple third-party tools. Magnet AXIOM supports timeline analysis and reconstructs events from digital evidence. It also supports keyword searches, data carving, and advanced filtering to help investigators quickly pinpoint relevant information. Finally, it streamlines report generation, supports collaboration, and specializes in mobile device analysis.

In conclusion, host and memory forensics are indispensable pillars in digital investigations. The analysis of artifacts on operating systems, coupled with the extraction of volatile memory data, allows digital forensic investigators to reconstruct digital trails, uncover hidden evidence, and decipher the story behind cyber incidents. Host forensics comprehensively explains a system's history and user activities.

In contrast, memory forensics enables real-time snapshots to be captured, exposing the inner workings of processes and potential threats. Intertwined with advanced tools and methodologies, these disciplines collectively contribute to the pursuit of truth and justice in the dynamic landscape of digital forensics. We will learn how to acquire disk and memory images from the cloud in *Chapter 10*. The following section focuses on techniques to perform live forensic analysis using various tools, as well as perform threat hunting, given that threat actors have evolved and use sophisticated techniques to hide malware in plain sight.

Live forensic analysis and threat hunting

Digital forensic investigators operate on the principle that malware must always run on memory; there is nowhere they can hide. However, in recent times, technology has evolved to make memory massive and less volatile, giving rise to fileless malware – that is, malware that does not touch the disk – which maintains this hidden nature until execution time. The following sections will cover some of the tools that modern corporate investigators utilize to identify malware and conduct threat hunting, helping you understand common persistence mechanisms that malware uses.

EDR-based threat hunting

Advancements in computational technologies, cloud infrastructure, and support for massive disk and memory sizes have made it necessary for a new set of tools that can continuously monitor a host and collect live telemetry data on disk and memory, capture every footprint of an application, spot malware, and stop the attack before it can get worse. This technology, known as **EDR**, is a new class of security tools (commercial tools) that collects advanced telemetry and uses various techniques beyond standard signature-based detection to identify and detect malware and respond to the threat tactically. We typically refer to EDRs as antiviruses on steroids as they can do much more than a simple antivirus, which threat actors can easily turn off or evade in terms of being detected.

EDRs generally operate at the operating system kernel level and can identify various activities on disk and memory beyond what a user can see. EDRs can track process calls, information regarding child processes, Windows **application programing interface (API)** usage, the command line passed to each process, network connections, process thread information, **Dynamic Link Libraries (DLLs)**, file handles, registry handles, and more.

Note that EDRs are not forensic tools. However, they do enhance forensic investigation by providing high-fidelity telemetry that would otherwise be missed if EDRs were not deployed within an organization. Most popular EDRs also offer forensic teams the ability to perform live queries on the host. You can query the host system using preset command-line parameters and perhaps even run a custom-built script to collect additional information or artifacts. Forensic investigators typically use live querying to download artifacts, logs, or even quick forensic packages for offline analysis.

Diving deep with EDR hunting

Let's assume that, as investigators, an EDR tool was deployed as part of the breach response. We are using the **SentinelOne Singularity platform** (used with permission) to demonstrate hunting using this method.

Once the SentinelOne agent has been installed on the infected system, it typically scans the system and starts breach containment, meaning any detected malware is contained. An alert is raised on the central Singularity console. This becomes the starting point for investigating or hunting, and investigators can continue to pursue their investigation via this EDR tool. In the following screenshot, notice that there's additional information under the **Threats** dashboard while providing options for kick-starting threat hunting. The **SHA1** hash also allows investigators to look at other threat intelligence sources, such as VirusTotal:

THREAT FILE NAME	2D9655C659970145AB3F2D74BB...		🗐 Copy Details 📄 Download Threat File
Path	\Device\HarddiskVolume3\Users\user\Downloads\2D9655C659970145...	Initiated By	Agent Policy
Command Line Arguments	N/A	Engine	SentinelOne Cloud
Process User	DESKTOP-M8S19S2\user	Detection type	Static
Publisher Name	N/A	Classification	Malware
Signer Identity	N/A	File Size	98.00 KB
Signature Verification	NotSigned	Storyline	Static Threat - View in DV
Originating Process	7zG.exe	Threat Id	1772371477498962493
SHA1	41e8db9bb005fce152e08c20e6392e0a5d44bb6e		

Figure 8.3 – Sample alert on SentinelOne EDR (produced with permission)

Once investigators can obtain enough information about the circumstances of the threat, they can begin to perform their threat hunting. SentinelOne offers multiple ways to hunt for threats. One of the easiest ways is through their Singularity **eXtended Detection and Response** (**XDR**) module, which presents additional telemetry data, allowing investigators to slice and dice them, more or less through a live flow of telemetry data. Based on the threat dashboard information, we can use the SHA1 hash to conduct deep dive hunting using Singularity XDR. We start by searching for the hash value that was identified earlier. The SentinelOne Singularity XDR module offers search filters for investigators to hunt through telemetry data easily. In the following example, we're using the following to search for the `tgt.file.sha1 = "41e8db9bb005fce152e08c20e6392e0a5d44bb6e"` SHA1 entry:

Event Time	Name	Event type	Event Source	Source Process Unique ID	Event Target	Event Details
Sep 12 2023 05: 48:02	SentinelOne	Pre Execution Detection	Agent UUID 273e248572d24254878249...	47C443E407D6070D	Target File Path C:\Users\user\Downloads\2...	Target File size 100352
Sep 12 2023 05: 48:02	SentinelOne	File Modification	Agent UUID 273e248572d24254878249...	47C443E407D6070D	Target File Path C:\Users\user\Downloads\2...	Target File size 100352
Sep 12 2023 05: 45:43	SentinelOne	Pre Execution Detection	Agent UUID 273e248572d24254878249...	846443E407D6070D	Target File Path C:\Users\user\Downloads\2...	Target File size 100352
Sep 12 2023 05: 45:20	SentinelOne	File Modification	Agent UUID 273e248572d24254878249...	846443E407D6070D	Target File Path C:\Users\user\Downloads\2...	Target File size 100352

Figure 8.4 – SHA1 hash-based hunting in the SentinelOne Singularity XDR module

Notice that each result has a checkbox that provides more information regarding the data collected. This includes information regarding the event itself, the account it was executed under, the SentinelOne agent's name and endpoint makeup, and details of the detection, including process information and command-line parameters supplied. Each entry can further be used to hunt deeper, which is especially useful for complex threat scenarios.

SentinelOne Singularity XDR natively presents a collection of all the fields in the telemetry data. The **FIELDS** view allows investigators to quickly jump in and investigate without spending time identifying their way around it. Here is an example of the field list that's part of the navigation options. It also provides aggregated field results for investigators to identify any anomalies. Each result can be clicked through to apply relevant search filters for hunts:

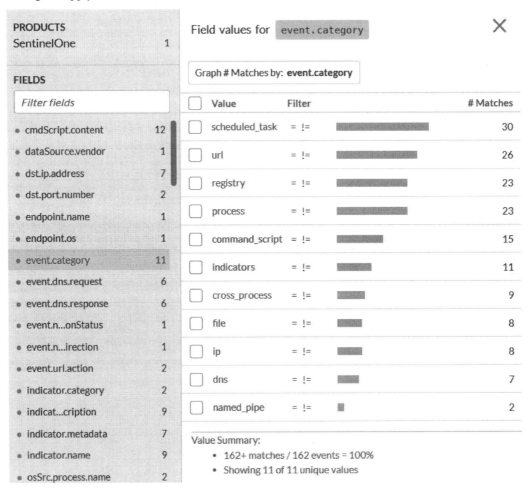

Figure 8.5 – SentinelOne Singularity XDR's fields

Once initial hunts have been performed using the Singularity XDR module, based on the results, investigators can quickly pivot to obtain more information regarding the activities around the detected threat. Through telemetric data, we know that the threat actor used PowerShell to attempt to access and execute the malware. The sample screenshot shows the event data identifying this threat actor's action, allowing investigators to pivot further to obtain more situational information about the event.

Investigators can use the **Event Details** tab when a relevant event entry is accessed (see *Figure 8.3*). **Event Details** provides more information about the event, including the commands for invoking the malware:

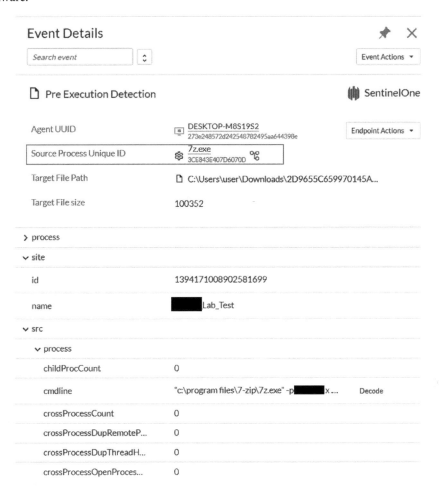

Figure 8.6 – Event Details based on the SigularityXDR search result

As we can see, EDR enhances the process of detecting and preventing malware from being executed. In the context of cloud forensics, having an EDR/XDR tool to investigate a cloud endpoint combined with the logs generated on the cloud console enhances the investigator's ability to analyze and identify how the threat occurred. Furthermore, from a legal standpoint, this allows investigators to corroborate the events from various sources, ensuring the identified investigations are forensically sound and legally acceptable.

Hunting for malware

Hunting for malware is a proactive approach to uncovering malicious applications/software within a host. This technique goes beyond traditional security measures by actively seeking signs of compromise, identifying root causes, and preventing future incidents. Incident responders analyze system behavior, employ threat intelligence, and leverage memory analysis to uncover signs of compromise. By scrutinizing logs, conducting sandboxing, and utilizing automated tools, they detect anomalies and patterns associated with malware. Here are some of the ways malware will commonly try to evade detection:

- **Service hijacking**: Service hijacking involves malicious actors gaining control over system services, enabling them to execute arbitrary code within the context of legitimate processes. By compromising trusted services, attackers can execute malicious commands or payloads, evading detection. One real-life example is the **Zeus** banking Trojan, which exploited the WMI service to execute malicious code and maintain persistence on infected systems.

- **Process injection**: Process injection is a technique that malware uses to insert its code into a legitimate process, effectively hiding its presence within a trusted application's memory space. Common injection methods include DLL injection, reflective DLL injection, and process hollowing. Detecting process injection involves monitoring memory regions for unexpected modifications, analyzing process memory for code inconsistencies, and examining API calls to identify signs of injected code execution. The **TrickBot** malware used process injection techniques such as reflective DLL injection to inject malicious code into legitimate processes, evading detection by security solutions.

- **Alternate Data Streams** (**ADS**): ADS provides a way to hide data within a legitimate file by attaching additional data streams. Malware can use ADS to store its code or configuration, making detection challenging. Hunting for ADS involves analyzing file metadata, checking for multiple data streams within files, and monitoring unusual data stream associations.

- **Web shells**: Web shells are malicious scripts or code snippets embedded within web applications or servers, allowing attackers to gain remote access and control. The **Shellshock** vulnerability allowed attackers to inject malicious code into web server environments, effectively deploying web shells to gain unauthorized access.

- **Packing**: Packing involves compressing or encrypting malware files to obfuscate their contents and prevent straightforward analysis. Malware typically unpacks in memory during runtime, making it difficult for investigators to sample it and identify its true nature. Detecting packing involves identifying packed executable headers, analyzing file entropy levels, and employing unpacking tools or techniques to reveal the original code. One of the most common application packers that legitimate applications and malware use is **UPX**.

- **Code signing**: Malware authors might sign their code with stolen or fraudulently obtained digital certificates to appear legitimate and avoid detection by security software. Detecting code signed with valid certificates involves checking the certificate's authenticity, examining the certificate chain, and monitoring for revoked certificates or anomalies in the certificate's usage. There have been multiple examples in recent history where attackers stole an organization's code signing certificate to sign malware and use it for downstream supply chain attacks.

- **Fileless malware**: Fileless malware operates in memory without leaving traces on disk, making detection difficult. This technique often involves leveraging scripting languages or exploiting system tools. Detecting these techniques requires collecting specific logs, such as PowerShell, and obtaining a memory image. EDRs are a great way to detect these attacks since they monitor and track filesystem changes and memory activities. Popular fileless malware methods use PowerShell's **IEX** cradle to download an application or additional scripts in memory and execute it at runtime without ever touching the disk. Recently, threat actors have been spotted using PowerShell Empire, a framework that allows fileless malware delivery techniques.

As we can see, threat actors can hide and evade detection on a host in various ways. While we discussed the most common and obvious ones, advanced threat actor groups use innovative techniques. To some extent, malware running in a cloud infrastructure may make an investigator's life easier because CSPs have integrated various security tools to identify and spot malicious activities.

Moreover, most CSPs partner with multiple security vendors that provide tooling and visibility into these hosts, thus helping investigators identify malware more quickly than traditional investigative methods. For example, AWS GuardDuty can scan the VMs directly without any agent installation and provide visibility into the malware detection capability. At the same time, GCP's CloudSCC and Azure's Security Center have similar features that monitor the VMs and notify the administrator of malicious programs. In either case, these detections are provided by CSP's partners yet available for investigators in the respective CSP security consoles. We'll cover these tools in *Chapters 4*, *5*, and *6*.

Common persistence mechanisms

We will now look at common persistence mechanisms that malware can typically employ. It is no different in the context of the cloud since malware will run irrespective of the underlying infrastructure:

- **AutoStart Extension Point (ASEP)**: ASEP is a concept in the Microsoft Windows operating system that allows applications and services to launch and run when the system starts up automatically. These extension points allow developers to integrate their software into the Windows startup process, ensuring their applications or services are available and operational as soon as the system boots up. However, given its features and the intent to help developers, it aids malware operators in persisting in an environment by automatically launching itself when a host is booted. Here are some common ASEPs:

  - **Service Control Manager (SCM) services**: System services are configured to start automatically during boot through SCM. These services run in the background and perform various system-level tasks.

- **Run keys in the Windows Registry**: Entries in the Run key of the Windows Registry start applications or scripts during every user login, allowing user-specific applications to launch automatically. Some of the common Registry keys to scan for are as follows:

```
Computer\HKEY_CURRENT_USER\Software\Microsoft\Windows\
CurrentVersion\Run
Computer\HKEY_CURRENT_USER\Software\Microsoft\Windows\
CurrentVersion\RunOnce
Computer\HKEY_LOCAL_MACHINE\SOFTWARE\Microsoft\Windows\
CurrentVersion\Run
Computer\HKEY_LOCAL_MACHINE\SOFTWARE\Microsoft\Windows\
CurrentVersion\RunOnce
```

- **Startup folders**: Applications placed in the user's or system's startup folders are automatically launched when a user logs in, enabling user-specific customization of startup behavior. One of the most common folders that's used by threat actors to maintain persistence is as follows:

```
%AppData%\Roaming\Microsoft\Windows\Start Menu\Programs\Startup
```

- **Scheduled tasks**: Scheduled tasks configured to run at system startup or user login times are managed by Windows Task Scheduler and can perform various actions, such as updates or maintenance tasks.

- **Group Policy Objects (GPOs)**: GPOs are one of the most common ways threat actors maintain persistence within an organization. They do this by creating a malicious GPO with the company's domain controller to prepare and dispatch malware copies for persistence and execution. Moreover, threat actors can tweak the GPO to control how malware is deployed across the enterprise centrally. Threat actors can also create a scheduled task when a condition is met and can either download scripts or trigger malware execution. Most ransomware operators use GPOs to centrally control and deploy ransomware across the organization, leaving no time for security administrators to stop the attack.

- **DLL hijacking**: DLL hijacking is a technique that's exploited by attackers to achieve malware persistence by manipulating how Windows loads DLLs. During DLL loading, Windows follows a specific order to locate the required DLLs, including standard directories such as the application's folder and system directories. Attackers identify a vulnerable application and place a malicious DLL with the same name as the needed one in a guide the application searches. When the application starts, the malicious DLL is loaded instead of the legitimate one, executing the attacker's code within the application's context. This allows the attacker to establish persistence, run arbitrary code, and potentially gain control over the compromised system. Due to the regular use of the targeted application, the malicious code executes consistently, ensuring persistence even after the system reboots.

- **WMI event consumers**: Malware persistence through WMI event consumers involves leveraging WMI's capabilities to execute malicious actions at specific trigger events. Here are the steps attackers might take to achieve this form of persistence. These steps are ultimately stored in a **Managed Object Format (MOF)** file, which is used to register new classes within the WMI repository:

  A. **Create a malicious event consumer**: Attackers create a WMI event consumer, a script or executable designed to execute when a specific WMI event occurs. System events such as startup, login, or other custom triggers could trigger this event. The malicious event consumer contains instructions to execute the attacker's payload.

  B. **Event filter and binding**: Attackers create an event filter that defines the conditions under which the malicious event consumer should execute. This filter is associated with a specific trigger event. They then bind the event filter to the malicious event consumer, establishing a link between the filter and the payload containing the script or executable.

  C. **Trigger event execution**: When the defined trigger event occurs, the associated event filter evaluates whether the conditions are met. If the conditions are satisfied, the WMI event consumer executes the payload, which could be malware, a script, or an executable. This payload runs in the context of the WMI service, allowing attackers to establish persistence, execute arbitrary code, and potentially gain control over the compromised system.

Investigators should refer to the following commands to query the WMI repository and determine malicious WMI:

```
> Get-WmiObject -Class __FilterToConsumerBinding -Namespace
root\subscription
> Get-WmiObject -Class __EventFilter -Namespace root\
subscription
> Get-WmiObject -Class __EventConsumer -Namespace root\
subscription
strings -q C:\windows\system32\wbem\repository\objects.data
```

In summary, the convergence of live forensics, EDR solutions, proactive malware hunting, and advanced persistence mechanisms underscore a comprehensive approach to modern cybersecurity. Live forensics, powered by cutting-edge tools and techniques, provides real-time insights into ongoing threats, enabling swift incident response.

We are now transitioning to the realm of network forensics. Network forensics is pivotal in uncovering cyber threats as it allows us to examine network activities, traffic patterns, and communication behavior. By delving into the intricacies of network data, we will gain invaluable insights into potential breaches, malicious activities, and the broader tactics employed by adversaries. This is highly vital in the context of cloud forensics.

Network forensics

As this section's title suggests, network forensics is an approach to forensically analyzing network protocols, packets, and any artifacts on the wire. Network forensics in the context of cloud environments involves analyzing network traffic, communication patterns, and data flows between CSP services and external users to uncover potential security breaches, data exfiltration, and unauthorized access. By examining network data within the cloud infrastructure, we can create a comprehensive picture of events, identify anomalies, and detect the traces left behind by cyber threats. Fundamentally, investigators must have access to network data to conduct this analysis. This deeper scrutiny allows us to respond to incidents effectively, mitigate risks, and maintain a resilient cloud security posture.

Basic networking concepts

In network forensics, investigators must always remember that any network communication is broken down into the layers outlined by the network communication model, which can be **Open Systems Interconnection** (**OSI**) or **Transmission Control Protocol/Internet Protocol** (**TCP/IP**). These models provide a clear picture to investigators of how a threat actor accessed a host and what protocols were used by the threat actor. Let's look at these two models in more detail. Note that we assume you are familiar with this area; this is only a refresher:

- **OSI model**: This model is a framework that standardizes the functions and interactions of various networking protocols, serving as a guide for designing and understanding how different networking technologies communicate. The model is divided into seven layers, each responsible for specific tasks and functions. The following figure outlines the seven layers and associated protocols that operate within each of those layers. In the context of the cloud, lower-level layers are managed by CSPs. This includes the **physical layer** and **data link layer**. In contrast, the **network layer** is a shared responsibility between cloud customers and CSPs since this layer allows customers to create their VPCs. To some extent, the **transport layer** is a shared responsibility if a specific IPsec needs to be configured, for example. On the other hand, the **session**, **presentation**, and **application layers** are the responsibility of cloud customers. While CSPs act as enablers, cloud customers are responsible for configuring and securing them:

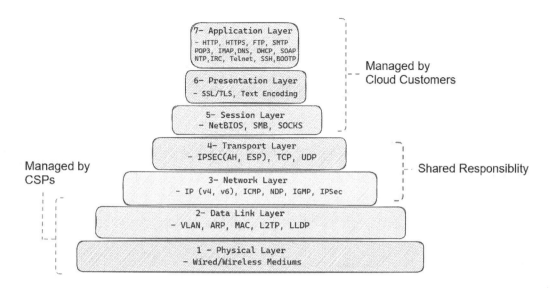

Figure 8.7 – OSI model and cloud responsibilities

- **TCP/IP reference model**: This model is a widely used framework for understanding and describing the functionalities of networking protocols that power the internet and many other networks. Unlike the seven-layer OSI model, the TCP/IP model consists of four layers, each with its own set of protocols and responsibilities; however, it closely aligns with the OSI model. The following figure shows a breakdown of the TCP/IP reference model's layers and supported protocols. In the context of the cloud, the reference models' lower layers, the **link layer** and the **CSPs**, typically handle the **internet layer**. In contrast, the customer and CSPs share responsibility for the **transport layer**, allowing customers to create their VPC subnets. Typically, it's the customer's responsibility to manage the **application layer**:

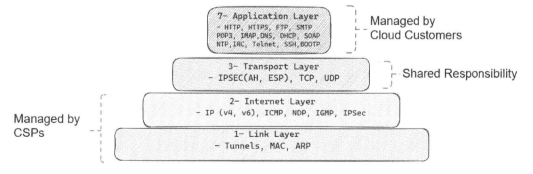

Figure 8.8 – TCP/IP reference model and cloud responsibilities

In the next section, we will explore log sources that are vital for investigative purposes, and we will also explore some tools for easier network analysis.

Cloud network forensics – log sources and tools

Let's look at some of the network artifacts that can be leveraged from CSPs and cloud instances:

- **VPC flow logs**: In the previous chapters (*Chapter 4*, *Chapter 5*, and *Chapter 6*), we looked at how to turn on and enable VPC flow logs. These are the most essential logs an investigator can access for network investigation. While VPC flow logs do not capture entire network traffic packets, analyzing and determining the source and destination nodes for malicious activities is vital.

- **tcpdump outputs**: In situations where VPC flow logs are not helpful, such as when examining data exfiltration and uncovering what data was exported by the threat actor, investigators need an entire packet dump. tcpdump is a widely popular network capture framework for collecting complete network packets and is vital for identifying threat actor activities on the network. With tcpdump outputs, investigators can trace the threat actor activities and sessions, determine transferred files or malware, and even reconstruct the files or malware from the packet capture for further analysis. With full packets, investigators can also replay and identify vulnerabilities exploited in the environment.

- **Logs from cloud-based firewalls and web application firewalls (WAFs)**: Most cloud-based organizations may also deploy a cloud-based firewall, which is a virtual firewall instance, or use CSP's native firewalling capabilities (with its limited features). Cloud-based firewalls generate logs that detail network traffic, including allowed and denied connections, while WAFs focus on web application-related traffic, filtering out malicious requests. Analyzing these logs can identify patterns of unauthorized access, attacks, and potential breaches. Investigators can reconstruct events, pinpoint vulnerabilities, and understand attackers' tactics by correlating firewall and WAF logs with other forensic data, such as system logs and packet captures. These logs serve as a crucial source of evidence in cloud network forensics, facilitating swift and accurate incident detection, response, and mitigation measures.

Now that we have an idea of the tools we can use to capture network traffic information, let's look at an example of using one of the popular network investigation tools available for investigators.

Network investigation tools

Network investigation tools in DFIR are essential resources that allow investigators to delve deep into network activities, analyze traffic patterns, and uncover potential security breaches. For example, investigators can tap the network to identify data exfiltration or use malicious code on a cloud instance. These tools provide the means to scrutinize network data, identify anomalies, trace the origins of threats, and reconstruct the sequence of events leading up to and during a security incident without accessing the host directly in the middle of an incident.

Not only do network investigations allow for a deeper dive, but they also provide essential IoCs that investigators can correlate with multiple sources, such as by using the IP address of the threat-actor-controlled remote server for data exfiltration, which can then be tracked within the SIEM tools to determine if there is any other evidence of exfiltration across the environment. Let's explore the diverse network investigation tools and techniques that are integral to modern DFIR practices.

Arkime

Arkime, formerly known as Moloch, is a powerful open source network investigation tool designed to capture, store, and analyze large volumes of network traffic data. Arkime provides investigators and incident responders with a comprehensive platform to investigate and understand network activities, detect anomalies, and uncover potential security threats. With its focus on scalability and flexibility, Arkime is particularly suited for analyzing vast network traffic in both on-premises and cloud environments.

Arkime offers several key features that make it a valuable tool in network investigation:

- **Packet capture and storage**: Arkime captures and stores network packets in a scalable and efficient manner, allowing for the retention of extensive historical traffic data for analysis.

- **Search and analysis**: The tool provides advanced search and filtering capabilities, enabling users to query and analyze network data based on various attributes, such as IP addresses, ports, protocols, and time ranges.

- **Session reconstruction**: Arkime can reconstruct network sessions from captured data, providing a holistic view of conversations and interactions between network nodes and understanding the context of communication.

- **Metadata extraction**: Arkime extracts metadata from network traffic and packet data, providing a higher-level overview of communications and facilitating efficient data analysis.

- **Visualization and reporting**: The tool visualizes network traffic patterns, helping analysts identify trends and anomalies. It also supports customizable reporting for documenting findings.

- **Customization and extensibility**: Arkime allows users to develop custom plugins and parsers to accommodate specific network protocols or applications, enhancing flexibility and adaptability.

- **Integration with other tools**: Arkime can integrate with other network and security tools, enabling seamless information sharing and enhanced analysis capabilities.

Arkime's ability to handle large-scale data analysis and its focus on aiding network investigations make it an indispensable tool in the DFIR toolkit. By leveraging its features, investigators can effectively detect, respond to, and mitigate network-related threats, ultimately bolstering their organization's cybersecurity posture. Let's look at an example of ingesting and analyzing a sample full packet capture from a cloud instance using Arkime.

Working with Arkime

Working with Arkime is easy; it has an intuitive **user interface** (**UI**) that allows you to perform slice-and-dice activities on network logs. Investigators have a choice of capturing the live network traffic or uploading an offline PCAP file that was collected from the infected systems. We assume investigators have access to a virtual Arkime environment. Arkime's UI can be accessed from any browser at the default location – that is, `http://<Arkime.ipAddress>:8005`:

1. The following figure represents the binary file that's shipped with Arkime, which is created explicitly for offline PCAP ingestion – `capture`:

```
user@arkime:/opt/arkime/bin$ ./capture --help
Usage:
  capture [OPTION?] - capture

Help Options:
  -h, --help              Show help options

Application Options:
  -c, --config            Config file name, default '/opt/arkime/etc/config.ini'
  -r, --pcapfile          Offline pcap file
  -R, --pcapdir           Offline pcap directory, all *.pcap files will be processed
  -m, --monitor           Used with -R option monitors the directory for closed files
  --packetcnt             Number of packets to read from each offline file
  --delete                In offline mode delete files once processed, requires --copy
  -s, --skip              Used with -R option and without --copy, skip files already processed
  --reprocess             In offline mode reprocess files, use the same files table entry
  --recursive             When in offline pcap directory mode, recurse sub directories
  -n, --node              Our node name, defaults to hostname.  Multiple nodes can run on same host
  --host                  Override hostname, this is what remote viewers will use to connect
  -t, --tag               Extra tag to add to all packets, can be used multiple times
  -F, --filelist          File that has a list of pcap file names, 1 per line
  --op                    FieldExpr=Value to set on all session, can be used multiple times
  -o, --option            Key=Value to override config.ini
  -v, --version           Show version number
  -d, --debug             Turn on all debugging
  -q, --quiet             Turn off regular logging
  --copy                  When in offline mode copy the pcap files into the pcapDir from the config file
  --dryrun                dry run, nothing written to databases or filesystem
  --flush                 In offline mode flush streams between files
  --insecure              Disable certificate verification for https calls
  --nolockpcap            Don't lock offline pcap files (ie., allow deletion)
```

Figure 8.9 – Arkime "capture" for processing PCAPs offline

2. Based on the options available, we will use the following command-line parameters to upload PCAP files to Arkime for further processing:

```
/opt/arkime/bin/capture -q --copy -r <PCAPFILENAME.PCAP> -t
<tagname>
```

3. Note that investigators must ensure that before uploading the PCAP file, all the associated dependency files are up to date. These include `ipv4-address-space.csv` (representing IPv4 address space ranges per **Regional Internet Registries** (**RIR**)) and **manuf** files (list of MAC address allocations per the **Network Interface Controller** (**NIC**) manufacturers). MAC addresses are unique identifiers that are assigned to NICs for network communication. In incident response, the MAC address helps identify the make of the NIC controller and

ultimately determine what computing systems this may have been used, taking it a step closer to the threat actor device.

4. Once uploaded to Arkime, we can jump onto the web browser to perform investigations. The following figure shows a real-life example of a ransomware attack captured on a cloud instance. The organization captured network traffic packets by mirroring their host network traffic and sending them to another host to record traffic. The following figure provides an overview of the UI and general feature sets. We can see activity spikes per session; you can slice the entries per time and perform additional searches. For each entry in the lower half of the page, there is a + option, which allows you to dig deeper into the particular TCP session. It also provides an entire conversation of the TCP stream (provided the TCP traffic was in clear text and not over SSL traffic):

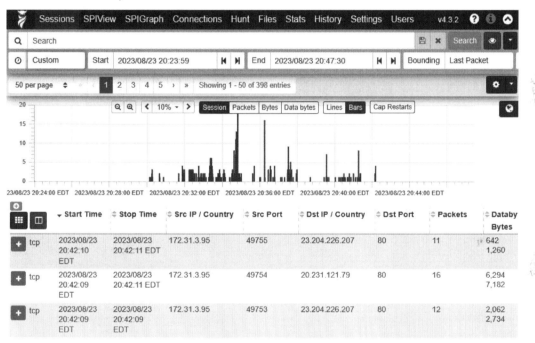

Figure 8.10 – Arkime main screen – post-PCAP ingestion and processing

5. As shown in the following screenshot, investigators also have the option of parsing the packets, depending on the requirements or nature of the traffic itself. It also provides the opportunity to decode packets:

Figure 8.11 – Arkime TCP session details (conversation)

As we can see from a session's detailed view, investigators can often view the individual packets that make up the session. This includes information about the packet size, timestamp, and packet payload, and this level of detail can be crucial for security analysts investigating network activities. Now, let's switch to session awareness and filtering capabilities in Arkime.

Session awareness – filtering

In this section, we'll look at the session awareness and filtering capabilities. Arkime has a **Session and Protocol Information** (**SPI**) view. This view is a critical component of Arkime's web-based interface and allows users to analyze and dissect network sessions and their associated protocols. Here are some of the use cases that investigators can leverage using SPI:

- **Session list**: The SPI view provides a list of network sessions that have been captured and indexed by Arkime. A session represents a sequence of network packets between a source and destination IP address and port.

- **Session detail**: Clicking on a specific session from the list will allow you to view detailed information about that session. This can include source and destination IP addresses, source and destination ports, protocol used, packet capture details, and more.

- **Protocol analysis**: Arkime's SPI view often provides protocol-specific information. This means you can analyze network sessions based on their protocols, including HTTP, DNS, and FTP. This can help in identifying suspicious or malicious activities.

- **Filters and searches**: Just like in other views of Arkime, the SPI view allows you to apply filters and search criteria to narrow down the sessions you're interested in. This can be helpful when you're dealing with large amounts of captured network data. With the SPI view and list of IP addresses, investigators can export the breakdown of the attributes and perform threat intelligence searches on each indicator to obtain more information. Some of the filtering capabilities are as follows:

    - **Simple filters**: You can filter sessions based on simple attributes such as IP addresses, ports, protocols, and timestamp ranges. For example, you can filter for all sessions involving a specific IP address or sessions that occurred within a specific time frame.

    - **Combining filters**: Moloch's query language allows you to combine multiple conditions using logical operators (AND, OR, NOT) to create more complex filters. This helps you narrow down your focus to specific scenarios.

    - **Regular expressions**: You can use regular expressions to match patterns within session attributes. For instance, you might want to filter sessions with URLs containing a specific keyword.

    - **Custom fields**: Arkime allows you to define and use custom fields, which can be extracted from session data or added during ingestion. You can then filter sessions based on these custom fields.

    - **Saved queries**: Once you've constructed a useful filter, you can save it as a named query for easy reuse in the future.

- **Session graphs**: Depending on the capabilities of the SPI view, you might also have access to visual representations of session data, such as graphs illustrating communication flows between hosts.

- **Threat detection**: Security analysts often use Arkime's SPI view to detect potential threats or anomalies within network traffic. Unusual patterns, unexpected protocols, or suspicious payloads can indicate malicious activity.

The following screenshot shows an example PCAP file. Here, Arkime will break down the sessions and protocols and provide a deeper dive into each packet. As we can see, the SPI view breaks down destination IPs and other protocols. Each result can be clicked, and further analysis can be performed:

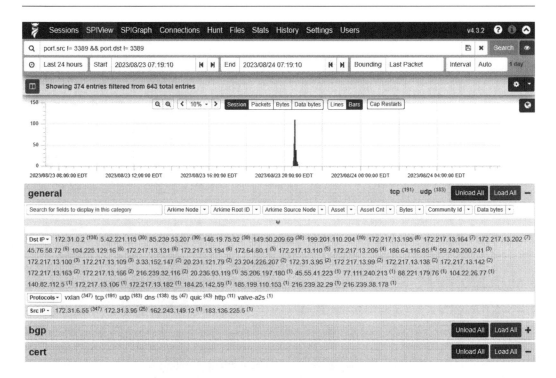

Figure 8.12 – Arkime's SPI view for session and protocol analysis

To summarize, Arkime is a powerful tool that allows you to break network traffic down for investigators to consume. It also has powerful enrichment capabilities. For example, Arkime can integrate an IP geolocation database to determine the location of origin IPs. Arkime also allows integration with other threat intelligence sources. Another feature is that it provides content extraction, meaning you can download files from Arkime for further manual analysis.

Wireshark/tcpdump

tcpdump and Wireshark are powerful tools that are commonly used in DFIR to capture and analyze network traffic. Both tools serve similar purposes but have distinct characteristics and use cases. Often, these tools are used to reverse engineer network protocols from a network investigation point of view.

tcpdump

tcpdump is a command-line packet analyzer that captures network packets in real time or from a previously captured file. It operates at the lower level of the network stack, allowing it to capture packets at a very granular level, including Ethernet frames, IP packets, TCP/UDP segments, and more. It's often used for network monitoring, troubleshooting, and security analysis. In DFIR, tcpdump is particularly useful for live packet capture during incident response, capturing network traffic for later analysis.

From a network investigation point of view, sometimes, investigators do not have full cloud access to set up a packet mirroring service that mirrors all the packets from the infected cloud instance to another instance under the organization's tenant. Knowledge of these tools certainly helps with preparing and initiating a network capture if access to the configuration elements is limited.

Investigators can initiate a full packet dump using the `sudo tcpdump` command (you will need administrator access). *Figure 8.13* shows the sample output of a tcpdump dump without any filters; it displays the following fields:

- **Current timestamp (local time)**: Displayed in `HH:MM:SS.microseconds`.

- **Source and destination ports**: `t2.lan.ssh` is the source IP/port sending data to `dfirlab.lan.27018`, and `dfirlab.lan.27018` is the source IP sending data to `t2.lan.ssh` as a response.

- **Flags**: `[P.]` indicates that the packet carries application data (PUSH flag set), while `[.]` indicates a regular acknowledgment (ACK flag set).

- **Sequence numbers**: `seq 188:440` indicates that the sequence numbers of the data in the packet range from `188` to `440`. This is used to keep track of the order of the data packets. `seq 6000:6256` indicates a subsequent sequence range.

- **Acknowledgment (ACK)**: `ack 1` indicates the acknowledgment number of the next expected byte. `ack 1148` are acknowledgments of the received data.

- **Window size**: `win 4097` and `win 501` indicate the receiver window size, which is the amount of data the receiver can buffer.

- **Length**: `length 252` indicates the packet's data payload length.

Note that you will have to explicitly indicate a filename to capture the packets to a file on the disk in a PCAP format for offline analysis:

```
11:41:01.971438 IP dfirlab.lan.27018 > t2.lan.ssh: Flags [.], ack 188, win 4097, length 0
11:41:02.024610 IP t2.lan.ssh > dfirlab.lan.27018: Flags [P.], seq 188:440, ack 1, win 501, length 252
11:41:02.066035 IP dfirlab.lan.27018 > t2.lan.ssh: Flags [.], ack 440, win 4096, length 0
11:41:02.113403 IP t2.lan.ssh > dfirlab.lan.27018: Flags [P.], seq 440:676, ack 1, win 501, length 236
11:41:02.159858 IP dfirlab.lan.27018 > t2.lan.ssh: Flags [.], ack 676, win 4095, length 0
11:41:02.217521 IP t2.lan.ssh > dfirlab.lan.27018: Flags [P.], seq 676:912, ack 1, win 501, length 236
11:41:02.271571 IP dfirlab.lan.27018 > t2.lan.ssh: Flags [.], ack 912, win 4100, length 0
11:41:02.321581 IP t2.lan.ssh > dfirlab.lan.27018: Flags [P.], seq 912:1148, ack 1, win 501, length 236
11:41:02.364912 IP dfirlab.lan.27018 > t2.lan.ssh: Flags [.], ack 1148, win 4099, length 0
```

Figure 8.13 – tcpdump in action

- **TCP dump filters**: Investigators should familiarize themselves with tcpdump filters. When applied during capture, these filters will only collect network packets that match the conditions specified in the filter. In the case of tcpdump, it uses **Berkeley Packet Filter** (**BPF**), which allows for low-level filtering and specifies requirements for capturing particular packets.

The following figure shows an example of using a BPF filter for capturing specific network packets – that is, sudo tcpdump -i <interface_name> proto 17. In this example, we filter packets based on protocol number 17, which refers to UDP traffic:

```
user@t2:~$ sudo tcpdump -i ens33 proto 17
[sudo] password for user:
tcpdump: verbose output suppressed, use -v[v]... for full protocol decode
listening on ens33, link-type EN10MB (Ethernet), snapshot length 262144 bytes
11:37:11.317634 IP android-80cb698ca5b3e555.lan.56082 > 239.255.255.250.1900: UDP, length
440
11:37:11.322938 IP android-80cb698ca5b3e555.lan.56082 > 239.255.255.250.1900: UDP, length
453
11:37:11.322962 IP android-80cb698ca5b3e555.lan.56082 > 239.255.255.250.1900: UDP, length
492
11:37:11.322964 IP android-80cb698ca5b3e555.lan.32804 > 239.255.255.250.1900: UDP, length
506
11:37:11.327242 IP android-80cb698ca5b3e555.lan.39407 > 239.255.255.250.1900: UDP, length
504
11:37:11.363017 IP t2.lan.46458 > unifi.lan.domain: 53977+ [1au] PTR? 250.255.255.239.in-a
ddr.arpa. (57)
11:37:11.420673 IP unifi.lan.domain > t2.lan.46458: 53977 NXDomain 0/1/1 (114)
11:37:11.420937 IP t2.lan.46458 > unifi.lan.domain: 53977+ PTR? 250.255.255.239.in-addr.ar
pa. (46)
11:37:11.423419 IP unifi.lan.domain > t2.lan.46458: 53977 NXDomain 0/0/0 (46)
11:37:11.424224 IP t2.lan.40326 > unifi.lan.domain: 54053+ [1au] PTR? 234.1.168.192.in-add
r.arpa. (55)
```

Figure 8.14 – tcpdump with BPF filter

Let's jump over to a more intuitive version of packet capture software – Wireshark. It has very similar functionality; however, you can do real-time analysis as packets are captured.

Wireshark

Wireshark, on the other hand, is a user-friendly graphical network protocol analyzer. It provides a detailed, visually rich interface for examining captured packets. Wireshark can open and analyze tcpdump capture files and packets directly from network interfaces. It operates at a higher level of abstraction than tcpdump, presenting dissected and decoded network protocols in a more human-readable format. Investigators widely use Wireshark to analyze network traffic for evidence of malicious activity, network anomalies, and data exfiltration. The following figure shows a simplistic view of the Wireshark user interface:

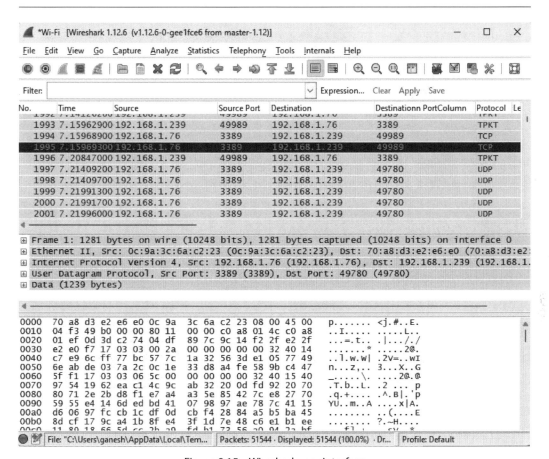

Figure 8.15 – Wireshark user interface

Wireshark offers many capabilities to filter packets and parse them through their UI and has clearly defined information on how to handle and filter packet information. Some of the cheat sheets have been referenced in the *Further reading* section of this chapter.

CyberChef

CyberChef is a powerful web-based tool for various data manipulation tasks that's often used in cybersecurity and digital forensics. It provides a user-friendly interface and recipes for encoding, decoding, transforming, and analyzing data in various formats. CyberChef can be incredibly useful for processing and analyzing network-related data in the context of network investigation. Here's how CyberChef can be used in network investigation:

- **Data transformation**: Network investigators often encounter encoded or obfuscated data in network traffic. CyberChef provides various data transformation operations, such as base64 encoding/decoding, URL encoding/decoding, XOR operations, and more. These transformations can help investigators unveil hidden information in network packets.

- **Data extraction**: When examining network traffic, extracting relevant information from raw data is essential. CyberChef's `grep` function can search for specific patterns, headers, or keywords within the traffic. This can help with identifying crucial details such as IP addresses, domain names, or file paths.

- **Hashing and encryption**: CyberChef supports various hashing and encryption/decryption techniques. Investigators can hash strings or files to check for matches with known malicious hashes. Additionally, they can attempt to decrypt encrypted data if they can access the necessary keys.

- **Parsing and decoding protocols**: CyberChef's capabilities can be extended using custom recipes. Investigators can create recipes that parse and decode network protocols such as HTTP, DNS, and SMTP. This can help in extracting meaningful information from protocol headers and payloads.

- **File carving**: CyberChef can be used to retrieve and reconstruct files from the captured data if network traffic contains file transfers. This is particularly useful when investigating potential data exfiltration or malware distribution.

- **Data visualization**: CyberChef can help visualize data transformations and conversions, making it easier to understand how data changes during its journey across the network. Visualizing data can assist in identifying anomalies or suspicious patterns.

- **Automating workflows**: CyberChef allows you to create and save recipes, enabling the automation of repetitive data manipulation tasks. This can significantly speed up the investigation process and ensure consistency in data processing.

- **Collaboration and sharing**: CyberChef recipes can be shared among investigators, allowing for collaboration and knowledge sharing within the investigative team. This can help less experienced team members benefit from the expertise of others.

- **Quick analysis**: For quick analysis of small pieces of data, CyberChef's easy-to-use interface can provide immediate insights without the need for complex scripting or coding.

The following figure demonstrates an example of CyberChef in use. As indicated earlier, it comes with predefined recipes (algorithms) to parse a given dataset. It is a helpful tool for network investigators and digital forensic investigators. In this example, we're taking a log export from AWS and parsing it in CyberChef. The log export was in JSON format; reading through it can be tricky if the export needs to be formatted correctly. Once the recipe has been defined, investigators can drag and drop the artifacts and review the output:

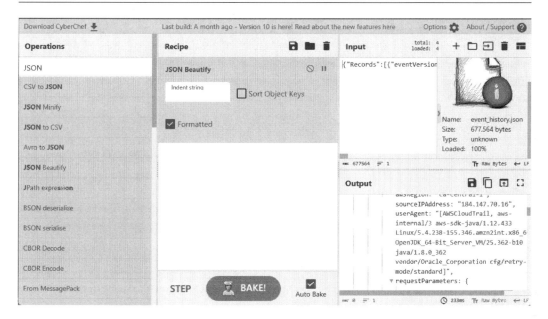

Figure 8.16 – CyberChef in use

As we can see, CyberChef is an enabler that extends an investigator's capabilities and creativity in solving an investigative challenge. Predefined recipes come with CyberChef, while other investigators have published a combination of recipes that can be applied to address a challenging forensic situation. We have included the cheat sheet in the *Further reading* section of this chapter for reference.

In the next section, we will switch gears and look at malware investigations. While a whole book could be written about this topic, the next section aims to provide a quick refresher on malware investigation concepts and how to explore some artifacts once you have captured them through host or network forensic investigation. We will look into setting up your lab environment and some essential tools that can be useful during an investigation.

Malware investigations

Malware investigations are a critical component of any incident response and involve the systematic process of identifying, analyzing, and responding to malicious software in an environment. The primary objective of a malware investigation is to understand the nature of the malware, its potential impact, and the extent of its infiltration. This information is essential for making informed decisions about containment, eradication, and recovery.

Malware analysts conduct in-depth analysis, dissecting the malware's code and behavior to reveal its capabilities, communication methods, and potential vulnerabilities that can be exploited. This information guides the understanding of the extent of compromise and aids in formulating appropriate countermeasures. An impact assessment evaluates the damage inflicted by the malware, including compromised data and affected systems, to prioritize response actions.

Eradication follows, which involves removing the malware using tailored antivirus signatures, removing files, and patching vulnerabilities. Post-eradication, recovery efforts commence, accompanied by an assessment of the incident response process and the integration of lessons learned into future strategies. For instances requiring legal action or a more profound understanding, forensic analysis preserves evidence, documents attack details, and facilitates potential collaboration with law enforcement. This comprehensive process ensures a thorough and effective response to malware incidents, safeguarding organizational integrity and security.

In the context of cloud environments, malware analysis introduces unique challenges and considerations due to the distributed and dynamic nature of cloud computing. Cloud-based malware analysis examines malicious software within virtualized or containerized environments hosted on cloud platforms.

As we can see, malware analysis closely follows the incident response process, providing critical indicators that are vital for containing and eradicating threats.

However, to perform malware analysis, you need a specialized set of tools and a completely isolated setup so that investigators do not detonate the malware on their devices and compromise the working papers of investigative information. For this reason, malware analysis is always performed in a lab environment.

Setting up your malware analysis lab

In this section, we will look at the basic architecture of setting up a malware analysis lab. For an on-premises lab, malware analysts typically use virtual infrastructure so that it is easier to tear it down and bring it back up as a fresh setup. Once malware is detonated in the lab, it leaves traces or artifacts that must be carefully studied. Similarly, investigators can set up a malware lab in the cloud. However, if you are detonating malware in the cloud, care must be taken that it does not compromise any other tenants and ensure that the malware lab is locked down.

The following figure illustrates an example of setting up a malware analysis lab and some key components. As indicated earlier, investigators must take utmost care while handling malware and associated artifacts. They are live and can also infect or compromise the investigator's computers. For this reason, most of the investigators will operate the malware in a lab. This is similar to handling an explosive and ensuring it does not cause damage. In the following figure, every connection is secured by a firewall and does not allow direct access to the detonation VM. This is where reverse engineers can explore malware and understand its capabilities:

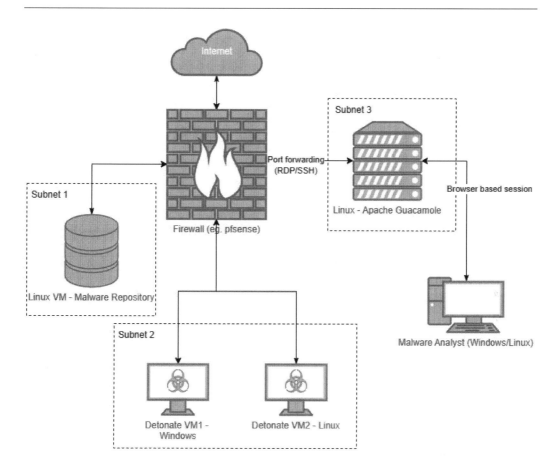

Figure 8.17 – Malware analysis lab architecture

Some of the critical components of the lab are as follows:

- **Firewalls**: Any firewall, physical or virtual, should be good. All the network connections to the malware-hosting VMs are secured and filtered. In our example, we use pfSense, a popular firewall appliance also available for virtual deployments. You can deploy a similar one if you plan to set up a lab in the cloud. In this example, the firewall and its subnet ensure that the malware lab is only accessible via specific port forwarding and not widely accessible on the internal network.

- **Malware repository**: A dedicated application with a database where malware can securely reside. We use a Python-based Viper framework application, which allows file and static malware analysis. It also has a database that stores malware and helps organize malware and exploit samples.

- **Detonation VMs**: These are dedicated VMs hosted on a separate and isolated subnet for detonating malware or enabling reverse engineers to explore the internal workings of the malware. It is important to note that investigators must securely configure the malware VMs, and all the network connections are carefully allowed. For example, for detonating malware, if it needs to connect to the internet, care must be taken when allowing internet access to the malware. Detonation VMs can come pre-built; you can use any freely available open source-based malware analysis VMs, such as Linux-based **Remnux** or **SANS SIFT workstation**, or you can build one based on your tools. You can also build on Windows, such as **Flare VM** from Mandiant, which offers scripts to set up the necessary software and harden the VM. You can also download a limited-time version of Windows 10 or Windows 11 directly from Microsoft at no cost; this provides a 90-day license and enables you to reinstall after the license's expiry date. This ensures that your Windows and malware analysis toolkits are up to date.

- **Apache Guacamole**: Apache Guacamole is an open source remote desktop gateway that provides web-based access to remote desktops and applications. It allows users to access their desktop environments and applications through a web browser session without requiring additional software installation on the client side. Guacamole supports various remote desktop protocols such as VNC, RDP, and SSH. The most crucial benefit of utilizing Apache Guacamole is enforcing additional controls, such as restrictions on copy-paste and limitations on the accessibility of network drives and printers. This is crucial as you do not want malware to spread or jump out of the VM's secure network zone.

- **Malware Analyst VM**: This is purely for securely accessing the malware network via Apache Guacamole over a web browser session. When accessing the malware lab, it is always recommended that a dedicated workstation is used to access this lab environment and for no other purposes.

Investigators can also choose to deploy similar architecture in the cloud by utilizing free and open source tools for malware analysis. Various renditions of malware analysis architecture can also be deployed if there is a requirement to set up a more oversized malware analysis workbench. One example is Japan's JPCERT group, which developed an architecture to deploy a lab in the cloud for memory forensics and analysis. A link to JPCERT's memory forensic lab is available in the *Further reading* section.

Let's dive deeper into some common malware traits that investigators often end up encountering with packed malware and multiple versions of the same malware.

Working with packed malware

One of the top challenges that malware reverse engineers encounter is packed malware. Packers are tools that enterprises, as well as threat actors, use to compress and encrypt any code. In the context of threats, malware code is packed and deployed in an environment that makes it harder for reverse engineers to analyze. Note that we indicated *harder* and not *impossible*. Threat actors aim to make it harder to detect and research so that investigators cannot create detection packages before the threat severely impacts organizations. These packers help obfuscate the code, making it challenging to understand malware functionality. Historically, some of the packers are commonly observed by investigators as preferred choices by threat actors:

- **Ultimate Packer for eXecutables** (**UPX**): This is a very popular and well-known tool for packing executable files. UPX is an open source tool that can protect executable packages. Unpacking a UPX-packed executable is relatively easy as well. Any commonly used **Portable Executable** (**PE**) file analyzer would provide results if a given executable is packed. The following figure shows a side-by-side example of real-world malware caught in the wild; the one on the left is UPX-packed, while the one on the right is unpacked or uncompressed. Note the size of each of the sections. Remember that UPX compresses the malware binary; therefore, the size and memory address locations of the unpacked binary differ when unpacked. While this is a simplistic version, sophisticated threat actors can make it more complex by applying multiple packing levels or numerous forms of packers:

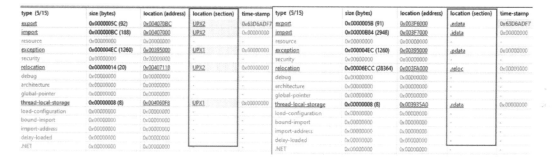

Figure 8.18 – UPX packed versus unpacked malware

- **Armadillo**: Armadillo is a commercial packer and employs code encryption, virtualization, anti-debugging measures, and dynamic unpacking to shield executable code from reverse engineering and analysis. Although intended for legitimate purposes, threat actors have exploited its features to obfuscate malware, making research and detection more challenging for security researchers.

- **Themida**: Themida is a commercial software protection tool that's commonly utilized by software developers to safeguard their applications against reverse engineering and unauthorized access. Like Armadillo, it employs sophisticated techniques such as code obfuscation, encryption, and anti-debugging measures to make it difficult for researchers to decipher the packed code's functionality. Additionally, Themida offers anti-tampering mechanisms and virtualization to fortify the protection further. While initially intended for legitimate purposes, we have seen threat actors repurposing Themida to cloak malware and complicate detection by security solutions.

While dealing with malware packers can be tricky, investigators must remember that whatever is executed in memory, at some point, the packed code must be unpacked and decoded before running in memory. Irrespective of the choice of packers used by threat actors, reverse engineers may choose a difficult road by manually debugging the packed malware to reveal unpacked code under it and adjust other associated parameters so that further analysis of the malware is possible.

Another challenging situation that investigators often encounter is multiple versions of the same binary. This raises concerns about the number of versions the threat actor may have deployed to evade detection; dealing with various versions of the same binary adds additional complexities to the investigation.

Binary comparison

Binary comparison is a process that's used in computer science and software engineering to determine the differences between two binary files, which are files containing compiled code or machine-readable data. This comparison involves analyzing the individual bytes or bits of the files to identify variations in content, structure, and code sequences or by evaluating the **Control Flow Graph** (**CFG**). Binary comparison is commonly employed in tasks such as version control, software debugging, malware analysis, and digital forensics. By identifying differences between binary files, developers, analysts, and researchers can understand code changes, track modifications, detect tampering, and uncover potential changes to the malware capabilities. The following screenshot shows an example of a Windows program represented in CFG format that demonstrates various decision trees, jump points, network access, and complexities of a program. We're using a free, open source tool known as **ProcDot** for this purpose. The following screenshot is just for illustration to demonstrate the code complexities:

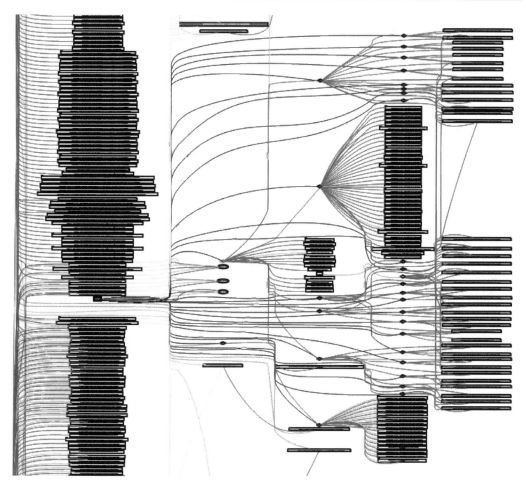

Figure 8.19 – Compressed view of an application CFG with read/write paths

CFG is a graphical representation that's used in computer science and software engineering to visualize control flow within a program or software application. It illustrates the various paths that a program's execution can take by depicting its basic blocks (individual segments of code with a single entry point and a single exit point) and the connections between them. Each basic block typically corresponds to a sequence of instructions executed sequentially without branching. CFGs use nodes to represent basic blocks and edges to represent the flow of control between them, indicating where the program can branch or jump to different sections of code based on conditions or loop constructs. CFGs are particularly useful for understanding program behavior, analyzing code paths, and detecting potential bugs or vulnerabilities, and especially useful when comparing similar versions of the executable files. They are commonly used in program analysis, optimization, debugging, and security research. Let's look at some of the specialized tools that are used to compare binaries.

BinDiff

BinDiff is a software comparison tool developed by **Zynamics**, a company acquired by Google. BinDiff is primarily used for analyzing and comparing binary files, such as executables, libraries, and other compiled code. It's widely employed in reverse engineering and malware analysis to identify similarities and differences between software versions or find common code patterns among different binaries.

To summarize, while we reflected upon some of the basic tools that are out there for malware investigations, researchers develop various tools that investigators must be prepared to stay up to date with so that they can leverage them when they notice complex malware that requires specialized tools. Knowing that there is a tool out there is more important than the knowledge of the tool itself. Given threat actors create malware differently all the time to make it difficult for us, it's important to stay on top of the technologies, techniques, and concepts utilized by malware developers. In the next section, we will compare traditional and cloud forensics, debunking a few myths.

Traditional forensics versus cloud forensics

Traditional and cloud forensics play critical roles in incident response but differ in focus and methodologies due to the distinct environments they address.

Here are their similarities:

- **Evidence collection**: Both traditional and cloud forensics involve collecting and preserving digital evidence to reconstruct events leading to an incident. This may include collecting memory dumps, log files, network traffic, and filesystem artifacts. Investigators often use cloud storage to store large volumes of artifacts, irrespective of the underlying CSP, as most breaches affect a cloud tenant at a CSP. In scenarios where the underlying CSP is believed to be compromised, it is recommended that investigators save all the necessary artifacts in a different CSP storage or offline for analysis.

- **Analysis techniques**: Both domains employ similar techniques for analyzing digital evidence, such as examining file structures, metadata, timestamps, and memory contents to understand the timeline and scope of an incident.

- **Chain of custody**: Maintaining the chain of custody is crucial in both scenarios to ensure the integrity and admissibility of evidence in legal proceedings.

Here are their differences:

- **Environment**: Traditional forensics involves physical devices such as computers, servers, and mobile devices. In contrast, cloud forensics focuses on virtualized and distributed environments, including **Infrastructure-as-a-Service (IaaS)**, **Platform-as-a-Service (PaaS)**, and **Software-as-a-Service (SaaS)**.

- **Evidence location**: In traditional forensics, evidence is often stored locally on physical devices. In cloud forensics, evidence might be distributed across multiple virtual instances and storage services, requiring different collection and preservation techniques.

- **Data ownership**: Data ownership and control can be complex due to shared resources in the cloud. Identifying which party is responsible for maintaining and providing access to evidence can be more challenging.

- **Data residency**: Data might be stored in various geographic locations in the cloud, potentially affecting legal and regulatory considerations in different jurisdictions.

- **Network traffic**: In traditional forensics, capturing network traffic is relatively straightforward. Network traffic might be harder to access in cloud environments due to virtualized networks and third-party services.

- **Logs and auditing**: Cloud environments often offer extensive logging and auditing capabilities, providing more detailed activity information. However, accessing and interpreting these logs can be complex.

- **Resource sharing**: In cloud environments, multiple tenants might share the same physical hardware, impacting the isolation and preservation of evidence.

- **Incident response tools**: Traditional incident response tools may not fully translate to cloud environments due to architectural differences and the need for specialized tools tailored to cloud forensics.

- **Legal and compliance**: Cloud forensics can involve additional legal and compliance challenges due to jurisdictional issues, cross-border data transfers, and varying cloud service provider terms.

In summary, while traditional and cloud forensics share common principles regarding evidence collection and analysis, cloud forensics introduces complexities related to cloud environments' virtualized and distributed nature (such as containerization and serverless architectures), shared resources, and legal considerations specific to the cloud. Incident responders and digital forensics experts must adapt their practices to effectively handle incidents in traditional and cloud-based systems.

Summary

As we've seen through this chapter, the basics of the incident response process and threat hunting largely remain the same, focusing on finding evil within the environment. Depending on the operating systems, investigators can customize what logs and artifacts should be collected and what must be investigated. We also saw how EDR deployments speed up the breach containment and incident response process. Remember, the incident response process is a discipline that investigators closely follow to ensure that all the investigative steps are performed. At the same time, the breach is contained, and there is no further risk to the organization and the endpoint under investigation. While this chapter aimed to introduce various elements of the breach investigation, it is undoubtedly encouraged that investigators stay up to date with the latest investigative tools and techniques.

In the next chapter, we will look at collecting these artifacts from the cloud environment. Recognizing that collecting necessary artifacts from the cloud environment is difficult, we will look at various cloud service providers and their support for collecting forensic packages. We will also look at the options for exporting full disk images versus quick forensic collections in the cloud.

Further reading

- *PE block*: https://archive.org/details/windowsntfilesys00naga/page/129

- *Overview of memory dump file options for Windows*: https://learn.microsoft.com/en-us/troubleshoot/windows-server/performance/memory-dump-file-options

- *Varieties of Kernel-Mode Dump Files*: Varieties of Kernel-Mode Dump Files - Windows drivers|Microsoft Learn

- *Awesome Threat Hunting*: https://github.com/0x4D31/awesome-threat-detection/tree/master

- *BPF – the forgotten bytecode*: https://blog.cloudflare.com/bpf-the-forgotten-bytecode/

- *BPF and tcpdump*: https://andreaskaris.github.io/blog/networking/bpf-and-tcpdump/

- *Transmission Control Protocol*: https://datatracker.ietf.org/doc/html/rfc793

- *Wireshark Cheat Sheet*: https://cdn.comparitech.com/wp-content/uploads/2019/06/Wireshark-Cheat-Sheet-1.jpg.webp

- *CyberChef*: https://gchq.github.io/CyberChef/

- *CyberChef Recipes*: https://github.com/mattnotmax/cyberchef-recipes

- *Flare VM*: https://github.com/mandiant/flare-vm

- *REMnux: A Linux Toolkit for Malware Analysis*: https://remnux.org/

- *SIFT Workstation*: https://www.sans.org/tools/sift-workstation/

- *JPCERT Coordination Center-Memory Forensics*: https://github.com/JPCERTCC/MemoryForensic-on-Cloud

- *Building a Custom Malware Analysis Lab Environment*: https://www.sentinelone.com/labs/building-a-custom-malware-analysis-lab-environment/

- *Get a Windows 11 development environment*: https://developer.microsoft.com/en-us/windows/downloads/virtual-machines/

- *Leveraging Microsoft Graph API for memory forensics*: https://medium.com/comae/leveraging-microsoft-graph-api-for-memory-forensics-7ab7f9ea4d06

- *Digital Forensic – Most Commonly used Tools*: https://medium.com/@KhalilAfridii/digital-forensic-most-commonly-used-tools-4a9dbb98f926

- *CyLR*: https://github.com/orlikoski/CyLR

- *Kansa*: https://github.com/davehull/Kansa

- *PSHunt*: https://github.com/Infocyte/PSHunt

- *PowerForensics*: https://github.com/Invoke-IR/PowerForensics

9

Common Attack Vectors and TTPs

As organizations increasingly rely on cloud infrastructures, security teams and incident responders find themselves confronting some unique vulnerabilities and attack patterns in the cloud. Attackers capitalize on these vulnerabilities and employ **Tactics, Techniques, and Procedures (TTPs)** that are sometimes tailored specifically to cloud environments.

This chapter dives deep into these common attack vectors in the cloud, offering insights to empower and refine our response strategies in the face of ever-evolving threats. Misconfigured virtual machine instances and storage buckets, unprotected API endpoints, and inadequate authentication protocols are just a few of the vulnerabilities that threat actors target. To exploit these weaknesses, attackers employ TTPs ranging from privilege escalation and server-side request forgery to zero-day exploits tailored for cloud infrastructures. Grasping these specific threats is indispensable for cloud security and effective incident response.

Specifically, we will discuss the following topics in this chapter:

- MITRE ATT&CK framework
- Forensic triage collections
- Host-based forensics
- Misconfigured virtual machine instances
- Misconfigured storage buckets
- Cloud administrator portal breach

Attack vectors and TTPs in the cloud, for the most part, echo those in on-premises environments. However, the decentralized nature of the cloud introduces distinct vulnerabilities. Misconfigured virtual machine instances can expose entire virtual environments, while improperly secured storage buckets can become gateways for data breaches. The cloud's accessibility brings forth issues such as weak authentication mechanisms, which can lead to unauthorized access. While the core principles of cybersecurity remain consistent, these cloud-centric issues demand specialized attention and understanding.

> **Important note**
>
> We'll look at common attack vectors and TTPs for cloud productivity suites in more detail in *Chapter 12*.

MITRE ATT&CK framework

The MITRE ATT&CK framework is a knowledge base of attacker tactics and techniques based on real-world observations from security researchers. It's a tool that's used by security teams to better understand attack behavior and to improve defense and response strategies. In the context of cloud environments, the MITRE ATT&CK framework outlines specific techniques that adversaries use against **cloud service providers** (**CSPs**) such as AWS, Azure, and GCP.

The MITRE ATT&CK framework is particularly useful for cloud forensics because it allows responders to anticipate attacker behavior and plan their forensic investigations accordingly. By aligning with this framework, organizations can identify gaps in their defensive posture and better understand how to detect, respond to, and mitigate cloud-specific threats.

Within the scope of cloud infrastructures, the MITRE ATT&CK framework provides a matrix of known attacker TTPs, which includes, but is not limited to, the following:

- **Initial access**: Techniques that use various entry vectors to gain a foothold within a cloud environment. For example, Exploit Public-Facing Application (T1190) could be linked to vulnerabilities in web applications hosted in the cloud.

- **Execution**: The execution phase encompasses techniques that result in adversary-controlled code running on a local or remote system. This could involve Server Software Component (T1505), where an attacker might execute code through a web server plugin.

- **Persistence**: In the cloud, attackers often exploit features to remain logged in to an environment, as seen in Create Cloud Instance (T1578), where an adversary creates a new instance within an existing account to maintain their operations.

- **Privilege escalation**: Techniques that allow an adversary to gain higher-level permissions on a system or network. An example is Abuse Elevation Control Mechanism (T1548), which could involve an attacker taking advantage of overly permissive **Identity and Access Management** (**IAM**) roles.

- **Defense evasion**: This involves techniques that adversaries use to avoid detection throughout their compromise. Techniques such as Disabling Security Tools (T1562) might be used to switch off monitoring and logging capabilities in the cloud.

To further illustrate how the MITRE ATT&CK framework fits within a cloud attack scenario, consider the following example:

- **Misconfiguration and Unauthorized Access (T1580)**: As discussed later in this chapter, attackers often take advantage of misconfigurations in cloud storage services such as AWS S3 buckets or Azure Blob Storage. By enumerating these services and exploiting open permissions, attackers can read, modify, or delete sensitive data stored in these resources.

By incorporating the MITRE ATT&CK framework into cloud security practices, organizations can more effectively structure their response to incidents and align their forensic efforts with industry-standard nomenclature and tactics. Doing so not only enhances the incident response plan but also aligns with global best practices, helping to ensure a more resilient defense against cloud-based attacks.

Incident responders will likely have to map all forensic findings to MITRE numbers in an easy tabular format for defense teams to better understand how an attack occurred in their environment. As an example, the following table demonstrates a sample MITRE ATT&CK table for a hypothetical cloud compromise:

MITRE ATT&CK Technique Number	Technique Name	Description
T1190	Exploit Public-Facing Application	Attacking a server or service that is accessible from the internet to gain access. For example, attackers could target specific web applications or services exposed to the internet, such as a web portal or API gateway hosted in the cloud. The focus is often on exploiting vulnerabilities in web modules or application code to gain unauthorized access to underlying cloud resources or sensitive data.
T1136.003	Use of Service Principal	Creating or compromising cloud identities to maintain access to cloud resources. This could involve creating or hijacking cloud identity services, such as Azure AD service principals or AWS IAM roles. Attackers may establish fake identities or compromise existing ones to gain persistent access to cloud resources, enabling them to access or manipulate workloads and services.

MITRE ATT&CK Technique Number	Technique Name	Description
T1580	Cloud Infrastructure Discovery	Scanning for information about cloud services and assets to plan further attacks. Attackers typically conduct reconnaissance on cloud environments, targeting specific cloud services such as AWS EC2 or Azure Virtual Machines. They scan for exposed APIs, unsecured storage buckets, or misconfigured cloud resources to identify potential entry points or valuable data.
T1078	Valid Accounts	Using stolen account credentials to gain unauthorized access to cloud systems.
T1090	Proxy	Utilizing intermediary systems to disguise the origin of malicious traffic. Attackers use intermediary cloud-based services or virtual machines as proxies to conceal their origin. This technique may involve spinning up cloud instances to route malicious traffic, making it harder to trace back to the source.
T1526	Cloud Service Dashboard	Gaining access to cloud service management interfaces for control or reconnaissance. By gaining access to cloud management interfaces, such as the AWS management console or the Azure portal, attackers can monitor and control cloud resources. This might involve tracking workloads, modifying configurations, or gaining insights into security controls.
T1548.004	Cloud Service Abuse	Exploiting cloud services or resources to support malicious operations.

MITRE ATT&CK Technique Number	Technique Name	Description
T1562.007	Disable or Modify Cloud Firewall	Modifying or disabling cloud-based firewalls to allow malicious traffic or block security responses. Attackers modify or disable cloud-based firewalls, such as AWS WAF or Azure Firewall, to permit malicious traffic or impede security responses. This could involve changing rules to allow access to specific ports or services, or disabling protective measures around critical cloud assets.
T1578	Modify Cloud Compute Infrastructure	Making changes to cloud compute services such as instances and virtual machines to establish persistence or escalate privileges, as well as making unauthorized alterations to cloud compute services, such as modifying virtual machine configurations or injecting malicious code into containerized applications. This technique aims to establish persistence, escalate privileges, or create backdoors in cloud environments.
T1583	Acquire Infrastructure: Cloud Accounts	Purchasing or otherwise obtaining cloud accounts for malicious purposes.
T1608.001	Stage Data for Exfiltration: Cloud Storage	Placing stolen data in cloud storage services in preparation for exfiltration, as well as placing stolen or illicitly obtained data in cloud storage services, such as Amazon S3 buckets or Azure Blob Storage, in preparation for exfiltration. This step often precedes large-scale data breaches or data theft operations, leveraging the cloud for staging and dissemination of compromised data.

Table 9.1 – Example of an incident MITRE ATT&CK table

> **Important note**
>
> All attacker TTPs can be mapped to the appropriate number under the ATT&CK framework. This can be found on the MITRE organization's site: `https://attack.mitre.org/`.

Forensic triage collections

One of the biggest pain points incident responders will face is data acquisition at the individual host level, especially when it pertains to operating system artifacts. CSPs such as Azure, AWS, and GCP offer various logging mechanisms to aid in monitoring and auditing actions on their resources. However, these logs often capture activities related to the infrastructure or services utilized. By default, they do not capture the granular details of user activities or system operations at the operating system level (except for cloud ecosystem-connected EDR agents such as Microsoft Defender for Endpoint). Even in a cyber incident that involves cloud resources, the reality is that most of an incident's **indicators of compromise (IoCs)** will come from host-level artifacts.

As we have seen throughout this book, cloud log sources primarily focus on the cloud resources' interactions. This means detailed host-level activities, such as specific Windows Event Logs, file modifications, memory operations, and user command executions are not captured (that is, accessible from the cloud) by default. The exception to this is if host artifacts and logs have been set to be forwarded to cloud services such as AWS CloudWatch or an Azure Log Analytics workspace. Most likely, incident responders will be responding to an incident that will require capturing all forensic artifacts at the host level (that is, the virtual machine instance hosted in the cloud environment). The operating system artifacts offer a more detailed picture of what happened on a virtual machine instance and piecing together the analysis of multiple virtual machines will allow incident responders to understand the extent to which their cloud infrastructure was impacted by the incident.

These artifacts can include the following:

- **Filesystem metadata**: Details about file creation, modification, or deletion
- **Memory artifacts**: Information about running processes, network connections, and loaded modules
- **Registry artifacts (for Windows)**: Details about installed applications, user activities, and system configurations
- **Shell histories (for Linux)**: Command execution histories, which can provide insights into user activities
- **Application logs**: Specific applications might generate logs that haven't been captured or aggregated by the CSP

The absence of these artifacts from the CSP makes it crucial to use tools such as **Kroll Artifact Parser and Extractor (KAPE**, `https://www.kroll.com/en/services/cyber-risk/incident-response-litigation-support/kroll-artifact-parser-extractor-kape`) or **Collect Your Logs Remotely (CyLR)** for triage and forensic analysis.

KAPE and CyLR are both free triage tools that collect and process forensically relevant artifacts swiftly. They are highly customizable and enable incident responders to target specific artifacts based on the nature of the cyber incident. They are lightweight and do not require much computational power to be run on a system.

> **Important note**
>
> KAPE requires an enterprise license when used on a third-party network and/or as part of a paid engagement. It is free for any local, state, federal, or international government agency, as well as educational and research uses.
>
> You can download KAPE and find its usage instructions at `https://www.kroll.com/en/services/cyber-risk/incident-response-litigation-support/kroll-artifact-parser-extractor-kape/`.
>
> You can download CyLR and find its usage instructions on GitHub at `https://github.com/orlikoski/CyLR/`.

Host-based forensics

In the context of the cloud, a host refers to a virtual or physical machine that runs user applications and serves as an endpoint for user and application activities. It can be an individual server, a virtual machine, or a container, depending on the specific cloud model being utilized. While in traditional on-premises scenarios, a host would often refer to a tangible physical server or machine, in the cloud, hosts can be ephemeral and rapidly spun up or down based on the demand and requirements.

> **Important note**
>
> In this chapter, we will concentrate on Windows-based systems. Linux systems will have different host-based artifacts that can be collected and analyzed.

Host-based forensics in the cloud focuses on retrieving and analyzing data from these individual hosts or endpoints, aiming to identify signs of intrusions, lateral movements, malicious code executions, and other TTPs. Given that a host is the primary point of execution for applications and often the entry or pivot point for attackers, it is a rich source of forensic data.

Several artifacts in the Windows operating system can provide a wealth of information regarding activities on a host:

- **Prefetch**: This is used to speed up the Windows boot process and application startup times. By examining prefetch files, incident responders can determine which programs were executed on a host and when.

- **AmCache**: AmCache contains information about executed applications and can provide insights into program execution and user activities.

- **ShimCache**: Also known as Application Compatibility Cache, ShimCache contains a list of recently executed applications. It is valuable for understanding what ran on a system, especially after a system reboot, as some other artifacts might be purged.

- **Windows Event Logs**: These logs, especially the security, system, and application logs, can offer a plethora of information about security-related events, system startups, shutdowns, application crashes, and more. They are critical for identifying patterns related to potential security incidents.

Many more artifacts can be analyzed, but these are the most useful from an incident responder's point of view. We will utilize these artifacts to analyze common intrusions on cloud resources discussed throughout this chapter.

> **Important note**
> Prefetch, AmCache, ShimCache, and Windows Event Logs are some of the many artifacts collected by KAPE and CyLR.

The process of analyzing host-based logs can be broken down into the following steps:

1. **Log collection**: Gather the data from the target host. This is the initial step where all the necessary entries are extracted for analysis. These logs are also captured when generating forensic triage packages.

2. **Data preparation**: Utilize a parsing tool to convert the raw data into a readable and analyzable format.

3. **Analysis and correlation**: This considers key aspects such as user activity, file paths, execution flags, file modification times, and file sizes/attributes for any anomalies or red flags. Cross-reference log data with other forensic artifacts to contextualize findings within the broader scope of the investigation.

4. **Outcome**: Document the analysis results, identifying any potential indicators of compromise. Based on the findings, determine the appropriate response actions, which could include further detailed investigation, system remediation, or initiating security protocols to prevent future breaches.

These steps can be visualized in the following process map:

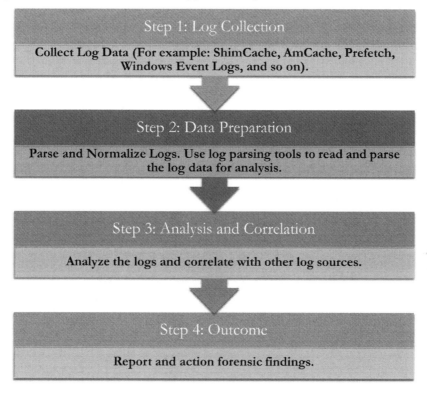

Figure 9.1 – Host-based forensic analysis process

Evidence of intrusion

Determining evidence of execution is often a crucial initial step in ascertaining evidence of intrusion on a host system. Threat actors, in their pursuit of system compromise and subsequent exploitation, frequently seek to execute unauthorized applications, particularly malware, to establish a foothold or gain elevated privileges. The unauthorized execution of these applications can serve as clear indicators of a breach or intrusion.

To pinpoint such unauthorized executions, incident responders rely on certain intrinsic artifacts, such as Prefetch, AmCache, and ShimCache. These artifacts store data about executed programs, offering invaluable insights into the history of application runs. By meticulously analyzing these artifacts, professionals can discern any discrepancies or anomalies pointing to unauthorized executions, thus revealing potential evidence of system intrusion by malicious actors. The focus is not just on identifying malware but also on understanding the breadth and depth of any intrusion, allowing for a more comprehensive security response.

In 2013, a large American retailer experienced a significant data breach where attackers stole credit card and personal information from millions of customers. In this incident, forensic artifacts such as Prefetch, AmCache, ShimCache, and Windows Event Logs were integral to the investigation. Prefetch files likely provided insights into the execution of malware and hacking tools used by the attackers, revealing patterns of malicious activity. AmCache entries, detailing executed programs, could have helped in identifying unauthorized binaries associated with the breach. ShimCache might have offered additional evidence of malicious executable runs, which would have been useful for understanding the malware's compatibility strategies across the retailer's systems. Windows Event Logs, which record a wide range of system activities, were crucial in reconstructing the breach's timeline, including login attempts, system changes, and network activities. These artifacts, when combined, enabled investigators to piece together the attackers' movements, ascertain the methods used in the breach, and comprehend the full extent of the intrusion, thus playing a pivotal role in unraveling one of the most significant cyberattacks in the retail sector.

Prefetch analysis

Prefetching is an optimization technique that's employed by the Windows operating system to expedite the startup of applications. It achieves this by predicting which files an application will need and loading them into memory pre-emptively. After an application's initial execution, the system populates the `Prefetch` directory with a corresponding `.pf` file. These files can be found in the `C:\Windows\Prefetch` directory on a standard Windows installation. The directory will contain files with the `.pf` extension, each named after the executable it corresponds to. For instance, if you have run `notepad.exe`, you might find a corresponding `NOTEPAD.EXE.pf` file in the `Prefetch` directory.

Analyzing these prefetch files provides insights into the applications that have been run on the system, making them valuable for both performance diagnostics and forensic investigations. These files are generated based on observations made by the cache manager, which keeps track of all the files and directories an application references during its run. Consequently, these `.pf` files become invaluable containers of historical data regarding application execution.

Forensic importance of prefetch files:

- **Execution history**: One of the most significant pieces of information that's extracted from prefetch files is the historical data on application execution. The `.pf` file records both the initial execution date and the last executed date for the respective application. These timestamps are crucial during forensic investigations as they can help trace back when a potentially malicious application was first introduced and subsequently run on a system.

- **Correlation with file metadata**: The date of creation and modification of the `.pf` file itself can also provide forensic clues. While the creation date often aligns with the first execution of the application, the modification date typically corresponds with the last execution date. By comparing these dates, investigators can ascertain the consistency and frequency of an application's usage.

One of the most popular open source tools for prefetch analysis is **PECmd**, which is written and maintained by Eric Zimmerman. This tool parses prefetch files and provides detailed output, including file paths, timestamps, run counts, and more. Another common (but licensed) tool to parse prefetch files is Magnet AXIOM.

> **Important note**
>
> You can download PECmd and find its usage details at `https://github.com/EricZimmerman/PECmd`.

Imagine a scenario where a suspicious file named `malicious.exe` was executed on a Windows-based virtual machine instance that is being hosted on an organization's cloud tenant. Upon retrieving the corresponding prefetch file (perhaps from one of the triage tools we discussed earlier), `MALICIOUS.EXE.pf`, and analyzing it with PECmd, the output might resemble something like this:

```
> PECmd.exe -f C:\Users\Mansoor\Downloads\MALICIOUS.EXE.pf
Processing C:\Users\Mansoor\Downloads\MALICIOUS.EXE.pf
----------------------------------
Source File: C:\Users\Mansoor\Downloads\MALICIOUS.EXE.pf
----------------------------------
Executable: C:\Users\Mansoor\Downloads\MALICIOUS.EXE
Run Count: 3
Volume Info:
    Volume Path: \\?\Volume{abcd1234-efgh-5678-ijkl-1234567890ab}\
    Creation Date: 2023-09-15 15:34:21 UTC
    Serial Number: 3A2B1C4D

Directories accessed:
    C:\Users\Mansoor\Downloads\
    C:\Windows\System32\
    C:\Temp\

Files accessed:
    C:\Users\Mansoor\Downloads\MALICIOUS.EXE
    C:\Windows\System32\somefile.dll
    C:\Temp\tempfile.tmp

Last Run Time: 2023-10-24 12:23:45 UTC

Trace Chains (Last 8 executions):
    1. 2023-10-24 12:23:45 UTC
    2. 2023-10-23 10:20:30 UTC
    3. 2023-10-22 14:15:15 UTC
```

The output provided by PECmd after analyzing a prefetch file such as `MALICIOUS.EXE.pf` is a rich source of forensic data. PECmd decodes the information stored within the prefetch file and presents it in a human-readable format, which includes a timestamp of the first and last time the application was run, the total number of times it was executed, and the files that were accessed during execution.

Here are some attacker TTPs to look out for when analyzing prefetch output:

- **Time stamping**: Prefetch files contain timestamps indicating the last time a particular application was run. This can help investigators correlate application execution times with other events on the system.

- **Application frequency**: By examining the run count within a prefetch file, analysts can determine how often an application is executed. Unusual frequencies can signal anomalous or malicious activity.

- **Volume information**: Prefetch files also store details about the volume from which an application was executed. This can be useful to trace back to potentially malicious external devices or volumes.

- **Application source path**: Identifying where an application was executed (for example, from a USB device or a specific directory) can help in piecing together an attacker's movement or actions on a host.

- **File and directory references**: Prefetch files list other files and directories that were accessed during the application's startup. This can highlight any dependent or associated files, which might also be malicious or compromised.

Prefetch files, though designed as a performance optimization feature, have cemented themselves as indispensable artifacts for incident responders.

AmCache analysis

AmCache, akin to prefetch, is a forensic artifact unique to Windows systems, particularly Windows 8 and above. The `AmCache.hve` file is a Windows registry hive that primarily serves the Windows Application Experience program, a feature aimed at ensuring software compatibility. Typically located at `C:\Windows\AppCompat\Programs\Amcache.hve`, this hive logs detailed metadata about executed applications, as well as information about connected hardware such as USB devices. While its primary function is software compatibility, the rich data it holds makes it an indispensable tool in forensic investigations.

Here's its forensic importance:

- **Binary metadata**: AmCache contains comprehensive metadata about executed binaries, such as the file path, last modification time, creation time, SHA-1 hash, and more. This helps forensic analysts trace the origin and history of executable files on the system.

- **Hardware footprints**: The hive also maintains records of plugged-in hardware devices, potentially allowing investigators to trace the insertion of malicious USB devices or external storage.

- **Correlation with execution**: By analyzing AmCache, forensic experts can correlate binary metadata with execution traces from other artifacts, offering a cohesive timeline of system activities.

One of the go-to tools for AmCache parsing is AmcacheParser, which is also part of Eric Zimmerman's suite of forensic tools. Like PECmd, it's open source and offers thorough parsing of the `AmCache.hve` file. Another licensed tool that offers robust AmCache parsing capabilities is Magnet AXIOM.

> **Important note**
>
> You can download AmcacheParser and find its usage details at `https://github.com/EricZimmerman/AmcacheParser`.

Imagine the execution of a malicious file named `malicious_mansoor.exe` on a Windows virtual machine hosted on a cloud. On obtaining the `AmCache.hve` file and parsing it with AmcacheParser, the output might look something like this:

```
> > AmcacheParser.exe -f C:\Users\Mansoor\Downloads\Amcache.hve
Processing C:\Users\Mansoor\Downloads\Amcache.hve
----------------------------------
Source File: C:\Users\Mansoor\Downloads\malicious_mansoor.exe
SHA-1: a1b2c3d4e5f67890a1b2c3d4e5f67890a1b2c3d4
File Created: 2023-09-14 12:01:12 UTC
File Last Modified: 2023-09-15 13:05:10 UTC
Run Count: 2
Associated Files:
    C:\Windows\System32\somefile.dll
    C:\Temp\tempfile.tmp
----------------------------------
```

Here are some key TTPs to look for when analyzing AmCache:

- **Binary hashes**: SHA-1 hashes in AmCache provide an opportunity to match known malicious hashes from threat intelligence feeds

- **File paths**: Unusual or suspicious file paths, especially ones located in temporary or uncommon directories, can hint toward malicious activities

- **File creation and modification**: Timestamps can be correlated with other system events to map out an attacker's actions

- **Associated files**: Like Prefetch, AmCache also provides references to files related to an executable, assisting in mapping out potentially malicious dependencies

AmCache hive, although created for compatibility, holds significant forensic potential. Alongside Prefetch, AmCache has proven its worth as a goldmine of information for incident response and digital forensics.

ShimCache analysis

ShimCache, formally known as Application Compatibility Cache, is a component of the Windows operating system that's designed to allow backward compatibility for applications designed for older versions of Windows. When Windows executes a program, it checks ShimCache to determine whether the application requires any "shims" or compatibility fixes to run correctly. ShimCache, in doing so, maintains a list of executables that have been run on the system, making it an invaluable resource for digital forensic analysts. The ShimCache information is stored within the Windows registry at `HKEY_LOCAL_MACHINE\SYSTEM\CurrentControlSet\Control\Session Manager\ AppCompatibility\AppCompatCache`.

Here's its forensic importance:

- **Execution history**: ShimCache maintains a list of the most recently executed applications, aiding forensic analysts in tracing which executables ran on the system. This list includes the file path, last modification time, and file size.

- **Persistence mechanism detection**: Malware often leverages various persistence mechanisms. Observing recurring entries in ShimCache for uncommon or suspicious paths can hint toward such persistence mechanisms.

- **Correlation with other artifacts**: Like AmCache, data from ShimCache can be cross-referenced with other forensic artifacts to provide a holistic view of the system's execution history and potential incidents.

A popular tool for extracting and parsing ShimCache entries is ShimCacheParser, also part of Eric Zimmerman's suite of forensic tools. It provides a structured output of the ShimCache entries, facilitating quick forensic analysis.

> **Important note**
> You can download ShimCacheParser and find its usage details at `https://github.com/ mandiant/ShimCacheParser`.

Consider a scenario where a malicious file named `malicious_mansoor.exe` is found on a Windows system. By extracting the ShimCache data and analyzing it using ShimCacheParser, the output might resemble the following:

```
> ShimCacheParser.exe -f SYSTEM
Processing SYSTEM hive...
---------------------------------
```

```
Source File: C:\Users\Mansoor\Downloads\malicious_mansoor.exe
File Last Modified: 2023-09-15 13:05:10 UTC
File Size: 24576 bytes
Execution Flag: Executed
----------------------------------
```

Based on this output, incident responders and forensic experts could say with high confidence that the malicious file was executed and at what point the malicious binary, `malicious_mansoor.exe`, may have been created or last changed on the filesystem.

Here are some key TTPs to look for when analyzing ShimCache:

- **File paths**: The presence of executables from uncommon or suspicious directories in ShimCache is often a red flag.

- **Execution flag**: While ShimCache logs executables, not all are necessarily executed. The execution flag distinguishes between mere presence and actual execution.

- **File modification time**: Anomalies in file modification times, especially if they correlate with known intrusion events, can be of significance.

- **File size and attributes**: Any deviations in file size or attributes from known good baselines can hint at potential tampering or malicious replacements.

ShimCache, which was designed for application compatibility, has evolved into an essential forensic artifact. Paired with other artifacts such as Prefetch and AmCache, ShimCache offers invaluable insights into system activities, aiding in thorough incident response and investigations.

Windows Event Logs

Windows Event Logs is a centralized system logging facility, inherent to Microsoft Windows systems. It provides detailed records of systems, security, applications, and other events. Whether it's tracking user activity, diagnosing system issues, monitoring security incidents, or ensuring regulatory compliance, Event Logs play a crucial role.

Here is the location:

- **Windows servers**: `C:\Windows\System32\winevt\Logs`
- **Windows 10 and Windows 11**: `C:\Windows\System32\winevt\Logs`

Here are some important Windows Event Logs:

- **Security logs**: Capture security-related events such as logons, logoffs, object access, account management, and more

- **System logs**: Reflect system components' activities, including drivers and services, capturing alerts on system failures, resource depletion, or other system-wide occurrences

- **Application logs**: Register application events, errors, warnings, and informational messages from installed applications and services

- **PowerShell logs**: Specifically record activities related to PowerShell commands, scripts, and modules

- **Terminal services (RDP)**: Pertain to **Remote Desktop Protocol** (**RDP**) sessions, capturing login successes and failures, disconnections, and other RDP-specific happenings

Here's the forensic importance:

- **Security logs**:

  - **Account logins**: Reveal when an account was authenticated

    - **Event ID 4624**: A successful logon

    - **Event ID 4625**: An account failed to log in

  - **Account management**: Show when user accounts or groups are created, changed, or deleted:

    - **Event ID 4720**: A user account was created

  - **Privilege use**: Indicate the use of special privileges

    - **Event ID 4672**: Special privileges assigned to a new logon

  - **Object access**: Detail when specific objects (files, directories) were accessed

    - **Event ID 4663**: An attempt was made to access an object

- **Terminal services (RDP)**:

  - **Event ID 4778**: A session was reconnected to a window station

  - **Event ID 4779**: A session was disconnected from a window station

- **PowerShell logs**:

  - **Event ID 4103**: Indicate that a PowerShell command or script block was executed

- **Lateral movement**:

  - **Event ID 5140**: A network share was accessed

  - **Event ID 5145**: A network share object was checked to see whether an object can be granted the desired access

- **Persistence via scheduled tasks**:

  - **Event ID 4698**: A scheduled task was created

- **Process/code execution**:

  - **Event ID 4688**: A new process has been created

To analyze Event Logs, you can use evtxECmd, an open source tool by Eric Zimmerman that provides extensive parsing capabilities.

> **Important note**
>
> You can download evtxECmd and find its usage details at `https://github.com/EricZimmerman/evtx`.

Here's a quick example of how you might determine which accounts have logged in to a host:

```
> evtxECmd.exe -f Security.evtx --csv out.csv
```

The output will be a CSV file with parsed Security Event Logs and columns corresponding to the fields:

	A	B	C	D	E	F
1	Timestamp	EventID	User	LogonType	SourceIP	Status
2	2023-10-24 12:01	4624	attackername	2	192.168.1.2	Success
3	2023-10-24 12:45	4625	admindoe	10	192.168.1.5	Failed

Figure 9.2 – Example of parsed security Event Logs (out.csv)

Here are some key TTPs to look for when analyzing Windows Event Logs:

- **Account enumeration**: A high volume of failed login attempts, especially with various usernames, can indicate account enumeration attempts. Look for multiple events with event ID 4625.

- **Suspicious RDP activity**: Frequent remote logins, especially during odd hours, can signal malicious activity. Event ID 4778 and event ID 4779 can assist.

- **Lateral movement**: A surge in network share access logs from unfamiliar systems may indicate lateral movement. Focus on event ID 5140 and event ID 5145.

- **Unusual PowerShell execution**: The execution of unexpected or rarely used PowerShell commands, tracked via event ID 4103, can hint at potential malicious activity.

- **Task scheduling for persistence**: Event ID 4698 indicates task scheduling. If a task is scheduled repeatedly, especially from unfamiliar sources or at high frequencies, it can signal a persistence mechanism.

- **Code execution outside norms**: Anomalies in process creation events, especially from uncommon directories or unknown binaries, can be a red flag. Use event ID 4688 for this.

Windows Event Logs are incredibly rich data sources that can provide a detailed view of nearly all activities on a system. Coupled with the right tools and an understanding of key events and indicators, they're indispensable in any serious forensic investigation or incident response.

Analyzing memory dumps

Memory dump forensics involves analyzing a snapshot of a system's volatile memory. It can reveal a treasure trove of evidence about a system's state at the time of the snapshot, from running processes to open network connections, in-memory artifacts, and even encryption keys or malware payloads that haven't been written to disk.

There are three types of memory dumps:

- **Full memory dump**: Captures the entire contents of physical memory (RAM)

- **Kernel memory dump**: Contains only the kernel-mode read/write pages

- **Small memory dump**: Records the smallest set of useful data, making it faster to save and easier to manage

Typically, memory dumps are first saved to the host's local disk, a choice driven by the speed and reliability of local storage, especially given the potentially large size of dump files. This is particularly relevant for full memory dumps, which capture the entire contents of physical memory (RAM) and thus are directly proportional in size to the amount of RAM in the system. For example, a system with 16 GB of RAM will result in a full memory dump of approximately the same size, necessitating substantial storage space.

Kernel memory dumps, containing only kernel-mode read/write pages, are smaller as they exclude user-mode applications and processes. Their size depends on the kernel footprint, usually much less than the total RAM but still sizeable. On the other hand, small memory dumps are significantly smaller, often just a few MBs, recording only the most essential data. They are quicker to save and manage, though they offer less comprehensive information.

Here's the forensic importance:

- **Active processes**: List all the processes running on the system, providing a real-time view of what was happening when the dump was taken.

- **Network connections**: Determine which remote systems the machine was communicating with.

- **Loaded modules**: Identify all drivers and dynamic link libraries (DLLs) loaded into memory. This can reveal injected DLLs or rootkits.

- **Decrypted data**: Sensitive data that might be encrypted on disk (e.g., passwords, encryption keys) can be found unencrypted in memory.

- **Malware artifacts**: Discover remnants of malware that might reside solely in memory and avoid being written to the filesystem.

Threat actors increasingly leverage techniques such as fileless malware, which operates entirely in memory, to evade traditional file-based detection methods. This makes memory forensics an essential component of incident response, especially in cases where not all evidence of compromise is written to the filesystem or captured in artifacts such as Prefetch, AmCache, ShimCache, and Event Logs. The importance of memory dump analysis depends on the nature of the compromise: for sophisticated attacks, especially those employing **advanced persistent threats** (**APTs**), memory analysis is often indispensable for uncovering the full extent of the compromise and the techniques used by the attackers. The caveat with memory forensics is that because they are run on the memory allocated by the RAM and not on the filesystem (and therefore the hard drive), they are cleared if the device is powered off.

The open source tool **Volatility** is a popular choice for memory dump forensics. It offers extensive plugin support, making it adaptable for various incident response tasks.

> **Important note**
>
> You can download Volatility and find its usage details at `https://www.volatilityfoundation.org/releases`.

Let's look at a sample analysis using Volatility:

1. Identify the image profile:

   ```
   > volatility -f memdump.raw imageinfo
   ```

   This will suggest suitable profiles for further analysis – for example, if there are profiles for Windows 10 architectures.

2. List the processes:

   ```
   > volatility -f memdump.raw --profile=Win10x86 pslist
   ```

   This displays active processes. Look for unusual or unexpected processes.

3. View network connections:

   ```
   > volatility -f memdump.raw --profile=Win10x86 netscan
   ```

   Review the established connections for any suspicious activity.

Here are the key TTPs to look for when analyzing memory dumps:

- **Process injection**: Unusual child processes or unexpected parent-child process relationships can indicate process injection.

- **Hidden processes**: Malware often tries to hide its processes. Detecting these can point to rootkit activity or evasion techniques.

- **Unexpected network connections**: Look out for those, especially to known malicious IPs or unfamiliar foreign addresses.

- **Hooks**: Some malware types use hooks to intercept system calls. Detecting these can be indicative of rootkits or certain types of spyware.

- **Strings analysis**: Extracting and analyzing strings from a memory dump can reveal paths, commands, URLs, and other malware indicators.

- **In-memory file extraction**: Extracting files that exist only in memory can unveil malicious payloads that avoid the filesystem or any artifacts that were deleted from the disk but linger in memory.

Memory dump forensics offers unique insights that aren't always obtainable from disk-based forensics. This form of analysis can be crucial, especially when dealing with advanced threats that use in-memory evasion or reside solely in volatile memory. Proper tools and a keen eye for anomalies make memory forensics a formidable weapon in the arsenal of every incident responder.

Misconfigured virtual machine instances

One of the prevalent entry points for attackers in cloud environments is through misconfigured virtual machine instances. The beauty of the cloud is how rapid the deployment of VMs can be. However, the downside of this is that configurations may be overlooked or improperly set. Such oversights grant threat actors unintended access or provide them with information to further their intrusions. Let's look at some common misconfigurations.

Unnecessary ports left open

Open ports function as communication endpoints for virtual machines. Each port allows a specific type of communication, such as HTTP traffic on port 80. However, leaving unused or unnecessary ports open expands the potential attack surface. An attacker can exploit open ports by identifying vulnerabilities associated with the services listening on these ports. It's essential to ensure that only required ports are open and accessible.

Here are some indicators to look for:

- **Host level (Windows)**:

  - Windows event ID 5156 (Windows Filtering Platform has permitted a connection) can be monitored to detect allowed network connections

- Windows event ID 5157 (Windows Filtering Platform has blocked a connection) can alert to blocked connection attempts

- **CSP**:

    - **AWS**: VPC Flow Logs, as discussed previously, can be used to observe the traffic that is reaching the virtual machine

    - **Azure**: NSG Flow Logs, as discussed previously, can offer insights into network traffic targeting the virtual machines

Default credentials left unchanged

Virtual machines often come with default administrator credentials for initial setup and access. While this is convenient for deployment, leaving these default credentials unchanged poses a significant security risk. Attackers are well aware of default credentials for many systems and can easily gain unauthorized access if they aren't updated.

Here's an indicator to look for:

- **Host level (Windows)**: Windows event ID 4625 (an account failed to log on) can be monitored to detect and respond to failed login attempts.

Outdated or unpatched software

Regularly updating and patching software and operating systems is a fundamental security practice. Over time, vulnerabilities in software are discovered, and patches are released to address them. Running outdated or unpatched software exposes the virtual machine to known vulnerabilities, creating opportunities for exploitation by attackers who target these weaknesses.

Here are some indicators to look for:

- **Host level (Windows)**:

    - Windows event ID 4375 (Windows Installer updated an installed product) can provide insights into patch installations and software updates

    - Software inventories and/or vulnerability scans using tools such as Nessus

- **CSP**:

    - **AWS**: AWS Systems Manager Patch Manager can be utilized for automated patching based on set policies.

    - **Azure**: Azure Security Center highlights unpatched virtual machines and recommends relevant security patches.

- **GCP:** GCP's operating system patch management service, Patch, allows for the scheduling and automation of patch deployment across virtual machine instances in Google Cloud. It provides features for patch compliance reporting and configuration of patch rollout schedules, ensuring that virtual machines are updated with the latest security patches.

Publicly exposed sensitive data (or metadata)

Data exposure is a critical issue, especially when sensitive or personal data is involved. Whether due to incorrect access controls, oversight, or misconfigured settings, public exposure of sensitive data can lead to data breaches, reputational damage, and potential regulatory repercussions. Ensuring strict access controls and regular audits is imperative to prevent unintentional data exposure. Let's take a closer look:

- **Host level (Windows):**

    - Windows event ID 4663 (an attempt was made to access an object) can be monitored to detect unusual or unexpected access attempts to sensitive files

    - Application logs at the software application level

- **CSP:**

    - **AWS:** Amazon has additional services that are designed to discover, classify, and safeguard sensitive data within AWS S3 – for example, Amazon Macie.

    - **Azure:** Azure storage logging through Azure Monitor helps monitor and analyze requests made to storage resources, ensuring only authorized access.

    - **GCP:** GCP's Sensitive Data Protection suite of services helps in discovering and classifying sensitive data across GCP services. Google Cloud Storage also offers detailed logging and monitoring capabilities through Cloud Audit Logs, allowing requests to storage resources to be tracked and analyzed.

By understanding these areas of misconfiguration and by actively monitoring for the associated indicators, organizations can greatly enhance their virtual machine security posture in the cloud.

Misconfigured storage buckets

Misconfigured storage buckets have emerged as a significant vulnerability in cloud environments. Cloud storage solutions, such as Amazon's S3 buckets or Azure Blob Storage, are often set up with ease and speed in mind. However, without rigorous security configurations, they can inadvertently become publicly accessible or easily breached. Such misconfigurations expose sensitive data, leading to potential data leaks and compromising organizational integrity. Let's look at some common misconfigurations that may allow unauthorized access.

Public permissions

Storage resources are typically created with a default private setting, ensuring that only properly authenticated and authorized entities can access the stored data. However, sometimes, these permissions are altered, either for convenience or by mistake, leading to unintentional public exposure.

Here are some indicators to look for:

- **AWS**:

  - Navigate to the Amazon S3 console. Check the **Access** column for each bucket. If any of them are labeled as **Public**, then there's potential exposure.

  - The AWS CLI can be used as follows:

    ```
    aws s3api get-bucket-acl --bucket YOUR_BUCKET_NAME
    ```

    If `Grantee: Group` has a URI of `http://acs.amazonaws.com/groups/global/AllUsers`, then the bucket has public permissions.

- **Azure**:

  - In the Azure portal, under **Blob Service | Containers**, check the **Public Access Level** property of each container.

  - We can use the Azure CLI as follows:

    ```
    az storage container show --name YOUR_CONTAINER_NAME
    --account-name YOUR_STORAGE_ACCOUNT --query 'properties.
    publicAccess'
    ```

    If the output is `Blob` or `Container`, there's public accessibility.

Exposed API keys or credentials

Storage buckets sometimes mistakenly contain sensitive files that hold API keys, credentials, or other secrets. If an attacker gains access to these, they could compromise systems or data associated with those keys.

Here are some indicators to look for:

- **AWS**:

  - Look for files with names such as `*.pem`, `*.json`, `credentials`, `keys`, and so on within your S3 buckets.

  - You can use the following AWS CLI sample to list all the files in a bucket:

    ```
    aws s3 ls s3://YOUR_BUCKET_NAME/ --recursive
    ```

- **Azure**:

  - Search within blob containers for files with extensions or names similar to `*.pfx`, `*.json`, `credentials`, `keys`, and so on

  - You can use the following Azure CLI sample to list blobs in a container:

```
az storage blob list --container-name YOUR_CONTAINER_NAME
--account-name YOUR_STORAGE_ACCOUNT --output table
```

Improper use of IAM policies

IAM controls who or what can perform actions on specific resources. Improper IAM configurations could give users or roles more access than they need, violating the principle of least privilege.

Here are some indicators to look for:

- **AWS**:

  - Review IAM policies attached to users, groups, and roles. In particular, scrutinize any policy allowing `s3:*` actions on `s3:::YOUR_BUCKET_NAME/*`.

  - You can use the following AWS CLI sample to list policies for a user:

```
aws iam list-attached-user-policies --user-name YOUR_USERNAME
```

- **Azure**:

  - Review **role-based access control** (**RBAC**) assignments on the storage account. Ensure there are no overly permissive roles such as Owner or Contributor assigned to identities that don't need them.

  - You can use the following Azure CLI sample to list role assignments for a storage account:

```
az role assignment list --assignee YOUR_OBJECT_ID --scope /
subscriptions/YOUR_SUBSCRIPTION_ID/resourceGroups/YOUR_RESOURCE_
GROUP/providers/Microsoft.Storage/storageAccounts/YOUR_STORAGE_
ACCOUNT
```

By regularly reviewing and ensuring the correct configurations of storage buckets and associated permissions, organizations can reduce the risk of data exposure and potential compromises.

Cloud administrator portal breach

Gaining access to the cloud administrator portal is akin to handing over the keys to the entire cloud kingdom. An attacker with such access can not only view sensitive data but can manipulate configurations, delete crucial resources, and potentially incur huge costs by spawning large amounts of resources. Let's take a closer look at what attacks can be performed:

- **Brute-force attacks**: Attackers use software to try as many combinations as possible to gain access

  Indicator: Multiple failed login attempts from the same IP address in a short period

- **Credential stuffing**: Attackers use previously breached usernames and passwords

  Indicator: Login attempts with multiple usernames from the same IP address

- **Phishing attacks**: Attackers deceive users into providing their login credentials

  Indicator: Users accessing cloud portals from unfamiliar referrer URLs or logging in from unfamiliar locations

- **Token theft**: Attackers steal authentication tokens or session cookies.

  Indicator: Unusual user agent strings or unexpected locations paired with familiar user accounts

AWS detections:

- **CloudTrail**: AWS CloudTrail provides the event history of your AWS account activity. Look for the following:

  - `eventName` such as `ConsoleLogin` paired with `errorMessage` such as `Failed authentication` for failed logins

  - Multiple `sourceIPAddresses` for the same `userIdentity` in a short period might suggest suspicious activity

  - AWS management console sign-in URL redirection, which can be an indicator of phishing attempts

- **GuardDuty**: This is a threat detection service. Check for findings such as `UnauthorizedAccess:IAMUser/ConsoleLogin`, which indicates suspicious console logins.

Azure detections:

- **Azure activity log**: Provides incident responders with insight into operations that were performed on resources. Search for the following:

  - Activities with a status of **Failed** linked with **Sign-in** operations

  - Unusual IP addresses or regions associated with successful sign-ins

- **Azure AD sign-ins**: This provides incident responders with access to the sign-in activity within the tenant. Look for the following:

  - Multiple failed sign-in attempts

  - Sign-in attempts from unfamiliar locations or unusual devices

By understanding the TTPs and regularly monitoring the relevant logs, incident responders and defenders can detect and potentially prevent breaches due to weak authentication in cloud environments. Even though secure multi-factor authentication has become more common, the cybersecurity landscape is fast evolving and new threats may emerge that may require incident responders to respond to complete administrator portal takeovers.

Summary

In this chapter, you learned about the challenges and risks that come with cloud security. We discussed how cloud environments, despite their advantages, have unique security issues. From misconfigured virtual machine instances to unprotected storage buckets, we highlighted the areas where mistakes can happen and how they can be exploited by attackers.

You've also gained insights into host-based forensics, diving into key indicators such as prefetch, AmCache, ShimCache, Windows Event Logs, and memory dumps. We touched on the importance of securing virtual machines, covering open ports, default credentials, and outdated software. Storage bucket configurations and their potential pitfalls were also discussed. Lastly, we delved into the crucial topic of authentication, emphasizing the serious outcomes of a cloud administrator portal breach.

As we transition to the next chapter on cloud evidence acquisition, we'll focus on collecting evidence in cloud environments.

Further reading

The MITRE ATT&CK matrix for cloud-based techniques: `https://attack.mitre.org/matrices/enterprise/cloud/`.

10

Cloud Evidence Acquisition

Until now, we have looked at investigating artifacts locally within the cloud using the tools provided by the **Cloud Service Provider** (CSP). We looked at AWS GuardDuty CloudTrail from a logging and investigation point of view. We also looked at GCP's Cloud Logging capability to investigate cloud logs emitted by various services, and Azure Monitor offers similar capabilities for services hosted within Microsoft Azure.

This chapter will take a step further in our cloud investigative journey and look at methods and techniques for securely collecting artifacts or forensic images of core services for offline analysis. Investigators will recognize that not all investigations can be performed using native cloud tools. Investigators may be required to use specialized tools that they have access to in a forensic environment, and the challenge will be to collect images from the cloud in a forensically sound and legally acceptable manner. We will explore these tools in the later sections of this chapter. We will be looking at forensic collections from the three significant CSPs:

- Forensic acquisition of AWS instances

- Forensic acquisition of Microsoft Azure Instances

- Forensic acquisition of GCP instances

Note that throughout this chapter, we will rely on some standard steps for collecting forensic images when investigators can access a Windows or a Linux operating system; these steps are standard irrespective of the underlying cloud platform.

Forensic acquisition of AWS instance

Let us jump right into the details of collecting forensic artifacts in a secure and forensically sound manner. We will assume that an organization received alerts for ransomware deployment on an **Elastic Compute Cloud** (EC2) instance. As a result, this instance was stopped. Forensic investigators would need to pull forensic artifacts out of the EC2 instance safely.

Any disks associated with an EC2 instance are referred to as **volumes** by AWS. To collect artifacts, investigators have to follow a specific sequence of steps. Firstly, investigators must record the infected instance's **instance ID** (unique identifier).

In this case, the infected instance name is CF2 and it has the instance ID i-00229ce2dd123a2e6.

Step 1 – creating EC2 volume snapshots

We will refer to these EC2 instances by their instance ID for the following steps:

1. Investigators must note storage volumes associated with i-00229ce2dd123a2e6 (CF2) and the volume IDs (a unique identifier for each volume):

Figure 10.1 – Volumes (disks) associated with 00229ce2dd123a2e (CF2)

2. We see two volumes attached to i-00229ce2dd123a2e (CF2). AWS will always assign the root drive (C:\) to /dev/sda1. This is an investigator's reference point if they only want to collect forensic images of the root drive.

3. We select the root drive, vol-061392d9abebf9433, attached to instance i-00229ce2dd123a2e (CF2), which takes us to the **Volumes** page, identified in the following screenshot:

Figure 10.2 – Selecting the volume that requires forensic imaging

4. Under the **Actions** tab, select the **Create snapshot** option. Snapshot creates a copy of the original volume without modifying the volume. We demonstrate this in *Figure 10.3*. Investigators must note that volumes associated with an EC2 instance cannot directly be downloaded or exported. It is always recommended to perform forensics on a copy or a snapshot of the original volume instead of the original volume to preserve artifacts.

Figure 10.3 – Selecting the AWS volume for the snapshot

5. Depending on the size of the volume, creating a snapshot may take seconds to a few minutes. Investigators must wait until proceeding further, ensuring snapshots are successfully created. In *Figure 10.4*, we see the successful completion of the snapshot. All the snapshots will be available under the **Snapshots** navigation tab within AWS EC2. Investigations must again record the unique snapshot ID. In this case, this is `snap-0857fc1efa85ae0ff`.

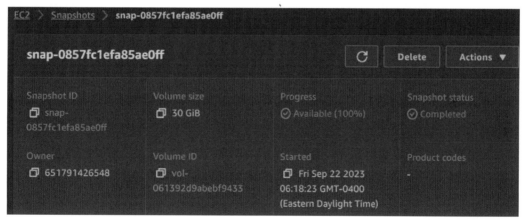

Figure 10.4 – Snapshot created of AWS Volume (vol-061392d9abebf9433)

Step 2 – acquiring OS memory images

Let us now look at methods of acquiring memory images of an EC2 instance forensically. Should there be a need for taking a memory image as part of the investigation, DFIR teams can consider some common steps as long as the infected instance is still running. Investigators have some form of interactive access to the infected instance via the command line (AWS **System Manager** (**SSM**) or GCP's Cloud Shell) or direct access to the instance via RDP or SSH. If possible, investigators must ensure that their identities are configured with the `AmazonSSMFullAccess` policy to allow complete access to the EC2 instance through Amazon SSM.

Taking a memory image is more complicated than a disk image. One of the simplest methods would be switching the EC2 instance into hibernation mode, which forces all the memory contents to be written to the disk in the form of `hyberfil.sys` before a complete disk evidence collection can be performed, allowing investigators to utilize a snapshot of the memory.

Step 2a – acquiring memory images via hibernation

One of the options that AWS allows within its EC2 dashboard is hibernation. Select the instance, choose **Instance state**, and select **Hibernation**. However, for AWS to hibernate the EC2 instance (on Windows or Linux), it must meet the following conditions:

- AWS supports the cloud native hibernation feature only on select instance families.

- When launching an EC2 instance, administrators should have enabled the **Hibernation** feature under **Advanced settings** to enable this behavior. This cannot be changed after an EC2 instance is created/launched.

- The EC2 instance must have root storage space to accommodate memory contents.

- Only specific **Elastic Block Storage** (**EBS**) volumes are supported, including General Purpose SSD (`gp2` and `gp3`) or Provisioned IOPS SSD (`io1` and `io2`)

AWS will not support cloud-native hibernation if the preceding conditions are not configured.

Once hibernation is enabled, investigators can capture memory contents by hibernating via the cloud console and collecting disk images for forensics.

Step 2b – common steps for acquiring memory images directly from OS

The process for memory acquisition is quite simple, but securely acquiring a forensic image is a manual process. You will note that there are various ways this can be automated; however, it depends on the level of access the investigators have and their roles (external (one-time) investigators or in-house corporate investigators). If it's in-house and organizations have a bigger footprint in the cloud, they can look into automating forensic collections and uploading to the cloud storage in various ways. In the *Further reading* section, we have included some ideas that leverage other cloud services. However, these steps provide you with a guide to make forensic data acquisition easier.

The following steps will provide a high-level overview of collecting memory images from relevant operating systems. Investigators must ensure that they can connect to the instance, either through an interactive RDP session or through a command line using cloud-native command line capabilities:

Collecting memory images from a Windows OS instance

Once investigators log into the infected Windows instance, they can begin their collections:

1. Specifically in AWS, this can be achieved by either directly logging into the affected virtual machine or via Amazon SSM.

2. Using `powershell.exe` with Windows Administrator privileges, create a folder to place all the memory dumps and artifacts in.

3. We then download the most recent version of `winpmem.exe` (we referred to this tool in *Chapter 8*) using the following command:

```
> Invoke-WebRequest -Uri https://github.com/Velocidex/WinPmem/
releases/download/v4.0.rc1/winpmem_mini_x64_rc2.exe -OutFile
"winpmem.exe"
```

4. Once it's been downloaded, we run it within the same PowerShell window. We run the tool and provide a file name as a parameter to save the memory into a file. Note that we are capturing the memory in RAW format:

```
> winpmem.exe memory.raw
```

5. The following screenshots demonstrate the in-progress memory collection. Depending upon the size of the memory, this may take anything from a few seconds to a few minutes:

```
 3 memory ranges:
Start 0x00001000 - Length 0x0009D000
Start 0x00100000 - Length 0x00002000
Start 0x00103000 - Length 0x3FEFD000
max_physical_memory_ 0x40000000
Acquitision mode PTE Remapping
Padding from 0x00000000 to 0x00001000
pad
 - length: 0x1000

00% 0x00000000 .
copy_memory
 - start: 0x1000
 - end: 0x9e000

00% 0x00001000 .
Padding from 0x0009E000 to 0x00100000
pad
 - length: 0x62000

00% 0x0009E000 .
copy_memory
 - start: 0x100000
 - end: 0x102000

00% 0x00100000 .
Padding from 0x00102000 to 0x00103000
pad
 - length: 0x1000

00% 0x00102000 .
copy_memory
 - start: 0x103000
 - end: 0x40000000

00% 0x00103000 .............................
```

Figure 10.5 – Memory dump using winpmem.exe

Once memory collections are complete, investigators must export the memory dump to a remote server or cloud-native storage area for offline access and processing. Alternatively, depending on an investigator's preference, you can also turn off the operating system and take a complete disk snapshot, and through forensic disk imaging, the memory images can later be exported as an artifact during the offline processing of the disk images.

Acquiring memory images from a Linux OS

Key differences investigators must know about are the different Linux and Windows operating system tools for memory acquisition. In some cases, investigators must first compile the specialized tools from the source to collect forensic images of the memory. This is because these tools make use of low-level libraries that are specific to the Linux kernel versions. For this purpose, we use **LiME**, which allows for full volatile memory acquisition in Linux.

Here are the steps for collecting memory images:

1. Once relevant access is secured, investigators must ensure they can download and compile tools from the source. They will also need access to the `sudo` command. In this case, we will use the LiME tool for memory capture. We will download them from GitHub using a command compile them. It is best if all the following commands are run with `sudo` privileges (meaning as `root`):

    ```
    # git clone https://github.com/504ensicsLabs/LiME.git
    # cd LiME/src
    # make
    ```

2. Once LiME is compiled within the virtual machine, you can collect memory images using the following command. Ensure you have a folder created to save your memory artifacts in. In our example, we will save the memory image within `/home/ubuntu/ir_forensics/` as `memory.dump`

    ```
    root@ip-172-31-2-215:/home/ubuntu/ir_forensics/LiME/src# insmod
    lime-$(uname -r).ko "path=/home/ubuntu/ir_forensics/memory.dump
    format=lime"
    ```

3. The following parameters are supplied for collecting the memory image. We are running LiME from the `src` folder, as the compiled version is saved in this folder:

    *   `insmod`: This command inserts a kernel module into a running Linux kernel.

    *   `lime-$(uname -r).ko`: This command part specifies the kernel module to load. It uses command substitution (`$(uname -r)`) to dynamically insert the current kernel version into the filename, loading a LiME module tailored to the currently running kernel version.

    *   `path=/home/ubuntu/ir_foreniscs/memory.dump`: This parameter specifies the path to save the memory dump.

    *   `format=lime`: This parameter specifies the format in which the memory dump should be saved, which is `lime` in this case.

4. Once the command executes completely and a memory dump is generated, investigators can export the artifacts and analyze them offline using the tool of their choice, including volatility.

Step 3 – creating a forensic collector instance

Once snapshots are successfully created, investigators must prepare a forensic collector instance. Some DFIR teams may already have their instance pre-created or use a templated virtual machine created for this purpose. Any of the preceding methods is suitable for forensically collecting the artifacts. Investigators must, however, note that when creating a forensic collector instance, the storage size of the collector instance must be appropriately configured. In general, it is recommended to configure a storage space for forensic data that is at least 120% or more of the original volume.

We are creating an **Ubuntu Linux** for our forensic collections since Ubuntu natively supports the dd tool and Windows and Linux filesystems. No other live forensic tools are installed on Ubuntu for this demonstration, and it's purely used for forensic collection. Investigators must, however, consider assigning higher CPU and memory for the instance since it will be doing bulk bit-by-bit copying, which requires more CPU cycles.

Some investigators may create vast storage space and save all their forensic images within the same storage space, treat it like a USB Drive, or create separate storage for specific volumes. Either way, as long as there's enough space for the forensic image to be saved, that is all that matters. We created a 100 GB storage volume to capture our forensic image in our target forensic collector instance, although we know the original infected system had only 30 GB of disk size. This should be good enough for all the bit-by-bit copying into the target storage.

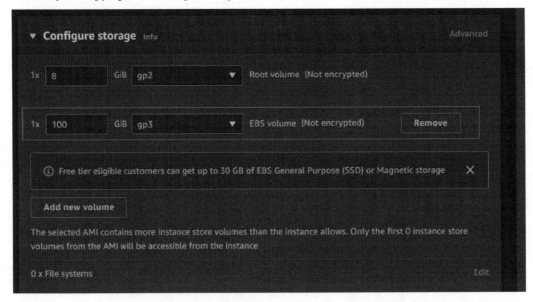

Figure 10.6 – Creating a new storage for forensic collections

Once the instance is created (`i-00747860d682ac481 (EC2_FORENSIC_CAPTURE)`) and additional storage is set up, we mount the disk, as indicated in the following screenshot. See `/dev/nvme1n1p1`, which is mounted as `/forensic`:

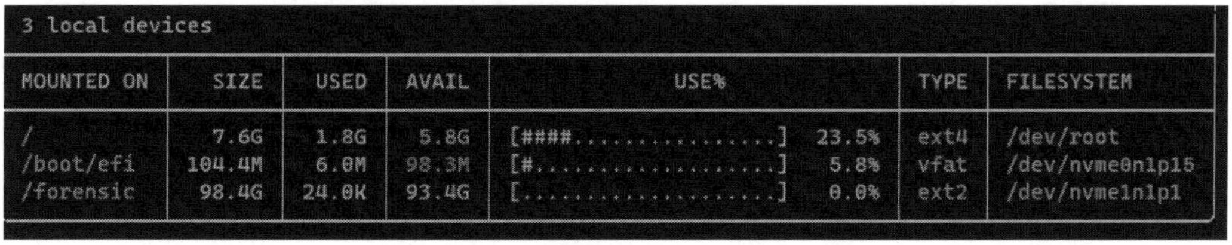

```
3 local devices

MOUNTED ON    SIZE    USED   AVAIL            USE%                TYPE   FILESYSTEM

/             7.6G    1.8G   5.8G   [####..............] 23.5%   ext4   /dev/root
/boot/efi     104.4M  6.0M   98.3M  [#.................]  5.8%   vfat   /dev/nvme0n1p15
/forensic     98.4G   24.0K  93.4G  [..................]  0.0%   ext2   /dev/nvme1n1p1
```

Figure 10.7 – Additional storage for forensic collections (initialized and mounted)

Refer to the *Further reading* section for information about initializing and mounting disks in Ubuntu Linux.

> **Note**
>
> Once the target EC2 instance is created (forensic collector), investigators must note the **availability zone** of this instance. We will explain the importance of this in *step 4*.

In our case, the forensic collector instance is hosted in `ca-central-1d`. This information is only made available once the EC2 instance is created.

Step 4 – creating and attaching infected volume from snapshots

Specifically for forensic purposes, we will create a volume from the snapshot we created in *step 1* and attach it to the target volume we created in *step 2*:

1. The first step is to initiate the volume creation process from the snapshot. As indicated in the following screenshot, we select the snapshot we created in *step 1* and then use the **Actions** option to **Create volume from snapshot**:

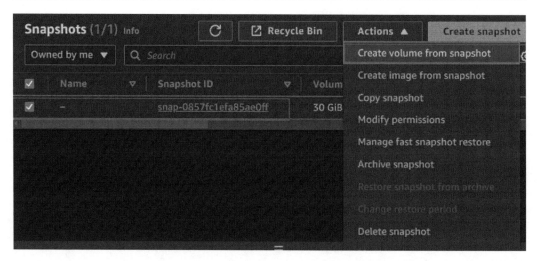

Figure 10.8 – Create volume from Snapshot (created in step 1)

2. As indicated in *step 2*, the forensic collector instance is created in the `ca-central-1d` availability zone. Investigators will require this information as volumes are assigned to an availability zone. If appropriate availability zones are not selected, the created volumes will not be available to attach to the target EC2 instance. We follow on-screen instructions on creating the volume; however, ensure that you map the volume to an availability zone that we recorded in *step 2* (`ca-central-1d`). Once a volume is created, availability zones cannot be changed, so it is essential to select the correct availability zone.

3. Record the volume ID upon creating the volume from the snapshot. In our case, the volume ID (as reflected in the following screenshot) is `vol-09ba3e6ad9ed12e5b`:

Figure 10.9 – Successful volume creation from snapshot

4. Once the volume is successfully created, we attach the new volume to the forensic collector EC2 instance (i-00747860d682ac481 (EC2_FORENSIC_CAPTURE)). We filter the new volume based on its unique identifier, select the volume, and under **Actions**, select **Attach volume**. No limitation exists on how many volumes can be attached to an EC2 instance:

Figure 10.10 – Attaching a volume to the EC2 instance

5. As indicated in the next screenshot, we follow on-screen instructions. However, one specific area that requires investigators to pay attention is mapping the volume to the correct instance; therefore, investigators must record the unique instance ID to ensure the volumes are attached correctly. In our case, we attach the volume (vol-09ba3e6ad9ed12e5b) to the EC2 instance (i-00747860d682ac481 (EC2_FORENSIC_CAPTURE)). As you can see, key elements are highlighted in the following screenshot. This is where everything comes together: the **Volume ID**, which reflects the new volume (vol-09ba3e6ad9ed12e5b) we created from the snapshot (snap-0957fc1efa85ae0ff) in *step 1*, the **Availability Zone** (ca-central-1d), which we recorded in *step 2* upon creating the EC2 instance and also when volume was created, and the **Instance** itself, which is the EC2 instance we created for forensic collections (i-00747860d682ac481 (EC2_FORENSIC_CAPTURE)):

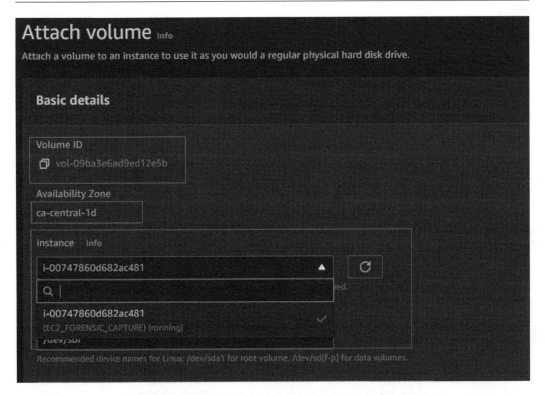

Figure 10.11 – Attaching volumes to EC2 instance for forensics

6.   Note that AWS will reference attached volumes as mount points; in this case, for AWS, the device name mount point is /dev/sdf, which may not be the same when accessing the volume within the Ubuntu Linux operating system.

7.   Now we switch to the Ubuntu Linux, our forensic collector system (i-00747860d682ac481 (EC2_FORENSIC_CAPTURE)).

Step 4a – common steps for acquiring instance disk images

Irrespective of the cloud service provider, the following steps are common steps that would be followed for collecting operating system forensic data. Before we start the forensic collection, ensure that pre-requisites are completed, which includes taking a snapshot, creating a forensic collector instance, and so on:

1.   Once infected volume snapshots are created within the cloud console, investigators can perform full disk forensic data collections. We will leverage the dd command natively available on Linux Ubuntu to do this.

2.   We will create a forensic collector instance on the same cloud platform to attach snapshots to the forensic collector instance as disk volumes.

3. We validate whether the new volume was correctly attached; see the following screenshot. We do this by running the `lsblk` command along with validating the filesystem information for the identified disk by running `sudo file -s /dev/nvme2n1p1`:

```
ubuntu@ip-172-31-45-98:/$ lsblk
NAME           MAJ:MIN RM   SIZE RO TYPE MOUNTPOINTS
loop0            7:0    0  24.4M  1 loop /snap/amazon-ssm-agent/6312
loop1            7:1    0  55.6M  1 loop /snap/core18/2745
loop2            7:2    0  63.3M  1 loop /snap/core20/1879
loop3            7:3    0 111.9M  1 loop /snap/lxd/24322
loop4            7:4    0  53.2M  1 loop /snap/snapd/19122
nvme0n1        259:0    0    8G  0 disk
├─nvme0n1p1    259:2    0   7.9G  0 part /
├─nvme0n1p14   259:3    0    4M  0 part
└─nvme0n1p15   259:4    0   106M  0 part /boot/efi
nvme1n1        259:1    0   100G  0 disk
└─nvme1n1p1    259:5    0   100G  0 part /forensic
nvme2n1        259:6    0   30G  0 disk
└─nvme2n1p1    259:7    0   30G  0 part
ubuntu@ip-172-31-45-98:/$ sudo file -s /dev/nvme2n1p1
/dev/nvme2n1p1: DOS/MBR boot sector, code offset 0x52+2, OEM-ID "NTFS    ", sectors/cluster 8, Media descriptor 0xf8, se
ctors/track 63, heads 255, hidden sectors 2048, dos < 4.0 BootSector (0x80), FAT (1Y bit by descriptor); NTFS, sectors/t
rack 63, sectors 62910463, $MFT start cluster 786432, $MFTMirror start cluster 2, bytes/RecordSegment 2^(-1*246), cluste
rs/index block 1, serial number 026702e69702e4043; contains bootstrap BOOTMGR
ubuntu@ip-172-31-45-98:/$
```

Figure 10.12 – Validating volumes attached to the EC2 instance

4. For entire disk forensic imaging, mounting disks to the instance (within the OS) is unnecessary; dd will image the whole volume directly. However, if investigations prefer to pull down specific artifacts (as outlined in *Chapter 8*), they can manually mount the disk to a mount point and extract relevant artifacts.

5. Before initiating the dd command, investigators must also ensure the target storage where the forensic images will be saved is created and mounted with read-write privileges. We run the following command to initiate forensic data collection. Ensure you have access to the sudo command, as this will be a low-level forensic collection:

```
$ sudo dd if=/dev/nvme2n1p1 of=/forensic/cf2.raw bs=4M
status=progress
```

Here are the details of the parameters supplied for the dd command:

- `if=/dev/nvme2n1p1`: This is the source disk that you need a copy of.

- `of=/forensic/cf2.raw`: We dump the forensic image in raw format at /forensic mount point. You can dump the forensic image in any format if the tool supports it. The forensic image is saved as cf2.raw (similar to the hostname of the infected EC2 instance) and is stored under the folder /forensic/.

- `bs=4M`: This sets the block size to 4 MB; you can adjust the value based on the needs.

The following screenshot reflects the completion of forensic acquisition via the dd command:

```
ubuntu@ip-172-31-45-98:~$ sudo dd if=/dev/nvme2n1p1 of=/forensic/cf2_image.raw bs=4M status=progress
32094814208 bytes (32 GB, 30 GiB) copied, 1759 s, 18.2 MB/s
7679+1 records in
7679+1 records out
32210157568 bytes (32 GB, 30 GiB) copied, 1761.28 s, 18.3 MB/s
```

Figure 10.13 – Outputs from the dd command

6. Optionally, once forensic imaging is completed, investigators can validate the accuracy by hashing both the source and destination points. For example, in the following snippet, we validate the hashes by running the md5sum command and confirming that the acquisition is accurate:

```
ubuntu@ip-172-31-45-98:~$ sudo md5sum /forensic/cf2_image.raw
e24806611c969189ec53a013e143f883  /forensic/cf2_image.raw
ubuntu@ip-172-31-45-98:~$ sudo md5sum /dev/nvme2n1p1
e24806611c969189ec53a013e143f883  /dev/nvme2n1p1
```

Once these steps are completed, investigators must determine their export options. Simply put, investigators can either upload these artifacts to the cloud-hosted storage (AWS S3, Azure Blob Storage, GCP Cloud Storage) or upload them to a remote server controlled by the investigator for offline analysis.

Step 5 – exporting collected images to AWS S3 for offline processing

Now that we have completed *steps 1–4*, our forensic image can be processed offline or offsite. However, before offline processing, you will have to export it. One of the most common methods investigators use is exporting via an S3 bucket:

1. Investigators must ensure that an S3 bucket is created and their account is configured with an AWS access key and secret key to access S3 buckets via the command line within EC2. Default configurations will not allow access to S3 buckets.

2. Once a bucket is created and access to AWS S3 is configured, you are all set to export. You can export by running the following command:

```
aws s3 cp /forensic/ s3://forensicbucket1/ --recursive
```

The following parameters are typically supplied with the aws s3 command:

- cp: Initiates the copy function, similar to the command available in most Linux variants

- /forensic/: The source folder name you would like to export

- S3://foreniscbucket1/: The destination S3 bucket where the files must be uploaded; command line parameters require using the s3:// nomenclature

- --recursive: Copy everything within the source folder, including sub-folders, to the destination bucket

The following screenshot reflects the copy process:

```
ubuntu@ip-172-31-45-98:~$ aws s3 cp /forensic/ s3://forensicbucket1/ --recursive
warning: Skipping file /forensic/lost+found. File/Directory is not readable.
upload: ../../forensic/cf2_image.raw to s3://forensicbucket1/cf2_image.raw
ubuntu@ip-172-31-45-98:~$
```

Figure 10.14 – Exporting files to AWS S3 from the command-line interface (CLI)

3. If the `aws s3` command is unavailable, run `sudo apt install aws-cli`, followed by the `aws configure` command, and follow on-screen instructions to configure the AWS access key and secret key.

4. Once uploads are completed, you can validate them via the S3 dashboard online. Investigators can download the file directly on the forensic workstations for further analysis. The next screenshot confirms successful uploads to the S3 bucket from the EC2 instance:

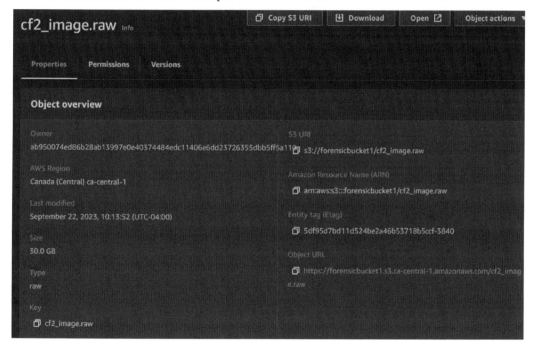

Figure 10.15 – Uploading forensic images to AWS S3

5. Most forensic tools can access RAW files; investigators can add this forensic image to their forensic case library and begin their offline processing.

As we can see here, there are steps within AWS Console that you are required to perform to ensure access to the operating systems and memory to capture images. However, complications are added when you export the artifacts or full disk images of these AWS instances, which requires specific steps to be followed.

Forensic acquisition of Microsoft Azure Instances

Like AWS, Microsoft Azure offers a similar approach when collecting the full disk image of an **Azure Virtual Machine** (**VM**) instance. You will have to specifically create a snapshot and then look to export the snapshot. Let us look at these specific steps in detail.

Step 1 – creating an Azure VM Snapshot

As indicated earlier, each cloud platform will have slight variations in terms of the steps to achieve an entire disk and memory imaging; familiarity with these variations will help investigators greatly to the point where they can automate basic tasks if the number of VMs for forensic acquisition is significant:

1. The first step is ensuring investigators have information about the infected Azure VM. This includes the VM name and operating system.

2. Investigators can create a full disk snapshot of this infected Azure VM. Investigators may prefer to turn off the VM entirely before taking the snapshot. Snapshots are accessible via the navigation page of the VM. Once on the snapshot page, we will select the **Create snapshot** option, as indicated in the following screenshot:

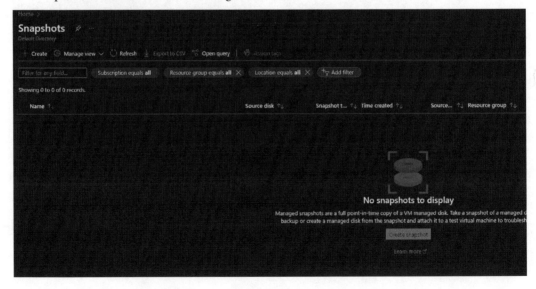

Figure 10.16 – Creating an Azure VM snapshot

3. Follow the on-screen instructions to create the snapshot of the infected Azure VM. As indicated in the next screenshot, ensure that you select the right resource group in which the infected VM resides and the specific **Instance details** (which we collected earlier):

Figure 10.17 – Creating an Azure VM snapshot (details)

4. In the same screen, select **Full** (*Figure 10.18*). Microsoft Azure also offers incremental snapshots that will only take a snapshot of the changes made within the filesystem. Since we intend to capture the disk image fully, we will select **Full** snapshot for a complete copy:

Figure 10.18 – Azure VM snapshot options

5. You will subsequently be asked to select the **Source disk** for which the snapshot will be created. As indicated in the following screenshot, ensure you select the correct disk. Typically, investigators will snapshot the root drive of the operating system; however, in some cases, investigators may want to take a snapshot of all the disks attached to the VM. Each disk attached to the infected VM will require a separate snapshot operation in these cases.

Figure 10.19 – Azure VM snapshot disk

6.   Once you have filled in all the required details, you can let Azure create the disk snapshot. Once completed, the snapshots will be available within the Azure subscription hosting the infected VM. You will notice the snapshot details within the snapshot dashboard, as indicated in the following screenshot:

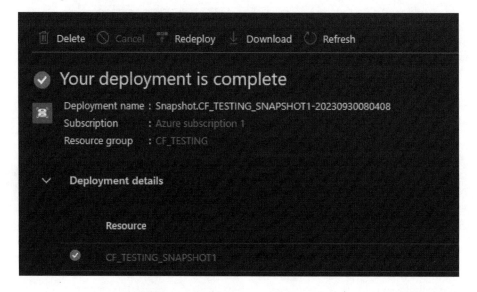

Figure 10.20 – Successful completion of Azure VM snapshot

Next, we look at exporting the newly created snapshot.

Step 2 – exporting an Azure VM snapshot directly

Once we complete *step 1*, investigators can attach this snapshot by creating a new disk, connecting to a VM to run a dd command, or using any of the commonly available tools discussed in *Chapter 8*. However, Microsoft Azure offers an option to download the snapshot directly once it's been created:

1.   Within the navigation menu, on the **Settings** tab, click on **Export snapshot**; this section offers the ability to export any snapshot directly via the browser:

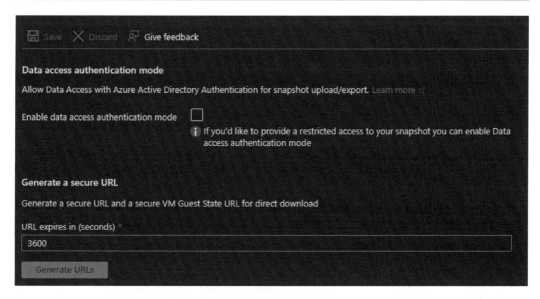

Figure 10.21 – Exporting Azure snapshots directly

2. Depending on the size of the infected volume, investigators may have to select the amount of time required for exporting snapshots, after which the secure URL will expire. They will not be available to resume or download any further. The maximum time that Microsoft Azure allows is 10 hours (36,000 seconds). In our example, we are downloading a 30 GB file, which takes less than one hour; therefore, we left it with the default value of 3,600 seconds. The Azure administrator may also configure specific authentication requirements instead of allowing the secure and unique URL to be publicly available online. Investigators must note URLs, which are displayed only once, before navigating away from the page. Even though they are publicly available, they are not widely available through search engines and require the investigators to know the full URL to access these artifacts.

3. Microsoft Azure typically generates two URLs, one with the **virtual hard disk** (**VHD**) file export and another with **VM guest state VHD** Export. These two links provide different files; however, investigators should download VHD files for investigative purposes.

Step 3 – connecting to an Azure VM for memory imaging

Microsoft Azure offers a couple of options to access the VMs; one of the most common is accessing the Azure VM via RDP or SSH. Alternatively, Azure offers a service called **Bastion**, which provides in-browser capabilities to access the Azure VM safely. See the next screenshot, which shows the options that are typically available. The choice on the left offers Bastion, which proxies RDP connection to the Azure VM through a browser session. The option on the right is the traditional approach to connecting with the Azure VM. To collect memory images, we will access the Azure VM via Bastion:

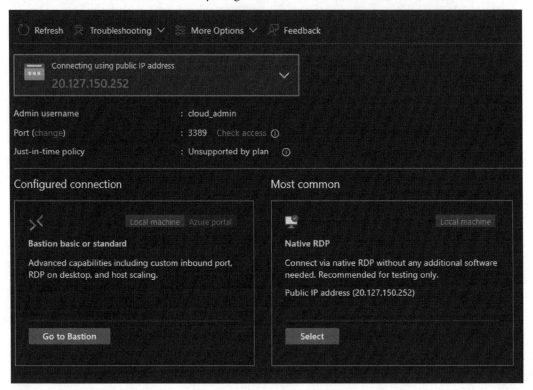

Figure 10.22 – Connection Option to Azure VM

After selecting **Go To Bastion**, Azure will automatically create a proxy tunnel service that allows connection to Azure VM. Investigators must supply a username and password to Bastion service to connect to the Azure VM, as indicated in the following screenshot. This service is similar to what Amazon calls its SSM service, which offers command-line access to the virtual machine:

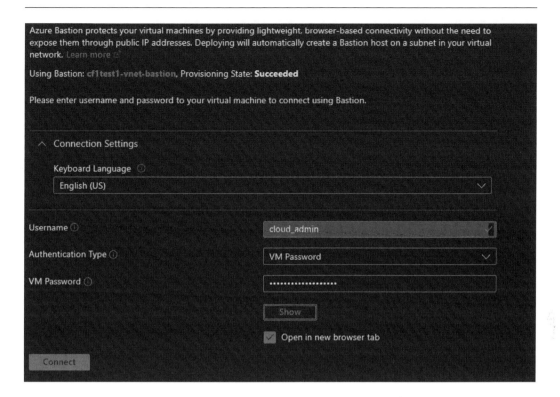

Figure 10.23 – Connecting to Azure VM via the Bastion service

Once connected to the Azure VM, investigators can follow the steps outlined in *step 2b* and *step 4a* for AWS.

Once all the relevant artifacts are collected, investigators can use their choice of export mechanism to export memory images or operating system artifacts using a third-party file-sharing service or through Azure Blob storage.

In the next section, we will review GCP's approach to allowing investigators to acquire and collect snapshots and memory images for offline forensic analysis.

Forensic acquisition of GCP instances

Like the steps we saw for AWS and Microsoft Azure, forensic acquisition of a GCP compute follows the same steps. We will first take a snapshot of the **compute engine** instance and then attach the snapshot as a separate drive to another forensic collector compute instance so we can do a bit-by-bit copy before exporting the disk image via cloud storage or any other data transfer means.

Step 1 – creating a snapshot of the compute engine instance

So, let us look at the pre-requisite steps to acquire a forensic image of a compute instance:

1. The first step is to create a disk snapshot of the compute engine instance; this can be done by accessing the navigation menu under **Storage** and selecting **Snapshots**. GCP offers two forms of snapshots. The first is regular snapshots, which include a complete disk snapshot of the compute engine instance, while the second is instant snapshots, which are more like an in-place backup of the disk used to create new disk volumes quickly. Instant snapshots are incremental, meaning after the first full snapshots, only the changes to the disk are recorded in instant snapshots. This is used for a more straightforward restoration of files. We will require a complete snapshot to copy everything from the operating system level for forensics.

2. When creating a snapshot, we must select the correct disk associated with the original infected instance, as indicated in the following screenshot. Similar to AWS and Microsoft Azure, each snapshot will associate with each disk, and therefore, when snapshotting a compute engine with multiple attached disks, investigators must note the number of disks attached to the instance and consider snapshotting them if all other disks are required. However, at minimum, the instance's root drive ($C:\backslash$) must be selected for snapshots:

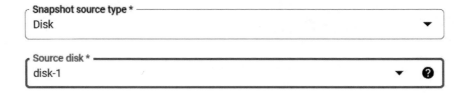

Figure 10.24 – Selecting a disk for a snapshot

Step 2 – attaching a snapshot disk for forensic acquisition

Once a snapshot is completed, investigators can create a new forensic instance within the same GCP tenant and attach this snapshot as a disk source. The following are some of the critical steps that investigators must take note of:

1. When creating a new instance, investigators must select the additional disk and choose the recently saved snapshot. As indicated in the following screenshot, investigators must ensure they attach the correct snapshots if multiple disk snapshots are taken:

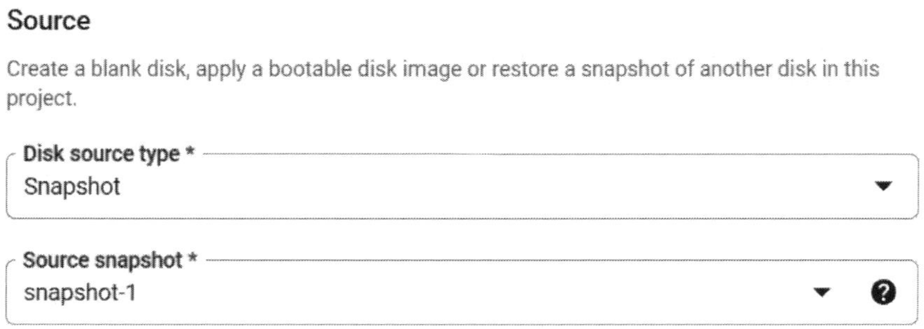

Source

Create a blank disk, apply a bootable disk image or restore a snapshot of another disk in this project.

Disk source type *

Snapshot ▼

Source snapshot *

snapshot-1 ▼ ❓

Figure 10.25 – Attaching a disk and restoring from a snapshot in GCP

2. Once a disk is attached, similar to the steps listed earlier for AWS, investigators can validate whether the disk is attached correctly by running the `lsblk -a` command, as illustrated in the following screenshot:

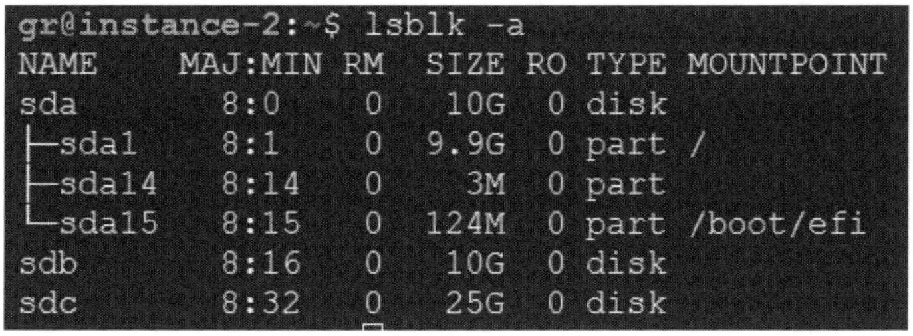

```
gr@instance-2:~$ lsblk -a
NAME      MAJ:MIN RM  SIZE RO TYPE MOUNTPOINT
sda         8:0    0   10G  0 disk
├─sda1      8:1    0  9.9G  0 part /
├─sda14     8:14   0    3M  0 part
└─sda15     8:15   0  124M  0 part /boot/efi
sdb         8:16   0   10G  0 disk
sdc         8:32   0   25G  0 disk
```

Figure 10.26 – Snapshot attached as a disk to the GCP compute instance

3. Once the disk is successfully attached, we follow the steps outlined in *step 4a* for AWS through the `dd` command.

Step 3 – connecting to the GCP compute engine instance for memory acquisition

Since all the cloud service providers operate in the same way, each cloud service provider offers a remote connection tool such as Cloud Shell or direct connection via IP. This section will utilize GCP Cloud Shell to connect to the infected host machine for memory acquisition:

1. Upon connecting to GCP's cloud shell, it will request an interactive logon to pass authentication tokens to the Cloud Shell session. Alternatively, administrators may create appropriate service accounts for investigators to handle the authentication process at the command line level without passing credentials interactively.

2.   When creating a service account, investigators must ensure that appropriate privileges are configured to the service account, specifically **Compute Admin** and **Storage Object Admin** privileges. **Compute Admin** privileges will allow investigators to access and modify the instance as required for forensic collections. In contrast, **Storage Object Admin** will allow the service account with privileges to upload artifacts to GCPs' cloud storage buckets. To create a service account, the following steps must be taken:

I.   Within the GCP's console, navigate to the **IAM & Admin** section.

II.   Click on **Service accounts** and then click on the **Create service account** button.

III. Give the service account a name description and select the role(s) that grant it the necessary permissions.

IV.   Click **Create** to create the service account.

For forensic collections, we created a service account, as indicated in the following screenshot, that will be used to interact with compute engine instances:

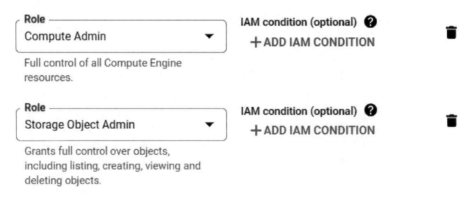

Figure 10.27 – Creating a service account for forensic acquisition

3. Next, we generate keys to access the compute engine instance using the service account:

   I.   Within the GCP's console, navigate to the **IAM & Admin** section.

   II.   Click on **Service accounts** and then click on the service account name that requires keys to be generated.

   III. On the **KEYS** tab, select **ADD KEY** and then **Create new key**.

   IV.   Select **JSON** as the option for the key file to be created. You will be presented with details once, with the option to download and save it on your computer.

4. Investigators can use this service account or their interactive accounts when connecting to a compute engine instance via Cloud Shell. Essentially, a service account offers a containerized set of roles that investigators can use to access the compute instance securely.

5. Once we have access to the compute instance via Cloud Shell or directly via RDP, we will follow the same steps as in *step 2b* for AWS for memory acquisition.

6. To export a memory image, investigators can upload the file to a remote server hosted by the DFIR team or to GCP's cloud storage bucket. To do this, you can use the service account that was created. We will take an example of exporting the memory image in a Windows device using PowerShell. We will first download the JSON file or copy the contents into a JSON file we generated in *step 3*.

7. Using PowerShell, we will run the following commands; you must ensure **gcloud** is installed on the Windows compute engine instance. The first thing is to activate the service account with `gcloud`:

```
gcloud auth activate-service-account forensic-collector@vaulted-
timing-390314.iam.gserviceaccount.com --key-file=./KEY.json
--project=vaulted-timing-390314
```

`gcloud` is the command we invoke to connect to the GCP console. The following parameters are utilized to establish a connection to GCP successfully:

- `gcloud auth activate-service-account`: This command is used to activate a service account for authentication.

- `forensic-collector@vaulted-timing-390314.iam.gserviceaccount.com`: This is the full email address of the service account (created under Google IAM) that requires activation.

- `key-file=./KEY.json`: This parameter specifies the path to the JSON key file associated with the service account. Ensure the JSON file path exists.

- `--project=vaulted-timing-390314`: This represents the project name assigned by GCP under which the service account is associated.

Once the service account is authenticated, investigators can upload memory images and other artifacts to the **GCP Cloud Storage** (**GCS**) bucket using the following command:

```
gsutil cp <memory.img> gs://<bucket_name>
```

The following are the parameters that are utilized for exporting the memory image to the storage area:

- `cp`: The sub-command of `gsutil` used for copying files and objects to and from GCS buckets
- `<memory.img>`: The filename and full path of the memory image stored on the host instance
- `gs://<bucket_name>`: The destination GCS bucket where the file will be exported

Once the memory image or any other artifacts are exported through `gsutil`, investigators can then proceed to acquire these artifacts from storage for their offline analysis. They can continue to retain these images in the storage area as long as it's not publicly accessible and access controls are strictly defined.

Summary

To summarize, the basic principles for collecting forensic artifacts, disk images, and memory dumps are similar when investigators have access to the operating system. The process is very similar if they have access to a computer or a device as part of the investigation. What is more important to learn are the steps to gain safe access to an operating system during an incident response situation.

Debunking cloud forensic acquisition is key; however, investigators must familiarize themselves with getting access to the full disk without making significant modifications to the instance, such as adding a new empty disk or installing tools only to create a full disk image and jumping through the challenges of exporting. Most cloud services have the option to snapshot your entire disk; this allows for more accessible collections. As for memory dump, unfortunately, there is no better option than jumping on the infected machine and running tools to dump memory. It is important for investigators to minimize their forensic footprint in volatile memory.

The next chapter will go over containerized instances, such as dockers and Kubernetes. In the forensic world, containerized instances offer different challenges, exacerbated when hosted on the cloud, and investigators are required to analyze them. The next chapter will look into demystifying container forensics on the cloud.

Further reading

- Make an Amazon EBS volume available for use on Linux: `https://docs.aws.amazon.com/AWSEC2/latest/UserGuide/ebs-using-volumes.html`

- How To Use LVM To Manage Storage Devices on Ubuntu 18.04: `https://www.digitalocean.com/community/tutorials/how-to-use-lvm-to-manage-storage-devices-on-ubuntu-18-04`

- Creating an IAM role with permissions for Session Manager and Amazon S3 and CloudWatch Logs (console): `https://docs.aws.amazon.com/systems-manager/latest/userguide/getting-started-create-iam-instance-profile.html#create-iam-instance-profile-ssn-logging`

- Create a Partition in Linux – A Step-by-Step Guide: `https://www.digitalocean.com/community/tutorials/create-a-partition-in-linux`

- Download a Windows VHD from Azure: `https://learn.microsoft.com/en-us/azure/virtual-machines/windows/download-vhd?tabs=azure-portal`

- Google Cloud (GCP) Forensics Best Practices and Tools: `https://medium.com/@cloud_tips/google-cloud-gcp-forensics-best-practices-and-tools-a99ed21e5ae5`

- How to automate forensic disk collection in AWS: `https://aws.amazon.com/blogs/security/how-to-automate-forensic-disk-collection-in-aws/`

- Computer forensics chain of custody in Azure: `https://learn.microsoft.com/en-us/azure/architecture/example-scenario/forensics/`

11

Analyzing Compromised Containers

Until this chapter, we looked at some standard methods and techniques to acquire and analyze forensic images of **virtual machines** (**VMs**) and cloud services. However, developing and analyzing a containerized environment introduces an entirely new challenge.

In today's technology landscape, containerization and Kubernetes orchestration have become fundamental to modern application deployment; therefore, ensuring these containers' security is paramount. Containers offer tremendous benefits in terms of efficiency and scalability, but they also present new challenges, with security being a top concern.

This chapter aims to understand containers' architecture and how containers are managed and orchestrated via Kubernetes.

In this chapter, we will be looking at the following topics:

- What are containers?
- Detecting and analyzing compromised containers

What are containers?

Containers are lightweight, standalone, and executable packages containing everything needed to run a piece of software, including the code, runtime, system tools, libraries, and settings. They are designed to provide consistency across different computing environments, from development and testing to deployment in production, by encapsulating the application and its dependencies in a containerized environment.

Some critical advantages of containerized deployments include the following:

- **Isolation**: Containers use operating system-level virtualization to create isolated environments. Each container shares the same OS kernel as the host but runs independently, ensuring separation from other containers on the same system.

- **Portability**: Containers are highly portable, allowing you to run the same application consistently across various platforms, such as Linux distributions or cloud providers. Containerization technologies such as Docker and container runtimes enable this portability.

- **Lightweight**: Containers are lightweight compared to traditional VMs. They consume fewer system resources because they do not require a full OS and only package the application and its dependencies.

- **Resource efficiency**: Containers start and stop quickly, making them efficient for scaling applications up and down dynamically in response to changes in workload.

- **Immutable infrastructure**: Containers are typically created from predefined images. When you want to update an application, you build a new container image with the changes, ensuring consistency and repeatability in your infrastructure.

- **Orchestration**: Container orchestration platforms such as Kubernetes provide automated management of containerized applications, including scaling, load balancing, and self-healing, making them suitable for deploying and managing microservices-based architectures.

- **Version control**: Container images can be versioned, making it easy to roll back to the previous version in case of issues. This supports a more controlled software development and deployment process.

- **Security isolation**: Containers offer a level of security isolation. However, it's essential to configure and manage them correctly to ensure proper security practices.

- **DevOps and CI/CD**: Containers are a fundamental tool in **DevOps** practices, as they facilitate **continuous integration and continuous deployment (CI/CD)** pipelines, allowing for streamlined and automated software development and delivery processes.

- **Microservices**: Containers are often used in a microservices architecture, where applications are broken down into small, independent services that can be easily deployed and scaled individually.

Docker versus Kubernetes

Although Docker and Kubernetes are the most popular containerization technologies, they serve different purposes:

- **Docker**: **Docker** is a containerization platform that allows developers to package applications and their dependencies into a single, portable container unit. Containers are lightweight and efficient, providing a consistent environment for running applications across different systems.

Docker simplifies the development process by encapsulating everything an application needs to run, ensuring it runs consistently from a developer's laptop to a production server.

Docker's ease of use and user-friendly **command-line interface** (**CLI**) have made it immensely popular among developers and operations teams. It's a valuable tool for local development, creating container images and sharing them via Docker Hub or private registries. Docker's primary focus is on application packaging and distribution, and it's often used as the foundation for building container images that can be run in various environments.

- **Kubernetes**: **Kubernetes**, often abbreviated as **K8s**, is an open source container orchestration platform that manages the deployment, scaling, and operation of containerized applications. While Docker is primarily concerned with packaging and running individual containers, Kubernetes takes a higher-level approach by orchestrating multiple containers into groups or services. It automates tasks such as load balancing, scaling, rolling updates, and self-healing, making it well suited for complex and distributed application architectures.

  Kubernetes is particularly valuable for microservices-based applications where multiple containers must work together seamlessly. It abstracts the underlying infrastructure and provides a unified API for managing containers across various environments, such as on-premises servers, public clouds, or hybrid setups. Kubernetes ensures **high availability** (**HA**), **fault tolerance** (**FT**), and resource efficiency, making it a cornerstone in modern containerized application deployment.

In short, Docker and Kubernetes are rather complementary technologies. Docker is ideal for creating and packaging individual containers, while Kubernetes is the go-to solution for orchestrating, scaling, and managing those containers within a larger ecosystem. They can be used together, with Docker providing container images deployed and orchestrated by Kubernetes, allowing organizations to build and manage resilient, scalable, and efficient containerized applications. The choice between Docker and Kubernetes largely depends on your specific needs and the application lifecycle stage you're addressing.

Containers have revolutionized how applications are developed, deployed, and managed, providing a consistent and efficient way to package and run software across various environments. In the next section, we will look into the types of containers and some of the use cases they serve.

Types of containers and their use cases

As indicated in the previous section, containers are packaged applications in various forms. Next are some forms of containers and their potential use cases:

- **Docker containers**: Docker containers are perhaps the most well-known and widely used type. Docker provides a platform for developing, shipping, and running container applications. Docker containers are highly portable and easy to manage, making them suitable for various use cases.

- **Linux Containers (LXC)**: LXC is an operating-system-level virtualization method that uses the Linux kernel's groups and namespaces to create isolated environments. LXC containers are less user-friendly than Docker but offer more flexibility and control, making them suitable for specific use cases where customization is crucial.

- **Rocket (rkt) containers**: Developed by CoreOS, `rkt` (pronounced *rocket*) is an alternative container runtime that focuses on security and simplicity. It is designed to be more secure and lightweight than Docker and is used in some Kubernetes deployments.

- **containerd**: `containerd` is an industry-standard core container runtime used by various container platforms and orchestration systems. It is designed to be a simple and reliable runtime for containers.

- **Podman containers**: Podman is an open source container management tool compatible with Docker but offers a more secure and rootless container experience. It is suitable for scenarios where you need Docker compatibility with added security.

- **OpenVZ containers**: OpenVZ is a containerization technology that provides a lightweight form of virtualization. It differs from traditional containers, as it uses a shared kernel and provides more isolation than typical containers but less than full virtualization.

- **FreeBSD jails**: FreeBSD jails are similar to Linux containers but are specific to the FreeBSD operating system. They provide lightweight virtualization on FreeBSD systems.

- **Windows containers**: Windows Server also supports containerization, while most containers are associated with Linux. Windows containers can run Windows-based applications within isolated environments.

- **systemd-nspawn**: `systemd-nspawn` is a containerization tool provided by the `systemd` `init` system. It offers lightweight OS-level virtualization, and it's commonly used for development and testing environments on Linux systems.

- **Kata Containers**: Kata Containers is an open source project that combines the security benefits of VMs with the efficiency and speed of containers. It's designed for workloads that require a high level of isolation.

The following are some use cases enterprises typically leveraged to deploy a containerized environment:

- **Application packaging and distribution**: Containers package applications and all their dependencies into a single, portable unit. This ensures consistent and reliable application deployment across different environments, from development to production.

- **Microservices architecture**: Containers are central to microservices, where applications are broken down into small, independent services. Each microservice runs in its own container, allowing scalability, flexibility, and easy maintenance.

- **Development and testing**: Developers use containers to create isolated development and testing environments that mirror production conditions. This ensures that applications work as expected and eliminates the "*it works on my machine*" problem.

- **CI/CD**: Containers enable streamlined CI/CD pipelines. Developers package their code and dependencies in containers, which are tested, deployed, and scaled automatically, improving software delivery speed and reliability.

- **Multi-cloud and hybrid cloud deployment**: Containers can run consistently across cloud providers and on-premises environments. This makes them suitable for multi-cloud and hybrid cloud strategies, allowing for cloud-agnostic application deployment.

- **Isolation and security**: Containers provide lightweight isolation between applications, enhancing security and minimizing the risk of conflicts or vulnerabilities between them.

- **Legacy application modernization**: Containers can wrap legacy applications, making them more portable and easier to manage. This helps organizations modernize existing systems without rewriting code.

- **Scalability and load balancing**: Containers can be quickly scaled up or down in response to changing workloads, making them ideal for applications that require elastic scaling and efficient resource utilization.

- **Stateful and statelessness**: Containers can be used for stateful and stateless applications. Stateful applications such as databases can run in containers, and stateless services can scale horizontally.

- **Resource efficiency**: Containers are lightweight, requiring fewer system resources than traditional VMs, resulting in better resource utilization and cost savings.

- **Orchestration**: Container orchestration platforms such as Kubernetes provide automated management of containers. They handle scaling, load balancing, and self-healing, making them suitable for complex application architectures.

- **HA and disaster recovery (DR)**: Containers can be orchestrated across multiple nodes and data centers to ensure HA and DR capabilities, reducing downtime and data loss.

- **Service discovery and load balancing**: Containers can be easily integrated with service discovery and load balancing solutions to ensure efficient communication and distribution of traffic among services.

- **Content delivery and content delivery networks (CDNs)**: CDNs use containers to cache and distribute content globally, reducing latency and improving content delivery performance.

- **Data processing and analytics**: Containers are used for running data processing and analytics workloads, providing a scalable and isolated environment for data-related tasks.

- **Internet of Things (IoT) and edge computing**: Containers can be employed for deploying and managing applications on edge devices and IoT devices, bringing computation closer to data sources.

- **Desktop virtualization**: Containers can be used for desktop virtualization, allowing users to run isolated desktop environments with specific applications and configurations.

In the following few sections, we will look into how to analyze a compromised container, what steps are required, and which forensic collection mechanism can be applied to collect forensic images of a containerized environment securely.

Detecting and analyzing compromised containers

Most organizations operate container architectures through Kubernetes since it offers many more scalable options and flexibility. Before we dive deeper into container analysis, it is essential to understand the components of Kubernetes, as they will play a pivotal role in your investigations.

About the Kubernetes orchestration platform

The following screenshot illustrates the basic architecture of a Kubernetes cluster; in summary, as we know, Kubernetes is an orchestration framework that manages one or more nodes that run one or more containers:

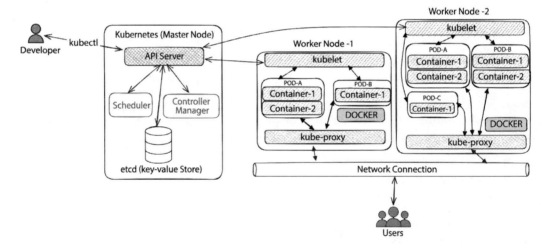

Figure 11.1 – Simple Kubernetes architecture

For the Kubernetes cluster, you need a master node that controls and orchestrates the cluster's operations and worker nodes that run the pods and tasks assigned by the master node. Here are some critical components of a Kubernetes cluster:

- **API server**: This is the frontend of the cluster; developers can connect to the Kubernetes cluster using the kubectl command. The API server operates as a RESTful API server, meaning it's a stateless protocol, with no information on previous requests being retained by the server.

- **Scheduler**: The scheduler is responsible for determining the optimal placement of pods onto available nodes in a cluster. Its primary function is to make intelligent scheduling decisions based on resource requirements, node affinity, and user-defined constraints. By evaluating the available resources on each node, the scheduler aims to balance the workload across the cluster, ensuring efficient resource utilization. The scheduler also supports features such as pod priority, preemption, affinity rules, and taints/tolerations, providing flexibility and customization for workload distribution. Additionally, Kubernetes allows for the creation of custom schedulers to address specific deployment requirements.

- **Controller manager**: One of the core components of Kubernetes architecture, it is responsible for managing various controllers that regulate the state of the cluster. Each controller is a separate process responsible for monitoring and reconciling the actual state of cluster objects with their desired state, as defined in the Kubernetes API server. Key controllers managed by the controller manager include the following:

  - **Replication controller**, which ensures the specified number of pod replicas are running

  - **Node controller**, which handles node lifecycle and the service account

  - **Token controller**, managing the lifecycle of service accounts and API access tokens

  The controller manager enhances the self-healing capabilities of Kubernetes by continuously monitoring and adjusting the cluster to maintain the desired configuration, ensuring HA and resilience of containerized applications.

- **etcd**: `etcd` is a distributed key-value store central to Kubernetes, serving as the primary data repository for cluster configuration and state. Employing the **Raft consensus** algorithm, `etcd` ensures strong consistency and HA across distributed nodes, providing reliability and FT. It plays a vital role in cluster coordination, enabling components such as the API server and controller manager to synchronize and share real-time information. Providing support for features such as data backup, secure communication, and a watch mechanism for dynamic updates, `etcd` contributes to the resilience and efficiency of Kubernetes clusters, serving as a critical foundation for managing containerized applications.

- **kubelet**: The kubelet is responsible for maintaining the container lifecycle and ensuring containers run as expected. Acting as an agent, the kubelet communicates with the Kubernetes control plane to receive pod specifications and then ensures the containers are started, stopped, and continuously monitored. It interacts with the container runtime (such as **Docker** or `containerd`) to manage the containers on the node, implementing the desired state described in the pod specifications. Additionally, the kubelet performs health checks on the containers, restarts failed containers when necessary, and reports the node's status back to the control plane.

- **Pod**: A pod is the smallest deployable and scalable unit in Kubernetes, representing a group of one or more containers that share the same network namespace and storage. Containers within a pod are scheduled together on the same node and can communicate with each other using `localhost`. This design allows them to share data and dependencies easily. Pods serve as the basic building blocks for deploying applications on Kubernetes, and they encapsulate one or more containers, along with shared storage resources and options for how the containers should be run. The Kubernetes API server manages pods and can be replicated, scaled, and updated to meet the dynamic demands of containerized applications.

- **kube-proxy**: kube-proxy is a vital component in Kubernetes responsible for network proxying and load balancing. Operating at the service level, it facilitates communication between pods and services by maintaining network rules and updating them based on changes in the cluster's services and endpoints. With capabilities for service discovery, load balancing, and managing NodePort services, kube-proxy ensures efficient and reliable network connectivity within the cluster. It abstracts the complexities of networking, playing a pivotal role in enabling seamless communication between different components of containerized applications in a Kubernetes environment.

You can explore the Kubernetes architecture by running the following command:

```
kubectl get pods -n kube-system --show-labels
```

The preceding command will print the name of the pod, its status, its age (uptime), and labels. Adapting kubectl command parameters based on your Kubernetes cluster configurations would be best. A snippet of the output can be seen in the next screenshot; you can see various parts of Kubernetes architecture, such as the **event exporter**, kube-dns, kube-proxy, the **metrics server**, and so on. Since this cluster is operating on **Google Cloud Platform** (**GCP**), you will notice pod associations and labels tagged with gke for **Google Kubernetes Engine** (**GKE**):

NAME	READY	STATUS	RESTARTS	AGE
container-watcher-hqf9p	1/1	Running	0	33m
container-watcher-rf5qv	1/1	Running	0	33m
event-exporter-gke-7bf6c99dcb-ff9bx	2/2	Running	0	35m
fluentbit-gke-jmffw	2/2	Running	0	33m
fluentbit-gke-kjpbg	2/2	Running	0	33m
gke-metrics-agent-b2gkg	2/2	Running	0	33m
gke-metrics-agent-xkk7d	2/2	Running	0	33m
konnectivity-agent-7bdcd55498-bvdpg	1/1	Running	0	33m
konnectivity-agent-7bdcd55498-l9vjb	1/1	Running	0	33m
konnectivity-agent-autoscaler-5d9dbcc6d8-861h5	1/1	Running	0	34m
kube-dns-5bfd847c64-gb4h9	4/4	Running	0	33m
kube-dns-5bfd847c64-gvkxh	4/4	Running	0	35m
kube-dns-autoscaler-84b8db4dc7-qk88q	1/1	Running	0	35m
kube-proxy-gke-cluster-1-default-pool-3ef40fb0-1f12	1/1	Running	0	33m
kube-proxy-gke-cluster-1-default-pool-3ef40fb0-5f5w	1/1	Running	0	33m
l7-default-backend-d86c96845-pb67c	1/1	Running	0	34m
metrics-server-v0.5.2-6bf74b5d5f-p2l7p	2/2	Running	0	33m
pdcsi-node-dzr69	2/2	Running	0	33m
pdcsi-node-zwfl9	2/2	Running	0	33m

Figure 11.2 – List of pods associated with the GKE cluster system (no application pods)

In the next section, we will focus on extracting logs for investigations. Now that we understand the Kubernetes architecture, accessing these logs will be much easier and simpler.

Acquiring forensic data and container logs for analysis

Now that we have an overview of key components of the Kubernetes architecture, let us look at how investigators can obtain logs/artifacts from a cluster.

Container logs

Various logs are typically available within Kubernetes clusters; some are operational logs, meaning they are related to the cluster's health, while some are associated with applications running within the containers. These can be specifically useful for **Digital Forensics and Incident Response (DFIR)** teams to investigate nefarious activities involving a Kubernetes cluster.

To understand logs, we break them down into two categories—operational and security logs—along with their use cases. You will notice that some of the logs offer operational insights and security logs:

Operational logs:

- **API server logs**: Reflecting upon the Kubernetes architecture, the API server plays a crucial role in ensuring the Kubernetes cluster operates efficiently. API server logs provide insights into API-related activity, including requests, responses, and authentication details. Specifically, API server logs help monitor API server health, track user activity, and troubleshoot API-related issues.

  You can access API server logs using the following command:
  ```
  kubectl logs -n kube-system <api-server-pod-name>
  ```

- **Controller manager logs**: Provides logs related to controller activities, such as node, replication, and cluster interactions. Useful for monitoring the controller's health, tracking controller decisions, and understanding replication and service-related events. You may access events related to the controller manager through the following command:
  ```
  kubectl logs -n kube-system <controller-manager-pod-name>
  ```

- **Scheduler logs**: Records logs associated with scheduling decisions made by the Kubernetes scheduler, such as pod placement. This log helps understand and monitor workload distribution, scheduling decisions, and node utilization. You can access logs specific to the Kubernetes controller through the following command:
  ```
  kubectl logs -n kube-system <scheduler-pod-name>
  ```

- **kubelet logs**: Provides details about pod lifecycle events, container runtime interactions, and heartbeats; logs associated with the kubelet provide insights into pod health and runtime issues. You can access logs related to a particular pod using the following command; note that this command will fetch operational events related to running the pod and not the application logs running within the pod:

```
kubectl logs -n kube-system <kubelet-pod-name>
```

- **kube-proxy logs**: as the name suggests, kube-proxy contains logs associated with proxying operations, network rules, and load-balancing activities. kube-proxy logs help monitor network-related issues and understand load-balancing issues. To access kube-proxy logs, the following command is utilized:

```
kubectl logs -n kube-system <kube-proxy-pod-name>
```

- **etcd logs**: Outlines the cluster changes, cluster state changes, and communication between etcd nodes. etcd logs provide critical insights into monitoring etcd health, tracking cluster state changes, and understanding etcd-related issues. You can access etcd logs using a similar command:

```
kubectl logs -n kube-system <etcd-pod-name>
```

- **Container runtime logs**: Capture container lifecycle events, image pulls, and runtime-specific details. Logs help monitor container health, runtime issues, and image-associated events. Container runtime logs can be accessed via journalctl -u docker or journalctl -u containerd. However, if you are running Kubernetes on a cloud platform such as GCP, the best way to access container runtime logs is via Logs Explorer or an equivalent log viewer offered by the **cloud service provider** (**CSP**).

- **Network plugin logs**: Provides information on network policies, pod routing, and communication between pods. Network plugin logs are helpful in troubleshooting network issues when clusters cannot communicate with each other. Another exciting use case for a network plugin is that DFIR teams can utilize the log to monitor and analyze traffic between pods. You can access network plugin logs via a similar kubectl command:

```
kubectl logs -n kube-system <network plugin pod name>
```

- **Ingress controller logs**: Instrumental in investigating issues when external network traffic does not connect to the intended Kubernetes pod. Typical reasons could be misconfigurations on the ingress controller itself. Ingress controllers are also responsible for terminating SSL/TLS connections; monitoring these events will provide crucial insights into service disruptions due to expired certificates. Similar to accessing other logs, ingress controller logs can be accessed through the following command:

```
kubectl logs -n kube-system <ingress controller pod name>
```

Security logs:

- **API server logs**: From a DFIR perspective, investigators can look into API server logs to identify unauthorized access attempts or authentication failures. You can also use API server logs to monitor for suspicious changes to critical resources such as pods through API server logs.

- **kubelet logs**: You can use kubelet logs to look for container anomalies. kubelet logs can provide insights into unexpected behaviors or network activity. You can also use kubelet logs to investigate node-level activities, resource exhaustion, or unusual activities.

- **etcd logs**: Useful for investigating changes to unauthorized cluster configurations or parameters. Investigators can also use `etcd` logs to identify data corruption or inconsistencies.

- **Network plugin logs**: You can use network plugin logs to analyze network traffic patterns. You can also do a `tcpdump` to verify the network traffic activity using this command:

```
kubectl exec -it <pod-name> -- tcpdump -i eth0
```

Network plugin logs provide insights into malicious network traffic between pods and identify evidence of lateral movements.

All in all, Kubernetes provides a framework to access these logs within each of the pods; however, if the cluster is running on a cloud platform, investigators can also leverage the native log viewer provided by each of the CSPs to quickly access the logs without accessing the logs directly via the cluster. In the following sections, we will look into both perspectives of accessing logs directly via the cluster and using the CSP's logging console to access Kubernetes cluster logs for investigation.

Examining the container runtime

Let's say you now have a Kubernetes cluster running on the cloud and a pod (applications) setup exposed to the internet accepting user connections. To explain the investigative approach, we are going to define a situation. We have a Kubernetes cluster deployed on Google Cloud, with WordPress and a MySQL server deployed as pods. As outlined in the next screenshot, we have three pods that frame the part of the application:

```
NAME                         READY   STATUS      RESTARTS   AGE
wordpress-1-deployer-vzv78   0/1     Completed   0          15d
wordpress-1-mysql-0          2/2     Running     0          15d
wordpress-1-wordpress-0      2/2     Running     0          15d
```

Figure 11.3 – Pods under the GKE cluster

These pods are configured so that MySQL will store the contents of the WordPress blog and authentication information. As investigators, we are tasked to investigate brute-force attempts on the MySQL server.

Now, there are multiple ways to address this. The most popular method is using Google's Log Explorer. While we walk through an investigation using a cloud tool, you can perform similar tasks with other CSPs as long as Kubernetes logs are configured to be ingested within the CSPs' cloud logging tools. Currently, there are two ways to investigate/gain access to logs. One is via Log Explorer, and the other is via the command line. It's up to the investigators to extract the logs and analyze them. We will explore both approaches and determine outcomes. Before investigating Kubernetes, investigators must understand how the organization has deployed the Kubernetes cluster and its architecture.

Option 1 – Log Explorer

1. Once investigators can access Log Explorer, we can directly start pinpointing activities relevant to the WordPress and MySQL servers. Remember that WordPress is a frontend tool, while the MySQL server provides the backend database as part of the complete application stack.

2. Through initial triage, we know that there were brute-force attempts; the resource usage dashboard can validate this. The following sample screenshot shows the general resource metrics associated with the Kubernetes cluster that highlight the increased resource usage:

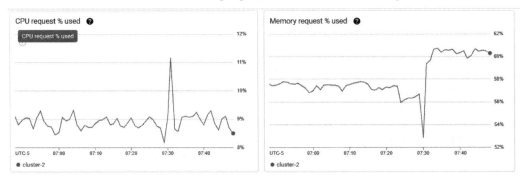

Figure 11.4 – Kubernetes cluster resource usage

3. Once we have established the basics, we jump onto the Log Explorer page. If you are familiar with querying Log Explorer, you can query the logs in the cluster's `default` namespace and where the container name is not `wordpress`. Next is the search query snippet that gathers all logs not associated with WordPress:

```
resource.labels.namespace_name="default"
-resource.labels.container_name="wordpress"
```

4. Typically, brute-force attempts can be identified through a series of failed logins followed by successful login attempts. We will modify the preceding query to pinpoint the investigator's failed MySQL access attempts. As investigators, if we are unfamiliar with Google's Log Explorer query capabilities, we can always click and select appropriate filters, and the query will automatically update itself:

```
resource.labels.namespace_name="default"
-resource.labels.container_name="wordpress"
--Show similar entries
textPayload=~"(\d{4}-(0[1-9]|1[0-2])-(0[1-9]|[12][0-9]|3[01]))
((\d{2}):(\d{2})(?::(\d{2}(?:\.\d*)?))?(?:([+-](?:\d{2}):?(?:\
d{2})?|Z)?))  ((?:\d[,.]?)*\d) \[Warning\] Access denied for user
'[^ =\t\n\r\f\"\(\)\[\]\|']+'@'localhost' \(using password: [^
=\t\n\r\f\"\(\)\[\]\|']+"
--End of show similar entries
```

5. Once you filter down the logs, you can quickly pinpoint logs associated with brute-force attacks. The next screenshot demonstrates the outcomes of the analysis using Log Explorer. In the screenshot, you can see multiple failed login attempts against MySQL before a successful one. Depending upon the deployed container, some logs may also collect granular information. In this case, we can use various usernames being tried by the threat actor before successfully connecting to the server using the `wp-admin` account:

Figure 11.5 – Analysis of brute-force attacks on Kubernetes pod

Next, we look into accessing logs directly via the command line.

Option 2 – Direct command-line access (kubectl)

In situations where access to the CSP's logger service is not available, as investigators, you can always `kubectl` to access these individual pod-based logs.

Accessing logs from pods is relatively easy. Once you have enumerated all the pods, you can use `kubectl logs <pod name>` to access entire logs. Logs are printed by default to the console; however, you can write the logs to disk for offline analysis. In this case, let's pull the logs associated with the MySQL pod—`kubectl logs wordpress-1-mysql-0`. The next screenshot extracts the logs associated with the brute-force attack:

```
[Warning] Access denied for user 'root'@'localhost' (using password: YES)
[Warning] Access denied for user 'admin'@'localhost' (using password: YES)
[Warning] Access denied for user 'wp-admin'@'localhost' (using password: YES)
[Warning] Access denied for user 'root'@'localhost' (using password: YES)
[Warning] Access denied for user 'root'@'localhost' (using password: YES)
[Warning] Access denied for user 'admin'@'localhost' (using password: YES)
[Warning] Access denied for user 'admin'@'localhost' (using password: YES)
[Warning] Access denied for user 'wp-admin'@'localhost' (using password: YES)
[Warning] Access denied for user 'wp-admin'@'localhost' (using password: NO)
[Warning] Access denied for user 'root'@'localhost' (using password: NO)
[Warning] Access denied for user 'wp-admin'@'localhost' (using password: NO)
[Warning] Access denied for user 'root'@'localhost' (using password: NO)
[Warning] Access denied for user 'root'@'localhost' (using password: YES)
[Warning] Access denied for user 'root'@'localhost' (using password: NO)
[Warning] Access denied for user 'root'@'localhost' (using password: YES)
[Warning] Access denied for user 'wp-admin'@'localhost' (using password: YES)
[Warning] Access denied for user 'wp-admin'@'localhost' (using password: YES)
[Warning] Access denied for user 'wp-admin'@'localhost' (using password: YES)
[Warning] Access denied for user 'wp-admin'@'localhost' (using password: YES)
[Warning] Access denied for user 'wp-admin'@'localhost' (using password: YES)
[Warning] Access denied for user 'wp-admin'@'localhost' (using password: YES)
[Warning] Access denied for user 'root'@'localhost' (using password: YES)
[Warning] Access denied for user 'root'@'localhost' (using password: YES)
[Warning] Access denied for user 'root'@'localhost' (using password: YES)
```

Figure 11.6 – Log extract of MySQL pod, evidencing brute-force attack

As investigators, we know the importance of logs; with Kubernetes, each pod will have its logs associated with the application it is running, along with other operational logs. However, knowing how to access these logs is vital, as investigators' access to the CSP's logging console will also immensely help as they can be maintained longer than hunting the pod itself.

Summary

This chapter explored the distinctions between Docker and Kubernetes, emphasizing their collaborative use for comprehensive container management. We delved into various types of containers and their specific use cases, highlighting their efficiency in scenarios such as microservices architectures.

Additionally, we looked at acquiring forensic data and logs for analysis in Kubernetes environments, emphasizing logging mechanisms, tools, and best practices for practical forensic analysis, including identifying security breaches and incident investigations. However, accessing Kubernetes logs is one of the most straightforward investigations. If Kubernetes is deployed in the cloud, CSPs are crucial for providing access to a centralized log explorer for longer-term log access.

In our next chapter, we will review the analysis of the cloud productivity suites hosted on Microsoft 365 and Google Workspace. The focus of this chapter is to understand how to analyze common threat vectors on productivity suites and which logs are available to investigators.

Further reading

- *The Raft Consensus Algorithm*: `https://raft.github.io/`

- *Cluster Networking*: `https://kubernetes.io/docs/concepts/cluster-administration/networking/`

- *Kubernetes Forensics*: `https://medium.com/@cloud_tips/kubernetes-forensics-c1e558b10d53#:~:text=This%20can%20involve%20looking%20for,command%2Dline%20interface%20for%20Kubernetes`

- *Incident response and forensics*: `https://aws.github.io/aws-eks-best-practices/security/docs/incidents/?source=post_page-----c1e558b10d53`

- *Image security*: `https://aws.github.io/aws-eks-best-practices/security/docs/image/`

- *CIS Kubernetes Benchmarks*: `https://www.cisecurity.org/benchmark/kubernetes`

- *10+ Top Kubernetes Security Tools in 2023*: `https://medium.com/@pdevsecops/10-top-kubernetes-security-tools-in-2023-df26642f995a`

- *Top Kubernetes Security Tools in 2023*: `https://www.armosec.io/blog/kubernetes-security-tools/`

12

Analyzing Compromised Cloud Productivity Suites

The reality is that most cloud-based security incidents within an organization will occur at the productivity suite level. As we discussed in *Chapter 7*, Microsoft 365 and Google Workspace are the most popular SaaS-based platforms in the industry. Organizations rely on Microsoft 365 and Google Workspace for business applications and services such as email, storage, office applications, and much more. Through the rise in the adoption of SaaS-based email solutions through Microsoft 365 and Google Workspace by corporations, these platforms have become a prime target for business email compromise attacks. Since these email accounts are integrally linked to other services within 365 and Workspace, such compromises also pose a risk to any additional service connected to the user's account, amplifying the potential for broader security breaches and a larger impact.

This chapter will dive into the details of compromised productivity suites, specifically Microsoft 365 and Google Workspace, from start to finish. We will discuss the following topics in this chapter:

- Business email compromise explained
- Initial scoping and remediation steps
- Microsoft 365 incident response
- Google Workspace incident response

Business email compromise explained

Business email compromise (**BEC**) is a sophisticated type of cyber fraud targeting organizations through deceptive practices involving email communications. This threat exploits the reliance of businesses on email for corporate correspondence, manipulating trust and authority to execute some sort of unauthorized fund transfers, obtain sensitive information, or move laterally into the IT network.

BEC attack phases

The phases that attackers utilize to conduct BEC attacks are demonstrated in *Figure 12.1*:

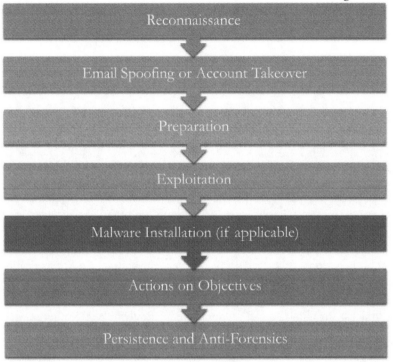

Figure 12.1 – BEC attack phases

Having observed the stages outlined in the figure, let's dive into each phase with a detailed breakdown:

- **Reconnaissance**: In this phase, attackers meticulously study the victim organization's hierarchy, communication patterns, and specific jargon used. If an attacker has access to an account already, they simply run searches within the email system to understand communication patterns and jargon at the organization. Otherwise, the attacker utilizes information that may be public about the company from various sources, such as LinkedIn and the victim organization's website. Attackers may use publicly available information, social engineering tactics, or even previous data breaches to collect data. This reconnaissance phase allows them to craft convincing emails mimicking users from inside the organization and spoof or target specific accounts of interest.

  BEC attacks are typically not random mass mailings but are directed at specific individuals within an organization, such as those with authority over finances or access to confidential data. As an example, the CFO of an organization is commonly targeted as they not only have access to confidential financial information, but they have the authority to approve transactions at the organization.

- **Email spoofing or account takeover**: Attackers either spoof a legitimate email address or gain unauthorized access to a legitimate account, often through phishing attacks or exploiting weak security practices.

Attackers frequently create "fake" websites that appear to look the same as the login pages of popular productivity suites (Microsoft 365 or Google Workspace). They achieve this by manipulating HTML and CSS to replicate the styling of these legitimate sites. The domains of these fake sites are often slightly altered versions of the real ones, designed to appear as if they belong to the organization's productivity suite tenant. For example, a fake domain for Microsoft 365 could be `microsoft365-login.com` instead of the legitimate `microsoft.com`, and for Google Workspace, it might be `googledocs-signin.com` instead of `google.com`. These fraudulent pages usually consist of forms designed to harvest and send back user credentials to the attackers. Unsuspecting users who enter their login details on these fake pages unintentionally provide attackers with access to their personal or corporate accounts, leading to account compromise.

If attackers cannot gain access to accounts in the organization, they typically purchase domains that appear to be very similar to the organization instead. As an example, instead of `ACME.com`, `AMCE.com` is purchased from domain registrars so that the attacker can also create email accounts sharing domains that closely resemble legitimate user emails at the victim organization. As an example, `Alice@AMCE.com` would be set up and used by attackers to mimic a legitimate user and account for Alice from ACME. Most users would not catch the subtle change in the domain from ACME to AMCE in their email correspondence.

- **Preparation**: In this phase, the attacker prepares the tools and methods they will use to execute the attack. This could include crafting convincing phishing emails, creating fake invoices, or setting up bank accounts for receiving fraudulent payments. This is based on their objective and the type of BEC, which we will discuss in the next section.

- **Exploitation**: In this stage, the victim interacts with the email, leading to the attacker's desired outcome. For BEC, this often means complying with the instructions in the email, such as transferring funds or providing confidential information.

- **Malware installation (if applicable)**: While not always a part of BEC, in some cases, the attacker might use the opportunity to install malware on the victim's system. This can be for long-term access, data exfiltration, or to facilitate further attacks. This is how attackers can pivot from the productivity suite account hosted and protected in the cloud to actual devices in the organization's IT network.

- **Actions on objectives**: The ultimate goal of the attacker is realized in this stage. For BEC, this usually involves the unauthorized transfer of funds to the attacker's account or the acquisition of sensitive information. The attacker's objectives are achieved once they receive the funds or information they were seeking.

- **Persistence and anti-forensics (if applicable)**: In sophisticated BEC schemes, attackers might try to maintain access to the victim's systems for future attacks or to hide evidence of their activities. This might involve setting up auto-forwarding rules outside the network, deletion of email evidence, creating backdoors in terms of application consents, or using other techniques to conceal their presence.

Common types of BECs

Now that we've explored the various phases of a BEC attack, let's discuss the common types of BECs that organizations frequently encounter:

- **Invoice fraud**: The scammer pretends to be a supplier or vendor of the target company, requesting payment for services or goods to a fraudulent account.

- **C-suite fraud**: Attackers pose as the company's CEO or any high-ranking executive and send emails to employees, usually in the finance department, instructing them to transfer funds to an account controlled by the attacker.

- **Attorney impersonation**: Attackers pose as a lawyer or legal representative involved with the company, often under the guise of urgent and confidential matters, to misdirect funds or gain sensitive information.

- **Data theft**: Here, the objective is not necessarily immediate financial gain but the theft of sensitive data, which could be employee tax information, intellectual property, or customer data.

- **Account compromise**: An employee's email account is hacked and then used to request payments from vendors listed in their email contacts.

- **Credentials harvesting**: An employee's email account is hacked and then used to further harvest more credentials from outside the organization to trusted contracts and vendors.

- **Motive for attackers**: The primary motivation behind BEC attacks is financial gain. Attackers exploit the trust within business communication channels to divert funds or obtain sensitive information that can be monetized. Additionally, the data harvested from such attacks, such as credentials and employee personal information or intellectual property, can be sold on the dark web or used for further attacks, including repeat BEC attacks and ransomware. The sophisticated and targeted nature of these attacks often leads to a higher success rate and potentially greater financial rewards for the attackers, making BEC a lucrative form of cybercrime.

A deep understanding of the varied BEC attack types, from invoice fraud to data theft, is essential for effective defense against these sophisticated and financially motivated cyber threats. Identifying types of BEC allows both technical and business controls to prevent these incidents. For example, organizations can implement controls to verbally verify transaction approvals over a set amount to prevent invoice and C-suite fraud.

Initial scoping and response

When responding to a BEC attack as an incident responder, the **initial scoping phase** is critical for understanding the breadth and depth of the incident. This phase involves gathering as much information as possible to assess the situation accurately. This initial scoping involves talking with the cloud productivity suite (Microsoft 365 or Google Workspace) IT administrators, organization general counsel, C-suite, and accounting staff to better understand the following, even before any technical forensic analysis:

- **Timeline of the attack**: Understanding when the attack started is crucial. Ask when the first signs of compromise were noticed and at what point users noticed anything suspicious. This could include unusual email activity, reports of suspicious emails from within or outside the organization, or financial transactions that were flagged as anomalous. If attackers were successful in transferring any unauthorized funds, note these dates in the timeline.

- **Extent of the compromise**: Determine which accounts have been compromised. This involves checking for signs of unauthorized access, such as login attempts from unfamiliar locations or devices, and changes in account settings or permissions that were not initiated by the account owners. If attackers were successful, IT administrators for the productivity suites would have already narrowed down on the accounts of interest. We will discuss how to determine evidence of compromise in the *Microsoft 365 incident response* and *Google Workspace incident response* sections.

- **Attack vectors**: Investigate how the attackers gained access. Was it through phishing emails, credential stuffing, or exploiting security vulnerabilities? Understanding the attack vector is essential for preventing future breaches. In some instances, users can recall at what points they may have entered their credentials to a phishing site. Furthermore, have the organization and/or individual users suffered a data breach in the past? If so, their username and credentials could be circulating on the dark web. It is not uncommon for employees to use their corporate email addresses for personal services. If those personal services suffer a data breach, the employee's corporate information may be exposed.

- **Data exfiltration**: Assess what information has been accessed or exfiltrated. This includes sensitive emails, attachments, and any data stored in the compromised accounts. Knowing the type of data exposed helps in understanding the potential impact of the breach.

- **Communication with affected parties**: Determine who has been affected by the breach, both internally and externally. This might include employees, customers, or business partners who have communicated with the compromised accounts.

- **Security measures in place**: Review the existing security measures. Were there any security protocols that were bypassed or ineffective? This could include multi-factor authentication, regular password changes, and employee training on recognizing phishing attempts.

- **Previous incidents**: Inquire if there have been previous similar incidents. Understanding past incidents can provide insights into potential weaknesses or repeated patterns of attacks. It has become much more common for repeat attacks, especially if attackers were successful in diverting funds in the past. They may see an organization as an easy repeat target.

- **Current response actions**: Check what actions have already been taken in response to the discovery of the attack. This can include changing passwords, disconnecting potentially compromised systems from the network, or notifying affected individuals.

- **Microsoft 365 access**: This is the most important step to actually kick off the response and investigation as an incident responder. You will require the organization's Microsoft 365 administrator to create an account in their 365 tenant with the following roles. For the most part, the accesses required to respond to a 365 compromise are as follows:

  - Azure AD:

    - Global reader

    - Security reader

  - Exchange online admin, a custom role with the following permissions:

    - Mail recipients

    - Security group creation and memberships

    - View only audit log

    - View only configuration

    - View only recipients

  - Microsoft Purview (compliance):

    - Compliance administrator

    - eDiscovery manager

These role names are likely to change within the Microsoft ecosystem; however, the key here is that you will require some sort of global reader or security reader role to allow you to run searches in the audit logs.

The initial scoping phase sets the stage for effective incident response by providing a clear picture of the attack. Next, we will dive a bit deeper into triaging and forensics for Microsoft 365 and Google Workspace.

Remediation steps

During the initial scoping of the incident, regardless of whether it's Microsoft 365 or Google Workspace, there are several steps that the organization can follow to ensure that the attacker is no longer in their environment prior to incident responders starting forensics. User interfaces and productivity suites change; however, the following steps are always relevant:

1. Reset the passwords of any accounts that were impacted or are suspected to be compromised.

2. Enable **multi-factor authentication (MFA)** organization-wide or, at the very least, for privileged accounts.

3. Remove any suspicious automation (i.e., email forwarding rules outside of the domain) and any suspicious inbox rules set inside the mailbox. We will discuss this further in the upcoming section.

4. Remove compromised accounts from any privileged or elevated role at the organization. For example, compromised accounts belonging to IT administrators should temporarily have their accesses limited to prevent further unauthorized activities.

Despite any changes in productivity suites such as Microsoft 365 or Google Workspace, these high-level steps, including password resets and access limitations, are universally applicable and crucial for safeguarding against cyber threats in a productivity suite environment. The product's UI and details may change; however, the steps remain the same.

Microsoft 365 incident response

After the initial scoping to understand the incident, the next step is to determine indicators of compromise and begin the threat hunt. This section delves into the tools and techniques that incident responders can employ to automate the log acquisition and analysis process, specifically to an organization that is utilizing Microsoft 365 as their cloud productivity suite. A key focus is on utilizing Microsoft 365's built-in security and compliance tools, such as Microsoft Purview, to rapidly gather logs and track suspicious activities.

Tooling

In *Chapter 7*, we discussed the various auditing and compliance features in Microsoft 365, one of which was Microsoft unified audit logs. These logs provide a consolidated view of all Microsoft 365 activity and are critical for investigating and understanding the extent of the compromise. Here's how incident responders can leverage the audit log search GUI in Microsoft 365 for this purpose:

1. **Accessing the audit log search**: The audit log search is accessible through Microsoft Purview. Incident responders need to navigate to the **Audit** section to begin.

2. **Scoping the incident**: Before running a search, it's crucial to complete the initial scoping of the incident, as we discussed in the previous section. This is because the initial scoping involves understanding the timeline of the incident, the suspected compromised accounts, and the

nature of the activities that are of interest. This initial scoping helps in applying the right filters. Otherwise, incident responders will have to run general searches, which may take a while to execute and can be difficult to quickly analyze and triage afterward.

3. **Apply filters**: The audit log search provides various filters to narrow down the search results:

   - **Date and time**: Specify the time frame for the incident

   - **Activities**: Filter by specific activities, such as file accesses, user logins, and administrative actions

   - **Users**: Focus the search on specific user accounts that are suspected to be compromised

   - **File, folder, and site**: Narrow down to specific files, folders, or SharePoint sites if relevant

4. **Running the search**: After applying the necessary filters, run the search. The GUI will display a list of events that match the criteria. Either classic or new searches can be used; however, note that classic searches will not save the history of the searches you conduct. Furthermore, classic searches are limited to only running concurrent search jobs.

5. **Exporting logs for detailed analysis**: For a more in-depth analysis, users can export the search results to a CSV file. This allows for additional analysis using external tools for archiving purposes. The exported data includes detailed information about each event, such as the source IP address, user agent, and the exact operations performed.

> **Important note**
>
> Exporting results through the audit search user interface is limited to only 10,0000 entries. As a result, it's important to ensure that your search results are refined under 10,000 or search jobs are broken down into multiple batches to ensure all entries are exported.

6. **Utilizing external tools**: Once the logs are exported, incident responders can utilize various data analysis tools to sift through the data. Tools such as Excel, Power BI, or specialized forensic tools can be used to analyze patterns, create timelines, and correlate events across different logs.

7. **Analyzing results**: Examine the results to identify any unusual or unauthorized activities. Look for patterns or anomalies that could indicate malicious behavior. We will discuss analysis further in the next section.

Searching for and extracting 365 audit logs

The following figures demonstrate how to run searches and extract the audit logs in CSV:

- The following screenshot demonstrates the audit log search tab with available filters to further refine queries:

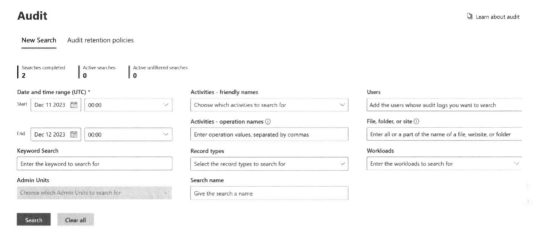

Figure 12.2 – Microsoft 365 Audit search log tab

- Search jobs are created on execution and listed below the audit log filters, as demonstrated:

Figure 12.3 – Audit log search jobs

- Once search jobs are completed, results are organized in a table, as shown:

Figure 12.4 – Audit log search results (UI)

- The next figure is an example of successful login and failed login events:

Date (UTC) ↓	IP Address	User	Record type	Activity
Dec 12, 2023 8:15 PM		Not Available	AzureActiveDirectoryStsLogon	User logged in
Dec 12, 2023 8:15 PM	...8...	mhaqanee@ :.ca	AzureActiveDirectoryStsLogon	UserLoginFailed
Dec 12, 2023 8:15 PM		mhaqanec⊖	AzureActiveDirectoryStsLogon	UserLoginFailed
Dec 12, 2023 8:14 PM:		mhaqanee@en⊐	AzureActiveDirectoryStsLogon	User logged in
Dec 12, 2023 8:13 PM	...0...	mhaqanee@er..:	AzureActiveDirectoryStsLogon	UserLoginFailed
Dec 12, 2023 8:13 PM	..3...	mhaqanee@er...	AzureActiveDirectoryStsLogon	UserLoginFailed

Figure 12.5 – Audit log search results – login events

- The following figure demonstrates an example of an event's **Details** pane:

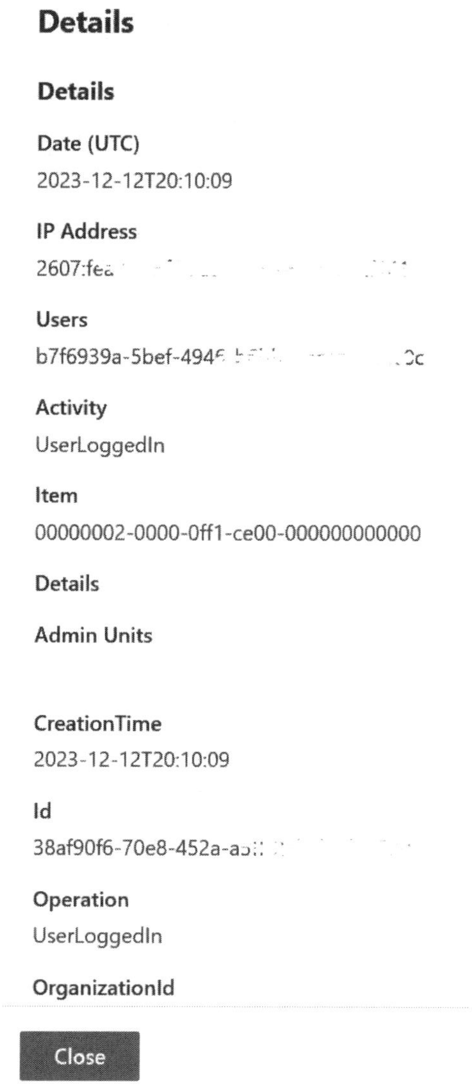

Details

Details

Date (UTC)
2023-12-12T20:10:09

IP Address
2607:fea

Users
b7f6939a-5bef-494⁵ ᵇ⁻¹⁻   ᴼᶜ

Activity
UserLoggedIn

Item
00000002-0000-0ff1-ce00-000000000000

Details

Admin Units

CreationTime
2023-12-12T20:10:09

Id
38af90f6-70e8-452a-aɔ:

Operation
UserLoggedIn

OrganizationId

Close

Figure 12.6 – Audit log event details

- All search results can be exported as a CSV file, as shown:

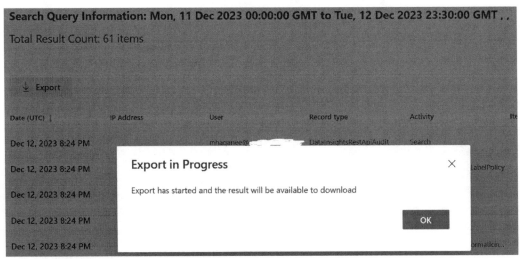

Figure 12.7 – Audit log export process

The resulting file is a CSV file; however, the majority of the fields will be stored in the `AuditData` column in the JSON format. The exported CSV is as follows:

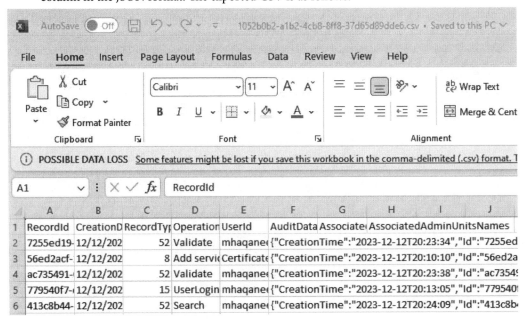

Figure 12.8 – Audit log export (CSV)

Extracting audit logs using PowerShell

The unified audit logs can also be programmatically extracted using PowerShell:

1. Open PowerShell as an administrator and navigate to your folder of choosing; for example, `C:\Incident Response\`.

2. Connect to the Microsoft 365 tenant with the following commands:

```
Install-Module ExchangePowerShell
Install-Module AzureAD
Import-Module AzureAD
Import-Module ExchangePowerShell
Connect AzureAD
```

3. Define a log time range (modify as needed; here, we will start with 30 days):

```
$StartDate = (Get-Date).AddDays(-30)
$EndDate = Get-Date
```

4. Retrieve the audit logs using the `Search-UnifiedAuditLog` cmdlet:

```
$AuditLogs = Search-UnifiedAuditLog -StartDate $StartDate
-EndDate $EndDate
```

5. Export the log as a CSV:

```
$AuditLogs | Export-Csv -Path "AuditLogs-last30.csv"
-NoTypeInformation
```

6. Release the 365 session (i.e., disconnect):

```
Disconnect-MsolService
```

The resulting CSV will be very similar to the export generated through the user interface in *Figure 12.8*.

Utilizing Microsoft Power Query

Whether exported through the Purview user interface or programmatically, a large amount of the data and useful fields will be stored in JSON. As a result, incident responders must complete the additional step of parsing this data for it to be useful (or easily searchable). Incident responders can utilize a JSON parsing tool of their choice, but in this example, we will utilize Microsoft Power Query. Power Query can be employed to drill down into the bulk of JSON data. The process involves importing the CSV file into Excel and then using Power Query's advanced data transformation capabilities to parse the JSON fields. This parsing translates the JSON data into a structured format that aligns with the traditional columns and rows of Excel. Users can expand the JSON fields into individual columns, making the data more accessible and easier to analyze. This transformation is crucial for incident responders who need to dissect and understand intricate details of user activities, security events, and system changes logged in the audit data column. By leveraging Microsoft's Power Query, organizations can efficiently convert the complex JSON data into a more manageable and analyzable format.

The steps to utilize Microsoft Power Query are as follows:

1. Starting with the unified audit log CSV, our next step is to create a new workbook in Microsoft Excel:

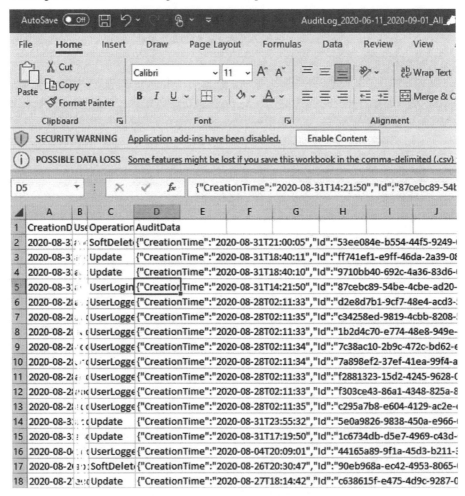

Figure 12.9 – Audit log results to be transformed

2. Create a new workbook:

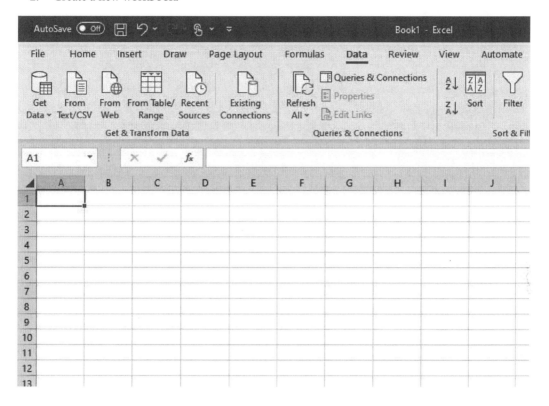

Figure 12.10 – New Excel workbook

3. Next, you will need to navigate to the **Data** tab and click on **Get Data | From File | From Text/CSV**.

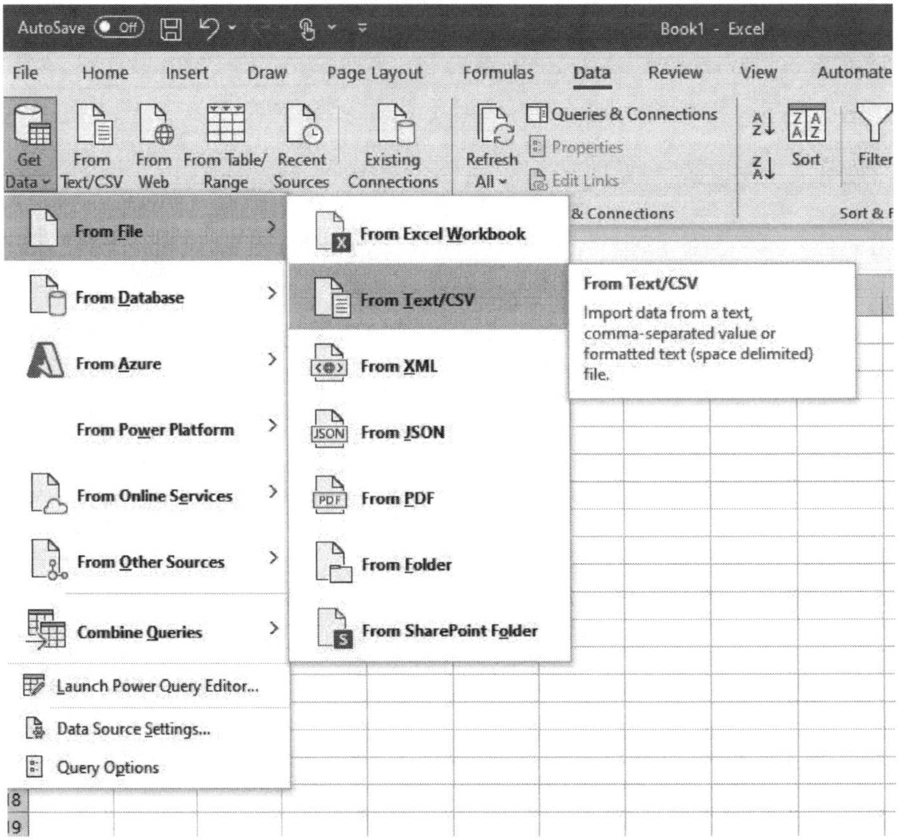

Figure 12.11 – Importing the audit data export

4. Next, you will import the unified audit log CSV and click **Transform Data** to further drill down into the `AuditData` column, which contains the JSON. Note that Power Query is limited to the maximum number of rows filled to a worksheet (i.e., 1,048,576).

AuditLog_2020-08-01_2020-08-31.csv

File Origin	Delimiter	Data Type Detection	
65001: Unicode (UTF-8) ▾	Comma ▾	Based on first 200 rows ▾	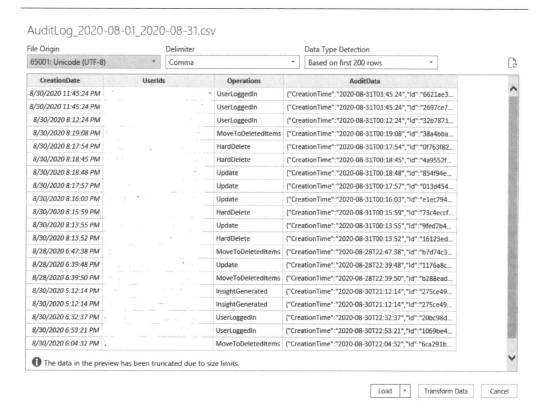

CreationDate	UserIds	Operations	AuditData
8/30/2020 11:45:24 PM		UserLoggedIn	{"CreationTime":"2020-08-31T03:45:24","Id":"6621ae3...
8/30/2020 11:45:24 PM		UserLoggedIn	{"CreationTime":"2020-08-31T03:45:24","Id":"2697ce7...
8/30/2020 8:12:24 PM		UserLoggedIn	{"CreationTime":"2020-08-31T00:12:24","Id":"32b7871...
8/30/2020 8:19:08 PM		MoveToDeletedItems	{"CreationTime":"2020-08-31T00:19:08","Id":"38a4bba...
8/30/2020 8:17:54 PM		HardDelete	{"CreationTime":"2020-08-31T00:17:54","Id":"0f763f82...
8/30/2020 8:18:45 PM		HardDelete	{"CreationTime":"2020-08-31T00:18:45","Id":"4a9552f...
8/30/2020 8:18:48 PM		Update	{"CreationTime":"2020-08-31T00:18:48","Id":"854f94e...
8/30/2020 8:17:57 PM		Update	{"CreationTime":"2020-08-31T00:17:57","Id":"013d454...
8/30/2020 8:16:03 PM		Update	{"CreationTime":"2020-08-31T00:16:03","Id":"e1ec794...
8/30/2020 8:15:59 PM		HardDelete	{"CreationTime":"2020-08-31T00:15:59","Id":"73c4eccf...
8/30/2020 8:13:55 PM		Update	{"CreationTime":"2020-08-31T00:13:55","Id":"9fed7b4...
8/30/2020 8:13:52 PM		HardDelete	{"CreationTime":"2020-08-31T00:13:52","Id":"16123ed...
8/28/2020 6:47:38 PM		MoveToDeletedItems	{"CreationTime":"2020-08-28T22:47:38","Id":"b7d74c3...
8/28/2020 6:39:48 PM		Update	{"CreationTime":"2020-08-28T22:39:48","Id":"1176a8c...
8/28/2020 6:39:50 PM		MoveToDeletedItems	{"CreationTime":"2020-08-28T22:39:50","Id":"b288ead...
8/30/2020 5:12:14 PM		InsightGenerated	{"CreationTime":"2020-08-30T21:12:14","Id":"275ce49...
8/30/2020 5:12:14 PM		InsightGenerated	{"CreationTime":"2020-08-30T21:12:14","Id":"275ce49...
8/30/2020 6:32:37 PM		UserLoggedIn	{"CreationTime":"2020-08-30T22:32:37","Id":"20bc98d...
8/30/2020 6:53:21 PM		UserLoggedIn	{"CreationTime":"2020-08-30T22:53:21","Id":"1069be4...
8/30/2020 6:04:32 PM		MoveToDeletedItems	{"CreationTime":"2020-08-30T22:04:32","Id":"6ca291b...

ⓘ The data in the preview has been truncated due to size limits.

Load ▾   Transform Data   Cancel

Figure 12.12 – Power Query options to load data

5. Next, audit data is transformed using the **Transform Data** option. The results are shown in the next figure:

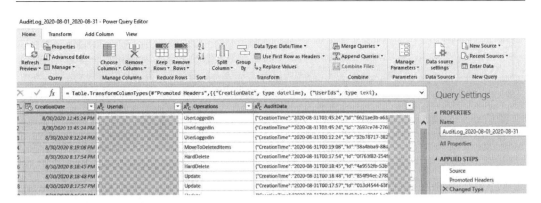

Figure 12.13 – Power Query results

6. Next, right-click on the AuditData column and click on **Transform | JSON**.

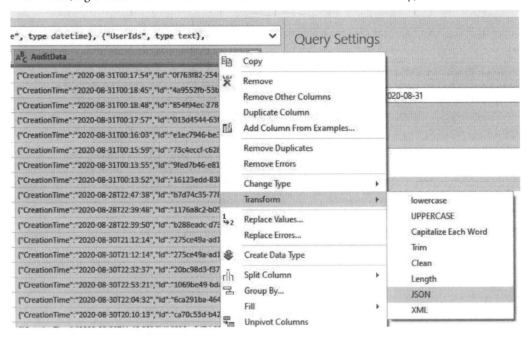

Figure 12.14 – Transforming the JSON data column

As shown next, your JSON data has now been transformed into CSV columns (for example, `AuditData.ClientIP`):

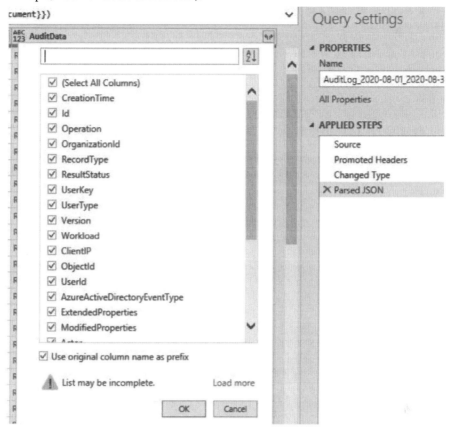

Figure 12.15 – Resulting CSV column

The following figure demonstrates the resulting data after the column has been transformed in Power Query:

fx	= Table.ExpandRecordColumn(#"Parsed JSON", "AuditData", {"CreationTime", "Id", "Operat		
AuditData.CreationTime	**AuditData.Id**	**AuditData.Operation**	**AuditData.Organiza**
2020-08-31T03:45:24	6621ae3b-a631	UserLoggedIn	
2020-08-31T03:45:24	2697ce74-2761	UserLoggedIn	
2020-08-31T00:12:24	32b78717-3829	UserLoggedIn	
2020-08-31T00:19:08	38a4bba9-88d.	MoveToDeletedItems	

Figure 12.16 – Expanding the transformed column

The result is a CSV file with all your audit data in a friendly, readable format to utilize Excel (or the tool of your choice) for further analysis.

Cloud forensics using HAWK

Incident responders can also utilize some open source tools based on the Microsoft 365 API, such as HAWK (`Github.com/T0pCyber/hawk`).

HAWK is a PowerShell-based tool for gathering information related to Microsoft 365 compromises. It searches and parses out a lot of useful information specific to a 365 compromise from the 365 configuration and the audit logs, such as the creation of new inbox rules, consent grants, a list of all users with administrator access, and much more. This simplifies the incident response process, as incident responders can find all information in their respective CSV as opposed to navigating to configurations in 365 or extracting it manually through the audit logs.

> **Important Note**
>
> The HAWK tool can be found on GitHub:
>
> `https://github.com/T0pCyber/hawk`
>
> Here is the HAWK Module PowerShell Gallery download:
>
> `https://www.powershellgallery.com/packages/HAWK/3.1.0`
>
> Here is the HAWK documentation:
>
> `https://cloudforensicator.com/`

To run HAWK, you require PowerShell on your system with administrator rights and an internet connection:

1. Open PowerShell as an administrator and navigate to the `C:\Incident Response\` folder using the `cd` command.

2. Install the HAWK module:

```
(Install-Module -Name Hawk)
```

3. Install and import the Microsoft 365 Exchange Online management module and the Microsoft 365 module:

```
Install-Module -Name ExchangeOnlineManagement
Install-Module MSOnline
Install-Module AzureAD
Install-Module ExchangePowerShell
Import-Module AzureAD
Import-Module ExchangeOnlineManagement
Import-Module ExchangePowerShell
```

4. Log in to the impacted 365 tenant with the following commands and authenticate with your Microsoft 365 username and password:

```
Connect-AzureAD
Connect-MsolService
```

5. Create a folder for your 365 files generated by HAWK. For this example, we will use `C:\Incident Response\`.

6. Run the HAWK tool:

```
Start-HawkTenantInvestigation
```

An example of the resulting files is shown in the following figure:

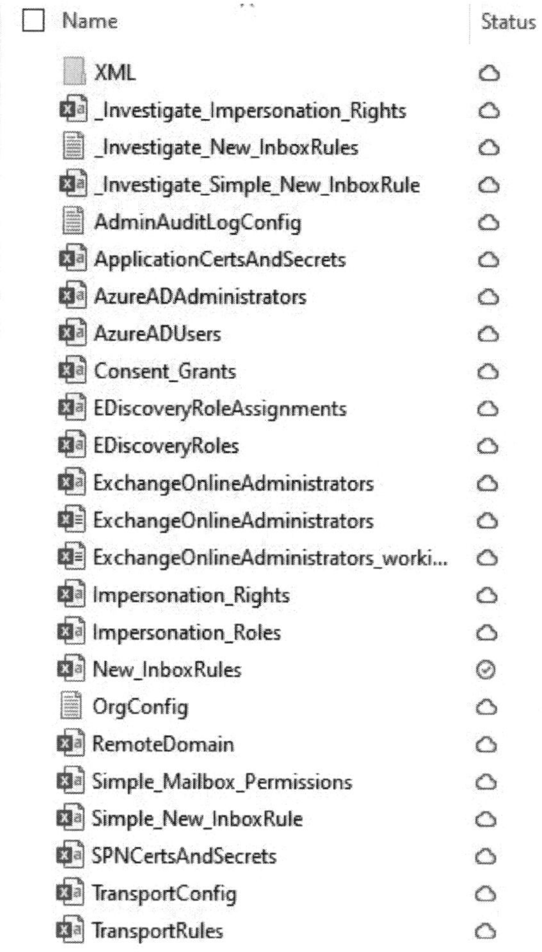

☐	Name		Status
	XML		☁
	_Investigate_Impersonation_Rights		☁
	_Investigate_New_InboxRules		☁
	_Investigate_Simple_New_InboxRule		☁
	AdminAuditLogConfig		☁
	ApplicationCertsAndSecrets		☁
	AzureADAdministrators		☁
	AzureADUsers		☁
	Consent_Grants		☁
	EDiscoveryRoleAssignments		☁
	EDiscoveryRoles		☁
	ExchangeOnlineAdministrators		☁
	ExchangeOnlineAdministrators		☁
	ExchangeOnlineAdministrators_worki...		☁
	Impersonation_Rights		☁
	Impersonation_Roles		☁
	New_InboxRules		⊘
	OrgConfig		☁
	RemoteDomain		☁
	Simple_Mailbox_Permissions		☁
	Simple_New_InboxRule		☁
	SPNCertsAndSecrets		☁
	TransportConfig		☁
	TransportRules		☁

Figure 12.17 – HAWK results

As mentioned in HAWK's GitHub, HAWK is designed to quickly get incident responders the data they need. It is not meant to complete the analysis for you. A full breakdown of all generated log files can be found on the HAWK documentation page.

Analysis

The goal of our analysis is to identify any evidence of compromise. The very first piece of analysis to be conducted is determining evidence of unauthorized access. This is best determined by identifying login events by using the `Activity` or `Operation` column in the unified audit logs in Microsoft 365. This column records the specific action that has been performed within the environment. In essence, it serves as a detailed ledger of activities, ranging from file access and sharing to administrative changes and login events. Each entry in the `Operation` column is tagged with a descriptive label that identifies the nature of the action, making it a valuable resource for incident responders.

> **Important note**
>
> All audited activities (i.e., operations) can be found in Microsoft's documentation at `https://learn.microsoft.com/en-us/purview/audit-log-activities`.

The first step to determine compromise is filtering for `UserLoggedIn` events, which is essential for monitoring and investigating unauthorized access. By analyzing these events, incident responders can track when and how users log into the system, providing crucial insights into threat actor behavior.

For instance, an unusual pattern of login activities, such as logins at unusual hours or from unexpected locations, can be early indicators of unauthorized access. This will allow incident responders to determine any indicators related to the compromise, such as login user agent strings and IP addresses.

The strongest indicator in terms of login activity will not be analyzing unusual login times but analyzing the location of IPs associated with the login events. This can be done by filtering the unified audit logs by the `UserLoggedIn` events and looking up the associated IP addresses (the `ClientIP` field in `AuditData`) with any bulk IP address lookup software (such as `ipinfo.io`). See *Figure 12.18* and *Figure 12.19* for an example of this:

"Parsed JSON", "AuditData", {"Creat

ABC 123 AuditData.ClientIP			▼
52.			
14			
69			
26	:t	93	52
67			
26	:t	93	52
52			

Figure 12.18 – Client IP audit data

These IPs can be copied to a lookup IP service that will give you the specific cities, regions, and countries associated with each IP. For example, looking up one of the IPs starting with 69 on IPinfo provides information stating that the user had logged in from an IP based in Minnesota, USA.

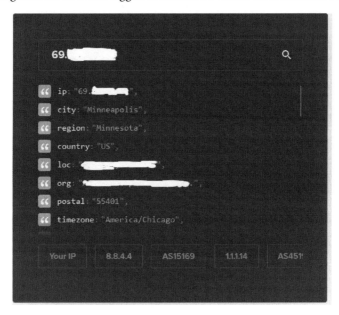

Figure 12.19 – IPInfo.io lookup results

The geographical information can be exported from your geo IP lookup service of choice and compared against all users in your audit log. As an incident responder, your next step is to determine whether the geographic location aligns with the organization's business operations or if the user was confirmed in the IP's location on that date. If the user had not traveled to the location, the user account can be deemed compromised. Incident responders can also analyze other pieces of the IP information, such as VPN/proxy use, or see if the hosting provider does not align with the user's normal (baseline) IP address.

Continuing from analyzing unusual login locations, another key threat-hunting task for incident responders is checking for changes in mailbox rules. **Mailbox rules** are automatic actions triggered by incoming emails. If attackers get into a user's account, they can secretly make or change rules. These unauthorized rules might redirect emails to other accounts, delete specific messages, or manage phishing emails to avoid being caught. The key operations to focus on are as follows:

- **New-InboxRule**: This operation is logged when a new mailbox rule is created. Incident responders should scrutinize any instance of this operation, paying close attention to rules that forward emails to external domains, automatically delete messages, or sort emails in a suspicious manner. A sudden increase in the creation of new rules, especially those with unusual criteria, should raise an alert.

- **Set-InboxRule**: This indicates modifications to existing mailbox rules. Alterations to established rules, especially those that change the rule's action or condition, can be a sign of an attacker trying to manipulate email flow subtly.

- **Remove-InboxRule**: The deletion of mailbox rules is captured under this operation. While it might seem benign, the removal of certain rules, particularly security-related ones, can be a tactic used by attackers to reduce detection of their activities.

- **New-TransportRule and Set-TransportRule**: These operations are associated with the creation and modification of transport rules, which are more complex and can control email flow at the organizational level. Unauthorized changes here could have widespread implications.

For example, the next screenshot is from a compromised 365 incident where threat actors had created a new inbox rule called zz. This inbox rule automatically deletes any emails that contain the following words in the subject line or body: "scam", "fraud", "phish", and an email address that has been sanitized for privacy reasons. This is because the attacker is trying to cover their tracks such that any emails or warnings from others related to their objective, that is, to "scam" or "fraud" the organization out of money, will be automatically deleted, and as a result, the threat attacker can complete their attack unnoticed.

ClientIP: [2001 .

CreationTime: 2020-07-28T18:54:55

ExternalAccess: false

Id: d647a926-2ae3--   . .

ObjectId: · ·   PROD.OUTLOOK.COM/Microsoft Exchange Hosted
                     Organizations/   '\zz

Operation: New-InboxRule

OrganizationId: 275ce49a ··

OrganizationName: ..onmicrosoft.com

OriginatingServer:

Parameters:

```
[
  {
    "Name": "AlwaysDeleteOutlookRulesBlob",
    "Value": "False"
  },
  {
    "Name": "Force",
    "Value": "False"
  },
  {
    "Name": "Name",
    "Value": "zz"
  },
  {
    "Name": "SubjectOrBodyContainsWords",
    "Value": "scam;fraud;phish;        f@            ·1.com"
  },
```

Figure 12.20 – Example malicious inbox rule

In addition to monitoring these specific operations, correlating this information with other login data, such as login locations and times, can provide a more comprehensive picture of the attacker's activities. For example, the creation of a new inbox rule immediately following a login from an unusual geographic location can be a strong indicator of a compromised account.

When addressing the issue of data exfiltration in Microsoft 365 compromises, incident responders need to focus on specific operations within the audit logs that can indicate unauthorized data movement or access. Data exfiltration can occur in various ways, such as through Outlook synchronization, accessing data via a web browser, or other activities. Understanding these nuances is vital for identifying potential breaches:

- **Outlook client synchronization (via SyncFolderItems operation)**: This operation is logged when a user's Outlook client syncs with the mailbox. Excessive or unusual sync activities, especially from unfamiliar devices or locations, can indicate that someone is trying to download a large amount of data. Comparing the volume and frequency of these sync operations against typical user behavior can reveal anomalies.

- **Web browser access (MailItemsAccessed operation)**: This operation is crucial for monitoring access to mail items via web browsers. An increase in the `MailItemsAccessed` events, especially from attacker IP addresses, suggests not only unauthorized access but that the threat actors viewed the contents of those mail items.

- **File and document access operations**: Operations such as `FileDownloaded`, `FileCopied`, `FileMoved`, and `FileDeleted` within SharePoint or OneDrive for Business are key indicators. These actions, particularly in high volumes or from atypical locations, can signal that someone is exfiltrating data.

- **Email forwarding rules (New-InboxRule, Set-InboxRule)**: As with mailbox compromises, the creation or modification of inbox rules that automatically forward emails to external addresses can be a method of data exfiltration.

- **eDiscovery search and export operations (SearchQueryInitiated, SearchQueryPerformed, ExportStarted)**: These operations indicate that someone is performing searches and possibly exporting data from eDiscovery, which can be a sophisticated way of extracting large datasets for malicious purposes.

- **Unusual sending patterns (Send and SendAs operations)**: A spike in email sending activities, especially those with large attachments or sent to external recipients, might indicate an attempt to exfiltrate data via email.

> **Important note**
>
> All mailbox audited activities (i.e., operations) can be found in Microsoft's documentation at https://learn.microsoft.com/en-us/purview/audit-mailboxes.

One of the key questions that organizations must answer during a productivity suite breach is whether data was exfiltrated by attackers. Analyzing the outlined operations will allow incident responders to better understand the scope of the incident from a data breach perspective.

Incident responders should also consider reviewing the following valuable sources of information in the context of a 365 compromise:

- **Impersonation rights**: These rights allow a user to perform actions on behalf of another user. Incident responders should check for unexpected or unauthorized assignments of impersonation rights. This can be done by reviewing the role assignments for each user.

- **List of Azure Active Directory administrators**: Reviewing the current Azure **Active Directory** (**AD**) administrators is important. You can view this list in the Azure AD admin center. Look for any unfamiliar accounts or changes in administrator roles, as attackers can elevate privileges to gain wider access in a 365 compromise.

- **List of Azure AD users**: Incident responders should audit a list of all users in Azure AD. Pay special attention to newly created users, especially those with high privileges. Check this list through the Azure AD admin center. Unexpected user accounts can be a sign that an attacker has created backdoors.

- **Consent grants**: These are permissions granted to applications to access user data. Review the consent grants in the Azure AD admin center for any unusual or broad permissions granted to unknown or suspicious applications. Excessive permissions can be abused for data access and exfiltration.

- **eDiscovery roles**: Users with eDiscovery roles can search and export content from mailboxes and sites. Check who has been assigned these roles in Microsoft Purview. Though unlikely, unauthorized eDiscovery role assignments can indicate an attempt to illicitly access and export sensitive data.

- **Exchange online administrators**: It's important to regularly review who has administrative privileges in Exchange Online, as these accounts have significant control over email operations. Check for any unexpected changes or additions in the Exchange admin center.

- **Transport rules (mail flow)**: These are rules set up in Exchange Online to control mail flow. Review the transport rules for any that redirect or copy emails to external domains, which can be a method of data exfiltration.

All of these sources for analysis can be reviewed by the CSVs that are generated by the HAWK tool, as demonstrated in *Figure 12.17*.

Google Workspace incident response

After understanding the basics of an incident as we have discussed in the *Initial scoping and response* section, incident responders using Google Workspace face the challenge of identifying compromises and starting threat hunting. **Google Workspace**, unlike Microsoft 365, offers fewer tools for this purpose, focusing mainly on its audit and reporting features. These tools, while not as extensive, are crucial for collecting logs and spotting unusual activities. This means responders often need to supplement these tools with external resources and more hands-on analysis to effectively track and investigate potential security breaches in Google Workspace environments.

Tooling

In a similar vein to our discussion on Microsoft 365, let's explore how incident responders can leverage audit logs in Google Workspace to investigate and understand the extent of compromises:

1. **Accessing the audit logs**: In Google Workspace, the audit logs are accessible through the Admin console. Incident responders can find these logs by navigating to the **Reports** section and then to the **Audit** subsection.

   As with Microsoft 365, the initial step involves understanding the incident's timeline, identifying potentially compromised accounts, and determining the nature of suspicious activities. This understanding helps to apply the right filters in the audit logs, making the search more efficient and focused.

2. **Applying filters in audit log search**: Google Workspace's audit log search offers various filters to refine searches:

   - **Date and time**: Set the specific time frame of interest

   - **Events**: Choose from a range of activities, such as email sent, file shared, admin activity, and more

   - **Users**: Focus on specific user accounts under suspicion

   - **Applications**: Filter by specific Google Workspace applications, such as Gmail, Drive, and Calendar, if relevant

3. **Running the search**: After setting the filters, run the search. The results will display a list of events that fit the criteria, which can then be reviewed for any suspicious activity.

4. **Exporting logs for analysis**: Google Workspace allows the exporting of search results for more detailed analysis. These exports can include comprehensive event information such as IP addresses, actions taken, and affected resources.

5. **Utilizing external tools for analysis**: Once exported, the logs can be further analyzed using tools such as Excel or other data analysis software. This step is crucial for spotting patterns, creating timelines, and correlating events across different logs.

6. **Analyzing results**: Carefully examine the audit log entries for unusual or unauthorized activities. Look for anomalies or patterns that could suggest malicious behavior, such as mass file downloads, unusual login times, or unexpected external sharing of documents. This is further discussed in the upcoming *Analysis* section.

> **Important note**
>
> Similar to Microsoft 365, exporting results from Google Workspace audit logs may have limitations in terms of the number of entries that one can export. It's important to ensure that your search is precise enough to capture all relevant data without exceeding these limits (typically 100,000 entries).

Searching and extracting Google Workspace logs

As discussed in *Chapter 7*, Google Workspace provides a range of audit logs, each tailored to different applications and activities. Key logs include the following:

- **Admin activity logs**: Track administrative actions such as changes to settings or user management
- **Login logs**: Monitor user sign-in attempts, successful or otherwise, which is crucial for identifying unauthorized access attempts
- **Drive audit logs**: Essential for tracking file sharing and access within Google Drive
- **Gmail logs**: Monitor for unusual email activities, such as mass deletions or forwarding rules

To export the Google Workspace's audit logs, incident responders can follow these steps:

1. In the Google Workspace admin console (`admin.google.com`), go to **Reports** and then **Audit and Investigations.**
2. Choose the specific audit log (e.g., admin log events, user log events, and group log events).
3. Apply the necessary filters and run the search.

Once the results are displayed, use the **Download** or **Export** option to save the data for further analysis.

The exported logs can be in the CSV format, making it easier to import into data analysis tools. When using tools such as Excel, responders can sort, filter, and use functions to analyze the data more effectively.

The following figures demonstrate the steps to export the audit events. Start by navigating to the **Reporting** and then going to the **Audit and investigation** tab, as shown:

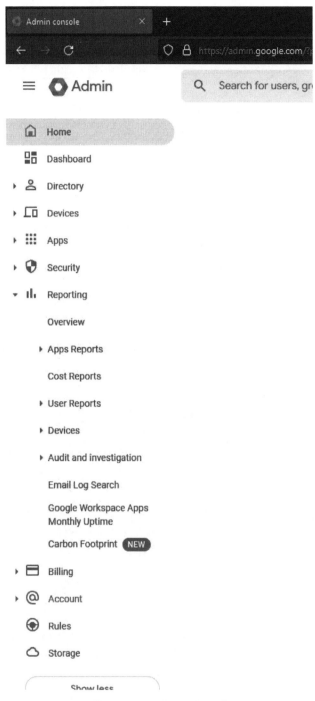

Figure 12.21 – Reporting tab

The following screenshot demonstrates all available logs under the **Audit and investigation** tab in the Google Workspace administrative console:

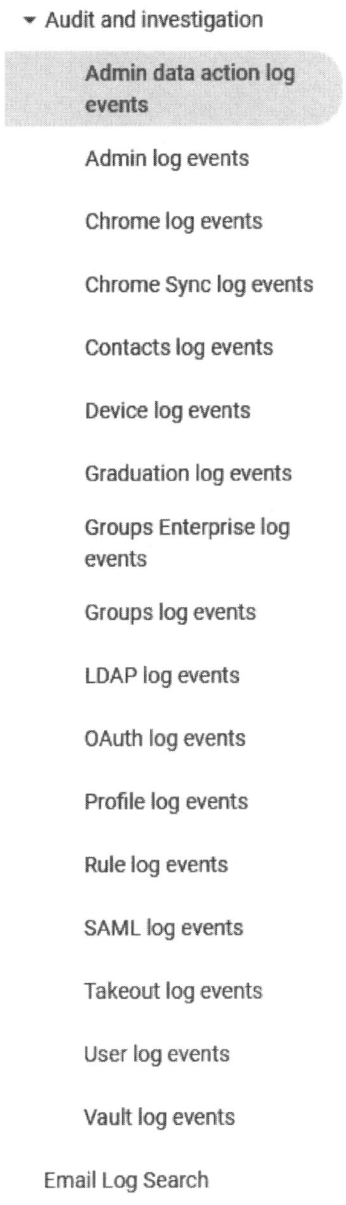

▾ Audit and investigation

Admin data action log
events

Admin log events

Chrome log events

Chrome Sync log events

Contacts log events

Device log events

Graduation log events

Groups Enterprise log
events

Groups log events

LDAP log events

OAuth log events

Profile log events

Rule log events

SAML log events

Takeout log events

User log events

Vault log events

Email Log Search

Figure 12.22 – Audit and investigations

Similar to Microsoft 365 audit log searches, filters can be set, as shown in this figure:

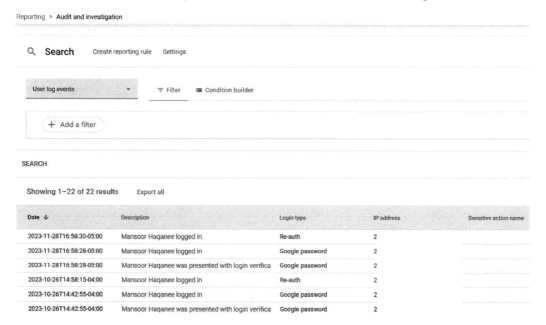

Figure 12.23 – User events

An example of the exported data is shown here:

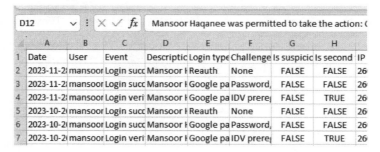

Figure 12.24 – Exported user events

Next, we will dive into the analysis portion of a Google Workspace compromise. A similar process to the Microsoft 365 analysis is to be followed for Google Workspace with a difference in audit logs and their syntax. The principles of verifying unusual logins remain the same.

Analysis

An analysis of a compromised Google Workspace environment requires focusing on mainly user and admin events. Incident responders need to thoroughly investigate these logs to identify evidence of unauthorized access and other indicators of compromise, similar to Microsoft 365, but this time in the Google ecosystem:

- **Login audit log analysis (user log events)**:

    - **Key events**: Focus on **Successful login** and **Login failure** events. These indicate successful and unsuccessful login attempts.

    - **Patterns to look for**: Repeated login failures followed by a success, particularly from varied IP addresses or geographic locations, could signal brute force attempts.

    - **IP and geolocation analysis**: Compare the IP addresses from the logs against the user's typical login locations. Discrepancies in geolocation data can be a strong indicator of unauthorized access.

- **Gmail (Email) log investigation**:

    - **Critical events**: Look for **Email sent**, **Email read**, and **Email deleted** activities.

    - **Anomalies to detect**: High volumes of outbound emails to unknown addresses, bulk deletion of emails, or opening numerous emails in a short time frame can suggest account takeover. Furthermore, look into the creation and modification of any inbox rules, similar to what we discussed in the *Microsoft 365 incident response* section.

- **Admin activity log review**:

    - **Significant events**: Monitor **User creation**, **User role change**, and **Service settings changed**.

    - **Red flags**: Unauthorized creation of new users, escalation of privileges, or alterations in security settings are critical areas of concern.

- **OAuth token activity monitoring**:

    - **Key events**: Track **Token granted** and **Token revoked** actions.

    - **Concerning observations**: The granting of tokens to unfamiliar third-party applications or an unusual pattern of token revocations can indicate that an attacker is trying to access data or services.

- **Groups audit log examination**:

  - **Crucial events**: Monitor **Group member added** and **Group settings changed**.

  - **Indicators of compromise**: An indicator is the addition of unknown members to critical groups or unauthorized changes in group settings, particularly in groups with access to sensitive information.

For each of these areas, incident responders should employ a context-driven approach. This involves looking beyond the mere occurrence of events to understanding their relevance in the broader context of user behavior and organizational norms. Analyzing the frequency, timing, and pattern deviations is crucial. We saw earlier in the *Microsoft 365 incident response* section how the login IPs can be looked up with an IP lookup service to better understand unauthorized access—the same process can be followed for Google Workspace.

> **Important note**
>
> Google Workspace's UI and syntax may change in the future, as these are active products being developed by their teams. As a result, some of the event names may change, but their principles are the same (for example, **Successful login** could change to **Login success** or vice versa).

Summary

In this final chapter on analyzing compromised cloud productivity suites, we explored how to tackle security incidents in the two most popular cloud-based productivity suites, Microsoft 365 and Google Workspace. These platforms, crucial for emails, storage, and office applications, are frequently targeted in BEC attacks. BEC, a sophisticated form of cyber fraud, often involves attackers gaining unauthorized access through email spoofing or account takeovers, leading to broader security breaches.

The chapter provided a guide to understanding BEC, its phases, and attacker methods. It then outlined crucial steps for initial scoping and remediation, essential for effective incident response. For Microsoft 365, it focused on using tools such as unified audit logs and Microsoft Purview for log analysis. It also discussed an open source PowerShell-based tool, HAWK, for streamlined data collection.

In contrast, Google Workspace incident response was discussed, with its more limited, yet vital, set of audit and reporting tools. The process involves using Google Workspace's audit logs to identify suspicious activities. This chapter equipped you with the knowledge to effectively respond to incidents in both Microsoft 365 and Google Workspace.

Further reading

- *Microsoft Purview*: https://learn.microsoft.com/en-us/purview/

- *What is a Business Email Compromise (BEC)*—Microsoft: https://www.microsoft.com/en-ca/security/business/security-101/what-is-business-email-compromise-bec

- *Identify and secure compromised accounts*—Google Workspace: https://support.google.com/a/topic/1355151?hl=en&ref_topic=1258984&sjid=10797876945924014941-NC

Index

www.packtpub.com

Subscribe to our online digital library for full access to over 7,000 books and videos, as well as industry leading tools to help you plan your personal development and advance your career. For more information, please visit our website.

Why subscribe?

- Spend less time learning and more time coding with practical eBooks and Videos from over 4,000 industry professionals

- Improve your learning with Skill Plans built especially for you

- Get a free eBook or video every month

- Fully searchable for easy access to vital information

- Copy and paste, print, and bookmark content

Did you know that Packt offers eBook versions of every book published, with PDF and ePub files available? You can upgrade to the eBook version at packtpub.com and as a print book customer, you are entitled to a discount on the eBook copy. Get in touch with us at customercare@packtpub.com for more details.

At www.packtpub.com, you can also read a collection of free technical articles, sign up for a range of free newsletters, and receive exclusive discounts and offers on Packt books and eBooks.

Other Books You May Enjoy

If you enjoyed this book, you may be interested in these other books by Packt:

Effective Threat Investigation for SOC Analysts

Mostafa Yahia

ISBN: 978-1-83763-478-1

- Get familiarized with and investigate various threat types and attacker techniques
- Analyze email security solution logs and understand email flow and headers
- Practically investigate various Windows threats and attacks
- Analyze web proxy logs to investigate C&C communication attributes
- Leverage WAF and FW logs and CTI to investigate various cyber attacks

Cloud Auditing Best Practices

Shinesa Cambric and Michael Ratemo

ISBN: 978-1-80324-377-1

- Understand the cloud shared responsibility and role of an IT auditor
- Explore change management and integrate it with DevSecOps processes
- Understand the value of performing cloud control assessments
- Learn tips and tricks to perform an advanced and effective auditing program
- Enhance visibility by monitoring and assessing cloud environments
- Examine IAM, network, infrastructure, and logging controls
- Use policy and compliance automation with tools such as Terraform

Packt is searching for authors like you

If you're interested in becoming an author for Packt, please visit `authors.packtpub.com` and apply today. We have worked with thousands of developers and tech professionals, just like you, to help them share their insight with the global tech community. You can make a general application, apply for a specific hot topic that we are recruiting an author for, or submit your own idea.

Share your thoughts

Now you've finished *Cloud Forensics Demystified*, we'd love to hear your thoughts! Scan the QR code below to go straight to the Amazon review page for this book and share your feedback or leave a review on the site that you purchased it from.

https://packt.link/r/1800564414

Your review is important to us and the tech community and will help us make sure we're delivering excellent quality content.

Download a free PDF copy of this book

Thanks for purchasing this book!

Do you like to read on the go but are unable to carry your print books everywhere?

Is your eBook purchase not compatible with the device of your choice?

Don't worry, now with every Packt book you get a DRM-free PDF version of that book at no cost.

Read anywhere, any place, on any device. Search, copy, and paste code from your favorite technical books directly into your application.

The perks don't stop there, you can get exclusive access to discounts, newsletters, and great free content in your inbox daily

Follow these simple steps to get the benefits:

1.   Scan the QR code or visit the link below

https://packt.link/free-ebook/9781800564411

2.   Submit your proof of purchase
3.   That's it! We'll send your free PDF and other benefits to your email directly